VHDL

Computer Engineering Series

DEWAR, SMOSNA • *Microprocessors* 0-07-016639-0

TRONTELJ, TRONTELJ, SHENTON • *Analog/Digital ASIC Design* 0-07-707300-2

VAN ZANT • *Microchip Fabrication* 0-07-067194-X

DI GIACOMO • *VLSI Handbook* 0-07-016903-9

DI GIACOMO • *Digital Bus Handbook* 0-07-016923-3

CLEMENTS • *68000 Sourcebook* 0-07-011321-1

ELLIOTT • *Integrated Circuit Fabrication Technology* 0-07-019339-8

MUN • *GaAs Integrated Circuits* 0-07-044025-5

BOSTOCK • *Programmable Logic Devices* 0-07-006611-6

TSUI • *LSI/VLSI Testability Design* 0-07-065341-0

ANTOGNETTI • *Semiconductor Device Modeling with SPICE* 0-07-002107-4, 0-07-002153-8 (pbk.)

CHORAFAS, STEINMANN • *Supercomputers* 0-07-010917-6

HWANG/DEGROOT • *Parallel Processing for Supercomputers and Artificial Intelligence* 0-07-031606-6

SHERMAN • *CD-ROM Handbook* 0-07-056578-3

SIEGEL • *Interconnection Networks for Large-Scale Parallel Processing* 0-07-057561-4

READ • *Gate Arrays* 0-07-051286-8

MICK, BRICK • *Bit-Slice Microprocessor Design* 0-07-041781-4

MITCHELL • *32-Bit Microprocessor* 0-07-042585-X

VHDL

Douglas L. Perry
San Ramon, California

McGraw-Hill, Inc.
New York St. Louis San Francisco Auckland Bogotá
Caracas Lisbon London Madrid Mexico Milan
Montreal New Delhi Paris San Juan São Paulo
Singapore Sydney Tokyo Toronto

Library of Congress Cataloging-in-Publication Data

Perry, Douglas L.
VHDL/Douglas Perry.
p. cm.
ISBN 0-07-049433-9
1. VHDL (Computer hardware description language) I. Title.
TK7885.7.P47 1991
621.39'2—dc20 90-44408
CIP

6 7 8 9 0 DOC/DOC 9 5 4 3 2

ISBN 0-07-049433-9

The sponsoring editor for this book was Theron Shreve, the editing supervisor was David E. Fogarty, the designer was Naomi Auerbach, and the production supervisor was Pamela A. Pelton.

Printed and bound by R. R. Donnelley & Sons Company.

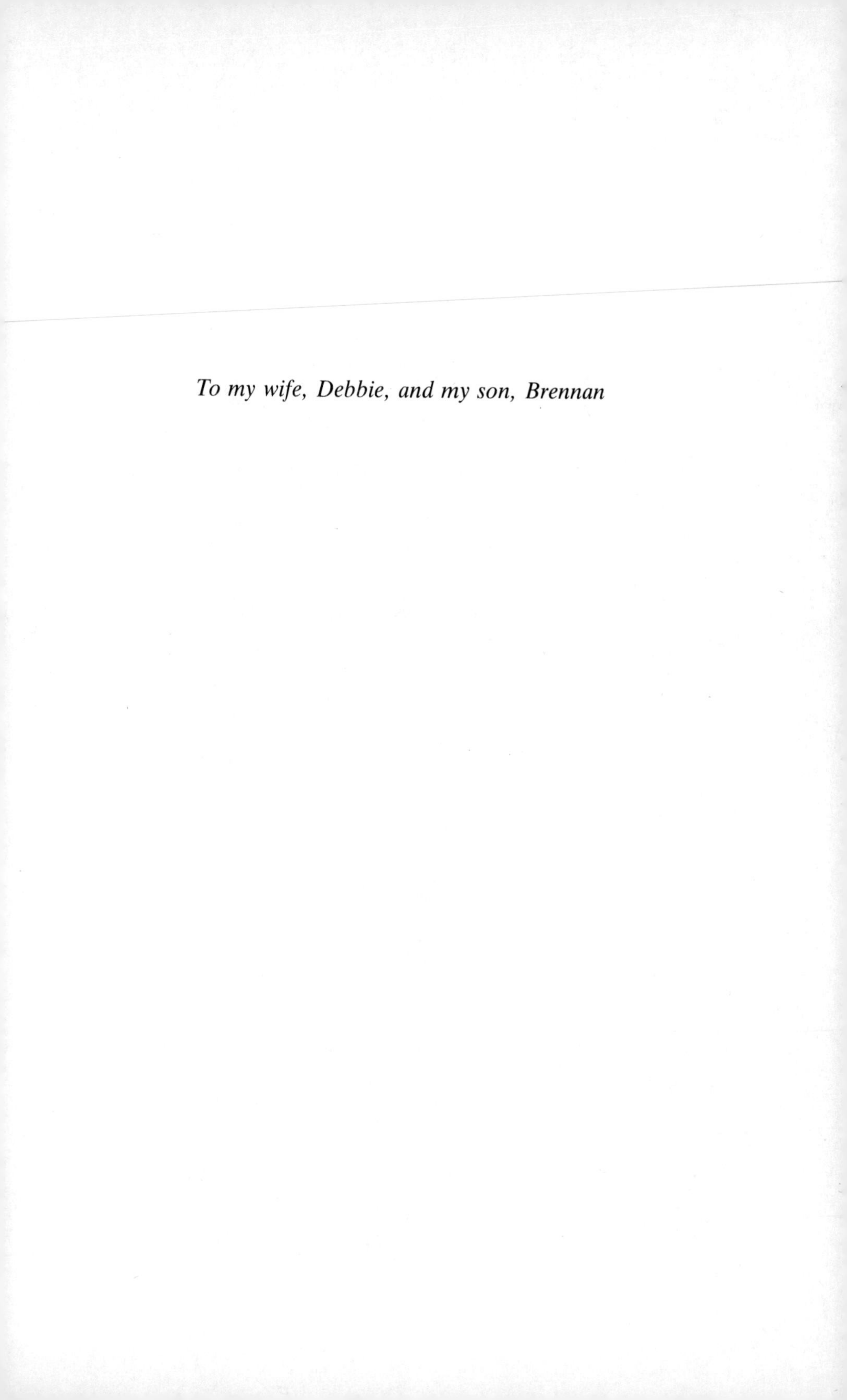

To my wife, Debbie, and my son, Brennan

Contents

Preface

This book was written to help hardware designers learn how to better model their designs. It will provide guidance in writing VHDL descriptions for every level of a hardware design, from the initial specification to the gate level implementation.

It will also attempt to bring the designer with little or no knowledge of VHDL, to the level of writing complex VHDL descriptions. It is not intended to show every possible construct of VHDL in every possible use, but rather to show the designer how to write concise, efficient, correct VHDL descriptions of hardware.

This book is organized into three logical parts. The first part of the book will introduce the features of VHDL, the second walks through a design example of a vending machine controller from initial specification to final implementation, and the final part discusses a standard package description used throughout the book.

In the first part VHDL features are introduced one or more at a time. As each feature is introduced, one or more real examples are given to show how the feature of the language would be used. The first part comprises Chapters 1 through 9, and each chapter introduces a basic description capability of VHDL. Chapter 1 discusses how VHDL design relates to typical computer-aided engineering (CAE) methodologies, and introduces the basic terms of the language. Chapter 2 describes some of the basic concepts of VHDL, including the different delay mechanisms available, how to use instance specific data, and talks about VHDL drivers. In Chapter 2, concurrent statements are discussed, while in Chapter 3 the reader is introduced to VHDL sequential statements. Chapter 4 talks about the wide range of types available for use in VHDL. Examples are given for each of the types showing how they would be used in a real example. In Chapter 5 the concepts of subprograms and packages are introduced. The different uses for functions are given, as well as the features available in VHDL packages.

Chapter 6 introduces the five kinds of predefined attribute categories available for use in VHDL. Each of the categories has examples describing how to use the specific attribute to the designer's best advantage. Examples are given which describe the purpose of each of the attributes. Chapter 7 discusses how configurations are used to specify how a design is constructed. Each of the types of configurations are discussed, along with some examples to illustrate the point. Chapter 8 walks the reader through some of the more advanced topics of VHDL. This chapter discusses overloading, user-defined attributes, generate statements, and TextIO. All of these topics are advanced features of the language that will be used when the designer becomes more familiar with VHDL. Chapter 9 provides a detailed discussion of value systems. This chapter will help show the differences between the varied value systems and point out which value system can be used for a particular type of design.

Chapters 10 through 14 walk the reader through a top-down design of a vending machine controller written in VHDL. The description begins at an algorithmic level in Chapter 10, and successively descends in description level, until in Chapter 14 the gate level description of the design is discussed.

There are three appendixes that provide the reader with more information about selected topics. Appendix A describes the STD_LOGIC package. The declarations contained in this package are used extensively in the examples in the book. Appendix B describes the technology-specific packages that allow the designer to write technology-independent models that can be made specific to a technology by including the appropriate package. Finally, Appendix C describes how to read the Bachus-Naur format (BNF) descriptions found in the *VHDL Language Reference Manual.*

Acknowledgments

This book would not have been possible without the help of a number of people, and I would like to express my gratitude to all of them. Rod Farrow, Cary Ussery, Alec Stanculescu, and Ken Scott answered a multitude of questions about some of the vagaries of VHDL. Ken Scott and Kjell Nielsen reviewed the manuscript. Their comments were both helpful and insightful. Rick Herrick supplied the idea of using a vending machine controller as an instructive example. It is an easy-to-understand example, yet still complex enough to show off some interesting features of the language. Paul Krol developed the chart in Chapter 7 that describes generics. Keith Irwin helped define the style of some of the chapters. Brent Gregory and Russ Segal of Synopsys contributed to the synthesis section of Chapter 14. Finally, I would like to thank all of the members of the team at Vantage Analysis Systems and Synopsys for providing tools that made verification of the concepts in the book possible.

VHDL

Chapter

1

Introduction to VHDL

The VHSIC Hardware Description Language is an industry standard language used to describe hardware from the abstract to the concrete level. VHDL is rapidly being embraced as the universal communication medium of design. Computer-aided engineering workstation vendors throughout the industry are standardizing on VHDL as input and output from their tools. These tools include simulation tools, synthesis tools, layout tools, etc.

In this chapter we will examine the basics of VHDL. The history of VHDL will be presented, and then some basic terms will be defined. Finally, VHDL design will be contrasted with traditional design methods.

1.1 VHSIC Program

VHDL is an offshoot of the very high speed integrated circuit (VHSIC) program that was funded by the Department of Defense in the late 1970s and early 1980s. The goal of the VHSIC program was to produce the next generation of integrated circuits. Program participants were urged to push technology limits in every phase of the design and manufacture of integrated circuits.

The goals were accomplished admirably, but in the process of developing these extremely complex integrated circuits the designers found out that the tools used to create these large designs were inadequate for the task. The tools that were available to the designers were mostly based at the gate level. Creating designs of hundreds of thousands of gates using gate level tools was an extremely challenging task, and therefore a new method of description was in order.

1.2 VHDL as a Standard

A new hardware description language was proposed in 1981 called the VHSIC Hardware Description Language, or as we know it now, VHDL. The goals of this new language were twofold. First the designers wanted a language that could describe the complex circuits that they were trying to describe. Secondly they wanted a language that was a standard so that all of the players in the VHSIC program could distribute designs to other players in a standard format. Also any subcontractors would be able to talk to their main contractors with a single standard format.

In 1986 VHDL was proposed as an IEEE standard. It went through a number of revisions and changes until it was adopted as the IEEE 1076 standard in December 1987. The IEEE 1076 -1987 standard VHDL is the VHDL that will be used in this book. All of the examples have been described in IEEE 1076 VHDL and compiled and simulated with the VHDL simulation environment from Vantage Analysis Systems.

1.3 Learning VHDL

VHDL can be a very difficult language to learn by reading the *VHDL Language Reference Manual* (also called the LRM) from cover to cover. The LRM describes VHDL for the VHDL implementor and was never intended to be a VHDL user's guide. VHDL itself is a large language, however, and learning all of it can be a very large task. The entire language does not need to be learned initially to write useful models. A subset of the language can be learned initially, and as more complex models are required the more complex features can be learned and used.

VHDL contains levels of representations that can be used to represent all levels of description from the bidirectional switch level to the system level, and any level in between. The best way to approach VHDL is to learn enough of the language to try some small designs. When you become familiar enough with this subset of VHDL that you feel very comfortable writing it, move on to some of the other features of the language and try new things.

1.4 VHDL Terms

Before we go any further let's define some of the terms that we will be using throughout the book. These are the basic VHDL building blocks that are used in almost every description, along with some terms that are redefined in VHDL to mean something different to the average designer.

- *Entity*. All designs are expressed in terms of entities. An entity is the most basic building block in a design. The uppermost level of the design is the top-level entity. If the design is hierarchical then the top-level description will have lower-level descriptions contained in it. These lower-level descriptions will be lower-level entities contained in the top-level entity description.
- *Architecture*. All entities that can be simulated have an architecture description. The architecture describes the behavior of the entity. A single entity can have multiple architectures. One architecture might be behavioral while another might be a structural description of the design.
- *Configuration*. A configuration statement is used to bind a component instance to an entity-architecture pair. A configuration can be considered like a parts list for a design. It describes which behavior to use for each entity much like a parts list describes which part to use for each part in the design.

- *Package*. A package is a collection of commonly used data types and subprograms used in a design. Think of a package as a toolbox that contains tools used to build designs.
- *Bus*. The term *bus* usually brings to mind a group of signals or a particular method of communication used in the design of hardware. In VHDL a bus is a special kind of signal that may have its drivers turned off.
- *Driver*. This is a source on a signal. If a signal is driven by two tristate inverters, when both inverters are active the signal will have two drivers.
- *Attribute*. An attribute is data that is attached to VHDL objects or predefined data about VHDL objects. Examples are the current drive capability of a buffer or the maximum operating temperature of the device.
- *Generic*. A generic is VHDL's term for a parameter that passes information to an entity. For instance, if an entity is a gate level model with a rise and a fall delay, values for the rise and fall delays could be passed into the entity with generics.
- *Process*. A process is the basic unit of execution in VHDL. All operations that are performed in a simulation of a VHDL description are broken into single or multiple processes.

1.5 Traditional Design Methods

When a design engineer develops a new piece of hardware today it is probably designed on a computer-aided engineering (CAE) workstation. To create a design on a typical CAE workstation the designer will create a schematic for the design.

A typical schematic consists of symbols representing the basic units of the design connected together with signals. The symbols come from a library of parts that the designer uses to build the schematic. The type of symbols available depends on the type of design that the designer is creating. If the designer is creating the schematic for a board design that uses transistor-transistor logic (TTL) parts, then the symbols used in the schematic represent the TTL parts that the designer has available. If the designer is creating a schematic for an application-specific integrated circuit (ASIC), then the symbols available are the library macros available for use on this specific type of ASIC.

The symbols are wired together using signals (or *nets*, short for networks). The interconnection of the symbols by signals creates the connections needed to specify the design such that a netlist can be derived from the connections. A netlist can be used to create a simulation model of the design to verify the design before it is built. Once the design has been verified, the netlist can be used to provide the information needed by a routing software package to complete the actual design. The routing software will create the physical connection data to either create the trace information needed for a PC board or the layer information needed for an ASIC.

Figure 1-1 illustrates an example of a symbol used in a schematic. It is the symbol for a reset-set flip-flop (RSFF). The symbol describes the following pieces of information to the designer:

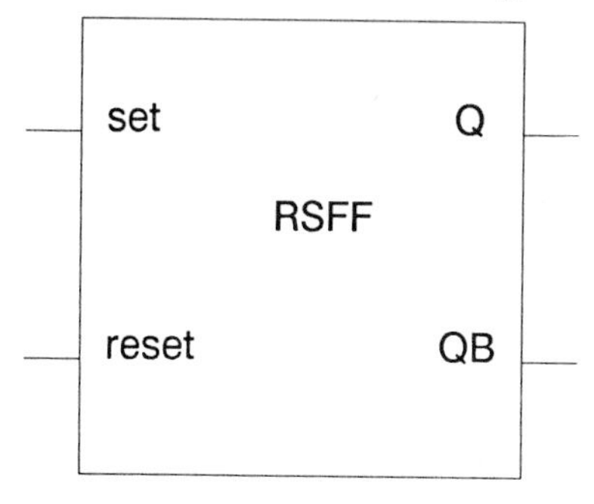

Figure 1-1

- *The number of input pins for the device.* In this example the number is 2, set and reset.
- *The number of output pins for the device.* In this example the number of output pins is 2, Q and QB.
- *The function of the device.* In this example the function of the device is described by the name of the symbol. In the case of simple gates the function of the symbol is described by the shape of the symbol.

Symbols specify the interface and the function to the designer. When the symbols are placed on a schematic sheet and wired together with

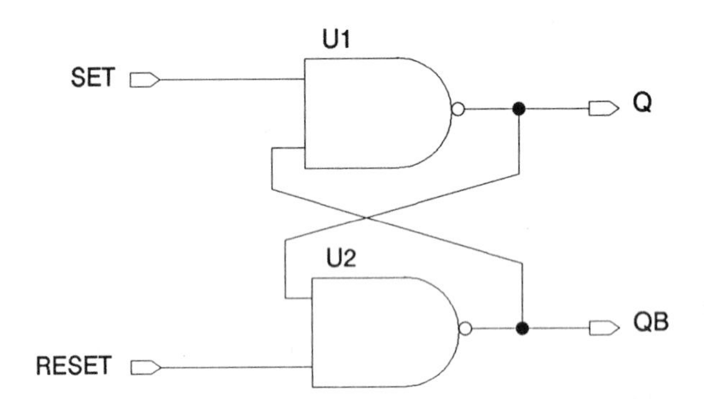

Figure 1-2

signals, a schematic for the design is formed. An example of a simple schematic for an RSFF is shown in Figure 1-2 .

1.6 Traditional Schematics

The schematic contains two nand gate symbol instances and four port instances. Four nets connect the symbols and ports together to form the RS flip-flop. Each port has a unique name which also specifies the name of the signal (net) connected to it. Each symbol instance has a unique instance identifier (U1, U2) . The instance identifier is used to uniquely identify an instance for reference.

When this schematic is compiled into a typical gate level simulator it will function as an RSFF. A '0' level on the reset port will cause the reset signal to have the value '0'. This will cause nand gate U2 to output a '1' value on signal QB independent of the value on the other input of the nand gate. The '1' value on QB feeds back to one input of the nand gate U1. If the set input is at an inactive value ('1') , then nand gate U1 will have two '1' values as input, causing it to output a value of '0' on the output Q. The RSFF will have been reset.

How would this same design look in VHDL? First of all, how do you represent a symbol in VHDL? What does a schematic look like in VHDL?

1.7 Symbols versus Entities

All designs are created from entities. An entity in VHDL corresponds directly to a symbol in the traditional CAE workstation design methodology. Let's look at the top-level entity for the *rsff* symbol described earlier. An entity for the *rsff* would look like this:

```
ENTITY rsff   IS
   PORT ( set, reset : IN BIT;
          q, qb : BUFFER BIT);
END rsff;
```

The keyword ENTITY signifies that this is the start of an entity statement. In the descriptions shown throughout the book, keywords of the language and types provided with the STANDARD package will be shown in all CAPITAL letters. For instance, in the example above the keywords are ENTITY, IS, PORT, IN, BUFFER, etc. The standard type provided is BIT. Names of user-created objects such as *rsff,* in the example above, will be shown in lower-case *italics*.

The name of the entity is *rsff*, as was the name of the symbol described earlier. The entity has four ports in the PORT clause. Two ports are of mode IN and two ports are of mode BUFFER. The reason for port mode BUFFER instead of just OUT will be described later. The two input ports correspond directly to the two input pins on the symbol from the CAE workstation. The two buffer ports correspond directly to the two output ports for the symbol. All of the ports have a type of BIT.

The entity describes the interface to the outside world. It specifies the number of ports, the direction of the ports, and the type of the ports. A lot more information can be put into the entity than is shown here, but this will give us a foundation upon which we can later build.

1.8 Schematics versus Architectures

The schematic for the *rsff* component also has a counterpart in VHDL. It is called an *architecture*. An architecture is always related to an entity and describes the behavior of that entity. An architecture for the *rsff* device described above would look like this:

```
ARCHITECTURE netlist OF rsff IS
   COMPONENT nand2
      PORT ( a, b : IN BIT;
               c    : OUT BIT);
   END COMPONENT;
BEGIN
   U1: nand2
      PORT MAP (set, qb, q);

   U2: nand2
      PORT MAP (reset, q, qb);
END netlist;
```

The keyword ARCHITECTURE signifies that this statement will describe an architecture for an entity. The architecture name will be *netlist*. The entity that the architecture is describing is called *rsff*. The reason for the connection between the architecture and the entity is that an entity can have multiple architectures describing the behavior of the entity. For instance, one architecture could be a behavioral description, and another, like the one shown above, could be a structural description.

The textual area between the keyword ARCHITECTURE and the keyword BEGIN is where local signals and components are declared for later use. In this example there are two instances of a *nand2* gate placed in the architecture. The compiler needs to know what the interface to the components placed in the architecture are. The component declaration statement will describe that information to the compiler.

The statement area of the architecture starts with the keyword BEGIN. All statements between the BEGIN and the END *netlist* statement are called concurrent statements, because all of the statements execute concurrently. This concept will be discussed in great detail later.

1.9 Component Instantiation

In the statement area are two component instantiation statements. Each statement creates an instance of a component in the model. In this example each statement creates an instance of a nand2 gate. The first instance U1 corresponds directly with the nand2 gate U1 in the schematic in Figure 1-2. The way to read the component instantiation statement is as follows. The first statement creates an instance called U1 of a nand2 component, with the first port connected to signal *set*, the second port connnected to signal *qb*, and the last port connected to signal *q*.

If we look again at the nand2 component declaration we will see that the first port is an IN port called *a*, the second port is an IN port called *b*, and the last port is an OUT port called *c*. Therefore the component instantiation would connect the *a* port of the nand2 component to signal *set*, the *b* port to signal *qb*, and the *c* port to signal *q*. We have thus matched the actual parameters *set*, *qb*, and *q* of the instantiation with the corresponding formal parameters *a*, *b*, and *c* of the declaration.

There is another way to map the ports, if the ports are not in a particular order. Component instantiation statements as demonstrated below can be used.

```
U1: nand2 port map (a <= set, b <= qb, c <= q );
```

This form is called *named association* and maps the ports directly without concern for the order. In fact the statement below would work perfectly well also.

```
U1: nand2 port map ( b <= qb, c <= q, a <= set);
```

The second component instantiation statement of architecture *netlist* creates another instance of the nand2 component with an instance identifier, U2. These instances correspond directly with the instance identifiers of the schematic in Figure 1-2 . This model matches the schematic in Figure 1-2 . This type of VHDL representation is called a structural model, or structural representation. What makes this description a structural one is the fact that it has components instantiated in it. In the next few chapters we will be discussing structural, behavioral, and mixed structural-behavioral descriptions.

The structural architecture *netlist* is very similar to a netlist in a typical CAE workstation simulator. Some of the examples in this book will use structural parts to describe the functionality, but behavioral modeling will be the main focus.

1.10 Behavioral Descriptions

Another way to describe this same circuit is by using a behavioral architecture. An example of a behavioral architecture is shown in the architecture example below. This architecture uses *concurrent signal assignment* statements. As the name implies the statements contained in the model assign values to signals. What makes these statements different from assignment statements in typical programming lanugages is the fact that these statements execute in parallel (concurrently), not serially.

```
ARCHITECTURE behave OF rsff IS
BEGIN
  q <= NOT( qb AND set ) AFTER 2 ns;
  qb <= NOT( q AND reset ) AFTER 2 ns;
END behave;
```

1.10.1 Concurrent Signal Assignment

In a typical programming language such as C or Pascal, each assignment statement executes one after the other and in a specified order. The order of execution is determined by the order of the statements in the source file. Inside a VHDL architecture, there is no specified ordering of the assignment statements. (We will look later at process statements in which signal assignment statements are ordered.) The order of execution is solely specified by events occurring on signals that the assignment statements are sensitive to.

Examine the first assignment statement from architecture *behave*, as shown below.

```
q <= NOT( qb AND set ) AFTER 2 ns;
```

A signal assignment is identified by the symbol < =. The logical AND of *qb* and *set* is complemented and assigned to signal *q*. This statement will be executed whenever either *qb* or *set* has an event occur on it. An event on a signal is a change in the value of that signal. A signal assignment statement is said to be sensitive to changes on any signals that are to the right of the < = symbol. This signal assignment statement is sensitive to *qb* and *set*. The other signal assignment statement in architecture *behave* is sensitive to signals *q* and *reset*.

The AFTER clause in the signal assignment is used to emulate propagation delay in the circuit. Any event (change in value) on *qb* or *set* may cause a change on signal *q* two nanoseconds later.

Let's take a look at how these statements actually work. Suppose that we have a steady state condition where both *set* and *reset* are at a '1' value, and signal *q* is currently at a '0' value. Signal *qb* will be at a '1' value because it will be opposite of *q* except when both *set* and *reset* are at a '0' value. Now assume that we place an event on the *set* signal that causes its value to change to a '0'. When this happens the first signal assignment statement will wake up and execute. This happens because *set* is on the right side of the < = and is therefore in the *implied sensitivity list* for the first signal assignment statement.

When the first statement executes it will compute the new value to be assigned to *q* from the current value of the signal expression on the right side of the < = symbol. The expression value calculation will use the current values for all signals contained in it.

What will the signal expression calculate? Signal *set* is now equal to '0' since its value just changed. Signal *qb* is equal to '1' because it did not change. The new value for signal *q* will be the complement of the two values, ANDed together. This will result in a '1' value to be assigned to signal *q*.

1.10.2 Event Scheduling

The assignment to signal *q* does not happen instantly, however. The AFTER clause we discussed earlier will delay the assignment of the new value to *q* by two nanoseconds. The mechanism for delaying the new value is called scheduling an event. By assigning *q* a new value an event was scheduled 2 nanoseconds in the future that contains the new value for signal *q*. When the event matures (2 nanoseconds in the future) signal *q* will receive the new value.

1.10.3 Statement Concurrency

The first assignment is the only statement to execute at the current time when the event on *set* happens. The second signal assignment statement will not execute until the event on signal *q* happens, or an event happens on signal *reset*. If no event happens on signal *reset*, then the second assignment statement will not execute for 2 nanoseconds. This will be when the event on signal *q* that was scheduled by the first signal assignment occurs.

When the event on signal *q* occurs, the second signal assignment statement will execute. It will calculate a new value from *q* and *reset*. Assuming *reset* stays at a '1' then the new value for *qb* will be a '0'. This value will be scheduled to occur on signal *qb* 2 nanoseconds in the future.

When the event occurs on signal *qb*, the first signal assignment will wake up, execute again, and calculate the new value for *q* based on the values of *qb* and *set*. If *set* is still a '0' then the '0' value of *qb* will not change the value of *q*. Signal *q* will already be at a '1' value from the *set* signal at a '0'. No new event will be scheduled on the *q* output signal, because signal *q* does not change its value.

The two signal assignment statements in the architecture *behave* form a behavioral model, or architecture, for the *rsff* entity. The *behave* architecture contains no structure. There are no components instantiated in the architecture. There is no further hierarchy and this architecture can be considered a leaf node in the hierarchy of the design.

1.11 Sequential Behavior

There is yet another way to describe the functionality of an *rsff* device in VHDL. The fact that VHDL has so many possible representations for similar functionality is what makes learning the entire language a big task. The third way to describe the functionality of the *rsff* will be to use a process statement to describe the functionality in an algorithmic representation. This is shown in architecture *sequential*, shown below.

```
ARCHITECTURE sequential OF rsff IS
BEGIN
   PROCESS (set, reset )
   BEGIN
      IF set = '1' AND reset = '0' THEN
         q <= '0' AFTER 2 ns;
         qb <= '1' AFTER 4 ns;
      ELSIF set = '0' AND reset = '1' THEN
         q <= '1' AFTER 4 ns;
         qb <='0' AFTER 2 ns;
      ELSIF set = '0' AND reset = '0' THEN
         q <= '1' AFTER 2 ns;
         qb  '1' AFTER 2 ns;
      END IF;
   END PROCESS;
END sequential;
```

The architecture contains only one statement, called a process statement. It starts at the line beginning with the keyword PROCESS and ends with the line that contains END PROCESS. All of the statements between these two lines are considered part of the process statement.

1.11.1 Process Statements

The process statement consists of a number of parts. The first part is called the *sensitivity list*. The second part is called the *process declarative part,* and the third is the *statement part*. In the example shown above, the list of signals in parentheses after the keyword PROCESS is called the sensitivity list. This list enumerates exactly which signals will cause the process statement to be executed. In this example the list consists of *set* and *reset.* Only events on these signals will cause the process statement to be executed.

1.11.2 Process Declarative Region

The process declarative part consists of the area between the end of the sensitivity list and the keyword BEGIN. In this example the declarative part is empty. This area is used to declare local variables or constants that can be used only inside of the process.

1.11.3 Process Statement Part

The statement part of the process starts at the keyword BEGIN and ends at the END PROCESS line. All of the statements enclosed by the process are sequential statements. This means that any statements enclosed by the process are executed one after the other in a sequential order just like a typical programming language. Remember that the order of the statements in the architecture did not make any difference; however, inside of the process this is not true. *The order of execution is the order of the statements in the model.*

1.11.4 Process Execution

Let's see how this works by walking through the execution of the example in architecture *sequential*, line by line. To be consistent let's assume that *set* changes to a '0' and *reset* remains at a '1'. Because *set* is in the sensitivity list for the process statement, the process will be invoked. Each statement in the process will then be executed sequentially. In this example however there is only one IF statement. Each check that the IF statement performs is done sequentially starting with the first in the model.

The first check is to see if *set* is equal to a '1' and *reset* is equal to a '0'. This statement will fail because *set* is equal to a '0' and *reset* is equal to a '1'. The two signal assignment statements that follow the first check will not be executed. Instead the next check will be performed. This check will succeed and the signal assignment statements following the check for *set* = '0' and *reset* = '1' will be executed. These statements are shown below.

```
q <= '1' AFTER 2 ns;
qb <= '0' AFTER 2 ns;
```

1.11.5 Sequential Statements

These two statements will execute sequentially. They may look exactly the same as previous signal assignment statements that we have examined, but because of the context (they are inside the process statement) they are different. These two assignment statements are called *sequential signal assignment* statements, and they execute one after the other inside the process statement. The first statement *may* schedule an event on signal *q* and then the second statement *may* schedule an event on signal *qb*. However, if signal *q* is already at a '1' value, no change in value will occur and therefore no event will be scheduled.

After these two statements are executed, the next check of the IF statement is not performed. Whenever a check succeeds no other checks are done. Since the IF statement was the only statement inside the process, the process terminates.

1.12 Architecture Selection

So far three architectures have been described for one entity. Which architecture should be used to model the *rsff* device? It depends on the accuracy wanted and if structural information is required. If the model is going to be used to drive a printed circuit board layout tool, then probably the structural architecture *netlist* is most appropriate. If a structural model is not wanted for some other reason, then a more efficient model can be used. Either of the other two methods (architectures *behave* and *sequential*) are probably more efficient in memory space required and speed of execution. How to choose between these two methods may come down to a question of programming style. Would the modeler rather write concurrent or sequential VHDL code? If the modeler wants to write concurrent VHDL code, then the style of architecture *behave* is the way to go; otherwise, architecture *sequential* should be chosen. Typically, modelers are more familiar with sequential coding styles, but concurrent statements are very powerful tools to write small efficient models, as we shall illustrate later.

1.12.1 Configuration Statements

An entity can have more than one architecture, but how does the modeler choose which architecture to use in a given simulation? The configuration statement maps component instantiations to entities. With this powerful statement the modeler can pick and choose which architectures are used to model an entity at every level in the design.

Let's look at a configuration statement using the *netlist* architecture of the *rsff* entity. An example configuration is shown below.

```
CONFIGURATION rsffcon1 OF rsff IS
  FOR netlist
    FOR U1,U2 : nand2 USE ENTITY
                  WORK.mynand(version1);
    END FOR;
  END FOR;
END rsffcon1;
```

The function of the configuration statement is to spell out exactly which architecture to use for every component instance in the model. This occurs in a hierarchical fashion. The highest-level entity in the design needs to have the architecture to use specified, as well as any components instantiated in the design.

The configuration statement shown above reads as follows. This is a configuration named *rsffcon1* for entity *rsff*. Use architecture *netlist* as the architecture for the topmost entity, which is *rsff*. For the two component instances U1 and U2 of type nand2 instantiated in the *netlist* architecture, use entity *mynand*, architecture *version1* from the library called WORK. All of the entities now have architectures specified for them. Entity *rsff* has architecture *netlist*, and component *nand2* has entity *mynand* and architecture *version1*.

1.12.2 Power of Configurations

By compiling the entities, architectures, and the configuration specified above, you can create a simulatable model. But what if you did not want to simulate at the gate level? What if you really wanted to use architecture BEHAVE instead? The power of the configuration is that you do not need to recompile your complete design; you only need to recompile the new configuration. An example configuration is shown below.

```
CONFIGURATION rsffcon2 OF rsff IS
  FOR behave
  END FOR;
END rsffcon2;
```

This is a configuration named *rsffcon2* for entity *rsff*. Use architecture *behave* for the topmost entity, which is *rsff*. By compiling this configuration, the architecture *behave* will be selected for entity *rsff* in this simulation.

This configuration is not necessary, in standard VHDL, but gives the designer the freedom to specify exactly which architecture will be used for the entity. The default architecture used for the entity is the last one compiled into the working library.

In this chapter we have had a basic introduction to VHDL, and some of the description styles available in the language. In the next chapter we will examine behavioral modeling in greater detail.

Chapter

2

Behavioral Modeling

In Chapter 1 we discussed structural modeling with traditional CAE systems and touched briefly on behavioral modeling. In this chapter we will discuss behavioral modeling more thoroughly as well as some of the issues relating to the simulation of VHDL models.

2.1 Introduction to Behavioral Modeling

The signal assignment statement is the most basic form of behavioral modeling in VHDL. An example is shown below.

```
a <= b;
```

This statement is read as follows: *a* gets the value of *b*. The effect of this statement is that the current value of signal *b* will be assigned to signal *a*. This statement will be executed whenever signal *b* changes value. Signal *b* is in the *sensitivity list* of this statement. Whenever a signal in the sensitivity list of a signal assignment statement changes value, the signal assignment statement is executed. If the result of the execution is a new value that is different than the current value of the signal, then an event is scheduled for the target signal. If the result of the execution is the same value, then no event will be scheduled but a transaction will still be generated (transactions are discussed later in Chapter 3) . A transaction is always generated when a model is evaluated, but only signal changes cause events to be scheduled.

The next example shows how to introduce a nonzero delay value for the assignment.

```
a <= b after 10 ns;
```

This statement is read as follows: *a* gets the value of *b* when ten nanoseconds of time have elapsed.

Both of the statements above are concurrent signal assignment statements. Both statements are sensitive to changes in the value of signal *b*. Whenever *b* changes value these statements will execute and new values will be assigned to signal *a*.

Using a concurrent signal assignment statement a simple AND gate can be modeled as follows:

```
ENTITY and2 IS
   PORT ( a, b : IN BIT;
      c : OUT BIT );
END and2;

ARCHITECTURE and2_behav OF and2 IS
BEGIN
   c <= a AND b AFTER 5 ns;
END and2_behav;
```

The AND gate has two inputs *a, b* and one output *c*, as shown in Figure 2-1. The value of signal *c* may be assigned a new value whenever either *a* or *b* changes value. With an AND gate, if *a* is a 0 and *b* changes from a 1 to a 0, output *c* will not change. If the output does change value, then a transaction occurs which causes an event to be scheduled on signal *c;* otherwise a transaction occurs on signal *c*.

The entity design unit describes the ports of the *and2* gate. There are two inputs *a* and *b*, as well as one output *c*. The architecture *and2_behav* for entity *and2* contains one concurrent signal assignment statement. This statement is sensitive to both signal *a* and signal *b* by the fact that

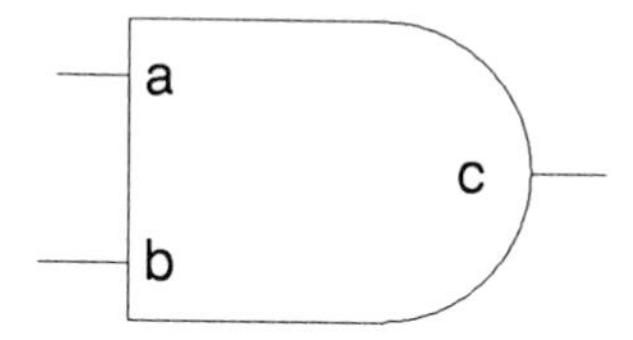

Figure 2-1

the expression to calculate the value of *c* includes both *a* and *b* signal values.

The value of the expression *a* and *b* will be calculated first, and the resulting value from the calculation will be scheduled on output *c*, 5 nanoseconds from the time the calculation is completed.

The next example shows more complicated signal assignment statements and demonstrates the concept of concurrency in greater detail. In Figure 2-2 the symbol for a four-input multiplexer is shown.

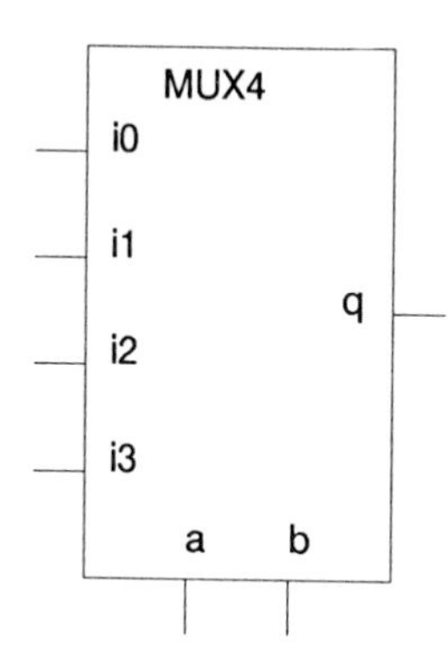

Figure 2-2

This is the behavioral model for the mux.

```
USE STD.std_logic.ALL;
USE STD.std_ttl.ALL;

ENTITY mux4 IS
   PORT ( i0, i1, i2, i3, a, b : IN t_wlogic;
                              q : OUT t_wlogic);
END mux4;
```

```
ARCHITECTURE mux4 OF mux4 IS
   SIGNAL sel: INTEGER;
BEGIN
   WITH sel SELECT
      q <= i0 AFTER 10 ns WHEN 0,
         i1 AFTER 10 ns WHEN 1,
         i2 AFTER 10 ns WHEN 2,
         i3 AFTER 10 ns WHEN 3,
         FX AFTER 10 ns WHEN OTHERS;

   sel <= 0 WHEN a = '0' AND b = '0' ELSE
         1 WHEN a = '1' AND b = '0' ELSE
         2 WHEN a = '0' AND b = '1' ELSE
         3 WHEN a = '1' AND b = '1' ELSE
         4 ;
END mux4;
```

The entity for this model has six input ports and one output port. Four of the input ports *(i0, i1, i2, i3)* represent signals that will be assigned to the output signal *q*. Only one of the signals will be assigned to the output signal *q* based on the value of the other two input signals *a* and *b*. The truth table for the multiplexer is shown in Figure 2-3 .

To implement the functionality described above we will use a conditional signal assignment statement and a selected signal assignment.

The second statement type in this example is called a conditional signal assignment statement. This statement will assign a value to the target signal based on conditions that are evaluated for each statement. The

a	b	q
0	0	I0
1	0	I1
0	1	I2
1	1	I3

Figure 2-3

statement WHEN conditions are executed one at a time in sequential order until the conditions of a statement are met. The first statement that matches the conditions required will assign the value to the target signal. The target signal for this example is the local signal *sel*. Depending on the values of signals *a* and *b*, the values 0 through 4 will be assigned to *sel*.

If more than one statement's conditions match, the first statement that matches will do the assign, and the other matching statements values will be ignored.

The first statement is called a selected signal assignment and will select among a number of options to assign the correct value to the target signal. The target signal in this example is the signal *q*.

The expression (the value of signal *sel* in this example) will be evaluated, and the statement that matches the value of the expression will assign the value to the target signal. All of the possible values of the expression *must* have a matching choice in the selected signal assignment (or an OTHERS clause must exist).

Each of the input signals can be assigned to output *q*, depending on the values of the two select inputs, *a* and *b*. If the values of *a* or *b* are unknown values, then the last value, FX (forcing unknown), is assigned to output *q*. The value FX is one of the values of the 46-state value system described in Chapter 9 and Appendix A. In this example when one of the select inputs is at an unknown value, the output is set to unknown.

Looking at the model for the multiplexer, it looks as though the model will not work as written. It looks as though the value of signal *sel* is used before it is computed. This impression is received from the fact that the second statement in the architecture is the statement that actually computes the value for *sel*. The model will work as written, however, because of the concept of concurrency.

The second statement is sensitive to signals *a* and *b*. Whenever either *a* or *b* changes value, the second statement is executed, and signal *sel* will be updated. The first statement is sensitive to signal *sel*. Whenever signal *sel* changes value, the first signal assignment will be executed.

2.2 Transport versus Inertial Delay

In VHDL there are two types of delay that can be used for modeling behaviors. Inertial delay is the most commonly used, while transport delay is used where a *wire* delay model is required.

2.2.1 Inertial Delay

Inertial delay is the default in VHDL. If no delay type is specified then inertial delay is used. Inertial delay is the default because in most cases it behaves similarly to the actual device.

In an inertial delay model, the output signal of the device has inertia which must be overcome in order for the signal to change value. The inertia value is equal to the delay through the device. If there are any spikes, pulses, etc. that have periods where a signal value is maintained for less than the delay through the device, the output signal value will not change. If a signal value is maintained at a particular value for longer than the delay through the device, the inertia is overcome and the device will change to the new state.

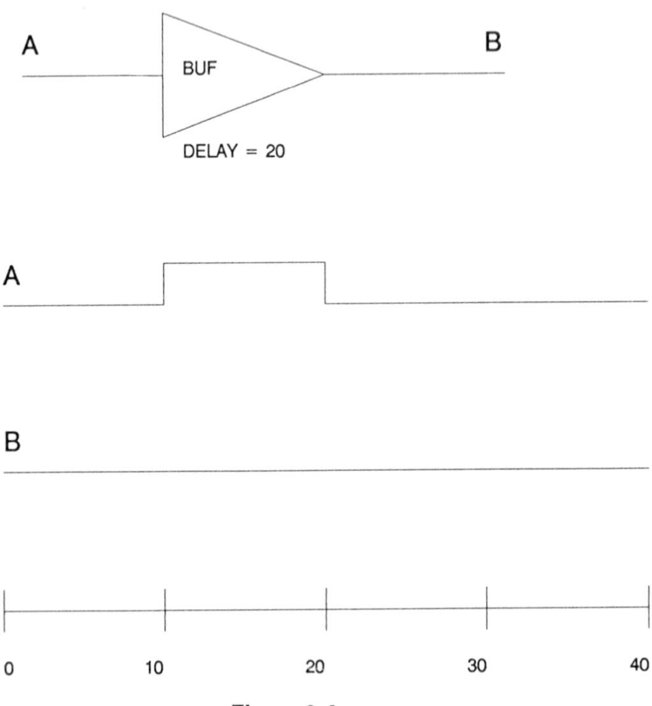

Figure 2-4

Figure 2-4 is an example of a very simple buffer symbol. The buffer has a single input A and a single output B. The waveforms are shown for input A and the output B. Signal A changes from a '0' to a '1' at time 10 ns and from a '1' to a '0' at 20 ns. This creates a pulse or *spike* that is 10 ns in duration. The buffer has a 20 ns delay through the device.

The '0' to '1' transistion on signal A causes the buffer model to be executed and will schedule an event with the value '1' to occur on output B at time 30 ns. At time 20 ns the next event on signal A occurs. This will execute the buffer model again. The buffer model will predict a new event on output B of a 0 value at time 40 ns. The event scheduled on output B for time 30 ns still has not occurred. The new event predicted by the buffer model clashes with the currently scheduled event, and the simulator will preempt the event at 30 ns.

The effect of the preemption is that the spike is swallowed. The reason for the cancellation is that according to the inertial delay model the first event at 30 ns did not have enough time to overcome the inertia of the output signal.

The inertial delay model is by far the most commonly used in all currently available simulators. Part of the reason for this is that in most cases the inertial delay model is accurate enough for the designer's needs. One more reason for the widespread use of inertial delay is that it prevents prolific propagation of spikes throughout the circuit. In most cases this is the behavior wanted by the designer.

2.2.2 Transport Delay

Transport delay is not the default in VHDL and must be specified. It represents a wire delay in which any pulse no matter how small is propagated to the output signal delayed by the delay value specified. Transport delay is especially useful for modeling delay line devices, wire delays on a PC board, and path delays on an ASIC.

If we look at the same buffer circuit that was shown in Figure 2-4 , but replace the inertial delay waveforms with the transport delay waveforms, we get the result shown in Figure 2-5. The same waveform is input to signal A but the output from signal B is quite different. With transport

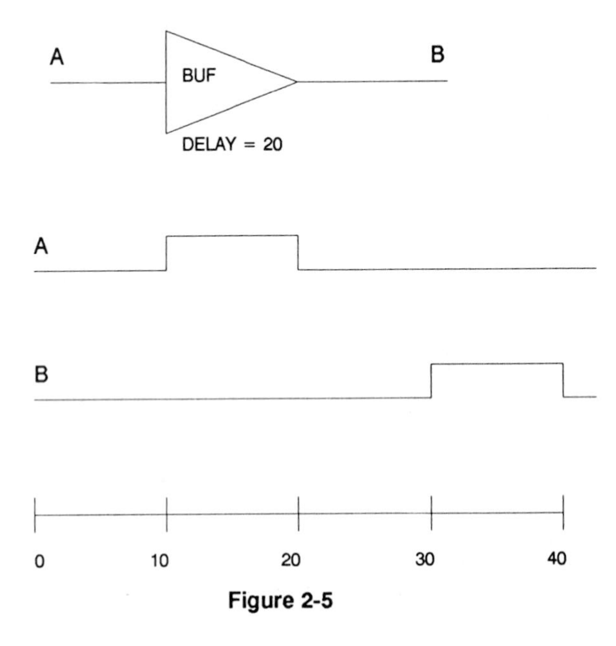

Figure 2-5

delay the spikes are not swallowed, but the events are ordered before propagation.

At time 10 ns the buffer model will be executed and will schedule an event for the output to go to a 1 value at 30 ns. At time 20 ns the buffer model will be reinvoked and predict a new value for the output at time 40 ns. With the transport delay algorithm the events are put in order. The event for time 40 ns will be put in the list of events after the event for time 30 ns. The spike is not swallowed but propagated intact after the delay time of the device.

2.2.3 Inertial Delay Model

The model below shows how to write an inertial delay model. It is the same as any other model that we have been looking at. The default delay type is inertial, therefore it is not necessary to specify the delay type to be inertial.

```
USE STD.std_logic.ALL;
ENTITY buf IS
   PORT ( a : IN t_wlogic;
```

```
        b : OUT t_wlogic);
END buf;

ARCHITECTURE buf OF buf IS
BEGIN
  b <= a AFTER 20 ns;
END buf;
```

2.2.4 Transport Delay Model

An example of a transport delay model is shown below. It is similar in every respect to the inertial delay model except for the keyword TRANSPORT in the signal assignment statement to signal *b*. When this keyword exists the delay type used in the statement is the transport delay mechanism.

```
USE STD.std_logic.ALL;
ENTITY delay_line IS
  PORT ( a : IN t_wlogic;
         b : OUT t_wlogic);
END delay_line;

ARCHITECTURE delay_line OF delay_line IS
BEGIN
  b <= TRANSPORT a AFTER 20 ns;
END delay_line;
```

2.3 Simulation Deltas

Simulation deltas are used to order some types of events during a simulation. Specifically, zero delay events must be ordered to produce consistent results. If zero delay events are not properly ordered, results can be disparate between different simulation runs. An example of this will be shown using the circuit shown in Figure 2-6. This circuit could be part of a clocking scheme in a complex device being modeled. It probably would not be the entire circuit, but only a part of the circuit used to generate the clock to the D flip-flop.

The circuit consists of an inverter, a NAND gate, and an AND gate driving the clock input of a flip-flop component. The NAND gate and AND gate are used to gate the clock input to the flip-flop.

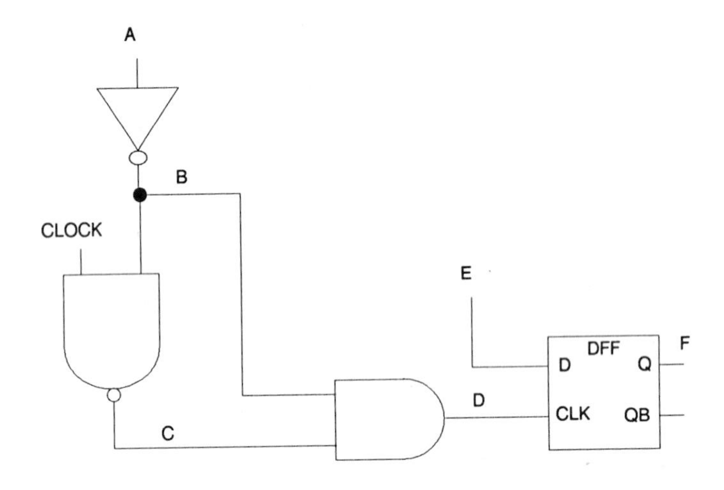

Figure 2-6

Let's examine the circuit operation, using a delta delay mechanism and using another mechanism. By examining the two delay mechanisms, we will better understand how a delta delay orders events.

To use delta delay, all of the circuit components must have zero delay specified. The delay for all three gates is specified as zero. (Real circuits do not exhibit such characteristics, but sometimes modeling is easier if all of the delay is concentrated at the outputs.) Let's examine the non-delta delay mechanism first.

When a falling edge occurs on signal A, the output of the inverter will change in 0 time. Let's assume that such an event occurred at time 10 ns. The output of the inverter, signal B, will change to reflect the new input value. When signal B changes, both the "and" gate and the nand gate will be reevaluated. For this example, the clock input is assumed to be a constant value '1'. If the nand gate is evaluated first, its new value will be '0'.

When the AND gate evaluates signal B will be a '0', and signal C will be a '1'; therefore the AND gate will predict a new value of '0'. But what happens if the AND gate evaluates first. The AND gate will see a '1' value on signal B, and a '1' value on signal C before the NAND gate has a chance to reevaluate. The AND gate will predict a new value of '1'.

The NAND gate reevaluates and calculates its new value as '0'. The change on the output of the NAND gate causes the AND gate to reevaluate again. The AND gate will now see the value of B, a '1' value, and the new value of signal C, a '0' value. The AND gate will now predict a '0' on its output. This process is summarized in Figure 2-7 :

AND first	NAND First
evaluate inverter	evaluate inverter
B < = 1	B < = 1
evaluate AND (C = 1)	evaluate NAND
D < = 1	C < = 0
evaluate NAND	evaluate AND
C < = 0	D < = 0
evaluate AND	
D < = 0	

Figure 2-7

Both circuits arrive at the same value for signal D. However, when the AND gate is evaluated first, a rising edge, one delta delay wide, occurs on signal D. This rising edge can clock the flip-flop, depending on how the flip-flop is modeled.

The point of this discussion is that without a delta synchronization mechanism, the results of the simulation can depend on how the simulator data structures are built. For instance, compiling the circuit the first time might make the AND gate evaluate first, while compiling again may make the NAND gate evaluate first—clearly not desireable results, and simulation deltas prevent this behavior from occurring.

The same circuit evaluated using the VHDL delta delay mechanism would evaluate as shown in Figure 2-8 :

The evaluation of the circuit does not depend on the order of evaluation of the NAND gate or AND gate. The sequence in Figure 2-8 will occur irrespective of the evaluation order of the AND or NAND gate.

Delta Delay Mechanism

time 10 ns	delta (1)	A < = 0
		evaluate inverter
	delta (2)	B < = 1
		evaluate AND
		evaluate NAND
	delta (3)	D < = 1
		C < = 0
		evaluate AND
	delta (4)	D < = 0
time 11 ns		

Figure 2-8

During the first delta time point of time 10 ns, signal A will receive the value '0'. This will cause the inverter to reevaluate, with the new value. The inverter will calculate the new value for signal B, which will be the value '1'. This value will not be propagated immediately, but will be scheduled for the next delta time point (delta 2).

The simulator will then begin execution of delta time point 2. Signal B will be updated to a '1' value, and the AND gate and NAND gate will be reevaluated. Both the AND gate and NAND gate will now schedule their new values for the next delta time point (delta 3).

When delta 3 occurs, signal D receives a '1' value, and signal C receives a '0' value. Since signal C also drives the "and" gate, the "and" gate will be reevaluated and will schedule its new output for delta time point 4.

To summarize, simulation deltas are an infinitesimal amount of time used as a synchronization mechanism when 0 delay events are present. Delta delay is used whenever 0 delay is specified, as shown below.

```
a <= b AFTER 0 ns;
```

Another case for using delta delay is when no delay is specified. This is shown below.

```
a <= b;
```

In both cases whenever signal *b* changes value from an event, signal *a* will have a delta-delayed signal assignment to it.

An equivalent VHDL model of the circuit shown in Figure 2-6, except for the flip-flop, is shown below:

```
ENTITY reg IS
   PORT( a, clock : in bit
         d : out bit);
END reg;

ARCHITECTURE test OF reg IS
   SIGNAL b, c : bit;
BEGIN
   b <= NOT(a);   -- notice no delay
   c <= NOT( clock AND b);
   d <= c AND b;
END test;
```

2.4 Drivers

VHDL has a unique way of handling multiply driven signals. Multiply driven signals are very useful for modeling a data bus, a bidirectional bus, etc. To correctly model these kinds of circuits in VHDL requires the concept of signal drivers. A VHDL driver is one contributor to the overall value of a signal.

A multiply driven signal has many drivers. The values of all of the drivers are resolved together to create a single value for the signal. The method of resolving all of the contributors into a single value is through a resolution function (resolution functions are discussed in Chapter 5). A resolution function is a designer-written function that will be called whenever a driver of a signal changes value.

2.4.1 Driver Creation

Drivers are created by signal assignment statements. A concurrent signal assignment inside of an architecture produces one driver for each signal assignment. Multiple signal assignments therefore produce multiple drivers for a signal. Consider the following architecture.

```
ARCHITECTURE test OF test IS
BEGIN
  a <= b AFTER 10 ns;
  a <= c AFTER 10 ns;
END test;
```

Signal *a* is being driven from two sources, *b* and *c*. Each concurrent signal assignment statement will create a driver for signal *a*. The first statement will create a driver that contains the value of signal *b* delayed by 10 ns. The second statement will create a driver that contains the value of signal *c* delayed by 10 ns. How these two drivers are resolved is left to the designer. The designers of VHDL did not want to arbitrarily add language constraints to signal behavior.

2.4.2 Bad Multiple Driver Model

Let's look at a model that looks correct enough at first glance, but will not function as the user intended. The model is for the four-to-one multiplexer discussed earlier.

```
USE STD.std_logic.ALL;
ENTITY mux IS
  PORT (i0, i1, i2, i3, a, b: IN t_wlogic;
    q : OUT t_wlogic);
END mux;

ARCHITECTURE bad OF mux IS
BEGIN
  q <= i0 WHEN a = '0' AND b = '0' ELSE F0;
  q <= i1 WHEN a = '1' AND b = '0' ELSE F0;
  q <= i2 WHEN a = '0' AND b = '1' ELSE F0;
  q <= i3 WHEN a = '1' AND b = '1' ELSE F0;
END BAD;
```

This model assigns *i0* to *q* when *a* is equal to a 0 and *b* is equal to a 0, *i1* when *a* is equal to a 1 and *b* is equal to a 0, etc. From a first glance the model looks as if it will work. However, each assignment to signal *q* creates a new driver for signal *q*. Four drivers to signal *q* will be created by this model.

Each driver will be driving either the value of one of the *i0, i1, i2, i3* inputs, or F0 (forcing 0). The value driven will be dependent on inputs *a* and *b*. If *a* is equal to '0', and *b* is equal to '0', the first assignment statement will put the value of *i0* into one of the drivers of *q*. The other three assignment statements will not have their conditions met, and therefore will be driving the value F0 (forcing 0). Three drivers will be driving the value 0, and one driver will be driving the value of *i0*. Typical resolution functions would have a difficult time predicting the desired output on *q*, which is the value of *i0*.

A better way to write this model is to create only one driver for signal *q*, as shown below:

```
ARCHITECTURE better OF mux IS
BEGIN
    q <= i0 WHEN a = '0' AND b = '0' ELSE
         i1 WHEN a = '1' AND b = '0' ELSE
         i2 WHEN a = '0' AND b = '1' ELSE
         i3 WHEN a = '1' AND b = '1' ELSE
         FX;         --- Forcing unknown
END better;
```

2.5 Generics

Generics are a general mechanism used to pass information to an instance of an entity. The information passed to the entity can be of most types allowed in VHDL. (Types are covered in detail later in Chapter 4.)

Why would a designer want to pass information to an entity? The most obvious, and probably most used, information passed to an entity are delay times for rising and falling delays of the device being modeled. Generics can also be used to pass any user-defined data types, including information such as load capacitance, resistance, etc.

All of the data passed to an entity is instance-specific information. The data values pertain to the instance being passed the data. In this way the designer can pass different values to different instances in the design.

The data passed to an instance is static data. Once the model has been elaborated (linked into the simulator), the data will not change during simulation. Generics cannot be assigned information as part of a simulation run. The information contained in generics passed into a component instance or a block can be used to alter the simulation results, but results cannot modify the generics.

The example shown below is an example of an entity for an AND gate that has three generics associated with it.

```
ENTITY and2 IS
   GENERIC(rise, fall : TIME; load : INTEGER);
   PORT( a, b : IN BIT;
      c : OUT BIT);
END AND2;
```

This entity would allow the designer to pass in a value for the rise and fall delays, as well as the loading that the device has on its output. With this information the model can correctly model the AND gate in the design. The architecture for the AND gate is shown below:

```
ARCHITECTURE load_dependent OF and2 IS
   SIGNAL internal : BIT;
BEGIN
   internal <= a AND b;
   c <= internal AFTER (rise + (load * 2 ns))
    WHEN internal = '1'
   ELSE internal AFTER (fall + (load * 3 ns));
END load_dependent;
```

The architecture declares a local signal called *internal* to store the value of the expression *a* and *b*. Precomputing values used in multiple instances is a very efficient method for modeling.

The generics *rise, fall,* and *load* contain the values that were passed in by the component instantiation statement. Let's look at a piece of a model that will instantiate the components of type AND2 in another model.

```
USE STD.std_logic.ALL;
ENTITY test IS
   GENERIC(rise, fall : TIME; load : INTEGER);
   PORT ( ina, inb, inc, ind : IN t_wlogic;
          out1, out2 : OUT t_wlogic);
```

```
END test;

ARCHITECTURE test_arch OF test IS
   COMPONENT AND2
   GENERIC(rise, fall : TIME; load : INTEGER);
   PORT ( a, b : IN t_wlogic;
          c : OUT t_wlogic);
   END COMPONENT;
BEGIN
   U1: AND2 GENERIC MAP(10 ns, 12 ns, 3 )
        PORT MAP (ina, inb, out1 );
   U2: AND2 GENERIC MAP(9 ns, 11 ns, 5 )
        PORT MAP (inc, ind, out2 );
END test_arch;
```

The architecture statement first declares any components that will be used in the model. In this example component AND2 is declared. Next, the body of the architecture statement contains a couple of component instantiation statements for components U1 and U2. Port *a* of component U1 is mapped to signal *ina,* port *b* is mapped to signal *inb,* and port *c* is mapped to *out1*. In the same way component U2 is mapped to signals *inc, ind,* and *out2.*

Generic *rise* of instance U1 is mapped to 10 ns, generic *fall* is mapped to 12 ns, and generic *load* is mapped to 3. The generics for component U2 are mapped to values 9 and 11 ns and value 5.

Generics can also have default values that are overridden if actual values are mapped to the generics. In the example below are two instances of component type AND2. In instance U1 actual values are mapped to the generics and these values will be used in the simulation. In instance U2, no values are mapped to the instance and therefore the default values will be used to control the behavior of the simulation if specified; otherwise an error will occur.

```
USE STD.std_logic.ALL;
ENTITY test IS
   GENERIC(rise, fall : TIME;
           load : INTEGER);
   PORT ( ina, inb, inc, ind : IN t_wlogic;
          out1, out2 : OUT t_wlogic);
END test;
```

```
ARCHITECTURE test_arch OF test IS
   COMPONENT and2
      GENERIC(rise, fall : TIME := 10 NS;
               load : INTEGER := 0);
      PORT ( a, b : IN t_wlogic;
              c : OUT t_wlogic);
   END COMPONENT;
BEGIN
   U1: and2 GENERIC MAP(10 ns, 12 ns, 3 )
         PORT MAP (ina, inb, out1 );
   U2: and2 PORT MAP (inc, ind, out2 );
END test_arch;
```

As we have seen, generics have many uses. The uses of generics are limited only by the creativity of the model writer.

2.6 Block Statements

Blocks are a partitioning mechanism within VHDL that allows the designer to logically group areas of the model. The analogy with a typical CAE system is a schematic sheet. In a typical CAE system, a level or a portion of the design can be represented by a number of schematic sheets. The reason for partitioning the design may relate to design standards about how many components are allowed on a sheet, or it may be a logical grouping that the designer finds more understandable.

The same analogy holds true for block statements. The statement area in an architecture can be broken into a number of separate logical areas. For instance, if you were designing a CPU, one block might be an ALU, another a register bank, and another a shifter.

Each block represents a self-contained area of the model. Each block can declare local signals, types, constants, etc. Any object that can be declared in the architecture declaration section can be declared in the block declaration section. An example is shown below.

```
USE STD.std_logic.ALL;
PACKAGE BIT32 IS
  TYPE tw32 IS ARRAY(31 DOWNTO 0)
     OF t_wlogic;
END BIT32;
```

```
USE STD.std_logic.ALL;
USE WORK.bit32.ALL;
ENTITY cpu IS
   PORT( clk, interrupt : IN t_wlogic;
         addr : OUT tw32; data : INOUT tw32 );
END cpu;

ARCHITECTURE cpu_blk OF cpu IS
   SIGNAL ibus, dbus : tw32;
BEGIN
   ALU : BLOCK
      SIGNAL qbus : tw32;
   BEGIN
      -- alu behavior statements
   END BLOCK ALU;

   REG8 : BLOCK
      SIGNAL zbus : tw32;
   BEGIN
      REG1: BLOCK
         SIGNAL qbus : tw32;
      BEGIN
         -- reg1 behavioral statements
      END BLOCK REG1;
      -- more REG8 statements
   END BLOCK REG8;
END cpu_blk;
```

Entity *cpu* is the outermost entity declaration of this model. (This is not a complete model, only a subset.) Entity *cpu* declares four ports that are used as the model interface. Ports *clk* and *interrupt* are input ports, *addr* is an output port, and *data* is an inout port. All of these ports are visible to any block declared in an architecture for this entity. The input ports can be read from and the output ports can be assigned values.

Signals *ibus* and *dbus* are local signals declared in architecture *cpu_blk*. These signals are local to architecture *cpu_blk* and cannot be referenced outside of the architecture. However, any block inside of the architecture can reference these signals. Any lower-level block can reference signals from a level above, but upper-level blocks cannot reference lower-level local signals.

Signal *qbus* is declared in the block declaration section of block ALU. This signal is local to block ALU and cannot be referenced outside of the block. All of the statements inside of block ALU can reference *qbus*, but statements outside of block ALU cannot use *qbus*.

In exactly the same fashion signal *zbus* is local to block REG8. Block REG1 inside of block REG8 has access to signal *zbus*, and all of the other statements in block REG8 also have access to signal *zbus*.

In the declaration section for block REG1 another signal called *qbus* is declared. This signal has the same name as the signal *qbus* declared in block ALU. Won't this cause a problem? To the compiler these two signals are separate, and this is a legal, although confusing, use of the language. The two signals are declared in two separate declarative regions and are valid only in those regions; therefore, they are considered to be two separate signals with the same name. Each *qbus* can be referenced only in the block that has the declaration of the signal , except as a fully qualified name, discussed later in this section.

Another interesting case is shown below.

```
BLK1 : BLOCK
   SIGNAL qbus : tw32;
BEGIN
   BLK2 : BLOCK
      SIGNAL qbus : tw32;
   BEGIN
      -- blk2 statements
   END BLOCK BLK2;

-- blk1 statements
END BLOCK BLK1;
```

In this example signal *qbus* is declared in two blocks. The interesting feature of this model is that one of the blocks is contained in the other. It would seem that BLK2 has access to two signals called *qbus*. The first from the local declaration of *qbus* in the declaration section of BLK2 and the second from the declaration section of BLK1. BLK1 is also the parent block of BLK2. However, BLK2 will see only the *qbus* signal from the declaration in BLK2. The *qbus* signal from BLK1 has been overridden by a declaration of the same name in BLK2.

The *qbus* signal from BLK1 can be seen inside of BLK2, if the name of signal *qbus* is qualified with the block name. For instance, in this example to reference signal *qbus* from BLK1, use *BLK1.qbus*.

In general, this can be a very confusing method of modeling. The problem stems from the fact that you are never quite sure which *qbus* is being referenced at a given time without fully analyzing all of the declarations carefully.

As mentioned earlier blocks are self-contained regions of the model. But blocks are unique because a block can contain ports and generics. This allows the designer to remap signals and generics external to the block to signals and generics inside the block. But why as a designer would I want to do that?

The capability of ports and generics on blocks allows the designer to reuse blocks written for another purpose in a new design. For instance let's assume that you are upgrading a CPU design and need extra functionality in the ALU section. Let's also assume that another designer has a new ALU model that performs the functionality needed. The only trouble with the new ALU model is that the interface port names and generic names are different than the names that exist in the design being upgraded. With the port and generic mapping ability within blocks, this is no problem. Map the signal names and the generic parameters in the design being upgraded to ports and generics created for the new ALU block. An example illustrating this is shown below.

```
PACKAGE math IS
   TYPE tw32 IS ARRAY(31 DOWNTO 0)
        OF t_wlogic;
   FUNCTION tw_add(a, b : tw32)
        RETURN tw32;
   FUNCTION tw_sub(a, b : tw32)
        RETURN tw32;
END math;

USE WORK.math.ALL;
USE STD.std_logic.ALL;
ENTITY cpu IS
   PORT( clk, interrupt : IN t_wlogic;
         addr : OUT tw32; cont : IN INTEGER;
```

```
          data : INOUT tw32 );
END cpu;

ARCHITECTURE cpu_blk OF cpu IS
   SIGNAL ibus, dbus : tw32;
BEGIN
   ALU : BLOCK
      PORT( abus, bbus : IN tw32;
            d_out : OUT tw32;
            ctbus : IN INTEGER);
      PORT MAP ( abus => ibus, bbus => dbus,
            d_out => data, ctbus => cont);
      SIGNAL qbus : tw32;
   BEGIN
      d_out <= tw_add(abus, bbus) WHEN
                     ctbus = 0 ELSE
               tw_sub(abus, bbus) WHEN
                     ctbus = 1 ELSE
               abus;

   END BLOCK ALU;
END;
```

Basically this is the same model shown earlier except for the port and port map statements in the ALU block declaration section. The port statement declares the number of ports used for the block, the direction of the ports, and the type of the ports. The port map statement maps the new ports with signals or ports that exist outside of the block. Port *abus* is mapped to architecture CPU_BLK local signal *ibus*, port *bbus* is mapped to *dbus*. Ports *d_out* and *ctbus* are mapped to external ports of the entity.

Mapping implies a connection between the port and the external signal such that whenever there is a change in value on the signal connected to a port, the port value changes to the new value. If a change occurs in the signal *ibus*, the new value of *ibus* will be passed into the ALU block and port *abus* will obtain the new value. The same is true for all ports.

2.7 Guarded Blocks

Block statements have another interesting behavior known as guarded blocks. A guarded block contains a *guard expression* which can enable and disable drivers inside the block. The guard expression is a boolean expression: when true, drivers contained in the block are enabled, and when false the drivers are disabled. Let's look at an example to show some more of the details.

```
USE STD.std_logic.ALL;
USE STD.std_ttl.ALL;
ENTITY latch IS
   PORT( d, clk : IN t_wlogic;
         q, qb : OUT t_wlogic);
END latch;

ARCHITECTURE latch_guard OF latch IS
BEGIN
   G1 : BLOCK( clk = '1')
   BEGIN
      q <= GUARDED d AFTER 5 ns;
      qb <= GUARDED NOT(d) AFTER 7 ns;
   END BLOCK G1;
END latch_guard;
```

This model illustrates how a latch model could be written using a guarded block. This is a very simpleminded model; however, more complex and more accurate models will be shown later. The entity declares the four ports needed for the latch, and the architecture has only one statement in it. The statement is a guarded block statement. A guarded block statement looks like a typical block statement except for the guard expression after the keyword BLOCK. The guard expression in this example is (*clk* = '1'). This is a boolean expression that will return TRUE when *clk* is equal to a '1' value and return FALSE when *clk* is equal to any other value.

When the guard expression is true, all of the drivers of guarded signal assignment statements will be enabled, or turned on. When the guard expression is false, all of the drivers of guarded signal assigment statements are disabled, or turned off. There are two guarded signal assignment statements in this model. One is the statement that assigns a value to *q* and the other is the statement that assigns a value to *qb*. A guarded signal assignment statement is recognized by the keyword GUARDED between the < = and the expression part of the statement.

When port *clk* of the entity has the value '1', the guard expression will be true, and the value of input *d* will be scheduled on the *q* output after 5 ns, and the NOT value of *d* will be scheduled on the *qb* output after 7 ns. When port *clk* has the value '0' or any other legal value of the type, outputs *q* and *qb* will turn off and the output value of the signal will be determined by the default value assigned by the resolution function. When *clk* is not equal to '1' the drivers created by the signal assignments for *q* and *qb* in this architecture are effectively turned off. The drivers do not contribute to the overall value of the signal.

Signal assignments can be guarded by using the keyword GUARDED. A new signal is implicitly declared in the block whenever a block has a guard expression. This signal is called GUARD. Its value is the value of the guard expression. This signal can be used to trigger other processes to occur.

Blocks are useful for partitioning the design into smaller, more manageable units. They allow the designer the flexibility to create large designs from smaller building blocks and provide a convenient method of controlling the drivers on a signal.

Chapter

3

Sequential Processing

In Chapter 2 we examined behavioral modeling using concurrent statements. We discussed concurrent signal assignment statements, as well as block statements and component instantiation. In this chapter we will focus on sequential statements. Sequential statements are statements that execute serially one after the other. Most programming languages such as C and Pascal support this type of behavior. In fact VHDL has borrowed the syntax for its sequential statements from ADA.

3.1 Process Statement

In an architecture for an entity, all statements are concurrent. So where do sequential statements exist in VHDL? There is a statement called the process statement that contains only sequential statements. The process statement is itself a concurrent statement. A process statement can exist in an architecture and define regions in the architecture where all statements are sequential.

A process statement has a declaration section and a statement part. In the declaration section types, variables, constants, subprograms, etc. can be declared (for a full list, see page A-13 in the LRM). The statement part contains only sequential statements. Sequential statements consist of CASE statements, IF THEN ELSE statements, LOOP statements, etc. We will examine these statements later in this chapter. First, let's look at how a process statement is structured.

3.1.1 Sensitivity List

The process statement can have an explicit sensitivity list. This list defines the signals that will cause the statements inside the process statement to execute whenever one or more elements of the list change value. The sensitivity list is a list of the signals that the process is sensitive to changes on. The process has to have an explicit sensitivity list or, as we will discuss later, a WAIT statement.

3.1.2 Process Example

Let's look at an example of a process statement in an architecture to see how the process statement fits into the big picture, and discuss some more details of how it works. Shown below is a model of a two-input nand gate.

```
USE STD.std_logic.ALL;
USE STD.std_ttl.ALL;
ENTITY nand2 IS
  PORT( a, b : IN t_wlogic;
        c : OUT t_wlogic);
END nand2;

ARCHITECTURE nand2 OF nand2 IS
BEGIN
  PROCESS( a, b )
    VARIABLE temp : t_wlogic;
  BEGIN
    temp := NOT (a and b);

    IF (temp = '1') THEN
      c <= temp AFTER 6 ns;
    ELSIF (temp = '0') THEN
      c <= temp AFTER 5 ns;
    ELSE
      c <= temp AFTER 6 ns;
    END IF;
```

```
   END PROCESS;
END nand2;
```

This example shows how to write a model for a simple two-input NAND gate using a process statement. The first two USE statements declare two VHDL packages that provide useful modeling tools in this example (these packages are described in Appendix B). We will discuss packages later in Chapter 5. These statements are used to provide technology information about the model. The USE statements were included so that the model could be simulated with a VHDL simulator without any modifications.

The entity declares three ports for the *nand2* gate. Ports *a* and *b* are the inputs to the *nand2* gate and port *c* is the output. The name of the architecture is the same name as the entity name. This is legal and can save some of the headaches of trying to generate unique names.

The architecture contains only one statement, a concurrent process statement. The process declarative part starts at the keyword PROCESS and ends at the keyword BEGIN. The process *statement* part starts at the keyword BEGIN and ends at the keywords END PROCESS. The process *declaration* section declares a local variable called *temp*. The process *statement* part has two sequential statements in it; a variable assignment statement

```
temp := NOT (a AND b);
```

and an IF THEN ELSE statement.

```
IF (temp = '1') THEN
   c <= temp AFTER 6 ns;
ELSIF (temp = '0') THEN
   c <= temp AFTER 5 ns;
ELSE
   c <= temp AFTER 6 ns;
END IF;
```

The process contains an explicit sensitivity list with two signals contained in it.

```
PROCESS( a, b )
```

The process is sensitive to signals *a* and *b*. In this example *a* and *b* are input ports to the model. Input ports create signals that can be used as inputs, output ports create signals that can be used as outputs, and inout ports create signals that can be used as both. Whenever port *a* or *b* has a change in value, the statements inside of the process will be executed. Each statement will be executed in serial order starting with the statement at the top of the process statement and working down to the bottom. After all of the statements have been executed once, the process will wait for another change in a signal or port in its sensitivity list.

The process declarative part declares one variable called *temp*. Its type is *t_wlogic*. This type will be explained in great detail in Chapter 9 and also in Appendix A, as it is used throughout the book. For now, assume that the type defines a signal that is a single bit and can assume the values 0, 1, and X. Variable *temp* is used as temporary storage in this model to save the precomputed value of the expression (*a* and *b*). The value of this expression is precomputed for efficiency.

3.2 Signal Assignment versus Variable Assignment

The first statement inside of the process statement is a variable assignment that assigns a value to variable *temp*. In the previous chapter we discussed how signals received values that were scheduled either after an amount of time or after a delta delay. A variable assignment happens immediately when the statement is executed. For instance, in this model the first statement has to assign a value to variable *temp* for the second statement to use. Variable assignment has no delay; it happens immediately.

Let's look at two examples that illustrate this point more clearly. Both examples are models of a four-to-one multiplexer device. The symbol and truth table for this device are shown in Figure 3-1. One of the four input signals is propagated to the output depending on the values on inputs *a* and *b*.

The first model for the multiplexer is an incorrect model and the second is a corrected version of the model.

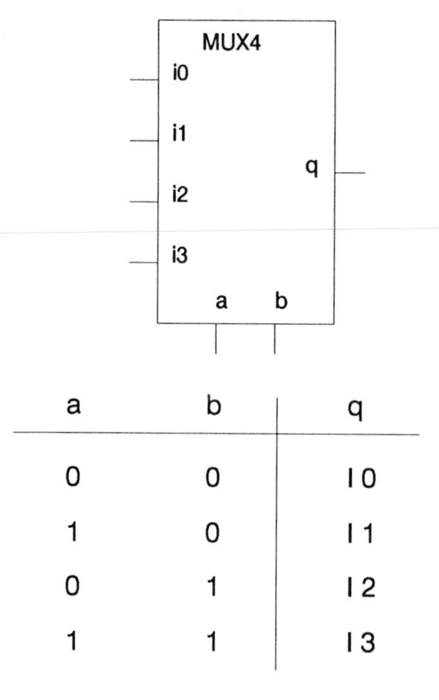

a	b	q
0	0	I0
1	0	I1
0	1	I2
1	1	I3

Figure 3-1

3.2.1 Incorrect Mux Example

The incorrect model of the multiplexer has a flaw in it that will cause the model to produce incorrect results. This is shown by the model below:

```
USE STD.std_logic.ALL;
ENTITY mux IS
   PORT (i0, i1, i2, i3, a, b : IN t_wlogic;
         q : OUT t_wlogic);
END mux;

ARCHITECTURE wrong of mux IS
   SIGNAL muxval : INTEGER;
BEGIN
   PROCESS ( i0, i1, i2, i3, a, b )
   BEGIN
      muxval <= 0;
      IF (a = '1') THEN
```

```
            muxval <= muxval + 1;
        END IF;

        IF (b = '1') THEN
            muxval <= muxval + 2;
        END IF;
        CASE muxval IS
            WHEN 0 =>
                Q <= I0 AFTER 10 ns;
            when 1 =>
                Q <= I1 AFTER 10 ns;
            when 2 =>
                Q <= I2 AFTER 10 ns;
            when 3 =>
                Q <= I3 AFTER 10 ns;
            when others =>
                null;
        END case;
    END PROCESS;
END wrong;
```

Whenever one of the input signals in the process sensitivity list changes value, the sequential statements in the process are executed. The process statement in the first example contains four sequential statements. The first statement initializes the local signal *muxval* to a known value (0). The subsequent statements add values to the local signal depending on the value of the *a* and *b* input signals. Finally, the case statement will choose an input to propagate to the output based on the value of signal *muxval.* This model has a significant flaw, however. The first statement

```
muxval <= 0;
```

causes the value 0 to be scheduled as an event for signal *muxval*. In fact, the value 0 is scheduled in an event for the next simulation delta because no delay was specified. When the second statement

```
IF (a = '1') THEN
    muxval <= muxval + 1;
END IF;
```

is executed, the value of signal *muxval* will be whatever was last propagated to it. The new value scheduled from the first statement will not have propagated yet. In fact, when multiple assignments to a signal occur within the same process statement, the last assigned value will be the value propagated.

The signal *muxval* will have a *garbage* value when entering the process. Its value will not be changed until the process has completed execution of all of the sequential statements contained in the process. In fact, if signal *b* is a '1' value, then whatever garbage value the signal had when entering the process will have the value 2 added to it.

A better way to implement this example is shown in the next example. The only difference between this next model and the previous one is the declaration of *muxval* and the assignments to *muxval*. In the previous model, *muxval* was a signal and signal assignment statements were used to assign values to it. In the next example, *muxval* is a variable and variable assignments are used to assign to it.

3.2.2 Correct Mux Example

In this example the incorrect model will be rewritten to reflect a solution to the problems with the last model.

```
USE STD.std_logic.ALL;
ENTITY mux IS
   PORT (I0, I1, I2, I3, A, B : IN t_wlogic;
         Q : OUT t_wlogic);
END mux;

ARCHITECTURE better OF mux IS
BEGIN
   PROCESS ( I0, I1, I2, I3, A, B )
      VARIABLE muxval : INTEGER;
   BEGIN

      muxval := 0;
      IF (A = '1') THEN
         muxval := muxval + 1;
      END IF;

      IF (B = '1') THEN
         muxval := muxval + 2;
      END IF;
      CASE muxval IS
         WHEN 0 =>
```

```
            Q <= I0 AFTER 10 ns;
        WHEN 1 =>
            Q <= I1 AFTER 10 ns;
        WHEN 2 =>
            Q <= I2 AFTER 10 ns;
        WHEN 3 =>
            Q <= I3 AFTER 10 ns;
        WHEN OTHERS =>
            NULL;
      END CASE;
    END PROCESS;
END better;
```

This simple coding difference makes a tremendous operational difference. When the first statement

```
muxval := 0;
```

is executed, the value 0 is placed in variable *muxval* immediately. The value is not scheduled because *muxval* in this example is a variable, not a signal. Variables represent local storage as opposed to signals, which represent circuit interconnect. The local storage is updated immediately, and the new value can be used later in the model for further computations.

Since *muxval* is initialized to 0 immediately, the next two statements in the process will use 0 as the initial value and add appropriate numbers, depending on the values of signals *a* and *b*. These assignments are also immediate, and therefore when the CASE statement executes, variable *muxval* contains the correct value. From this value the correct input signal can be propagated to the output.

3.3 Sequential Statements

Sequential statements exist inside the boundaries of a process statement as well as in subprograms. In this chapter we are most concerned with sequential statements inside of process statements. In Chapter 5 we will discuss subprograms and the statements contained within them.

The sequential statements that we will discuss are

- IF
- CASE

- LOOP
- ASSERT
- WAIT

3.4 IF Statements

In Appendix A of the LRM all VHDL constructs are described using a variant of the Bachus-Naur format (BNF) that is used to describe typical programming languages. If you are not familiar with BNF, Appendix C in this book gives a cursory description. Becoming familiar with the BNF will help you to better understand how to construct complex VHDL statements.

The BNF description of the IF statement is listed on page A-9 of the LRM and looks like this:

```
if_statement ::=
  IF condition THEN
    sequence_of_statements
  {ELSIF condition THEN
    sequence_of_statements}
  [ELSE
    sequence_of_statements]
  END IF;
```

From the BNF description we can conclude that the IF statement starts with the keyword IF and ends with the keywords END IF spelled out as two separate words. There are also two optional clauses; they are the ELSIF clause and the ELSE clause. The ELSIF clause is repeatable such that more than one ELSIF clause is allowed, but the ELSE clause is optional, and only one is allowed. The condition construct in all cases is a boolean expression. This is an expression that evaluates to either true or false. Whenever a condition evaluates to a true value, the sequence of statements following is executed. If no condition is true, then the sequence of statements for the ELSE clause is executed, if one exists. Let's analyze a few examples to get a better understanding of how the BNF relates to the VHDL code.

The first example shows how to write a simple IF statement.

```
IF (x < 10) THEN
   a := b;
END IF;
```

The IF statement starts with the keyword IF. Next is the condition (x < 10), followed by the keyword THEN. The condition will be true when the value of *x* is less than 10, otherwise it will be false. When the condition is true, the statements between the THEN and END IF will be executed. In this example the assignment statement *(a := b)* will be executed whenever *x* is less than 10. What happens if *x* is greater than or equal to 10? In this example there is no ELSE clause, so no statements will be executed in the IF statement. Instead control will be transferred to the statement after the END IF.

Let's look at another example where the ELSE clause is useful.

```
IF (day = sunday) THEN
   weekend := TRUE;
ELSIF (day = saturday) THEN
   weekend := TRUE;
ELSE
   weekday := TRUE;
END IF;
```

In this example there are two variables *weekend* and *weekday* that get set depending on the value of a signal called *day*. Variable *weekend* gets set to TRUE whenever *day* is equal to *saturday* or *sunday*. Otherwise, variable *weekday* gets set to TRUE. The execution of the IF statement starts by checking to see if variable *day* is equal to *sunday*. If this is true, then the next statement is executed and control is transferred to the statement following END IF. Otherwise, control is transferred to the ELSIF statement part and *day* is checked for *saturday*. If variable *day* is equal to *saturday*, then the next statement is executed and control is again transferred to the statement following the END IF statement. Finally if *day* is not equal to *sunday* or *saturday*, then the ELSE statement part is executed.

The IF statement can have multiple ELSIF statement parts, but only one ELSE statement part. Between each statement part can exist more than one sequential statement.

3.5 CASE Statements

The CASE statement is used whenever a single expression value can be used to select between a number of actions. The BNF for the CASE statement is shown below:

```
case_statement ::=
   CASE expression IS
      case_statement_alternative
      {case_statement_alternative}
   END CASE;

case_statement_alternative ::=
   WHEN choices =>
      sequence_of_statements


sequence_of_statements ::=
   {sequential_statement}

choices ::=
   choice{| choice}

choice ::=
   SIMPLE_expression|
   discrete_range|
   ELEMENT_simple_name|
   OTHERS
```

A CASE statement consists of the keyword CASE followed by an expression and the keyword IS. The expression will either evaluate to a value that matches one of the CHOICES in a WHEN statement part, or match an OTHERS clause. If the expression matches the CHOICE part of a WHEN *choices* = > clause, the *sequence_of_statements* following will be executed. After these statements are executed control is transferred to the statement following the END CASE clause.

Either the CHOICES clause must enumerate every possible value of the type returned by the expression, or the *last* choice must contain an OTHERS clause.

Let's look at some examples to reinforce what the BNF states.

```
CASE instruction IS
   WHEN load_accum =>
      accum <= data;
   WHEN store_accum =>
      data_out <= accum;
   WHEN load|store =>
      process_IO(addr);
   WHEN OTHERS =>
      process_error(instruction);
END CASE;
```

The CASE statement will execute the proper statement depending on the value of input *instruction.* If the value of *instruction* is one of the choices listed in the WHEN clauses, then statement following the WHEN clause is executed. Otherwise the statement following the OTHERS clause is executed. In this example when the value of *instruction* is *load_accum*, the first assignment statement is executed. If the value of *instruction* is *load* or *store*, the *process_IO* procedure is called.

If the value of *instruction* is outside the range of the choices given, then the OTHERS clause will match the expression and the statement following the OTHERS clause will be executed. It is an error if an OTHERS clause does not exist and the choices given do not cover every possible value of the expression type.

In the next example a more complex type (types are discussed in Chapter 4) is returned by the expression. The CASE statement uses this type to select among the choices of the statement.

```
TYPE vectype IS ARRAY(0 TO 1) OF BIT;
VARIABLE bit_vec : vectype;

CASE bit_vec IS
   WHEN "00" =>
      RETURN 0;
   WHEN "01" =>
      RETURN 1;
   WHEN "10" =>
      RETURN 2;
   WHEN "11" =>
   RETURN 3;
END CASE;
```

This example shows one way to convert an array of bits into an integer. When both bits of variable *bit_vec* contain '0' values the first choice "00" will match and the value 0 will be returned. When both bits are '1' values, the value 3, or "11", will be returned. This CASE statement does not need an OTHERS clause because all possible values of variable *bit_vec* are enumerated by the choices.

3.6 LOOP Statements

The LOOP statement is used whenever an operation needs to be repeated. LOOP statements are used when powerful iteration capability is needed to implement a model. The BNF for the LOOP statement is shown below:

```
loop_statement ::=
  [LOOP_label : ] [iteration_scheme] LOOP
    sequence_of_statements
  END LOOP[LOOP_label];

iteration_scheme ::=
  WHILE condition |
  FOR LOOP_parameter_specification

LOOP_parameter_specification ::=
  identifier IN discrete_range
```

The LOOP statement has an optional label, which can be used to identify the LOOP statement. The LOOP statement has an optional *iteration_scheme* that determines which kind of LOOP statement is being used. The *iteration_scheme* includes two types of LOOP statements, a WHILE condition LOOP statement and a FOR identifier IN *discrete_range* statement. The FOR loop will loop as many times as specified in the *discrete_range*, unless the loop is exited from (discussed later). The WHILE condition LOOP statement will loop as long as the condition expression is TRUE.

Let's look at a couple of examples to see how these statements work.

```
WHILE (day = weekday) LOOP
  day := get_next_day(day);
END LOOP;
```

This example uses the WHILE condition form of the LOOP statement. The condition is checked each time before the loop is executed. If the condition is TRUE the LOOP statements are executed. Control will then be transferred back to the beginning of the loop. The condition will be checked again. If TRUE, the loop will be executed again; if not, statement execution will continue on the statement following the END LOOP clause.

The other version of the LOOP statement is the FOR loop.

```
FOR i IN 1 to 10 LOOP
  i_squared(i) := i * i;
END LOOP;
```

This loop will execute 10 times whenever execution begins. Its function is to calculate the squares from 1 to 10 and insert them into the *i_squared* signal array. The index variable, *i*, will start at the leftmost value of the range and will be incremented until the rightmost value of the range.

In some languages the loop index, in this example *i*, can be assigned a value inside the loop to change its value. VHDL *does not* allow any assignment to the loop index. This also precludes the loop index existing in any return values of a function, or out and inout parameters of a procedure.

Another interesting point about FOR LOOP statements is the fact that the index value *i* is locally declared by the FOR statement. The variable *i* does not need to be declared explicitly in the process, function, or procedure. By virtue of the FOR LOOP statement, the loop index is declared locally. If another variable of the same name exists in the process, function, or procedure, then these two variables are treated as separate variables and are accessed by context. Let's look at an example to illustrate this point.

```
PROCESS(i)
BEGIN

  x <= i + 1; -- x is a signal

  FOR i IN 1 to a/2 LOOP
    q(i) := a; -- q is a variable
  END LOOP;
```

```
END PROCESS;
```

Whenever the value of the signal *i* in the process sensitivity list changes value, the process will be invoked. The first statement will schedule the value $i + 1$ on the signal x. Next the FOR loop will be executed. The index value *i* is not the same object as the signal *i* that was used to calculate the new value for signal *x*. These are separate objects that are each accessed by context. Inside the FOR loop, when a reference is made to *i*, the local index is retrieved. But outside the FOR loop, when a reference is made to *i*, the value of the signal *i* in the sensitivity list of the process is retrieved.

The values used to specify the range in the FOR loop need not be specific integer values, as has been shown in the examples. The range can obtain any discrete range. A *discrete_range* can be expressed as a *subtype_indication* or a range statement. Let's look at a few more examples of how FOR loops can be constructed with ranges.

```
PROCESS(clk)
   TYPE day_of_week IS (sun, mon, tue, wed,
                        thur, fri, sat);
BEGIN
   FOR i IN day_of_week LOOP
      IF i = sat THEN
         son <= mow_lawn;
      ELSIF i = sun THEN
         church <= family;
      ELSE
         dad <= go_to_work;
      END IF;
   END LOOP;
END PROCESS;
```

In this example the range is specified by the type. By specifying the type as the range the compiler will determine that the leftmost value is *sun*, and the rightmost value is *sat*. The range will then be determined as from *sun* to *sat*.

If an ascending range is desired, use the *to* clause. The *downto* clause can be used to create a descending range. An example is shown below.

```
PROCESS(x, y)
BEGIN
   FOR i IN x downto y LOOP
      q(i) := w(i);
   END LOOP;
END PROCESS;
```

When different values for *x* and *y* are passed in, different ranges of the array *w* are copied to the same place in array *q*.

3.6.1 NEXT Statement

There are cases when it is necessary to stop executing the statements in the loop for this iteration and go to the next iteration. VHDL includes a construct that will accomplish this. The NEXT statement allows the designer to stop processing this iteration and skip to the successor. When the NEXT statement is executed, processing of the model stops at the current point and is transferred to the beginning of the LOOP statement. Execution will begin with the first statement in the loop but the loop variable will be incremented to the next iteration value. If the iteration limit has been reached, processing will stop. If not, execution will continue.

An example showing this behavior is shown below:

```
PROCESS(A, B)
   CONSTANT max_limit : INTEGER := 255;
BEGIN
   FOR i IN 0 TO max_limit LOOP
      IF (done(i) = TRUE) THEN
         NEXT;
      ELSE
         done(i) := TRUE;
      END IF;
      q(i) <= a(i) AND b(i);
   END LOOP;
END PROCESS;
```

The process statement contains one LOOP statement. This LOOP statement will logically "and" the bits of arrays *a* and *b* and put the results in array *q*. This behavior will continue whenever the flag in array *done* is not true. If the *done* flag is already set for this value of the index *i*, then the NEXT statement is executed. Execution will continue with the first statement of the loop, and index *i* will have the value *i* + 1. If the value of the *done* array is not true, then the NEXT statement is not executed, and execution will continue with the statement contained in the ELSE clause for the IF statement.

The NEXT statement allows the designer the capability to stop execution of this iteration and go on to the next iteration. There are other cases when the need exists to stop execution of a loop completely. This capability is provided with the EXIT statement.

3.6.2 EXIT Statement

During the execution of a LOOP statement, it may be necessary to jump out of the loop. This can occur because a significant error has occurred during the execution of the model or all of the processing has finished early. The VHDL EXIT statement allows the designer to exit or jump out of a LOOP statement currently in execution. The EXIT statement causes execution to halt at the location of the EXIT statement. Execution will continue at the statement following the LOOP statement.

An example illustrating this point is shown below:

```
PROCESS(a)
   variable int_a : integer;
BEGIN
   int_a := a;
   FOR i IN 0 TO max_limit LOOP
      IF (int_a <= 0) THEN -- less than or
         EXIT;                -- equal to
      ELSE

         int_a := int_a -1;
         q(i) <= 3.1416 / REAL(a * i); -- signal
      END IF;                          -- assign
   END LOOP;
   y <= q;
END PROCESS;
```

Inside this process statement, the value of *int_a* is always assumed to be a positive value greater than 0. If the value of *int_a* is negative or zero, then an error condition results and the calculation should not be completed. If the value of *int_a* is less than or equal to 0, then the IF statement will be true and the EXIT statement will be executed. The loop will be immediately terminated and the next statement executed will be the assignment statement to *y* after the LOOP statement.

If this were a complete example, the designer would also want to alert the user of the model that a significant error had occurred. A method to accomplish this function would be with an ASSERT statement, which is discussed later in this chapter.

The EXIT statement has three basic types of operations. The first involves an EXIT statement without a loop label, or a WHEN condition. If these conditions are true then the EXIT statement will behave as follows:

The EXIT statement will only exit from the most current LOOP statement encountered. If an EXIT statement is inside a LOOP statement that is nested inside another LOOP statement, the EXIT statement will only exit the inner LOOP statement. Execution will still remain in the outer LOOP statement. The exit statement will only exit from the most recent LOOP statement.

If the EXIT statement has an optional loop label, then the EXIT statement, when encountered, will transfer control to the loop label specified.

If the EXIT statement has an optional WHEN condition, then the EXIT statement will only exit the loop if the condition specified is true. The next statement executed depends on whether the EXIT statement has a loop label specified or not. If a loop label is specified, the next statement executed will be contained in the LOOP statement specified by the loop label. If no loop label is present, the next statement executed is in the next outer loop.

The EXIT statement provides a quick and easy method of exiting a LOOP statement when all processing is finished or an error or warning condition occurs.

3.7 ASSERT Statement

The ASSERT statement is a very useful statement for reporting textual strings to the designer. The ASSERT statement checks the value of a boolean expression for true or false. If the value is true, the statement does nothing. If the value is false the ASSERT statement will output a user-specified text string to the standard output to the terminal.

The designer can also specify a severity level with which to output the text string. The four levels are, in increasing level of severity, *note, warning, error, failure*. The severity level allows the designer the capability to classify messages into proper categories.

The *note* category is useful for relaying information to the user about what is currently happening in the model. For instance, if the model had a giant loop that took a long time to execute, an assertion of severity level *note* could be used to notify the designer when the loop was 10 percent complete, 20 percent complete, 30 percent complete, etc.

Assertions of category *warning* can be used to alert the designer of conditions that, while not catastrophic, can cause erroneous behavior later. For instance, if a model expected a signal to be at a known value while some process was executing, but the signal was at a different value, it may not be an error as in the exit statement example, but a warning to the user that results may not be as expected.

Assertions of severity level *error* are used to alert the designer of conditions that will cause the model to work incorrectly, or not work at all. If the result of a calculation was supposed to return a positive value, but instead returned a negative value, depending on the operation, this could be considered an error.

Assertions of severity level *failure* are used to alert the designer of conditions within the model that can have disastrous effects. An example of such a condition was discussed in the EXIT statement section. Division by 0 is an example of an operation that could cause a failure in the model. Another is addressing beyond the end of an array. In both cases the severity level *failure* can let the designer know that the model is behaving incorrectly.

The severity level is a good method for classifying assertions into informational messages to the designer that can describe conditions during execution of the model.

3.7.1 Assertion BNF

The BNF description for the ASSERT statement is shown below:

```
assert_statement ::=
   ASSERT condition
   [REPORT expression]
   [SEVERITY expression];
```

The keyword ASSERT is followed by a boolean-valued expression called a condition. The condition determines whether the text expression specified by the REPORT clause is output or not. If false, the text expression is output if true; the text expression is not output.

There are two optional clauses in the ASSERT statement. The first is the REPORT clause. The REPORT clause allows the designer the capability to specify the value of a text expression to output. The second is the SEVERITY clause. The SEVERITY clause allows the designer to specify the severity level of the ASSERT statement. If the report clause is not specified, the default value for the ASSERT statement is *assertion violation*. If the severity clause is not specified, the default value is *error*.

Let's look at an example of an ASSERT statement in a practical use to illustrate how it works. The example performs a data setup check between two signals that control a D flip-flop. Most flip-flops require the *din* (data) input to be at a stable value a certain amount of time before a clock edge appears. This time is called the *setup* time and will guarantee that the *din* value will be clocked into the flip-flop if the setup time is met. This is shown in the model below. The assertion example will issue an error message to the designer if the setup time is violated (*assertion is false*).

```
PROCESS(clk, din)
   VARIABLE last_d_change   : TIME := 0 ns;
   VARIABLE last_d_value    : t_wlogic := U;
   VARIABLE last_clk_value  : t_wlogic := U;
BEGIN
   IF (last_d_value /= din) THEN -- /= is
      last_d_change := NOW;      --  not equal
      last_d_value := din;
   END IF;

   IF (last_clk_value /= clk) THEN
      last_clk_value := clk;

      IF  (clk = '1') THEN
```

```
            ASSERT (NOW - last_d_change = 20 ns)
            REPORT "setup violation"
            SEVERITY WARNING;
         END IF;
      END IF;
   END PROCESS;
```

The process makes use of three local variables to record the time and last value of signal *din* as well as the value of the *clk* signal. By storing the last value of *clk* and *din* we can determine if the signal has changed value or not. By recording the last time that *din* changed we can measure from the current time to the last *din* transistion to see if the setup time has been violated or not.

Whenever either *din* or *clk* changes, the process is invoked. The first step in the process is to see if the *din* signal has changed. If it has, the time of the transistion is recorded using the predefined function NOW. This function returns the current simulation time. Also the latest value of *din* is stored for future checking.

The next step is to see if signal *clk* has made a transistion. If the *last_clk_value* variable is not equal to the current value of *clk* then we know that a transistion has occurred. If signal *clk* is a '1' value, then we know that a rising edge has occurred. Whenever a rising edge occurs on signal *clk*, we need to check the setup time for a violation. If the last transistion on signal *d* was less than 20 ns ago then the expression

```
   (NOW - last_D_change)
```

will return a value that is less than 20 ns. The ASSERT statement will trigger and report the assertion message *setup violation* as a warning to the designer. If the last transistion on signal *d* occurred more than 20 ns in the past, then the expression will return a value larger than 20 ns and the ASSERT statement will not write out the message. Remember, the ASSERT statement writes out the message when the assert condition is false.

The message reported to the user will have at a minimum the user string and the error classification. Some simulators will also include the time of the assertion report as well as the line number in the file of the assertion.

The ASSERT statement used in this example was a sequential ASSERT statement, because it was included inside of a PROCESS statement. A concurrent version of the ASSERT statement also exists. It has exactly the same format as the sequential ASSERT statement and only exists outside of a PROCESS statement or subprogram.

The concurrent ASSERT statement will execute whenever any signals that exist inside of the condition expression have an event upon them. This is as opposed to the sequential ASSERT statement in which execution occurs when the sequential ASSERT statement is reached inside the PROCESS statement or subprogram.

3.8 WAIT Statements

The WAIT statement allows the designer the capability of suspending the sequential execution of a process or subprogram. The conditions for resuming execution of the suspended process or subprogram can be specified by three different means. These are

- WAIT ON signal changes
- WAIT UNTIL an expression is true
- WAIT FOR a specific amount of time

The main use of WAIT statements is either to delay process execution for a time amount or to modify the sensitivity list of the process dynamically. A WAIT statement can be used to control the signals a process or subprogram is sensitive to at any point in the execution. An example is shown below:

```
PROCESS
BEGIN
   WAIT ON a; -- 1.
      .
      .
   WAIT ON b; -- 2.
      .
      .
END PROCESS;
```

Execution of the statements in the PROCESS statement proceeds until point 1 in the VHDL fragment shown above. The WAIT statement will cause the process to halt execution at that point. The process will not continue execution until an event occurs on signal *a*. The process is therefore sensitive to changes in signal *a* at this point in the the execution. When an event occurs on signal *a*, execution will start again at the statement directly after the WAIT statement at point 1. Execution will proceed until the WAIT statement at point 2 is encountered. Once again execution is halted, and the process is now sensitive to events on signal *b*. Therefore, by adding in two WAIT statements, we can alter the process sensitivity list dynamically.

Next let's discuss the three different options available to the WAIT statement. They are again:

```
WAIT ON signal [,signal]

WAIT UNTIL boolean_expression

WAIT FOR time_expression
```

3.8.1 WAIT ON Signal

We have already seen an example of the first type in the process example above. The WAIT ON signal clause specifies a list of one or more signals that the WAIT statement will wait for events upon. If any signal in the signal list has an event occur on it, execution will continue with the statement following the WAIT statement. An example is shown below:

```
WAIT ON a, b;
```

When an event occurs on either *a* or *b*, the process will resume with the statement following the WAIT statement.

3.8.2 WAIT UNTIL Expression

The WAIT UNTIL *boolean_expression* clause will suspend execution of the process until the expression returns a value of true. This statement will effectively create an implicit sensitivity list of the signals used in the expression. When any of the signals in the expression have events occur upon them, the expression will be evaluated. The expression must return a boolean type or the compiler will complain. When the expression returns a true value, execution will continue with the statement following the WAIT statement. Otherwise the process will continue to be suspended. An example is shown below:

```
WAIT UNTIL (( x * 10 ) < 100 );
```

In this example, as long as the value of signal *x* is greater than or equal to 10, the WAIT statement will suspend the process or subprogram. When the value of *x* is less than 10, execution will continue with the statement following the WAIT statement.

3.8.3 WAIT FOR time_expression

The WAIT FOR *time_expression* clause will suspend execution of the process for the time specified by the time expression. After the time specified in the time expression has elapsed, execution will continue on the statement following the WAIT statement. A couple of examples are shown below:

```
WAIT FOR 10 ns;

WAIT FOR ( a * ( b + c ));
```

In the first example the time expression is a simple constant value. The WAIT statement will suspend execution for 10 ns. After 10 ns has elapsed execution will continue with the statement following the WAIT statement.

In the second example, the time expression is an expression that first must be evaluated to return a time value. Once this value is calculated, the WAIT statement will use this value as the time value to wait for.

3.8.4 Multiple WAIT Conditions

The WAIT statement examples that we have examined so far have shown the different options of the WAIT statement used separately. The different options can be used together. A single statement can include an ON signal, UNTIL expression, and FOR *time_expression* clauses. An example is shown below:

```
WAIT ON nmi,interrupt UNTIL ((nmi = TRUE) or
     (interrupt = TRUE)) FOR 5 usec;
```

This statement will wait for an event on signals *nmi* and *interrupt* and will continue only if *interrupt* or *nmi* is true at the time of the event, or until 5 microseconds of time has elapsed. Only when one or more of these conditions are true will execution continue.

When using a statement such as below:

```
WAIT UNTIL (interrupt = TRUE) OR
           ( old_clk = '1');
```

be sure to have at least one of the values in the expression contain a signal. This is necessary to insure that the WAIT statement does not wait forever. If both *interrupt* and *old_clk* are variables, the WAIT statement will not reevaluate when these two variables change value. (In fact, the variables cannot change value because they are declared in the suspended process.) Only signals have events on them, and only signals can cause a WAIT statement or concurrent signal assignment to reevaluate.

3.8.5 WAIT Time-Out

There are instances while designing a model when you are not sure that a condition will be met. To prevent the WAIT statement from waiting forever, add a time-out clause. The time-out clause will allow execution to proceed whether or not the condition has been met. Be careful, though, because this method can cause erroneous behavior unless properly handled. The following example shows this problem.

```
ARCHITECTURE wait_example of wait_example IS
  SIGNAL sendB, sendA : t_wlogic;
BEGIN
  sendA <= F0;
  A : PROCESS
  BEGIN
    WAIT UNTIL sendB = F1;
    sendA <= F1 AFTER 10 ns;
    -- F1 is a forcing 1 value, discussed in
    -- appendix A

    WAIT UNTIL sendB = F0;
    sendA <= F0 AFTER 10 ns;
    -- F0 is a forcing 0 value

  END PROCESS A;
```

```
    B : PROCESS
    BEGIN
      WAIT UNTIL sendA = F0;
      sendB <= F0 AFTER 10 ns;

      WAIT UNTIL sendA = F1;
      sendB <= F1 AFTER 10 ns;
    END PROCESS B;
  END wait_example;
```

This architecture has two processes that communicate through two signals *sendA* and *sendB*. This example does not do anything real but is a simple illustration of how WAIT statements can wait forever, a condition commonly referred to as *deadlock.*

During simulator initialization all processes are executed exactly once. This allows the processes to always start at a known execution point at the start of simulation. In this example the process labeled *A* will execute at start-up and stop at the line shown below:

```
WAIT UNTIL sendB = F1;
```

The process labeled *B* will also execute at start-up. Execution starts at the first line of the process and continues until the line shown below:

```
WAIT UNTIL sendA = F1;
```

Execution will stop at the first WAIT statement of the process even though the expression sendA = F0 is satisfied by the first signal assignment of signal *sendA*. This is because the WAIT statement needs an event to occur on signal sendA to cause the expression to be evaluated. Both processes are now waiting on each other. Neither process can continue because they are both waiting for a signal set by the other process. If a time-out interval is inserted on each WAIT statement, execution can be allowed to continue. There is one catch to this last statement. Execution will continue when the condition is not met. An ASSERT statement can be added to check for continuation of the process without the condition being met. The example below shows the architecture *wait_example* above rewritten to include time-out clauses.

```
ARCHITECTURE wait_timeout OF wait_example IS
  SIGNAL sendA, sendB : t_wlogic;
  BEGIN
    A : PROCESS
```

```
    BEGIN
      WAIT UNTIL (sendB = F1) FOR 1 us;
      ASSERT (sendB = F1)
        REPORT "sendB timed out at F1"
        SEVERITY ERROR;
      sendA <= F1 AFTER 10 ns;

      WAIT UNTIL (sendB = F0) FOR 1 us;
        ASSERT (sendB = F0)
        REPORT "sendB timed out at F0"
        SEVERITY ERROR;
      sendA <= F0 AFTER 10 ns;
    END PROCESS A;

    B : PROCESS
    BEGIN
      WAIT UNTIL (sendA = F0) FOR 1 us;
      ASSERT (sendA =  F0)
        REPORT "sendA timed out at F0"
        SEVERITY ERROR;
      sendB <= F0 AFTER 10 ns;

      WAIT UNTIL (sendA = F1) FOR 1 us;
      ASSERT (sendA = F1)
        REPORT "sendA timed out at F1"
        SEVERITY ERROR;
      sendB <= F1 AFTER 10 ns;
    end PROCESS B;
  END wait_timeout;
```

Each of the WAIT statements now has a time-out expression specified as 1 usec. However, if the time out does happen the ASSERT statement will report an error that the WAIT statement in question has timed out.

3.8.6 Sensitivity List versus WAIT Statement

A process with a sensitivity list is an implicit WAIT ON the signals in the sensitivity list. This can be shown by the example below:

```
  PROCESS (clk)
    VARIABLE last_clk : t_wlogic := U;
  BEGIN
    IF (clk /= last_clk ) AND (clk = F1) THEN
      q <= din AFTER 25 ns;
```

```
      END IF;

      last_clk := clk;

   END PROCESS;
```

This example can be rewritten using a WAIT statement as below:

```
PROCESS
   VARIABLE last_clk : t_wlogic := U;
BEGIN
   IF (clk /= last_clk ) AND (clk = F1) THEN
      q <= din AFTER 25 ns;
   END IF;

   last_clk := clk;

   WAIT on clk;
END PROCESS;
```

The WAIT statement at the end of the process is equivalent to the sensitivity list at the beginning of the process. But why is the WAIT statement at the end of the process and not at the beginning? During initialization of the simulator all processes are executed once. To mimic the behavior of the sensitivity list, the WAIT statement must be at the end of the process to allow the PROCESS statement to execute once.

3.8.7 Concurrent Assignment Problem

One of the problems that most designers using sequential signal assignment statements will encounter is that the value assigned in the last statement will not appear immediately. This can cause erroneous behavior in the model if the designer is depending on the new value. An example with this problem is shown below:

```
USE STD.std_logic.ALL;
ENTITY mux IS
   PORT (I0, I1, I2, I3, A, B : IN t_wlogic;
         Q : OUT t_wlogic);
END mux;

ARCHITECTURE mux_behave OF mux IS
   SIGNAL sel : INTEGER RANGE 0 TO 3;
BEGIN
```

```
B : PROCESS(A, B, I0, I1, I2, I3)
BEGIN

   sel <= 0;
   IF (A = F1) THEN sel <= sel + 1; END IF;
   IF (B = F1) THEN sel <= sel + 2; END IF;

   CASE sel IS
      WHEN 0 =>
         Q <= I0;
      WHEN 1 =>
         Q <= I1;
      WHEN 2 =>
         Q <= I2;
      WHEN 3 =>
         Q <= I3;
   END CASE;
 END PROCESS;
END mux_behave;
```

This model is for four-to-one multiplexer. Depending on the values of *A* and *B* one of the four inputs, *I0-I3*, will be transferred to output *Q*.

The architecture starts processing by initializing internal signal *sel* to the value 0. Then, based on the values of *A* and *B* the values 1 or 2 are added to *sel* to select the correct input. Finally, a CASE statement selected by the value of *sel* will transfer the value of the input to output *Q*.

This architecture will not work as presently implemented. The value of signal *sel* will never be initialized by the first line in the architecture:

```
sel <= 0;
```

This statement inside of a process statement will schedule an event for signal *sel* on the next delta time point, with the value 0. However, processing will continue in the process statement with the next sequential statement. The value of *sel* will remain at whatever value that it had at the entry to the process. Only when the process has completed will this current delta have finished and the next delta time point be started. Only then will the new value of *sel* be reflected. By this time, however, the rest of the process will have already been processed using the wrong value of *sel*.

There are two ways to fix this problem. The first is to insert WAIT statements after each sequential signal assignment statement as shown below:

```
ARCHITECTURE mux_fix1 OF mux IS
   SIGNAL sel : INTEGER RANGE 0 TO 3;
BEGIN
   PROCESS
   BEGIN
      sel <= 0;
      WAIT FOR 0 ns;   -- or wait on sel

      IF (a = F1) THEN sel <= sel + 1; END IF;
      WAIT for 0 ns;

      IF (b = F1) THEN sel <= sel + 2; END IF;
      WAIT FOR 0 ns;

      CASE sel IS
         WHEN 0 =>
            Q <= I0;
         WHEN 1 =>
            Q <= I1;
         WHEN 2 =>
            Q <= I2;
         WHEN 3 =>
            Q <= I3;
      END CASE;

      WAIT ON A, B, I0, I1, I2, I3;
   END PROCESS;
END mux_fix1;
```

The WAIT statements after each signal assignment cause the process to wait for one delta time point before continuing with the execution. By waiting for one delta time point, the new value has a chance to propagate. Therefore, when execution continues after the WAIT statement, signal *sel* has the new value.

One consequence of the WAIT statements, however, is that the process can no longer have a sensitivity list. A process with WAIT statements contained within it or within a subprogram called from within the process cannot have a sensitivity list. A sensitivity list implies that execution will start from the beginning of the procedure, while a WAIT statement allows suspending a process at a particular point. The two are mutually exclusive.

Since the process can no longer have sensitivity list, a WAIT statement has been added to the end of the process that will exactly imitate the behavior of the sensitivity list. This is the statement below:

```
WAIT ON A, B, I0, I1, I2, I3;
```

The WAIT statement will proceed whenever any of the signals on the right side of the keyword ON have an event upon them.

This method of solving the sequential signal assignment problem will cause the process to work, but a better solution is to use an internal variable instead of the internal signal, as shown below:

```
ARCHITECTURE mux_fix2 OF mux IS
BEGIN
  PROCESS(A, B, I0, I1, I2, I3)
    VARIABLE sel : INTEGER RANGE 0 TO 3;
  BEGIN
    sel := 0;
    IF (A = F1) THEN sel := sel + 1; END IF;
    IF (B = F1) THEN sel := sel + 2; END IF;

    CASE sel IS
      WHEN 0 =>
        Q <= I0;
      WHEN 1 =>
        Q <= I1;
      WHEN 2 =>
        Q <= I2;
      WHEN 3 =>
        Q <= I3;
    END CASE;
  END PROCESS;
END mux_fix2;
```

The signal *sel* from the example above has been converted from an internal signal to an internal variable. This was accomplished by moving the declaration from the architecture declaration section to the process declaration section. Variables can only be declared in the process or subprogram declaration section.

Also the signal assignments to *sel* have been changed to variable assignment statements. Now when the first assignment to *sel* is executed, the value is updated immediately. Each successive assignment is also executed immediately so that the correct value of *sel* is available in each statement of the process.

3.9 Passive Processes

Passive processes are processes that exist in the entity statement part of an entity. They are different from a normal process in that no signal assignment is allowed. These processes are used to do all sorts of checking functions. For instance, one good use of a passive process is to check the data setup time on a flip-flop.

The advantage of the passive process over the example discussed in the ASSERT statement section is that since the passive process exists in the entity, it can be applied to any architecure of the entity. Take a look at the example below:

```
USE STD.std_logic.ALL;
ENTITY dff IS
   PORT( CLK, din : IN t_wlogic;
       Q, QB : OUT t_wlogic);
   BEGIN
     PROCESS(CLK, din)
        VARIABLE last_d_change : TIME := 0 ns;
        VARIABLE last_clk,
              last_d_value : t_wlogic := U;
     BEGIN
        IF (din /= last_d_value) THEN
           last_d_change := now;
           last_d_value := din;
        END IF;

        IF (CLK /= last_clk) THEN
           IF  (CLK = F1) THEN
             ASSERT(now - last_d_change = 15 ns)
                REPORT "setup error"
                SEVERITY ERROR;
```

```
         END IF;

         last_clk := CLK;
      END IF;
   END PROCESS;
END dff;

ARCHITECTURE behave OF dff IS
BEGIN
   .
   .
   .
   .
END behave;

ARCHITECTURE struct OF dff IS
BEGIN
   .
   .
   .
   .
END struct;

ARCHITECTURE switch OF dff IS
BEGIN
   .
   .
   .
   .
END switch;
```

This example shows the entity for a D flip-flop with a passive process included in the entity that performs a data setup check with respect to the clock. This setup check function was described in detail in the ASSERT statement description. What this example shows is that when the setup check function is contained in the entity statement part, each of the architectures for the entity will have the data setup check performed automatically. Without this functionality, each of the architectures would have to have the setup check code included. This introduces more code to maintain, and can introduce inconsistencies between architectures.

The only restriction on these processes, as mentioned earlier, is that no signal assignment is allowed in a passive process. In the example above a process statement was used to illustrate a passive process. A passive process can also exist as a concurrent statement that does not do any signal assignment. Examples of such statements are concurrent assert statements and concurrent subprogram invocations. An example of two concurrent assert statements as passive processes are shown below:

```
ENTITY adder IS
   PORT( A, B : IN INTEGER;
         X : OUT INTEGER);
BEGIN
   ASSERT (A < 256)
      REPORT "A out of range"
      SEVERITY ERROR;

   ASSERT  (B < 256)
      REPORT "B out of range"
      SEVERITY ERROR;

END adder;
```

The first ASSERT statement checks to make sure that input *A* is not out of range, and the second assertion checks that input *B* is not out of the range of the adder. Each of these statements acts as an individual process that is sensitive to the signal in its expression. For instance, the first assertion is sensitive to signal *A* since that signal is contained in its expression.

In this chapter we discussed the sequential statements available in VHDL. These included IF statements, LOOP statements, CASE statements, etc. All of the sequential statements had to be encased in a PROCESS statement. In the next chapter we will discuss the varied data types available in VHDL for high- and low-level description.

Chapter

4

Types and Attributes

In this chapter we will examine the object types used in VHDL. The types allowed in VHDL consist of everything from scalar numeric types, to composite arrays and records, to file types. The first step in looking at the varied VHDL types, will be to review the VHDL objects that can attain the varied types. Then we will use examples to show how many types of descriptions can be made easier to read by using the power of enumerated and composite data types.

4.1 Object Types

A VHDL object consists of one of the following:

- Signal, which represents interconnection wires that connect component instantiation ports together.
- Variable, which is used for local storage of temporary data, visible only inside a process.
- Constant, which names specific values.

4.1.1 Signal

Signal objects are used to connect entities together to form models. Signals are the means for communication of dynamic data between entities. A signal declaration looks like this:

```
SIGNAL signal_name : signal_type
     [:= initial_value];
```

The keyword SIGNAL is followed by one or more signal names. Each signal name will create a new signal. Separating the signal names from the signal type is a colon. The signal type specifies the data type of the information that the signal will contain. Finally, the signal can contain an initial value specifier so that the signal value may be initialized.

Signals can be declared in entity declaration sections, architecture declarations, and package declarations. Signals in package declarations are also referred to as *global* signals because they can be shared among entities.

An example of signal declarations is shown below:

```
USE STD.std_logic.ALL;
PACKAGE sigdecl IS
  TYPE bus_type IS ARRAY(0 to 7) OF t_wlogic;

  SIGNAL vcc    : t_wlogic := F1;
  SIGNAL ground : t_wlogic := F0;

  FUNCTION magic_function( a : IN bus_type)
    RETURN bus_type;

END sigdecl;

USE WORK.sigdecl.ALL;
USE STD.std_logic.ALL;
USE STD.std_ttl.ALL;
ENTITY board_design is
  PORT( data_in : IN bus_type;
        data_out : OUT bus_type);

  SIGNAL sys_clk : t_wlogic := F1;
END board_design;
```

```
ARCHITECTURE data_flow OF board_design IS
   SIGNAL int_bus : bus_type;
   CONSTANT disconnect_value : bus_type
        := (D, D, D, D, D, D, D, D);
BEGIN
   int_bus <= data_in WHEN sys_clk = '1'
   ELSE int_bus;

   data_out <= magic_function(int_bus)
   WHEN sys_clk = '0'
   ELSE disconnect_value;

   sys_clk <= NOT(sys_clk) after 50 ns;
END data_flow;
```

Signals *vcc* and *ground* are declared in package *sigdecl.* Because these signals are declared in a package, they can be referenced by more than one entity and are therefore *global* signals. For an entity to reference these signals the entity will need to use the package. To use the package requires a VHDL USE clause as shown below:

```
USE work.sigdecl.vcc;
USE work.sigdecl.ground;
```

or,

```
USE work.sigdecl.ALL;
```

In the first example the objects are included in the entity by specific reference. In the second example the entire package is included in the entity. In the second example problems may arise because more than what is absolutely necessary is included. If more than one object of the same name results because of the USE clause, none of the objects is visible, and a compile operation that references the object will fail.

4.1.1.1 Signals Global to Entities

Inside the entity declaration section for entity *board_design* is a signal called *sys_clk*. This signal can be referenced in entity *board_design* and any architecture for entity *board_design*. In this example there is only one architecture, *data_flow*, for *board_design*. The signal *sys_clk* can therefore be assigned to and read from in entity *board_design* and architecture *data_flow*.

4.1.1.2 Architecture Local Signals

Inside of architecture *data_flow* is a signal declaration for signal *int_bus*. Signal *int_bus* is of type *bus_type*, a type defined in package *sigdecl*. The *sigdecl* package is used in entity board, therefore the type *bus_type* is available in architecture *data_flow*. Since the signal is declared in the architecture declaration section, the signal can only be referenced in architecture *data_flow* or in any process statements in the architecture.

4.1.2 Variables

Variables are used for local storage in process statements and subprograms (subprograms are discussed in Chapter 6). As opposed to signals which have their values scheduled, all assignments to variables occur immediately. A variable declaration looks as follows:

```
VARIABLE variable_name {,variable_name} :
  variable_type [:= value];
```

The keyword VARIABLE is followed by one or more variable names. Each name creates a new variable. The construct *variable_type* defines the data type of the variable, and an optional initial value can be specified.

Variables can be declared in the process declaration section and subprogram declaration sections only. An example using two variables is shown below:

```
USE STD.std_logic.ALL;
USE STD.std_ttl.ALL;
ENTITY and5 IS
  PORT ( a, b, c, d, e : IN  t_wlogic;
         q : OUT t_wlogic);
END and5;

ARCHITECTURE and5 OF and5 IS
BEGIN
  PROCESS(a, b, c, d, e)
    VARIABLE state : t_wlogic;
    VARIABLE delay : time;
  BEGIN
    state := a AND b AND c AND d AND e;
    IF state = '1' THEN
      delay := 4.5 ns;
```

```
      ELSIF state = '0' THEN
         delay := 3 ns;
      ELSE
         delay := 4 ns;
      END IF;
      q <= state AFTER delay;
   END PROCESS;
END and5;
```

This example is the architecture for a five-input AND gate. There are two variable declarations in the process declaration section, one for variable *state* and one for variable *delay*. Variable *state* is used as a temporary storage area to hold the value of the AND function of the inputs. Temporary-storage value *delay* is used to hold the delay value that will be used when scheduling the output value. Both of these values cannot be static data because their values depend on the values of inputs *a, b, c, d,* and *e*. Signals could have been used to store the data, but there are several reasons why a signal was not used.

- Variables are inherently more efficient because assignments happen immediately, while signals must be scheduled to occur.
- Variables take less memory, while signals need more information to allow for scheduling and signal attributes.
- Using a signal would have required a WAIT statement to synchronize the signal assignment to the same execution iteration as the usage.

When any of the input signals *a, b, c, d,* or *e* change, the process is invoked. Variable *state* is assigned the AND of all of the inputs. Next, based on the value of variable *state*, variable *delay* is assigned a delay value. Based on the delay value assigned to variable *delay*, output signal *q* will have the value of variable *state* assigned to it.

4.1.3 Constants

Constant objects are names assigned to specific values of a type. Constants allow the designer the capability to have a better-documented model, and a model that is easy to update. For instance, if a model requires a fixed value in a number of instances, a constant should be used.

By using a constant the designer can change the value of the constant and recompile, and all of the instances of the constant value will be updated to reflect the new value of the constant.

A constant also provides a better-documented model by providing more meaning to the value being described. For instance, instead of using the value 3.1414 directly in the model, the designer should create a constant as shown below:

```
CONSTANT PI: REAL := 3.1414;
```

Even though the value is not going to change, the model becomes more readable.

A constant declaration looks like this:

```
CONSTANT  constant_name {,constant_name} :
        type_name[:= value];
```

The value specification is optional, because VHDL also supports deferred constants. These are constants declared in a package declaration, whose value is specified in a package body.

A constant has the same scoping rules as signals. A constant declared in a package can be global if the package is used by a number of entities. A constant in an entity declaration section can be referenced by any architecture of that entity. A constant in an architecture can be used by any statement inside the architecture, including a process statement. A constant declared in a process declaration can be used only in a process.

4.2 Data Types

All of the objects that we have been discussing until now—the signal, the variable, and the constant—can be declared using a type specification to specify the characteristics of the object. VHDL contains a wide range of types that can be used to create simple or complex objects.

To define a new type, you must create a type declaration. A type declaration defines the name of the type and the range of the type. Type declarations are allowed in package declaration sections, entity declaration sections, architecture declaration sections, subprogram declaration sections, and process declaration sections.

A type declaration looks like this:

```
TYPE type_name IS type_mark;
```

A *type_mark* construct encompasses a wide range of methods for specifying a type. It can be anything from an enumeration of all of the values of a type to a complex record structure. In the next few sections type marks will be examined. All of the scoping rules that were defined for signals and variables apply to type declarations also.

Figure 4-1 is a diagram showing the types available in VHDL. The four broad categories are scalar types, composite types, access types, and file types. Scalar types include all of the simple types such as integer and real. Composite types include arrays and records. Access types are the equivalent of *pointers* in typical programming languages. Finally, file types give the designer the capability to declare file objects with designer-defined file types.

4.3 Scalar Types

Scalar types describe objects that can hold at most one value at a time. The type itself can contain multiple values, but an object that is declared to be a scalar type will hold at most one of the scalar values at any point in time. Referencing the name of the object references the entire object. Scalar types encompass these four classes of types:

- Integer types
- Real types
- Enumerated types
- Physical types

4.3.1 Integer Types

Integer types are exactly like mathematical integers. All of the normal predefined mathematical functions like add, subtract, multiply, and divide apply to integer types. The VHDL LRM does not specify a maximum range for integers, but does specify the minimum range: from -2,147,483,647 to +2,147,483,647. The mimimum range is specified by the Standard package which is contained in the Standard Library.

The Standard package defines all of the predefined VHDL types provided with the language. The Standard library is used to hold any

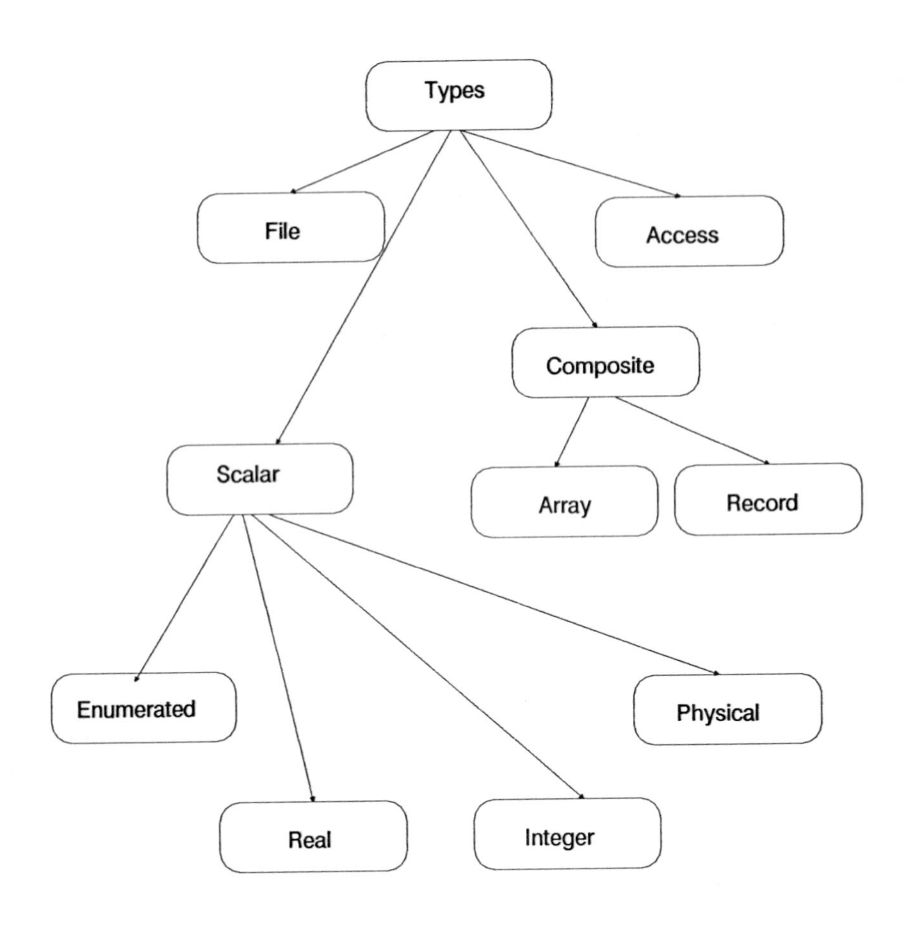
Types
File
Access
Composite
Scalar
Array
Record
Enumerated
Physical
Real
Integer

Figure 4-1

packages or entities provided as standard with the language. The Standard package appears on page 14-9 of the *VHDL Lanugage Reference Manual.*

It may seem strange to some designers who are familiar with two's complement representations that the integer range is specified from -2,147,483,647 to +2,147,483,647 when two's complement integer representations usually allow one smaller negative number, -2,147,483,648. The language defines the integer range to be symmetric around 0.

Some examples of integer values are shown below:

```
ARCHITECTURE test OF test IS
BEGIN
   PROCESS(X)
      VARIABLE a : INTEGER;
      VARIABLE b : int_type;
   BEGIN
      a := 1;      -- Ok     1
      a := -1;     -- Ok     2
      a := 1.0;    -- error  3
   END PROCESS;
END test;
```

The first two statements (1 and 2) show examples of a positive integer assignment and a negative integer assignment. Line 3 shows a noninteger assignment to an integer variable. This line will cause the compiler to issue an error message. Any numeric value with a decimal point is considered a real number value. Because VHDL is a strongly typed language, for the assignment to take place either the base types must match or a type-casting operation must be performed .

4.3.2 Real Types

Real types are used to declare objects that emulate mathematical real numbers. They can be used to represent numbers out of the range of integer values as well as fractional values. The minimum range of real numbers is also specified by the Standard package in the Standard Library, and is from -1.0E+38 to +1.0E+38. These numbers are represented by the following notation:

```
+ or - number.number[E + or - number]
```

A few examples of some real numbers are shown below:

```
ARCHITECTURE test OF test IS
SIGNAL a : REAL;
  BEGIN
    a <= 1.0;          -- Ok    1
    a <= 1;            -- error 2
    a <= -1.0E10;      -- Ok    3
    a <= 1.5E-20;      -- Ok    4
    a <= 5.3 ns;       -- error 5
  END test;
```

Line 1 shows how to assign a real number to a signal of type REAL. All real numbers have a decimal point to distinguish them from integer values. Line 2 is an example of an assignment that will not work. Signal *a* is of type REAL, and a real value must be assigned to signal *a*. The value 1 is of type INTEGER, so a type mismatch will be generated by this line.

Line 3 shows a very large negative number. The numeric characters to the left of the character E represent the mantissa of the real number, while the numeric value to the right represents the exponent.

Line 4 shows how to create a very small number. In this example the exponent is negative so the number is very small.

Line 5 shows how a type TIME cannot be assigned to a real signal. Even though the numeric part of the value looks like a real number, because of the units after the value, the value is considered to be of type TIME.

4.3.3 Enumerated Types

An enumerated type is a very powerful tool for abstract modeling. A designer can use an enumerated type to represent exactly the values required for a specific operation. All of the values of an enumerated type are user-defined. These values can be identifiers or single-character literals. An identifier is like a name. Examples are a, abc, and black. Character literals are single characters enclosed in quotes, such as 'X', '1', and '0'.

A typical enumerated type for a four-state simulation value system is shown below:

```
TYPE fourval IS ( 'X', '0', '1', 'Z' );
```

This type contains four character literal values that each represent a unique state in the four-state value system. The values represent the following conditions:

- 'X' – an unknown value
- '0' – a logical 0 or false value
- '1' – a logical 1 or true value
- 'Z' – a tristate or open collector value

Character literals are needed for values '1' and '0' to separate these values from the integer values 1 and 0. It would be an error to use the values 1 and 0 in an enumerated type, because these are integer values. The characters X and Z do not need quotes around them because they do not represent any other type, but the quotes were used for uniformity.

Another example of an enumerated type is shown below:

```
TYPE color IS ( red, yellow, blue, green,
                orange );
```

In this example the type values are very abstract, that is, not representing physical values that a signal might attain. The type values in type *color* are also all identifiers. Each identifier represents a unique value of the type; therefore all identifiers of the type must be unique.

Each identifier in the type has a specific position in the type determined by the order in which the identifier appears in the type. The first identifier will have a position number of 0, the next a position number of 1,and so on.(In Chapter 5 are some examples using position numbers of a type.)

A typical use for an enumerated type would be representing all of the instructions for a microprocessor as an enumerated type. For instance, an enumerated type for a very simple microprocessor could look as follows:

```
TYPE instruction IS ( add, sub, lda, ldb,
                      sta, stb, outa, xfr );
```

The model that uses this type might look like this:

```
PACKAGE instr IS
  TYPE instruction IS ( add, sub, lda, ldb,
                        sta, stb, outa, xfr );
END instr;

USE WORK.instr.ALL;
ENTITY mp IS
  PORT (instr : IN instruction;
        addr  : IN INTEGER;
        data  : INOUT INTEGER);
END mp;

ARCHITECTURE mp OF mp IS
BEGIN
  PROCESS(instr)
    TYPE regtype IS ARRAY(0 TO 255) OF INTEGER;
    VARIABLE a, b : INTEGER;
    VARIABLE reg : regtype;
  BEGIN
                        -- select instruction to
  CASE instr is         -- execute
      WHEN lda =>
         a := data;  -- load a accumulator
      WHEN ldb =>
         b := data;  -- load b accumulator
      WHEN add =>
         a := a + b; -- add accumulators
      WHEN sub =>
         a := a - b; -- subtract accumulators
      WHEN sta =>
         reg(addr) := a; -- put a accum in
                            reg array
      WHEN stb =>
         reg(addr) := b; -- put b accum in
                            reg array
      WHEN outa =>
         data <= a;      -- output a accum
      WHEN xfr =>         -- transfer b to a
         a := b;
    END CASE;
  END PROCESS;
END mp;
```

The model receives an instruction stream (*instr*), an address stream (*addr*), and a data stream (*data*). Based on the value of the enumerated value of *instr*, the appropriate instruction is executed. A CASE statement is used to select the instruction to execute. The statement is executed and the process will then wait for the next instruction.

4.3.4 Physical Types

Physical types are used to represent physical quantities such as distance, current, time, etc. A physical type provides for a base unit, and successive units are then defined in terms of this unit. The smallest unit representable is one base unit; the largest is determined by the range specified in the physical type declaration. An example of a physical type for the physical quantity *current* is shown below:

```
TYPE current IS RANGE 0 to 1000000000
  UNITS
    na;                 -- nano amps
    ua = 1000 na;       -- micro amps
    ma = 1000 ua;       -- milli amps
    a  = 1000 ma;       -- amps
  END UNITS;
```

The type definition begins with a statement that declares the name of the type (*current*) and the range of the type (0 to 1,000,000,000). The first unit declared in the UNITS section is the *base unit*. In the example above the base unit is *na*. After the base unit is defined, other units can be defined in terms of the base unit or other units already defined. In the example above the unit *ua* is defined in terms of the base unit as 1000 base units. The next unit declaration is *ma*. This unit is declared as 1000 *ua*. The units declaration section is terminated by the END UNITS clause.

More than one unit can be declared in terms of the base unit. In the example above, the *ma* unit can be declared as 1000 ma or 1,000,000 na. The range constraint limits the minimum and maximum values that the physical type can represent in base units. The unit identifiers all must be unique within a single type. It is illegal to have two identifiers with the same name.

4.3.4.1 Predefined Physical Types

The only predefined physical type in VHDL is the physical type TIME. This type is shown below:

```
TYPE TIME IS RANGE <implementation defined>
  UNITS
    fs;                  -- femtosecond
    ps    =  1000 fs;    -- picosecond
    ns    =  1000 ps;    -- nanosecond
    us    =  1000 ns;    -- microsecond
    ms    =  1000 us;    -- millisecond
    sec   =  1000 ms;    -- second
    min   =  60 sec;     -- minute
    hr    =  60 min;     -- hour
  END UNITS;
```

The range of time is implementation-defined but has to be at least the range of integer, in base units. This type is defined in the Standard package.

An example using a physical type is shown below:

```
PACKAGE example IS
  TYPE current IS RANGE 0 TO 1000000000
    UNITS
      na;               -- nano amps
      ua = 1000 na;     -- micro amps
      ma = 1000 ua;     -- milli amps
      a  = 1000 ma;     -- amps
    END UNITS;

  TYPE load_factor IS (small, med, big );

END example;

USE WORK.example.ALL;
ENTITY delay_calc IS
  PORT ( out_current : OUT current;
         load : IN load_factor;
         delay : OUT time);
END delay_calc;

ARCHITECTURE delay_calc OF delay_calc IS
BEGIN
```

```
    delay <= 10 ns WHEN (load = small) ELSE
             20 ns WHEN (load = med) ELSE
             30 ns WHEN (load = big) ELSE
             10 ns;

    out_current <= 100 ua WHEN (load = small)ELSE
                   1 ma   WHEN (load = med) ELSE
                   10 ma  WHEN (load = big) ELSE
                100 ua;
END delay_calc;
```

In this example two examples of physical types are represented. The first is of predefined physical type TIME and the second of user-specified physical type *current*. This example will return the *current* output and delay value for a device based on the output load factor.

4.4 Composite Types

Looking back at the VHDL types diagram in Figure 4-1, we see that composite types consist of array and record types. Array types are groups of elements of the same type, while record types allow the grouping of elements of different types. Arrays are useful for modeling linear structures such as RAMs and ROMs, while records are useful for modeling data packets, instructions, etc.

Composite types are another tool in the VHDL toolbox that allows very abstract modeling of hardware. For instance, a single array type can represent the storage required for a ROM.

4.4.1 Array Types

Array types group one or more elements of the same type together as a single object. Each element of the array can be accessed by one or more arrray indices. Elements can be of any VHDL type. For instance, an array can contain an array or a record as one of its elements.

In an array all elements are of the same type. The example below shows a type declaration for a single dimensional array of bits.

```
TYPE data_bus IS ARRAY(0 TO 31) OF BIT;
```

This declaration declares a data type called *data_bus* that is an array of 32 bits. Each element of the array is the same as the next. Each element of the array can be accessed by an array index. An example of how to access elements of the array is shown below:

```
VARIABLE X: data_bus;
VARIABLE Y: BIT;

Y := X(0);    -- line 1
Y := X(15);   -- line 2
```

This example represents a small VHDL code fragment, not a complete model. In line 1 the first element of array *X* is being accessed and assigned to variable *Y*, which is of bit type. The type of *Y* must match the base type of array *X* in order for the assignment to take place. If the types do not match, the compiler will generate an error.

In line 2 the sixteenth element of array *X* is being assigned to variable *Y*. Line 2 is accessing the sixteenth element of array *X* because the array index starts with 0. Element 0 is the first element, element 1 is the second, and so on.

Another more comprehensive example of array accessing is shown below:

```
PACKAGE array_example IS
  TYPE data_bus IS ARRAY(0 TO 31) OF BIT;
  TYPE small_bus IS ARRAY(0 TO 7) OF BIT;
END array_example;

USE WORK.array_example.ALL;
ENTITY extract IS
  PORT (data : IN data_bus;
        start : IN INTEGER;
        data_out : OUT small_bus);
END extract;

ARCHITECTURE test OF extract IS
BEGIN
  PROCESS(data, start)
  BEGIN
    FOR i IN 0 TO 7 LOOP
      data_out(i) <= data(i + start);
    END LOOP;
  END PROCESS;
END test;
```

This entity will take in a 32-bit array element as a port and return 8 bits of the element. The 8 bits of the element returned depend on the value of index *start*. The 8 bits are returned through output port *data_out* (there is a much easier method to accomplish this task, with functions, described in Chapter 5).

A change in value of *start* or *data* will trigger the process to execute. The FOR loop will loop 8 times, each time copying a single bit from port *data* to port *data_out*. The starting point of the copy takes place at the integer value of port *start*. Each time through the loop the ith element of *data_out* is assigned the (i + start) element of *data*.

The examples shown so far have been simple arrays with scalar base types. In the next example the base type of the array will be another array.

```
USE STD.std_logic.ALL;
PACKAGE memory IS
   CONSTANT width   : INTEGER := 3;
   CONSTANT memsize : INTEGER := 7;

   TYPE data_out IS ARRAY(0 TO width)
        OF t_wlogic;
   TYPE mem_data IS ARRAY(0 TO memsize)
        OF data_out;
END memory;

USE STD.std_logic.ALL;
USE WORK.memory.ALL;
ENTITY rom IS
   PORT( addr : IN INTEGER;
         data : OUT data_out;
         cs   : IN t_wlogic);
END rom;

ARCHITECTURE basic OF rom IS
   CONSTANT z_state : data_out :=
                      (ZX, ZX, ZX, ZX);
   CONSTANT x_state : data_out :=
                      (FX, FX, FX, FX);
   CONSTANT rom_data : mem_data :=

     ( ( F0, F0, F0, F0),
```

```
          ( F0, F0, F0, F1),
          ( F0, F0, F1, F0),
          ( F0, F0, F1, F1),
          ( F0, F1, F0, F0),
          ( F0, F1, F0, F1),
          ( F0, F1, F1, F0),
          ( F0, F1, F1, F1) );
BEGIN
  ASSERT addr <= memsize
    REPORT "addr out of range"
    SEVERITY ERROR;
  data <= rom_data(addr) AFTER 10 ns
            WHEN cs = '1' ELSE

         z_state AFTER 20 ns
            WHEN cs = '0' ELSE

         x_state AFTER 10 ns;
END basic;
```

Package *memory* uses two constants to define two data types that form the data structures for entity *rom*. By changing the constant *width* and recompiling, we can change the output width of the memory. The initialization data for the ROM would also have to change to reflect the new width.

The data types from package memory are also used to define the data types of the ports of the entity. In particular the *data* port is defined to be of type *data_out*.

The architecture defines three constants used to determine the output value. The first defines the output value when the *cs* input is a '0'. The value output is consistent with the *rom* being not selected. The second constant defines the output value when *rom* has an unknown value on the *cs* input. The value output by *rom* will be unknown as well. The last constant defines the data stored by *rom* (this is a very efficient method to model the ROM, but if the ROM data changes, the model will need to be recompiled). Depending on the address to *rom* an appropriate entry from this third constant will be output. This will happen when the *cs* input is a '1' value.

The *rom* data type in this example is organized as 8 rows (0 to 7) and 4 columns (0 to 3). It is a two-dimensional structure, as shown in Figure 4-2.

	3	2	1	0
0	0	0	0	0
1	0	0	0	1
2	0	0	1	0
3	0	0	1	1
4	0	1	0	0
5	0	1	0	1
6	0	1	1	0
7	0	1	1	1

Figure 4-2

To initialize the constant for the *rom* data type an aggregate initialization is required. The table after the *rom_data* constant declaration is an aggregate used to initialize the constant. The aggregate value is constructed as a table for readability; it could have been all on one line. The structure of the aggregate must match the structure of the data type for the assignment to occur. A simple example of an aggregate assignment is shown below:

```
PROCESS(X)
   TYPE bitvec IS ARRAY(0 TO 3) OF BIT;
   VARIABLE Y : bitvec;
BEGIN
   Y := ('1', '0', '1', '0');
   .
   .
   .
END PROCESS;
```

Variable *Y* has an element of type BIT in the aggregate for each element of its type. In this example the variable *Y* is 4 bits wide, and the aggregate is 4 bits wide as well.

The constant *rom_data* from the *rom* example is an array of arrays. Each element of type *mem_data* is an array of type *data_out*. The aggregate assignment for an array of arrays can be represented by the form shown below:

```
value := ((e1, e2,...,en),...,(e1, e2,...,en));
                E1              ...          En
```

However a much more readable form is shown below:

```
value := ((e1, e2,..., en),   -- E1
          (e1, e2,..., en),   -- E2
           .    . ...  .
           .    . ...  .
          (e1, e2,..., en) ) -- En
```

In the statement part of the *rom* example there is one conditional signal assignment statement. The output port *data* is assigned a value based on the value of the *cs* input. The data type of the value assigned to port *data* must be of type *data_out* because port *data* has a type of *data_out*. By addressing the *rom_data* constant with an integer value, a data type of *data_out* will be returned.

A single value can be returned from the array of arrays by using the syntax shown below:

```
bit_value := rom_data(addr) (bit_index);
```

The first index (*addr*) will return a value with a data type of *data_out*. The second index (*bit_index*) will index the *data_out* type and return a single element of the array.

4.4.1.1 Multidimensional Arrays

The constant *rom_data* in the *rom* example was represented using an array of arrays. Another method for representing the data is with a multidimensional array, as shown in the example below:

```
TYPE mem_data_md IS
  ARRAY(0 TO memsize, 0 TO width) OF t_wlogic;

CONSTANT rom_data_md : mem_data :=
  ( ( F0, F0, F0, F0),
    ( F0, F0, F0, F1),
    ( F0, F0, F1, F0),
```

```
( F0, F0, F1, F1),
( F0, F1, F0, F0),
( F0, F1, F0, F1),
( F0, F1, F1, F0),
( F0, F1, F1, F1) );
```

The declaration shown above declares a two-dimensional array type *mem_data_md*. When constant *rom_data_md* is declared using this type, the initialization syntax remains the same but the method of accessing an element of the array is different. In the example below, a single element of the array is accessed.

```
X := rom_data_md(3, 3);
```

This access will return the fourth element of the fourth row, which in this example is an F1.

4.4.1.2 Unconstrained Array Types

An unconstrained array type is a type whose range or size is not completely specified when the type is declared. This allows multiple subtypes to share a common base type. Entities and subprograms can then operate on all of the different subtypes with a single subprogram, instead of a subprogram or entity per size.

An example of an unconstrained type declaration is shown below:

```
TYPE BIT_VECTOR IS ARRAY(NATURAL RANGE <>)
   OF BIT;
```

This is the type declaration for type BIT_VECTOR from the Standard package. This type declaration declares a type that is an array of type BIT. However, the number of elements of the array is not specified. The notation that depicts this is shown below:

```
RANGE <>
```

This notation specifies that the type being defined has an unconstrained range. The word NATURAL before the keyword RANGE, in the type declaration, specifies that the type is bounded only by the range of NATURAL. Type NATURAL is defined in the Standard package to have a range from 0 to integer'high. Type BIT_VECTOR, then, can range in size from 0 elements to integer'high elements. Each element of the BIT_VECTOR type is of type BIT.

Unconstrained types are typically used for types of subprogram arguments, or entity ports. These entities or subprograms can be passed items of any size within the range of the unconstrained type if it has a bounding range.

For instance let's assume that a designer wants a shift-right function, for type BIT_VECTOR. The function will use the unconstrained type BIT_VECTOR as the type of its ports, but it can be passed any type which is a subtype of type BIT_VECTOR. Let's walk through an example to illustrate how this works. An example of an unconstrained shift-right function is shown below:

```
PACKAGE mypack IS
   SUBTYPE eightbit IS BIT_VECTOR(0 TO 7);
   SUBTYPE fourbit IS BIT_VECTOR(0 TO 3);
   FUNCTION shift_right(val : BIT_VECTOR)
      RETURN BIT_VECTOR;
END mypack;

PACKAGE BODY mypack IS
   FUNCTION shift_right(val : BIT_VECTOR)
      RETURN BIT_VECTOR IS
      VARIABLE result : BIT_VECTOR(0 TO
         (val'LENGTH - 1));
   BEGIN
      result := val;
      IF (val'LENGTH > 1) THEN
         FOR i IN 0 TO (val'LENGTH - 2) LOOP
            result(i) := result(i + 1);
         END LOOP;
         result(val'LENGTH - 1) := 0;
      ELSE
         result(0) := 0;
      END IF;
      RETURN result;
   END shift_right;
END mypack;
```

The package declaration (the first five lines of the model) declares two subtypes, *eightbit*, and *fourbit*. These two subtypes are subtypes of the unconstrained base type BIT_VECTOR. These two types constrain the base type to range 0 to 7 for type *eightbit* and range 0 to 3 for type *fourbit*.

In a typical hardware description language without unconstrained types, two different shift-right functions would need to be written to handle the two different-sized subtypes. One function would work with type *eightbit*, and the other would work with type *fourbit*. With unconstrained types in VHDL, a single function can be written that will handle both input types and return the correct type.

Based on the size of input argument *val*, the internal variable *result* is created to be of the same size. Variable *result* is then initialized to the value of input argument *val*. This is necessary because the value of *val* can only be read in a function; it cannot have a value assigned in the function. If the size of input argument *val* is greater than 1, then the shift-right function will loop through the length of the subtype value passed into the function. Each loop will shift one of the bits of variable *result* one bit to the right. If the size of input argument *val* is less than 2, we will treat this as a special case and return a single bit whose value is '0'.

4.4.2 Record Types

Record types group objects of many types together as a single object. Each element of the record can be accessed by its field name. Record elements can include elements of any type, including arrays and records. The elements of a record can be of the same type or different types. Like arrays, records are used to model abstract data elements.

An example of a record type declaration is shown below:

```
TYPE optype IS ( add, sub, mpy, div, jmp );

TYPE instruction IS
  RECORD opcode : optype;
         src    : INTEGER;
         dst    : INTEGER;
  END RECORD;
```

The first line declares the enumerated type *optype*, which will be used as one of the record field types. The second line starts the declaration of the record. The record type declaration begins with the keyword RECORD and ends with the clause END RECORD. All of the declarations between these two keywords are field declarations for the record.

Each field of the record represents a unique storage area which can be read from and assigned data of the appropriate type. This example declares three fields, *opcode* of type *optype*, and *src* and *dst* of type INTEGER. Each field can be referenced by using the name of the record, followed by a period, and the field name. An example of this type of access is shown below:

```
PROCESS(X)
  VARIABLE inst : instruction;
  VARIABLE source, dest : INTEGER;
  VARIABLE operator : optype;
BEGIN
  source := inst.src;-- Ok line 1
  dest   := inst.src;-- Ok line 2

  source := inst.opcode;-- error line 3
  operator := inst.opcode;-- Ok line 4

  inst.src  := dest;-- Ok line 5
  inst.dst := dest;-- Ok line 6

  inst := (add, dest, 2);-- Ok line 7
  inst := (source);-- error line 8
END PROCESS;
```

This example declares variable *inst*, which is of type *instruction*. Also variables matching the record field types are declared. Lines 1 and 2 show fields of the record being assigned to local process variables. The assignments are legal because the types match. Notice the period after the name of the record to select the field.

Line 3 shows a case which is illegal. The type of field *opcode* does not match the type of variable source. The compiler will flag this statement as a type mismatch error. Line 4 shows the correct assignment occurring between the field *opcode* and a variable which matches its type.

Lines 5 and 6 show that not only can record fields be read from, but they can be assigned to as well. In these two lines, two of the fields of the record are assigned the values from variable *dest*.

Line 7 shows an example of an aggregate assignment. In this line all of the fields of the record are being assigned at once. The aggregate assigned contains three entries: an *optype* value, an INTEGER variable value, and an INTEGER value. This is a legal assignment to variable record *inst*.

Line 8 shows an example of an illegal aggregate value for record *inst*. There is only one value present in the aggregate, which is an illegal type for the record.

In the examples so far all of the elements of the records have been scalars. Let's examine some examples of records that have more complex field types. A record for a data packet is shown below:

```
TYPE word IS ARRAY(0 TO 3) OF t_wlogic;
TYPE t_word_array IS ARRAY(0 TO 15) OF word;
TYPE addr_type IS
   RECORD
      source : INTEGER;
      key    : INTEGER;
   END RECORD;

TYPE data_packet IS
   RECORD
      addr : addr_type;
      data : t_word_array;
      checksum : INTEGER;
      parity : BOOLEAN;
   END RECORD;
```

The first two type declarations define type *word* and *addr_type,* which are used in the record *data_packet*. Type *word* is a simple array and type *addr_type* is a simple record. Record type *data_packet* contains four fields using these two types in combination with two VHDL predefined types.

The example below shows how a variable of type *data_packet* would be accessed.

```
PROCESS(X)
   VARIABLE packet : data_packet;
BEGIN

   packet.addr.key := 5;     -- Ok line 1
   packet.addr := (10, 20);    -- Ok line 2
```

```
    packet.data(0) :=
       (F0, F0, F0, F0);      -- Ok line 3

    packet.data(10)(4) := F1; -- error line 4
    packet.data(10)(0) := F1;-- Ok line 5

END PROCESS;
```

This example shows how complex record types are accessed. In line 1 a record field of a record is accessed. Field *key* is a record field of record *addr_type,* which is a field of record *data_packet.* This line assigns the value 5 to that field. Line 2 assigns an aggregate to the whole field called *addr* in record *data_packet.*

In line 3 the *data* field is assigned an aggregate for the 0th element of the array. Line 4 tries to assign to only one bit of the eleventh element of the data array field in record *data_packet,* but the second index value is *out of range.* Finally, line 5 shows how to assign to a single bit of the array correctly.

Composite types are very powerful tools for modeling complex and abstract data types. By using the right combination of records and arrays, you can make models easy to understand and efficient.

4.5 Access Types

Most hardware design engineers using VHDL will probably never use access types directly (a hardware designer may use the TextIO package, which uses access types, thereby an indirect use of access types), but access types provide very powerful programming language type operations. An access type in VHDL is very similar to a *pointer* in a language like Pascal or C. It is an address, or a handle to a specific object.

Access types allow the designer to model objects of a dynamic nature. For instance dynamic queues, fifos, etc. can be modeled easily using access types. Probably the most common operation using an access type would be creating and maintaining a linked list.

Only variables can be declared as access types. By the nature of access types they can only be used in sequential processing.

When an object is declared to be of an access type, two predefined functions are automatically available to manipulate the object. These functions are named NEW and DEALLOCATE. Function NEW will allocate memory of the size of the object in bytes and return the access value. Function DEALLOCATE takes in the access value and returns the memory back to the system. An example to show how this all works is shown below:

```
PROCESS(X)
  TYPE fifo_element_t IS ARRAY(0 TO 3)
    OF t_wlogic; -- line 1

  TYPE fifo_el_access IS
    ACCESS fifo_element_t; -- line 2

  VARIABLE fifo_ptr : fifo_el_access
    := NULL; -- line 3

  VARIABLE temp_ptr : fifo_el_access
    := NULL; -- line 4
BEGIN
  temp_ptr := new fifo_element_t;   -- Ok line 5
  temp_ptr.ALL := (F0, F1, F0, F1);-- Ok line 6

  temp_ptr.ALL := (F0, F0, F0, F0); --Ok line 7
  temp_ptr.ALL(0) := F0; -- Ok line 8

  fifo_ptr := temp_ptr; -- Ok line 9
  fifo_ptr.ALL := temp_ptr.ALL; -- Ok line 10
END PROCESS;
```

In line 2 an access type is declared using the type declared in line 1. Lines 3 and 4 declare two access type variables of *fifo_el_access* type from line 2. This process now has two access variable objects that can be used to access objects of type *fifo_element_t*.

Line 5 calls the predefined function NEW, which allocates enough memory for a variable of type *fifo_element_t* and returns an access value to the memory allocated. The access value returned is then assigned to variable *temp_ptr*. Variable *temp_ptr* is now pointing to an object of type *fifo_element_t*. This value can be read from or assigned to using variable assignment statements.

In line 6 a value is assigned to the object pointed to by *temp_ptr*. Line 7 shows another way to assign a value using an access value. The keyword .ALL specifies that the entire object being accessed. Subelements of the object can be assigned by using a subelement name after the access variable name. Line 8 shows how to reference a subelement of an array pointed to by an access value. In this example the first element of the array will have a value assigned to it.

In the next few statements we will examine how access values can be copied among different objects. In line 9 the access value of *temp_ptr* is assigned to *fifo_ptr*. Now both *temp_ptr* and *fifo_ptr* are pointing to the same object. This is shown in Figure 4-3 :

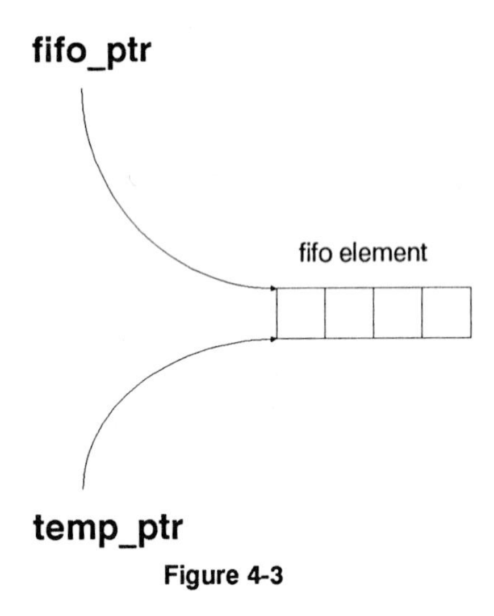

Figure 4-3

Both *temp_ptr* and *fifo_ptr* can be used to read from and assign to the object being accessed.

Line 10 shows how one object value can be assigned to another using access types. The value of the object pointed to by *temp_ptr* will be assigned to the value pointed to by *fifo_ptr*.

4.5.1 Incomplete Types

When implementing recursive structures such as linked lists, you need another VHDL language feature to complete the declarations. This feature is called the *incomplete type*. The incomplete type allows the declaration of a type to be defined later.

An example that demonstrates why this would be useful is shown below:

```
PACKAGE stack_types IS
   TYPE data_type IS ARRAY(0 TO 7)
      OF t_wlogic; -- line 1

   TYPE element_ptr;  -- incomplete type line 2

   TYPE element_rec IS -- line 3
      RECORD -- line 4
         data : data_type; -- line 5
         nxt  : element_ptr; -- line 6
      END RECORD; -- line 7

   TYPE element_ptr IS
      ACCESS element_rec; -- line 8

END stack_types;

USE WORK.stack_types.ALL;
ENTITY stack IS
   PORT(din : IN data_type;
        clk : IN t_wlogic;
        dout : OUT data_type;
        r_wb : IN t_wlogic);
END stack;

ARCHITECTURE stack OF stack IS
BEGIN
   PROCESS(clk)

      VARIABLE list_head : element_ptr
         := NULL;-- line 9
```

```
      VARIABLE temp_elem : element_ptr
         := NULL;-- line 10

      VARIABLE last_clk : t_wlogic
         := U;  -- line 11
    BEGIN
      IF (clk = '1') AND
         (last_clk = '0') THEN -- line 12

         IF (r_wb = '0') THEN --  line 13

             -- line 14
             temp_elem := NEW element_rec;

             temp_elem.data := din; -- line 15

             -- line 16
             temp_elem.nxt := list_head;

             list_head := temp_elem; -- line 17
         -- read mode line 18
         ELSIF (r_wb = '1') THEN
             dout <= list_head.data; -- line 19
             temp_elem := list_head; -- line 20

             -- line 21
             list_head := temp_elem.nxt;

             DEALLOCATE (temp_elem); -- line 22
         ELSE
             ASSERT FALSE
             REPORT "read/write
                unknown while clock active"
             SEVERITY WARNING; -- line 23
         END IF;
      END IF;
      last_clk := clk; -- line 24
    END PROCESS;
  END stack;
```

This example implements a stack using access types. The package *stack_types* declares all of the types needed for the stack. In line 2 is a declaration of the incomplete type *element_ptr*. The name of the type is specified, but no specification of the type is present. The purpose of this declaration is to reserve the name of the type and allow other types to gain access to the type when it is fully specified. The full specification for this incomplete type appears in line 8.

The fundamental reason for the incomplete type is to allow self-referencing structures as linked lists. Notice that type *element_ptr* is used in type *element_rec* in line 6. In order to use a type it must first be defined. Notice also that in the declaration for type *element_ptr* in line 8 that type *element_rec* is used. Since each type uses the other in its respective declarations, neither type can be declared first without a special way of handling this case. The incomplete type allows this scenario to exist.

Lines 3 through 7 declare the record type *element_rec*. This record type will be used to store the data for the stack. The first field of the record is the data field, and the second is an access type that will point to the next record in the stack.

The entity for stack declares port *din* for data input to the stack, a *clk* input on which all operations are triggered, a *dout* port which transfers data out of the stack, and finally a *r_wb* input which causes a read operation when high and a write operation when low. The process for the stack is only triggered when the *clk* input has an event occur. It is not affected by changes in *r_wb*.

Lines 9 through 11 declare some variables used to keep track of the data for the stack. Variable *list_head* will be the head of the linked list of data. It will always point to the first element of the list of items in the stack. Variable *temp_elem* will be used to hold a newly allocated element until it is connected into the stack list. Variable *last_clk* is used to hold the previous value of *clk* to enable transitions on the clock to be detected (this behavior can be duplicated with attributes, which are discussed in Chapter 7).

Line 12 checks to see if a 0 to 1 transistion has occurred on the *clk* input. If so, then the stack needs to do a read or write depending on the *r_wb* input. Line 13 checks to see if *r_wb* is set up for a write to the stack. If so lines 14 to 17 create a new data storage element and connect this element to the list.

Line 14 uses the predefined function NEW to allocate a record of type *element_rec* and return an access value to be assigned to variable *temp_elem*. This creates a structure that is shown graphically in Figure 4-4.

Lines 15 and 16 fill in the newly allocated object with the data from input *din* and the access value to the head of the list. After line 16 the data structures look as shown in Figure 4-5.

Finally in line 17 the new element is added to the head of the list. This is shown in Figure 4-6.

Lines 18 to 22 of the model provide the behavior of the stack when an element is read from the stack. Line 19 copies the data from the stack element to the output port. Lines 20 to 22 disconnect the element from the stack list and return the memory to the system.

Line 20 assigns the *temp_elem* access variable to point to the head of the list. This is shown in Figure 4-7.

Line 21 moves the head of the list to the next element in the list. This is shown in Figure 4-8.

Finally in line 22, the element that had its data transferred out is deallocated and the memory returned to the memory pool. This is shown in Figure 4-9.

Access types are very powerful tools for modeling complex and abstract types of systems. Access types bring programming language types of operations to VHDL processes.

4.6 File Types

A file type allows declarations of objects that have a type FILE. A file object type is actually a subset of the variable object type. A variable object can be assigned with a variable assignment statement, while a file object cannot be assigned. A file object can be read from, written to, and checked for end of file only with special procedures and functions.

Files consist of sequential streams of a particular type. A file whose base object type is integer will consist of a sequential stream of integers. This is shown in Figure 4-10.

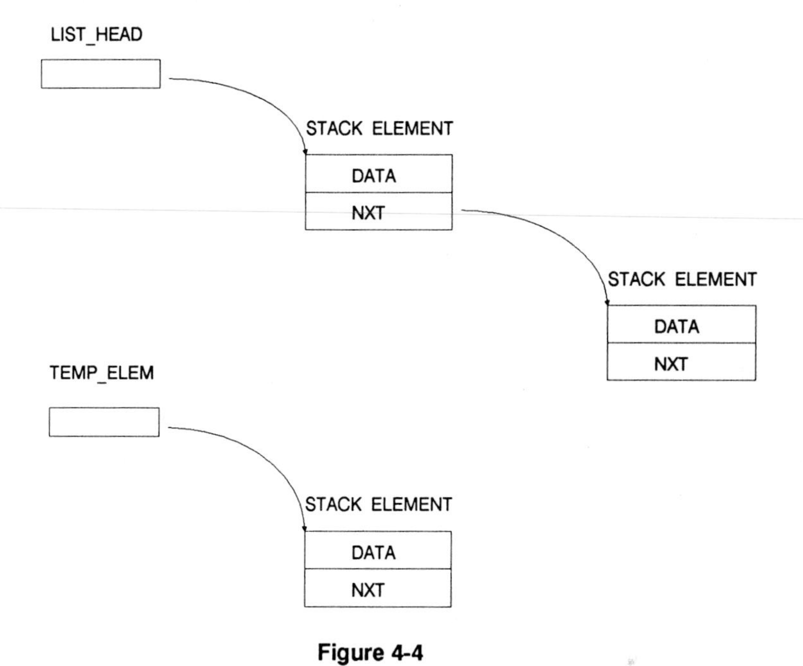

Figure 4-4

LIST_HEAD

STACK ELEMENT

DATA

NXT

STACK ELEMENT

DATA

NXT

TEMP_ELEM

STACK ELEMENT

DATA

NXT

Figure 4-5

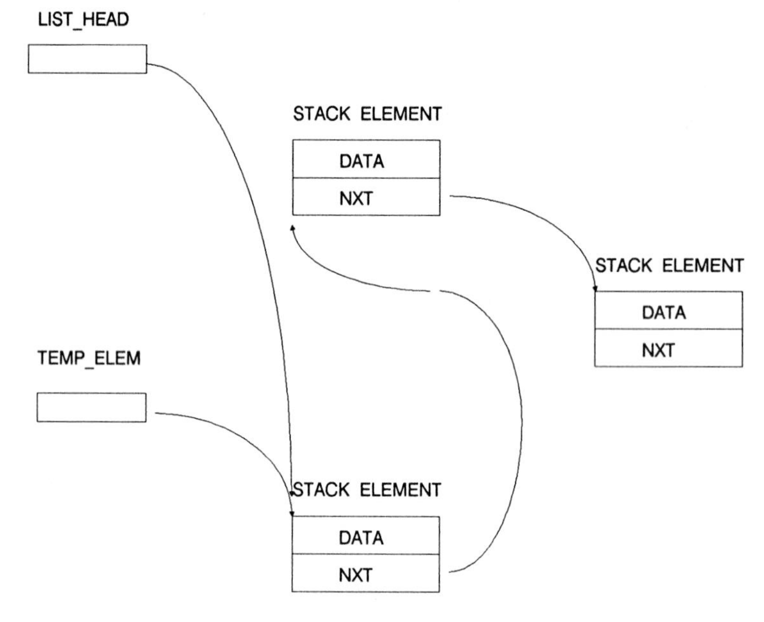

Figure 4-6

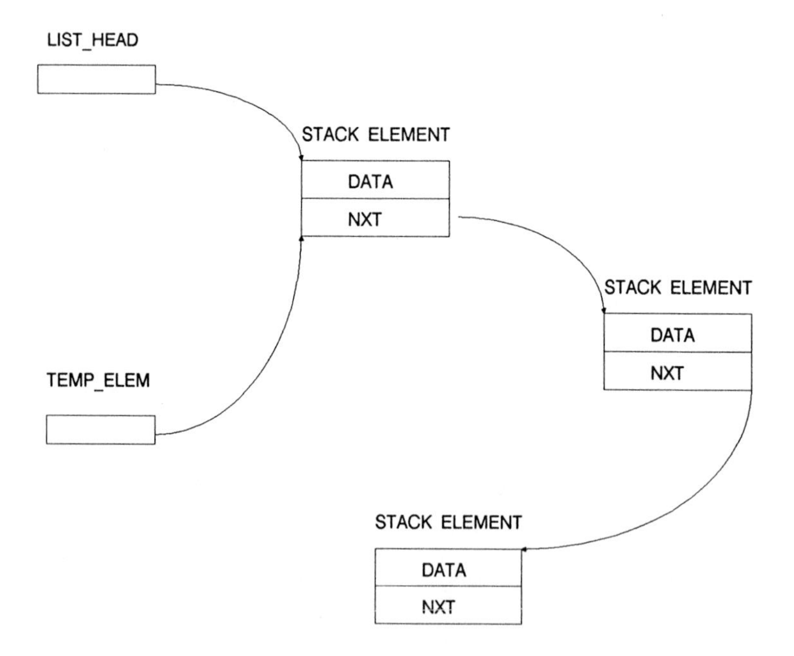

Figure 4-7

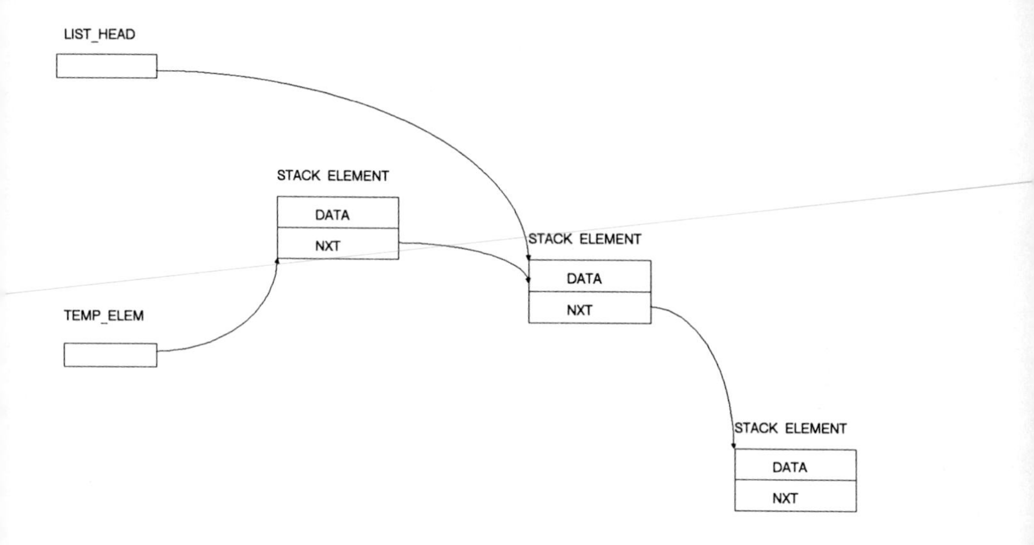

Figure 4-8

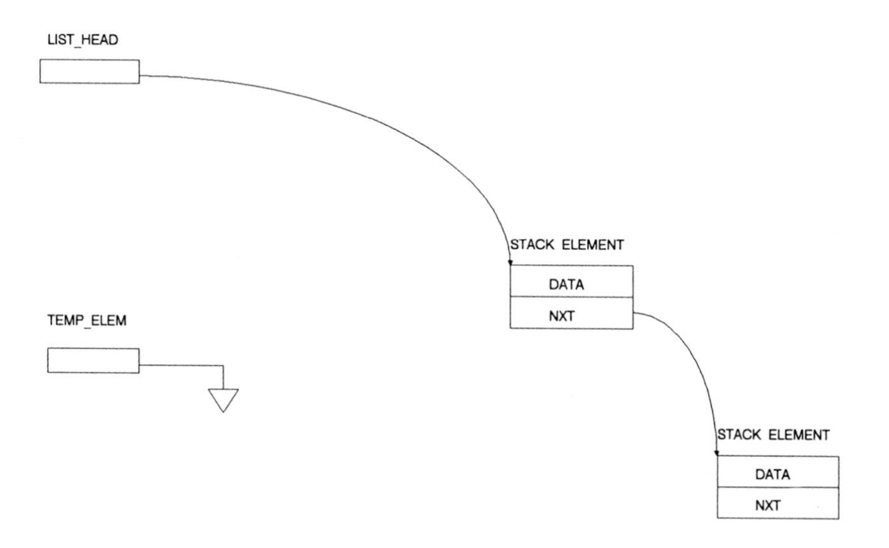

Figure 4-9

INTEGER 1	INTEGER 2	....	INTEGER N	END OF FILE

Figure 4-10

A file whose object type is a complex record type will consist of a sequential stream of complex records. An example of how this might look is shown in Figure 4-11.

COMPLEX FILE

RECORD 1	RECORD 2		RECORD N	
OPCODE	OPCODE	....	OPCODE	END OF FILE
ADDRMODE	ADDRMODE		ADDRMODE	
SRC	SRC		SRC	
DST	DST		DST	

Figure 4-11

At the end of the stream of data is an end-of-file mark. Two procedures and one function allow operations on file objects. They are as follows:

- READ (file, data) – Procedure
- WRITE (file, data) – Procedure
- ENDFILE (file) – Function, returns boolean

Procedure READ will read an object from the file and return the object in argument *data*. Procedure WRITE will write argument *data* to the file specified by the file argument. Finally function ENDFILE will return true when the file is currently at the end-of-file mark.

To use these procedures and functions requires a file type declaration and a file object declaration.

4.6.1 File Type Declaration

A file type declaration specifies the name of the file type and the base type of the file. An example of a file type declaration is shown below:

```
TYPE integer_file IS FILE OF INTEGER;
```

This declaration specifies a file type whose name is *integer_file* and is of type INTEGER. This declaration corresponds to the file in Figure 4-10.

4.6.2 File Object Declaration

A file object makes use of a file type and declares an object of type FILE. The file object declaration specifies the name of the file object, the mode of the file, and the physical disk path name. The file mode can be IN or OUT. If the mode is IN, then the file can be read with the READ procedure. If the mode is OUT, then the file can be written with the WRITE procedure. An example is shown below:

```
FILE myfile : integer_file IS IN
  "/doug/test/examples/data_file";
```

This declaration declares a file object called *myfile* that is an input file of type *integer_file*. The last argument is the path name on the physical disk where the file is located (in most implementations this is true, but it is not necessarily so) .

4.6.3 File Type Examples

To read the contents of a file, you can call the READ procedure within a loop statement. The loop statement can perform read operations until an end of file is reached, at which time the loop will be terminated. An example of a file read operation is shown below:

```
USE STD.std_logic.ALL;
ENTITY rom IS
  PORT(addr : IN INTEGER;
       cs   : IN t_wlogic;
       data : OUT INTEGER);
END rom;

ARCHITECTURE rom OF rom IS
BEGIN
  PROCESS(addr, cs)
    VARIABLE rom_init : BOOLEAN
      := FALSE;-- line 1

    TYPE rom_data_file_t IS
```

```
        FILE OF INTEGER;-- line 2

    FILE rom_data_file : rom_data_file_t IS IN
        "/doug/dlp/test1.dat"; --line 3
    TYPE dtype IS ARRAY(0 TO 63)
        OF INTEGER;
    VARIABLE rom_data : dtype; -- line 4

    VARIABLE i : INTEGER := 0;-- line 5
  BEGIN
    IF (rom_init = false) THEN-- line 6

        -- line 7
        WHILE NOT ENDFILE(rom_data_file)
            AND (i < 64) LOOP

            -- line 8
            READ(rom_data_file, rom_data(i));

            i := i + 1;-- line 9
        END LOOP;
        rom_init := true;-- line 10
    END IF;
    IF (cs = '1') THEN-- line 11
        data <= rom_data(addr);-- line 12
    ELSE
        data <= -1;-- line 13
    END IF;
  END PROCESS;
END rom;
```

This example shows how a *rom* can be initialized from a file the first time the model is executed and never again. A variable called *rom_init* is used to keep track of whether the *rom* has been initialized or not. If false, the *rom* has not been initialized; if true, the *rom* has already been initialized.

Line 2 of the example declares a file type *rom_data_file_t* that will be used to declare a file object. In line 3 a *rom_data_file* object is declared. In this example the physical disk path name was *hard-coded* into the model, but a generic could have been used to pass a different path name for each instance of the *rom*.

Line 6 of the example tests variable *rom_init* for true or false. If false, the initialization loop is executed. Line 7 is the start of the initialization loop. The loop test makes use of the predefined function ENDFILE. The loop will execute until there is no more data in the file or when the *rom* storage area has been filled.

Each pass through the loop calls the predefined procedure READ. This procedure will read one integer at a time and place it in the element of *rom_data* that is currently being accessed. Each time through the loop the index *i* is incremented to the next element position.

Finally, when the loop finishes the variable *rom_init* is set to true. The next time that the process is invoked, variable *rom_init* will be true, so the initialization loop will not be invoked again.

Writing a file is analogous to reading except that the loop will not test every time through for an end-of-file condition. Each time a loop writing data is executed, the new object is appended to the end of the file. When the model is writing to a file, the file must have been declared with mode OUT.

4.6.4 File Type Caveats

In general, the file operations allowed are limited. Files cannot be opened, closed, or accessed in a random sequence. All that VHDL provides is a simple sequential capability.

For textual input and output, there is another facility that VHDL provides called TextIO. This facility provides for formatted textual input and output and is discussed in Chapter 8.

4.7 Subtypes

Subtype declarations are used to define subsets of a type. The subset can contain the entire range of the base type but does not necessarily need to. A typical subtype adds a constraint(s) to an existing type.

The type integer encompasses the minimum range -2,147,483,647 to +2,147,483,647. In the Standard package (a designer should never redefine any of the types used in the Standard package; this can result in incompatible VHDL, because of type mismatches) there is a subtype called NATURAL whose range is from 0 to +2,147,483,647. This subtype is defined as shown below:

```
TYPE INTEGER IS -2,147,483,647 TO
   +2,147,483,647;
SUBTYPE NATURAL IS
   INTEGER RANGE 0 TO +2,147,483,647;
```

After the keyword SUBTYPE is the name of the new subtype being created. The keyword IS is followed by the base type of the subtype. In this example the base type is INTEGER. An optional constraint on the base type is also specified.

So why would a designer want to create a subtype? There are two main reasons for doing so.

- To add constraints for selected signal assignment statements or case statements.
- To create a resolved subtype (resolved types will be discussed along with resolution functions in Chapter 5).

When a subtype of the base type is used, the range of the base type can be constrained to be what is needed for a particular operation. Any functions that work with the base type will also work with the subtype.

Subtypes and base types also allow assignment between the two types. A subtype can always be assigned to the base type because the range of the subtype is always less than or equal to the range of the base type. The base type may or may not be able to be assigned to the subtype, depending on the value of the object of the base type. If the value is within the value of the subtype, then the assignment will succeed; otherwise, a range constraint error will result.

A typical example where a subtype is useful is adding a constraint to a numeric base type. In the example above, the NATURAL subtype constrained the integer base type to the positive values and zero. But what if this range is still too large? The constraint specified can be a user-defined expression that matches the type of the base type. In the example below, an 8-bit multiplexer is modeled with a much smaller constraint on the integer type.

```
PACKAGE mux_types IS
   SUBTYPE eightval IS
```

```
      INTEGER RANGE 0 TO 7; -- line 1
END mux_types;

USE WORK.mux_types.ALL;
USE STD.std_logic.ALL;
ENTITY mux8 IS
   PORT(I0, I1, I2, I3, I4, I5,
        I6, I7: IN t_wlogic;
        sel : IN eightval;   -- line 2
        q : OUT t_wlogic);
END mux8;

ARCHITECTURE mux8 OF mux8 IS
BEGIN
   WITH sel SELECT        -- line 3
      Q <= I0 AFTER 10 ns WHEN 0, -- line 4
           I1 AFTER 10 ns WHEN 1,     -- line 5
           I2 AFTER 10 ns WHEN 2,     -- line 6
           I3 AFTER 10 ns WHEN 3,     -- line 7
           I4 AFTER 10 ns WHEN 4,     -- line 8
           I5 AFTER 10 ns WHEN 5,     -- line 9
           I6 AFTER 10 ns WHEN 6,     -- line 10
           I7 AFTER 10 ns WHEN 7;     -- line 11
END mux8;
```

The package *mux_types* declares a subtype *eightval,* which adds a constraint to base type INTEGER. The constraint allows an object of *eightval* to take on values from 0 to 7.

The package is included in entity *mux8*, which has one of its input ports, *sel,* declared using type *eightval.* In the architecture at line 3, a selected signal assignment statement uses the value of *sel* to determine which output is transferred to the output *Q*. If *sel* was not of the subtype *eightval*, but was strictly an integer type, then the selected signal assignment would need a value to assign for each value of the type, or an OTHERS clause. By adding the constraint to the integer type, all values of the type can be directly specified.

In this chapter we have examined the different types available in VHDL to the designer. The scalar types are types such as integer, and bit, useful for modeling of simple data structures. We expanded our discussion to include some of the higher-level types, such as arrays and records. We discussed the access type, the pointer equivalent in VHDL, and finally concluded with a discussion of subtypes.

In the next chapter we will focus on another method of sequential statement modeling, the subprogram.

Chapter

5

Subprograms and Packages

In this chapter subprograms and packages will be discussed. Subprograms consist of procedures and functions used to perform common operations. Packages are mechanisms that allow sharing data among entities. Subprograms, types, and component declarations are the tools to build designs with, and packages are the toolboxes.

5.1 Subprograms

Subprograms consist of procedures and functions. A procedure can return more than one argument, while a function always returns just one. In a function all parameters are input parameters, while a procedure can have input parameters, output parameters, and inout parameters.

There are two versions of procedures and functions: a concurrent procedure and concurrent function, and a sequential procedure and sequential function. The concurrent procedure and function exist outside of a process statement or another subprogram, while the sequential function and procedure exist *only* in a process statement or another subprogram statement.

All statements inside of a subprogram are sequential. The same statements that exist in a process statement can be used in a subprogram, including WAIT statements. The WAIT statements only pertain to the outer process statement, however.

A procedure exists as a separate statement in an architecture or process, while a function is usually used in an assignment statement or expression.

5.1.1 Function

In the example below is a function that takes in an array of the *t_wlogic* type (this is described in Chapter 9 and Appendix A) and returns an integer value. The integer value represents the numeric value of all of the bits treated as a binary number.

```
USE STD.std_logic.ALL;
PACKAGE num_types IS
  TYPE log8 IS ARRAY(0 TO 7)
           OF t_wlogic;-- line 1
END num_types;

USE STD.std_logic.ALL;
USE WORK.num_types.ALL;
ENTITY convert IS
  PORT(I1 : IN log8;-- line 2
       O1 : OUT INTEGER);-- line 3
END convert;

ARCHITECTURE behave OF convert IS

  FUNCTION vector_to_int(S : log8) -- line 4
       RETURN INTEGER is-- line 5

  VARIABLE result : INTEGER := 0;-- line 6

BEGIN
  FOR i IN 0 TO 7 LOOP-- line 7
    result := result * 2;-- line 8
    IF S(i) = '1' THEN-- line 9
```

```
        result := result + 1;-- line 10
      END IF;
    END LOOP;
    RETURN result;-- line 11
  END vector_to_int;

  BEGIN
    O1 <= vector_to_int(I1);-- line 12
  END behave;
```

Line 1 of the example declares the array type used throughout the example. Lines 2 and 3 show the input and output ports of the *convert* entity, and their types. Lines 4 through 11 describe a function that is declared in the declaration region of the architecture *behave.* By declaring the function in the declaration region of the architecture, the function is visible to any region of the architecture.

Lines 4 and 5 declare the name of the function, the arguments to the function, and the type that the function returns. In line 6 a variable local to the function is declared. Functions have declaration regions very similar to process statements. Variables, constants, and types can be declared, but no signals.

Lines 7 through 10 declare a loop statement that will loop once for each value in the array type. The basic algorithm of the function is to do a shift and add for each bit position in the array. The result is first shifted (by multiplying by 2), and then if the bit position is a logical 1, a 1 value is added to the result.

At the end of the loop statement, variable *result* will contain the integer value of the array passed in. The value of the function is passed back via the RETURN statement. An example RETURN statement is shown in line 11.

Finally, line 12 shows how a function is called. The name of the function is followed by its arguments enclosed in parentheses. The function will always return a value; therefore the calling process, concurrent statement, etc. must have a place for the function to return the value to. In this example, the output of the function is assigned to an output port.

Parameters to a function are always *input only*. No assignment can be done to any of the parameters of the function. In the example above the parameters were of a *constant* kind because no explicit kind was specified and the default is constant. The arguments are treated as if they were constants declared in the declaration area of the function.

The other kind of parameter that a function can have is a *signal* parameter. With a signal parameter, the attributes (attributes are discussed in Chapter 6) of the signal are passed in and are available for use in the function. The exception to this statement are attributes 'STABLE, 'QUIET, 'TRANSACTION, and 'DELAYED, which create special signals.

An example showing a function that contains signal parameters is shown below:

```
USE STD.std_logic.ALL;
ENTITY dff IS
   PORT(d, clk : IN t_wlogic;
        q : OUT t_wlogic);

   FUNCTION rising_edge
      (SIGNAL S : t_wlogic)   -- line 1
      RETURN BOOLEAN IS     -- line 2
   BEGIN
      -- this function makes use of attributes
      -- 'event and 'last_value discussed
      -- in Chapter 6
      IF (S'EVENT) AND (S = '1') AND   -- line 3
         (S'LAST_VALUE = '0') THEN     -- line 4

         RETURN TRUE;    -- line 5
      ELSE
         RETURN FALSE;    -- line 6
      END IF;
   END rising_edge;
END dff;

ARCHITECTURE behave OF dff IS
BEGIN
   PROCESS( clk)
   BEGIN
```

```
      IF rising_edge(clk) THEN    -- line 7
        q <= d;    -- line 8
      END IF;
    END PROCESS;
  END behave;
```

This example provides a rising edge detection facility for the D flip-flop being modeled. The function is declared in the entity declaration section and is therefore available to any architecture of the entity.

Lines 1 and 2 show the function declaration. There is only one parameter (*S*) to the function, and it is of a signal type. Lines 3 and 4 show an IF statement that determines whether the signal has just changed or not, if the current value is a '1', and whether the previous value was a '0'. If all of these conditions are true, then the IF statement will return a true value, signifying that a rising edge was found on the signal.

If any one of the conditions is not true, the value returned will be false, as shown in line 6. Line 7 shows an invocation of the function using the signal created by port *clk* of entity *dff.* If there is a rising edge on the signal *clk,* then the *d* value is transferred to the output *q*.

The most common use for a function is to return a value in an expression; however there are two more classes of use available in VHDL. The first is a *conversion function* and the second is a *resolution function*. Conversion functions are used to convert from one type to another. Resolution functions are used to resolve bus contention on a multiply-driven signal.

5.1.2 Conversion Functions

Conversion functions are used to convert an object of one type to another. They are used in component instantiation statements to allow mapping of signals and ports of different types. This type of situation usually arises when a designer wants to make use of an entity from another design that uses a different data type.

Assume that designer A was using a data type that had the four values shown below:

```
TYPE fourval IS (X, L, H, Z);
```

Designer B was using a data type that also contained four values, but the value identifiers were different, as shown below:

```
TYPE fourvalue IS ('X', '0', '1', 'Z');
```

Both of these types can be used to represent the states of a four-state value system for a VHDL model. If designer A wanted to use a model from designer B, but designer B used the values from type *fourvalue* as the interface ports to the model, then designer A cannot use the model without converting the types of the ports to the value system used by designer B. This problem can be solved through the use of conversion functions.

First, let's write the function that will convert between these two value systems. The values from the first type represent these distinct states.

- X – unknown value
- L – logical 0 value
- H – logical 1 value
- Z – high-impedance or open-collector value

The values from the second type represent these states.

- 'X' – unknown value
- '0' – logical 0 value
- '1' – logical 1 value
- 'Z' – high-impedance or open-collector value

From the description of the two value systems, the conversion function will be trivial. An example of one is shown below:

```
FUNCTION convert4val(S : fourval)
      RETURN fourvalue IS
BEGIN
   CASE S IS
      WHEN X =>
         RETURN 'X';
      WHEN L =>
         RETURN '0';
      WHEN H =>
         RETURN '1';
```

```
      WHEN Z =>
         RETURN 'Z';
   END CASE;
END convert4val;
```

This function will accept a value of type *fourval* and return a value of type *fourvalue*. The example below shows where such a function might be used.

```
PACKAGE my_std IS
   TYPE fourval IS (X, L, H, Z);
   TYPE fourvalue IS ('X', '0', '1', 'Z');

   TYPE fvector4 IS ARRAY(0 TO 3) OF fourval;
END my_std;

USE WORK.my_std.ALL;
ENTITY reg IS
   PORT(a : IN fvector4;
        clr : IN fourval;
        clk : IN fourval;
        q : OUT fvector4);

   FUNCTION convert4val(S : fourval)
        RETURN fourvalue IS
   BEGIN
      CASE S IS
         WHEN X =>
            RETURN 'X';
         WHEN L =>
            RETURN '0';
         WHEN H =>
            RETURN '1';
         WHEN Z =>
            RETURN 'Z';
      END CASE;
   END convert4val;

   FUNCTION convert4value(S : fourvalue)
        RETURN fourval IS
   BEGIN
      CASE S IS
         WHEN 'X' =>
```

```
            RETURN X;
         WHEN '0' =>
            RETURN L;
         WHEN '1' =>
            RETURN H;
         WHEN 'Z' =>
            RETURN Z;
      END CASE;
   END convert4value;
END reg;

ARCHITECTURE structure OF reg IS
   COMPONENT dff
      PORT(d, clk, clr : IN fourvalue;
            q : OUT fourvalue);
   END COMPONENT;
BEGIN
   U1 : dff PORT MAP(convert4val(a(0)),
                     convert4val(clk),
                     convert4val(clr),
                     convert4value(q) => q(0));

   U2 : dff PORT MAP(convert4val(a(1)),
                     convert4val(clk),
                     convert4val(clr),
                     convert4value(q) => q(1));

   U3 : dff PORT MAP(convert4val(a(2)),
                     convert4val(clk),
                     convert4val(clr),
                     convert4value(q) => q(2));

   U4 : dff PORT MAP(convert4val(a(3)),
                     convert4val(clk),
                     convert4val(clr),
                     convert4value(q) => q(3));

END structure;
```

This example is a 4-bit register built out of flip-flops. The type used in the entity declaration for the register is a vector of type *fourval.* However the flip-flops being instantiated have ports which are of type *fourvalue.*

A type mismatch error will be generated if the ports of entity register are mapped directly to the component ports. Therefore a conversion function is needed to convert between the two value systems.

If the ports are all of mode IN, then only one conversion is needed to map from the containing entity type to the contained entity type. In this example if all of the ports were of mode input, then only function *convert4val* would be required.

If the component has output ports as well, then the output values of the contained entity need to be converted back to the containing entity type. In this example, the *q* port of component *dff* is an output port. The type of the output values will be *fourvalue*. These values cannot be mapped to the type *fourval* ports of entity *xregister*. Function *convert4value* will convert from a *fourvalue* type to a *fourval* type. Applying this function on the output ports will allow the port mapping to occur.

There are four component instantiations that use these conversion functions, components U1 through U4. Notice that the input ports use the *convert4val* conversion function while the output ports use the *convert4value* conversion function.

Using the named association form of mapping for component instantiation, U1 would look like this:

```
U1: dff PORT MAP (
    d   => convert4val( a(0) ),
    clk => convert4val( clk ),
    clr => convert4val( clr ),
    convert4value(q) => q(0) );
```

What this notation shows is that for the input ports the conversion functions are applied to the appropriate input signals (ports) before being mapped to the *dff* ports, and the output port value is converted with the conversion function before being mapped to the output port *q(0)*.

Conversion functions free the designer from generating a lot of temporary signals or variables to perform the conversion. The example below shows another method for performing conversion functions.

```
temp1 <= convert4val( a(0) );
temp2 <= convert4val( clk );
```

```
temp3 <= convert4val( clr );

U1: dff PORT MAP (
   d   => temp1,
   clk => temp2,
   clr => temp3,
   q   => temp4);

q(0) <=  convert4value(temp4);
```

This method is much more verbose, requiring an intermediate temporary signal for each port of the component being mapped. This clearly is not the preferred method.

If a port is of mode INOUT, conversion functions cannot be used with positional notation. The ports must use named association because two conversion functions must be associated with each inout port. One conversion function will be used for the input part of the inout port and the other will be used for the output part of the inout port.

In the example below, two bidirectional transfer devices are contained in an entity called *trans2*.

```
PACKAGE my_pack IS
   TYPE nineval IS (Z0, Z1, ZX,
                    R0, R1, RX,
                    F0, F1, FX);

   TYPE nvector2 IS ARRAY(0 TO 1) OF nineval;
   TYPE fourstate IS (X, L, H, Z);

   FUNCTION convert4state(a : fourstate)
        RETURN nineval;

   FUNCTION convert9val(a : nineval)
        RETURN fourstate;

END my_pack;

PACKAGE body my_pack IS
   FUNCTION convert4state(a : fourstate)
        RETURN nineval IS
   BEGIN
```

```
      CASE a IS
         WHEN X =>
            RETURN FX;
         WHEN L =>
            RETURN F0;
         WHEN H =>
            RETURN F1;
         WHEN Z =>
            RETURN ZX;
      END CASE;
   END convert4state;

   FUNCTION convert9val(a : nineval)
        RETURN fourstate IS
   BEGIN
      CASE a IS
         WHEN Z0 =>
            RETURN Z;
         WHEN Z1 =>
            RETURN Z;
         WHEN ZX =>
            RETURN Z;
         WHEN R0 =>
            RETURN L;
         WHEN R1 =>
            RETURN H;
         WHEN RX =>
            RETURN X;
         WHEN F0 =>
            RETURN L;
         WHEN F1 =>
            RETURN H;
         WHEN FX =>
            RETURN X;
      END CASE;
   END convert9val;
END my_pack;

USE WORK.my_pack.ALL;
ENTITY trans2 IS
   PORT( a, b : INOUT nvector2;
         enable : IN nineval);
```

```
END trans2;

ARCHITECTURE struct OF trans2 IS
   COMPONENT trans
      PORT( x1, x2 : INOUT fourstate;
               en : IN fourstate);
   END COMPONENT;
BEGIN
   U1 : trans PORT MAP(
      convert4state(x1) => convert9val(a(0)),
      convert4state(x2) => convert9val(b(0)),
      en => convert9val(enable) );

   U2 : trans PORT MAP(
      convert4state(x1) => convert9val(a(1)),
      convert4state(x2) => convert9val(b(1)),
      en => convert9val(enable) );
END struct;
```

Each component is a bidirectional transfer device called *trans*. The *trans* device contains three ports. Ports *x1* and *x2* are inout ports and port *en* is an input port. When port *en* is an H value, *x1* is transferred to *x2* and when port *en* is an L value, *x2* is transferred to *x1*.

The *trans* components use type *fourstate* for the port types, while the containing entity uses type *nineval*. Conversion functions are required to allow the instantiation of the *trans* components in architecture *struct* of entity *trans2*.

The first component instantiation statement for the *trans* component labeled U1 shows how conversion functions are used for inout ports. The first port mapping maps port *x1* to *a(0)*. Port *a(0)* is a *nineval* type; therefore the signal created by the port is a *nineval* type. When this signal is mapped to port *x1* of component *trans*, it must be converted to a *fourstate* type. Conversion function *convert9val* must be called to complete the conversion. When data is transferred out to port *x1* for the out portion of the inout port, conversion function *convert4state* must be called.

The conversion functions are organized such that the side of the port mapping clause that changes contains the conversion function that must be called. When *x1* changes, function *convert4state* is called to convert the *fourstate* value to a *nineval* value before it is passed to the containing entity *trans2.* Conversely, when port *a(0)* changes, function *convert9val* is called to convert the *nineval* value to a *fourstate* value that can be used within the *trans* model.

Conversion functions are used to convert a value of one type to a value of another type. They can be called explicitly as part of execution or implicitly from a mapping in a component instantiation.

5.1.3 Resolution Functions

A resolution function is used to return the value of a signal when the signal is driven by multiple drivers. It is illegal in VHDL to have a signal with multiple drivers without a resolution function attached to that signal.

A resolution function consists of a function that is called whenever one of the drivers for the signal has an event occur on it. The resolution function will be executed and will return a single value from all of the driver values; this value will be the new value of the signal.

In typical simulators, resolution functions are built in, or fixed. With VHDL the designer has the capability to define any type of resolution function desired, wired-or, wired-and, average signal value, etc.

A resolution function has a single-argument input and returns a single value. The single-input argument consists of an unconstrained array of driver values for the signal that the resolution function is attached to. If the signal has two drivers, the unconstrained array will be two elements long; if the signal has three drivers, the unconstrained array will be three elements long. The resolution function will examine the values of all of the drivers and return a single value called the *resolved value* of the signal.

Let's examine a resolution function for the type *fourval* that was used in the conversion function examples. The type declaration for *fourval* is shown below:

```
TYPE fourval IS (X, L, H, Z);
```

Four distinct values are declared that represent all of the possible values that the signal can obtain. The value L represents a logical 0, the value H represents a logical 1, the value Z represents a high-impedance or open-collector condition, and finally the value X represents an unknown condition in which the value can represent an L or an H, but we're not sure which. This condition can occur when two drivers are driving a signal, one driver driving with an H, and the other driving with an L.

Listed by order of strength, with the weakest at the top, the values are as follows:

- Z – weakest, H, L, or X can override
- H,L – medium strength, only X can override
- X – strong, no override

Using this information a truth table for two inputs can be developed as shown in Figure 5-1.

Four-State Truth Table

	Z	L	H	X
Z	Z	L	H	X
L	L	L	X	X
H	H	X	H	X
X	X	X	X	X

Figure 5-1

This truth table is for two input values, it can be expanded to more inputs by successively applying it to two values at a time. This can be done because the table is commutative and associative. An L and a Z, or a Z and an L will give the same results. An (L, Z) with H will give the same results as an (H, Z) with an L. These principles are very important, because the order of driver values within the input argument to the resolution function is nondeterministic from the designer's point of view. Any dependence on order can cause nondeterministic results from the resolution function.

Using all of this information a designer can write a resolution function for this type. The resolution function will maintain the highest strength seen so far, and compare this value with new values a single element at a time, until all values have been exhausted. This algorithm will return the highest-strength value.

An example of such a resolution function is shown below:

```
PACKAGE fourpack IS
   TYPE fourval IS (X, L, H, Z);
   TYPE fourval_vector IS
      ARRAY (natural RANGE <> ) OF fourval;

   FUNCTION resolve( s: fourval_vector)
      RETURN fourval;
END fourpack;

PACKAGE BODY fourpack IS
   FUNCTION resolve( s: fourval_vector)
         RETURN fourval IS
      VARIABLE result : fourval := Z;
   BEGIN
      FOR i IN s'RANGE LOOP
         CASE result IS
            WHEN Z =>
               CASE s(i) IS
                  WHEN H =>
                     result := H;
                  WHEN L =>
                     result := L;
                  WHEN X =>
                     result := X;
                  WHEN OTHERS =>
                     NULL;
               END CASE;

            WHEN L =>
               CASE s(i) IS
                  WHEN H =>
                     result := X;
                  WHEN X =>
                     result := X;
```

```
                    WHEN OTHERS =>
                       NULL;
                 END CASE;

              WHEN H =>
                 CASE s(i) IS
                    WHEN L =>
                       result := X;
                    WHEN X =>
                       result := X;
                    WHEN OTHERS =>
                       NULL;
                 END CASE;

              WHEN X =>
                 result := X;
            END CASE;
        END LOOP;
        RETURN result;
     END resolve;
  END fourpack;
```

The input argument is an unconstrained array of the driver-base type, *fourval*. The resolution function will examine all of the values of the drivers passed in argument *s* one at a time and return a single value of *fourval* type to be scheduled as the signal value.

Variable *result* is initialized to a Z value to take care of the case of zero drivers for the signal. In this case the loop will never be executed, and the result value returned will be the initialization value. It is also a good idea to initialize the result value to the weakest value of the value system to allow overwriting by stronger values.

If a nonzero number of drivers exists for the signal being resolved, then the loop will be executed once for each driver value passed in argument *s*. Each driver value is compared with the current value stored in variable *result*. If the new value is stronger according to the rules outlined earlier, then the current result will be updated with the new value.

Let's look at some example driver values to see how this works. Assuming that argument *s* contained the driver values shown in Figure 5-2, what would the result be?

Since there are two drivers, the loop will be executed twice. The first time through the loop variable *result* contains the initial value Z. The first driver value is also a Z value. Value Z compared with value Z will produce a resulting value Z.

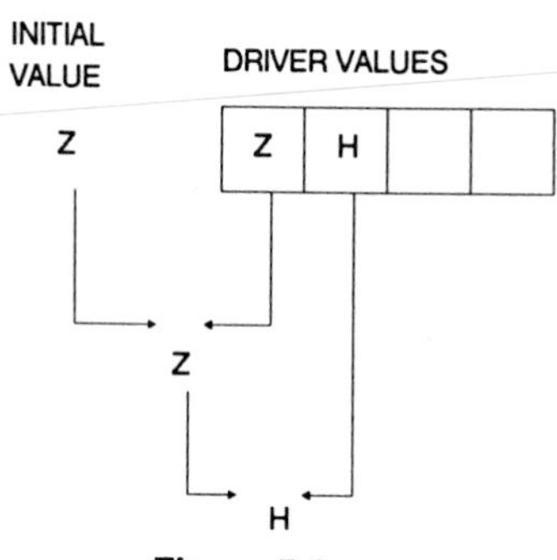

Figure 5-2

The next iteration through the loop will retreive the next driver value, which is H. The value H compared with value Z will return value H. The function will therefore return the value H as the resolved value of the signal.

Another case is shown in Figure 5-3. In this example there are three drivers, and the resolution function will execute the loop three times. The first iteration of the loop the initial value of *result* (Z) will be compared with the first driver value (H). The value H will be assigned

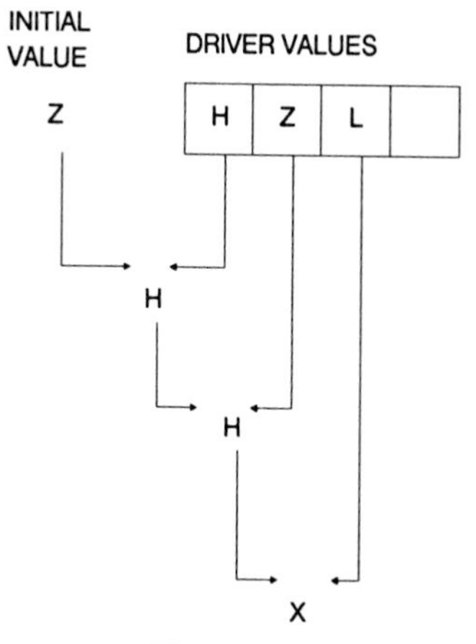

Figure 5-3

to *result*. In the next iteration *result* (H) will be compared with the second driver (Z). The value H will remain in *result* because the value Z is weaker. Finally, the last iteration *result* (H) will be compared with the last driver value (L). Since these values are of the same strength, the value X will be assigned to *result*. The value X will be returned from the function as the resolved value for the signal.

5.1.3.1 Nine-Value Resolution Function

Some simulators use more complex types to represent the value of a signal. For instance, what might a resolution function look like for a nine-value system, typical of most workstation-based simulators in use currently. The nine values in the value system are shown below:

```
    Z0, Z1, ZX, R0, R1, RX, F0, F1, FX
weakest-----------------------------strongest
```

The system consists of three strengths and three logic values. The three strengths represent the following:

- Z – high impedance strength, few hundred k of resistance
- R – resistive, few k of resistance
- F – forcing, few ohms of resistance

The three logic levels are represented as follows:

- 0 – logical 0 or false
- 1 – logical 1 or true
- X – logical unknown

The nine states are described as follows:

- Z0 – high-impedance 0
- Z1 – high-impedance 1
- ZX – high-impedance unknown
- R0 – resistive 0
- R1 – resistive 1
- RX – resistive unknown
- F0 – forcing 0

- F1 – forcing 1
- FX – forcing unknown

A few simple rules can be used to define how the resolution function should work.

- Strongest strength always wins
- If strengths are the same and values are different, return same strength but X value

The type declarations needed for the value system are shown below:

```
PACKAGE ninepack IS
   TYPE strength IS (Z, R, F);
   TYPE nineval IS ( Z0, Z1, ZX,
                     R0, R1, RX,
                     F0, F1, FX );

   TYPE ninevalvec IS ARRAY(natural RANGE <>)
        OF nineval;

   TYPE ninevaltab IS ARRAY(nineval'LOW TO
        nineval'HIGH) OF nineval;
   TYPE strengthtab IS ARRAY(strength'LOW TO
        strength'HIGH) OF nineval;

   FUNCTION resolve9( s: ninevalvec)
      RETURN nineval;

END ninepack;
```

The package body contains the resolution function (package bodies are discussed near the end of this chapter).

```
PACKAGE BODY ninepack IS
   FUNCTION resolve9( s: ninevalvec)
        RETURN nineval IS
      VARIABLE result: nineval;
      CONSTANT get_strength : ninevaltab :=
         (Z,    --Z0
          Z,    --Z1
          Z,    --ZX
          R,    --R0
          R,    --R1
```

```
            R,      --RX
            F,      --F0
            F,      --F1
            F);     --FX

        CONSTANT x_tab :  strengthtab :=
            (ZX,    --Z
             RX,    --R
             FX);   --F
    BEGIN
        IF s'LENGTH = 0 THEN RETURN ZX; END IF;
        result := s(0);
        FOR i IN s'RANGE LOOP
            IF get_strength(result) <
                    get_strength(s(i)) THEN
                result := s(i);

            ELSIF get_strength(result) =
                    get_strength(s(i)) THEN
                IF result /= s(i) THEN
                    result :=
                        x_tab(get_strength(result));
                END IF;

            END IF;
        END LOOP;

        RETURN result;
    END resolve9;
END ninepack;
```

The package *ninepack* declares a number of types used in this example, including some array types to make the resolution function easier to implement. The basic algorithm of the function is the same as the *fourval* resolution function; however, the operations with nine values are a little more complex. Function *resolve9* still does a pairwise comparison of the input values to determine the resultant value. With a nine-value system, the comparison operation is more complicated, and therefore some constant arrays were declared to make the job easier.

The constant *get_strength* returns the driving strength of the driver value. The constant *x_tab* will return the appropriate unknown nine-state value, given the strength of the input. These constants could have been implemented as IF statements or CASE statements, but constant arrays are much more efficient.

In the nine-value system there are three values at the lowest strength level, so the variable *result* has to be initialized more carefully to predict correct results. If there are no drivers the range attribute of argument *s* will return 0 and the default value (ZX) will be returned.

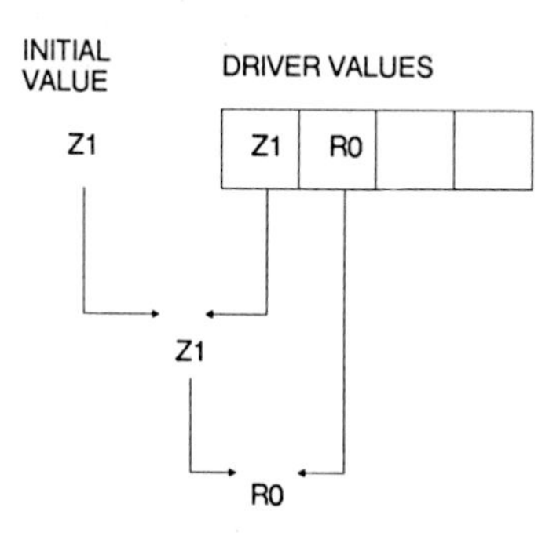

Figure 5-4

Let's look at a few examples of driver-input arguments, and see what the resolution function will predict. An example of two drivers is shown in Figure 5-4.

This example contains two driver values, Z1 and R0. Variable *result* is initialized to the first driver value, and the loop will execute as many times as there are drivers. The first time through the loop, *result* will equal Z1 and the first driver will equal Z1. Variable *result* will remain at Z1 because the values are equal. The next time through the loop, variable *result* contains Z1 and the second driver contains R0. The constant *get_strength* will return strength R. The constant *get_strength* for variable *result* will return strength Z. Strength R is lexically greater than strength Z. This is because value R has a higher position number than Z, because R is listed after Z in the type declaration for type *strength*. The fact that the new driver has a stronger strength value than variable *result* will cause variable *result* to be updated with the stronger value, R0.

Another example will show how the constant *x_tab* is used to predict the correct value for conflicting inputs. The driver values are shown in the array in Figure 5-5.

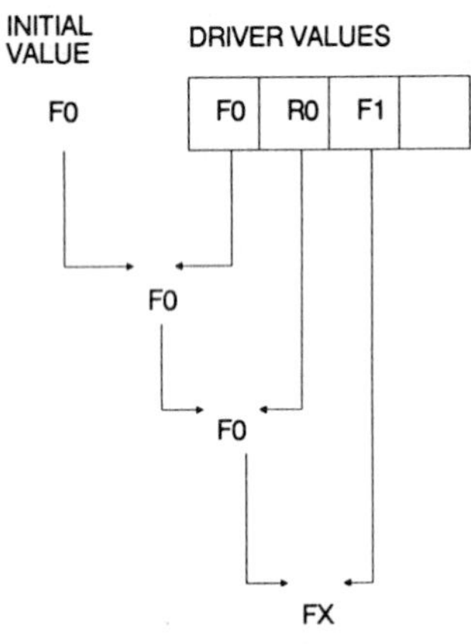

Figure 5-5

In this example variable *result* is initialized to F0. The first iteration of the loop will do nothing because the first driver and the result-initialization value are the same value. The next iteration starts with variable *result* containing the value F0, and the next driver value as R0. Since the value in variable *result* is greater in strength than the value of the new driver, no action is implemented, except to advance the loop to the next driver.

The last driver contains the value F1. The strength of the value contained in variable *result* and the new driver value are the same. Therefore the IF statement checking this condition will be executed and succeed. The next IF statement will check to see if the logical values are the same for both variable *result* and the new driver. Variable *result* contains an F0, and the new driver value contains an F1. The values are not the same, and the *x_tab* table will be used to return the correct unknown value for the strength of the driver values. The *x_tab* table will return the value FX, which will be returned as the resolved value.

A more efficient method to implement the loop would be to skip the first iteration where the first driver is compared to itself, because the value in variable *result* is initialized to the first driver value. It is left as an exercise to the reader to write this new loop iteration mechanism.

5.1.3.2 Composite Type Resolution

For simple signal values such as the *nineval* and *fourval* types it is easy to see how to create the resolution function. But for signals of composite types it is not so obvious. How can one value of a composite type be stronger than another?

The answer is that one value must be *designated* as weaker than all of the other values. Then the principle is the same as any other type being resolved. In the *fourval* type the value Z was considered the weakest state, and any of the other values could overwrite this value. In the *nineval* type, all values with a strength of Z could be overridden by values with a strength of R or F, and all values with strength R could be overridden by strength F.

To resolve a composite type, designate one value of the composite type as unusable except to indicate that the signal is not currently being driven. The resolution function will check how many drivers have this value and how many drivers have a driving value. If only one driving value exists, then the resolution function can return this value as the resolved value. If more than one driving value is present, then an error condition probably exists and the resolution function can announce the error.

A typical application for a Composite Type Resolution Function is shown in Figure 5-6.

Signal XBUS can be driven from a number of sources, but hopefully only one at a time. The resolution function must determine how many drivers are trying to drive XBUS and return the correct value for the signal.

Shown below is the type declarations and resolution function for a composite type used in such a circuit.

```
PACKAGE composite_res IS
   TYPE xtype IS
      RECORD
         addr : INTEGER;
```

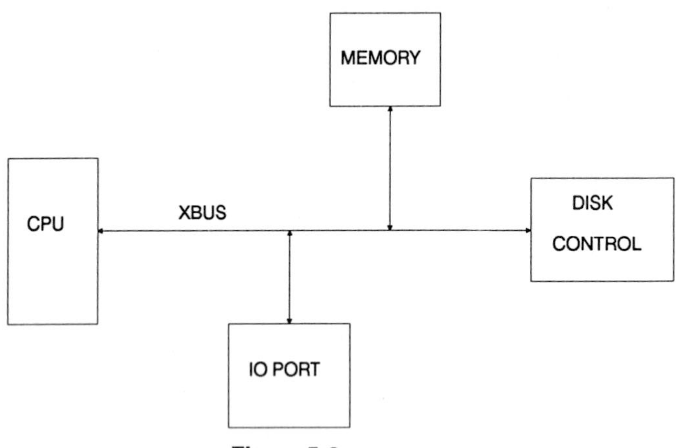

Figure 5-6

```
        data : INTEGER;
      END RECORD;
    TYPE xtypevector IS ARRAY( natural RANGE <>)
        OF xtype;
    CONSTANT notdriven : xtype := (-1,-1);
    FUNCTION cresolve( t : xtypevector)
        RETURN xtype;
  END composite_res;

  PACKAGE BODY composite_res IS
    FUNCTION cresolve( t : xtypevector)
      RETURN xtype IS
      VARIABLE result : xtype := notdriven;
      VARIABLE drive_count : INTEGER := 0;
    BEGIN
      IF t'LENGTH = 0 THEN RETURN notdriven;
      END IF;

      FOR i IN t'RANGE LOOP
        IF t(i) /= notdriven THEN
          drive_count := drive_count + 1;
          IF drive_count = 1 THEN
            result := t(i);
          ELSE
            result := notdriven;
            ASSERT FALSE
```

```
                  REPORT "multiple drivers detected"
                  SEVERITY ERROR;
               END IF;
            END IF;
         END LOOP;
         RETURN result;
      END cresolve;
   END composite_res;
```

Type *xtype* declares the record type for signal *xbus*. Type *xtypevector* is an unconstrained array type of *xtype* values used for the resolution function input argument *t*. Constant *notdriven* declares the value of the record that will be used to signify that a signal driver is not driving. Negative number values were used to represent the *notdriven* state because in this example only positive values will be used in the *addr* and *data* fields. But what happens if all of the values must be used for a particular type? The easiest solution is probably to declare a new type which is a record, containing the original type as one field of the record, and a new field which is a boolean that determines whether the driver is driving or not driving.

In this example resolution function *cresolve* first checks to make certain that at least one driver value is passed in argument *t* (drivers can be turned off using guarded signal assignment). If at least one driver is driving, the loop statement will loop through all driver values, looking for driving values. If a driving value is detected, and it is the first, then this value is assumed to be the output resolved value, until proven otherwise. If only one driving value occurs, that value will be returned as the resolved value.

If a second driving value appears, the output is set to the nondriven value, signifying that the outcome is uncertain, and the ASSERT statement will write out an error message to that effect.

In this example the negative numbers of the integer type were not used except to indicate whether the signal was driving or not. We reserved one value to indicate this condition. Another value could be reserved to indicate the multiply-driven case such that when multiple drivers are detected on the signal, this value would be returned as the resolved value. An example might look like this:

```
CONSTANT multiple_drive : xtype := (-2,-2);
```

This constant provides the capability of distinguishing between a non-driven signal and a multiply-driven signal.

5.1.4 Resolved Signals

So far we have discussed how to write resolution functions that can resolve signals of multiple drivers, but we have not discussed how all of the appropriate declarations are structured to accomplish this.

Resolved signals are created using one of two methods. The first is to create a resolved subtype and declare a signal using this type. The second is to declare a signal specifying a resolution function as part of the signal declaration.

Let's discuss the resolved subtype method first. To create a resolved subtype, the designer declares the base type, then declares the subtype specifying the resolution function to use for this type. An example would look like this:

```
TYPE fourval IS (X, L, H, Z); -- won't compile
SUBTYPE resfour IS resolve fourval; -- as is
```

The first declaration declares the enumerated type *fourval*. The second declaration is used to declare a subtype named *resfour*, that uses a resolution function named *resolve* to resolve the base type *fourval*. This syntax will not compile as is because the function *resolve* is not visible. To declare a resolved subtype requires a very specific combination of statements, in a very specific ordering.

A correct example of the resolved type is shown below:

```
PACKAGE fourpack IS
  TYPE fourval IS (X, L, H, Z); -- line 1
  TYPE fourvalvector IS ARRAY(natural RANGE <>)
    OF fourval;      -- line 2

  FUNCTION resolve( s: fourvalvector)
    RETURN fourval; -- line 3

  SUBTYPE resfour IS resolve fourval; -- line 4
END fourpack;
```

The statement in line 2 declares an unconstrained array of the base type that will be used to contain the driver values passed to the resolution function. The statement in line 3 declares the definition of the resolution function *resolve* so that the subtype declaration can make use of it. The body of the resolution function is implemented in the package body. Finally, the statement in line 4 declares the resolved subtype using the base type and the resolution function declaration.

The order of the statements is important, because each statement declares something that is used in the next statement. If the unconstrained array declaration is left out, the resolution function could not be declared, and if the resolution function was not declared, the subtype could not be declared.

The second method of obtaining a resolved signal is to specify the resolution function in the signal declaration. In the example below, a signal is declared using the resolution function *resolve*.

```
PACKAGE fourpack IS
   TYPE fourval IS (X, L, H, Z);
   TYPE fourvalvector IS ARRAY(natural RANGE <>)
      OF fourval;
   FUNCTION resolve( s: fourvalvector)
      RETURN fourval;
   SUBTYPE resfour IS resolve fourval;
END fourpack;

USE WORK.fourpack.ALL;
ENTITY mux2 IS
   PORT( i1, i2, a : IN fourval;
         q : OUT fourval);
END mux2;

ARCHITECTURE different OF mux2 IS
   COMPONENT and2
      PORT( a, b : IN fourval;
            c : OUT fourval);
   END COMPONENT;

   COMPONENT inv
      PORT( a : IN fourval;
            b : OUT fourval);
```

```
    END COMPONENT;
    SIGNAL nota : fourval;

    -- resolved signal
    SIGNAL intq : resolve fourval := X;

BEGIN
    U1: inv
       PORT MAP(a, nota);
    U2: and2
       PORT MAP(i1, a, intq);
    U3: and2
       PORT MAP(i2, nota, intq);
    q <= intq;
END different;
```

The package *fourpack* declares all of the appropriate types and function declarations so that the resolution function *resolve* is visible in the entity. In the architecture declaration section signal *intq* is declared of type *fourval*, using the resolution function *resolve*. This signal is also given an initial value of X.

Signal *intq* is required to have a resolution function because it is the output signal for components U2 and U3. Each component provides a driver to signal *intq*. Resolution function *resolve* is used to determine the end result of the two driver values. Signal *nota* is not required to have a resolution function because it only has one driver, component U1.

5.2 Procedures

In the section describing functions above, we discussed how functions can have a number of input parameters and always return one value. In contrast, procedures can have any number of in, out, and inout parameters. A procedure call is considered a statement of its own, while a function usually exists as part of an expression. The most usual case of using a procedure is when more than one value is returned.

Procedures have basically the same syntax and rules as functions. A procedure declaration begins with the keyword PROCEDURE, followed by the procedure name, and finally the argument list. The main difference between a function and a procedure is that the procedure argument list will most likely have a direction associated with each parameter, while the function argument list does not. In a procedure some of the arguments can be mode IN, OUT, or INOUT, while in a function all arguments are of mode IN by default and can only be of mode IN.

A typical example where a procedure is very useful is during the conversion from an array of a multivalued type to an integer. A procedure showing an example of how to accomplish this is shown below:

```
USE STD.std_logic.ALL;
PROCEDURE vector_to_int
        (z : IN t_wlogic_vector;
         x_flag : OUT BOOLEAN;
         q : INOUT INTEGER) IS
BEGIN
   q := 0;
   x_flag := false;

   FOR i IN z'RANGE LOOP
      q := q * 2;

      IF z(i) = F1 THEN
         q := q + 1;
      ELSIF z(i) /= F0 THEN
         x_flag := TRUE;
      END IF;

   END LOOP;
END vector_to_int;
```

The behavior of this procedure is to convert the input argument *z* from an array of a type to an integer. However, if the input array has unknown values contained in it, an integer value cannot be generated from the array. When this condition occurs, output argument *x_flag* is set to true, indicating that the output integer value is unknown. A procedure was required to implement this behavior because more than one output value results from the procedure. Let's examine what the result from the procedure will be from the input array value shown below:

```
F0 F0 F1 F1
```

The first step for the procedure is to initialize the output values to known conditions, in case a zero length input argument is passed in.

Output argument *x_flag* is initialized to false, and will stay false until proven otherwise.

The loop statement will loop through the input vector *z* and progressively add each value of the vector until all values have been added. If the value is an F1 (logical 1) then it is added to the result. If the value is an F0 (logical 0) then no addition is done. If any other value is found in the vector, the *x_flag* result is set true, indicating that an unknown condition was found on one of the inputs.

5.2.1 Procedure with Inout Parameters

The examples we have discussed so far have dealt mostly with in and out parameters, but procedures can have inout parameters also. The example below shows a procedure that has an inout argument that is a record type. The record contains an array of eight integers, along with a field used to hold the average of all of the integers. The procedure will calculate the average of the integer values, write the average in the average field of the record, and return the updated record.

```
PACKAGE intpack IS
   TYPE bus_stat_vec IS ARRAY(0 to 7)
      OF INTEGER;

   TYPE bus_stat_t IS
      RECORD
         bus_val: bus_stat_vec;
         average_val : INTEGER;
      END RECORD;

   PROCEDURE bus_average
        ( x : inout bus_stat_t );

END intpack;

PACKAGE BODY intpack IS
   PROCEDURE bus_average
        ( x : inout bus_stat_t ) IS
      VARIABLE total : INTEGER := 0;
   BEGIN
      FOR i IN 0 TO 7 LOOP
         total := total + x.bus_val(i);
```

```
      END LOOP;
      x.average_val := total / 8;
   END bus_average;
END intpack;
```

A process calling the procedure might look as shown below:

```
PROCESS( mem_update )
   VARIABLE bus_statistics : bus_stat_t;
BEGIN
   bus_statistics.bus_val :=
         (50, 40, 30, 35, 45, 55, 65, 85 );
   bus_average(bus_statistics);
   average <= bus_statistics.average_val;
END PROCESS;
```

The variable assignment to *bus_statistics.bus_val*, fills in the appropriate bus utilization values to be used for the calculation. The next line is the call to the *bus_average* procedure, which will perform the averaging calculation. Initially, the argument to the *bus_average* procedure is an input value, but after the procedure has finished, the argument becomes an output value that can be used inside the calling process. The output value from the procedure is assigned to an output signal in the last line of the process.

5.2.2 Side Effects

Procedures have an interesting problem that is not shared by their function counterparts. Procedures can cause side effects to occur. A side effect is the result of changing the value of an object inside a procedure when that object was not an argument to the procedure. For instance, a signal of an architecture can be assigned a value from within a procedure, without that signal being an argument passed into the procedure. For instance, if two signals are not declared in the argument list of a procedure, but are assigned from within a procedure called from the current procedure, any assignments to these signals are side effects.

This is not a recomended method for writing a model. The debugging and maintenance of a model of this type can be very difficult. This feature was presented so that the reader would understand the behavior if such a model were examined.

5.3 Packages

The primary purpose of a package is to encapsulate elements that can be shared (globally) among two or more design units. A package is a common storage area used to hold data to be shared among a number of entities. Declaring data inside of a package allows the data to be referenced by other entities; thus the data can be shared.

A package consists of two parts: a package declaration section and a package body. The package declaration defines the interface for the package, much the same way that the entity defines the interface for a model. The package body specifies the actual behavior of the package in the same method that the architecture statement does for a model.

5.3.1 Package Declaration

The package declaration section can contain the following declarations:

- Subprogram declaration
- Type, subtype declaration
- Constant, deferred constant declaration
- Signal declaration – creates a global signal
- File declaration
- Alias declaration
- Component declaration
- Attribute declaration, a user-defined attribute (Chapter 8)
- Attribute specification
- Disconnection specification
- Use clause

All of the items declared in the package declaration section are visible to any design unit that *uses* the package with a USE clause. The interface to a package consists of any subprograms or deferred constants declared in the package declaration. The subprogram and deferred constant declarations must have a corresponding subprogram body and deferred constant value in the package body or an error will result.

5.3.2 Deferred Constants

Deferred constants are constants which have their name and type declared in the package declaration section but have the actual value specified in the package body section. An example of a deferred constant in the package declaration is shown below:

```
PACKAGE tpack IS
   CONSTANT timing_mode : t_mode;
END tpack;
```

This example shows a deferred constant called *timing_mode* being defined as type *t_mode*. The actual value of the constant will be specified when the package body for package *tpack* is compiled. This feature allows late binding of the value of a constant so that the value of the constant can be specified at the last possible moment and can be changed easily. Any design unit that uses a deferred constant from the package declaration need not be recompiled if the value of the constant is changed in the package body. Only the package body needs to be recompiled.

5.3.3 Subprogram Declaration

The other item that forms the interface to the package is the subprogram declaration. A subprogram declaration allows the designer to specify the interface to a subprogram separately from the subprogram body. This functionality allows any designers using the subprogram to start or continue with the design, while the specification of the internals of the subprograms are detailed. It also gives the designer of the subprogram bodies freedom to change the internal workings of the subprograms, without affecting any designs that use the subprograms. An example of a subprogram declaration is shown below:

```
PACKAGE cluspack IS
   TYPE nineval IS (Z0, Z1, ZX,
                    R0, R1, RX,
                    F0, F1, FX );
   TYPE t_cluster IS ARRAY(0 to 15) OF nineval;
   TYPE t_clus_vec IS ARRAY(natural range <>)
        OF t_cluster;
```

```
    FUNCTION resolve_cluster( s: t_clus_vec )
          RETURN t_cluster;

    SUBTYPE t_wclus IS resolve_cluster t_cluster;

    CONSTANT undriven : t_wclus;
  END cluspack;
```

The subprogram declaration for *resolve_cluster* specifies the name of the subprogram, any arguments to the subprogram, their types and modes, and the return type if the subprogram is a function. This declaration can be used to compile any models that intend to use it, without the actual subprogram body specified yet. The subprogram body must exist before the simulator is built, during elaboration.

5.3.4 Package Body

The main purpose of the package body is to define the values for deferred constants, and specify the subprogram bodies for any subprogram declarations from the package declaration. However the package body can also contain the following declarations:

- Subprogram declaration
- Subprogram body
- Type, subtype declaration
- Constant declaration, which fills in the value for the deferred constant
- File declaration
- Alias declaration
- Use clause

All of the declarations in the package body, except for the constant declaration that is specifying the value of a deferred constant, and the subprogram body declaration, will be local to the package body.

Let's examine a package body for the package declaration that was discussed in the last section:

```
PACKAGE BODY cluspack IS
   CONSTANT undriven : t_wclus :=
```

```
        (ZX, ZX, ZX, ZX,
         ZX, ZX, ZX, ZX,
         ZX, ZX, ZX, ZX,
         ZX, ZX, ZX, ZX);

    FUNCTION resolve_cluster ( s: t_clus_vec )
      return t_cluster IS
    VARIABLE result : t_cluster;
    VARIABLE drive_count : INTEGER;
  BEGIN
    IF s'LENGTH = 0 THEN RETURN undriven;
    END IF;
    FOR i in s'RANGE LOOP
      IF s(i) /= undriven THEN
        drive_count := drive_count + 1;
        IF drive_count = 1 THEN
          result := s(i);
        ELSE
          result := undriven;
          ASSERT FALSE
          REPORT "multiple drivers detected"
          SEVERITY ERROR;
        END IF;
      END IF;
    END LOOP;
    RETURN result;
    END resolve_cluster;
  END cluspack;
```

The package body statement is very similar to the package declaration except for the keyword BODY after package. The contents of the two design units are very different, however. This package body example contains only two items, the deferred constant value for deferred constant *undriven*, and the subprogram body for subprogram *resolve_cluster.* Notice how the deferred constant value specification matches the deferred constant declaration in the package declaration, and the subprogram body matches the subprogram declaration in the package declaration. The subprogram body must match the subprogram declaration exactly, in the number of parameters, the type of parameters, and the return type.

A package body can also contain local declarations that are used only within the package body to create other subprogram bodies, or deferred constant values. These declarations are not visible outside of the package body but can be very useful within the package body. An example of a complete package making use of this feature is shown below:

```
USE STD.std_logic.ALL;
PACKAGE math IS
  TYPE tw16 IS ARRAY(0 TO 15) OF t_wlogic;

  FUNCTION add(a, b: IN tw16) RETURN tw16;
  FUNCTION sub(a, b: IN tw16) RETURN tw16;

END math;

PACKAGE BODY math IS
  FUNCTION vect_to_int(S : tw16)
          RETURN INTEGER IS
    VARIABLE result : INTEGER := 0;
  BEGIN
    FOR i IN 0 TO 7 LOOP
      result := result * 2;

      IF S(i) = '1' THEN
        result := result + 1;
      END IF;
    END LOOP;

    RETURN result;
  END vect_to_int;

  FUNCTION int_to_tw16(s : INTEGER)
          RETURN tw16 IS
    VARIABLE result : tw16;
    VARIABLE digit : INTEGER := 2**15;
    VARIABLE local : INTEGER;
  BEGIN
    local : = s;
    FOR i IN 15 DOWNTO 0 LOOP
      IF local/digit >= 1 THEN
```

```
            result(i) := F1;
            local := local - digit;
         ELSE
            result(i) := F0;
         END IF;

         digit := digit/2;

      END LOOP;
      RETURN result;
   END int_to_tw16;

   FUNCTION add(a, b: IN tw16) RETURN tw16 IS
      VARIABLE result : INTEGER;
   BEGIN
      result := vect_to_int(a) + vect_to_int(b);
      RETURN int_to_tw16(result);
   END add;

   FUNCTION sub(a, b: IN tw16) RETURN tw16 IS
      VARIABLE result : INTEGER;
   BEGIN
      result := vect_to_int(a) - vect_to_int(b);
      RETURN int_to_tw16(result);
   END sub;
END math;
```

The package declaration declares a type, *tw16,* and two functions, *add* and *sub,* that work with this type. The package body has function bodies for function declarations *add* and *sub* and also includes two functions that are only used in the package body. These functions are *int_to_tw16* and *vect_to_int.* These functions are not visible outside of the package body. To make these functions visible, a function declaration would need to be added to the package declaration, for each function.

Functions *vect_to_int* and *int_to_tw16* must be declared ahead of function *add* to compile correctly. All functions must be declared before they are used to compile correctly.

In this chapter we discussed the different kinds of subprograms and some of the uses for them. These included conversion functions and resolution functions. We discussed how procedures are similar to functions, but have more than one return value. We concluded the chapter with a discussion of how packages are used to contain types and subprograms. The contained information can then be shared among entities. In the next chapter we will discuss how attributes can make some descriptions easier to read, and more compact.

Chapter

6

Predefined Attributes

This chapter will discuss VHDL predefined attributes, and the way that concise readable models can be written using attributes. Predefined attributes are data that can be obtained from blocks, signals, and types or subtypes. The data obtained will fall into one of the categories shown below:

- *Value kind.* A simple value is returned.
- *Function kind.* A function call is performed to return a value.
- *Signal kind.* A new signal is created whose value is derived from another signal.
- *Type kind.* A type mark is returned.
- *Range kind.* A range value is returned.

Predefined attributes have a number of very important applications. Attributes can be used to detect clock edges, perform timing checks in concert with ASSERT statements, return range information about unconstrained types, and much more. All of these applications will be examined in this chapter. First we will discuss each of the predefined attribute kinds and the ways that these attributes can be applied to modeling.

6.1 Value Kind Attributes

Value attributes are used to return a particular value about an array of a type, a block, or a type in general. Value attributes can be used to return the length of an array or the lowest bound of a type. Value attributes can be further broken down into three subclasses:

- Value type attributes, which return the bounds of a type
- Value array attributes, which return the length of an array
- Value block attributes, which return block information

6.1.1 Value Type Attributes

Value type attributes are used to return the bounds of a type. For instance, a type defined as shown below would have a low bound of 0 and a high bound of 7.

```
TYPE state IS (0 TO 7);
```

There are four predefined attributes in the value type attribute category. They are:

- T'LEFT, which returns the left bound of a type or subtype
- T'RIGHT, which returns the right bound of a type or subtype
- T'HIGH, which returns the upper bound of a type or subtype
- T'LOW, which returns the lower bound of a type or subtype

Attributes are specified by the character ' and then the attribute name. The object preceding the ' is the object that the attribute is attached to. The capital T in the description above means that the object that the attribute is attached to is a type. The ' character is pronounced *tick* among VHDL hackers. Therefore the first attribute above is specified by T *tick* left.

The left bound of a type or subtype is the leftmost entry of the range constraint. The right bound is the rightmost entry of the type or subtype.

In the example below, the left bound is -32,767 and the right bound is 32,767.

```
TYPE smallint IS -32767 TO 32767;
```

The upper bound of a type or subtype is the bound with the largest value, and the lower bound is the bound with the lowest value. For the type *smallint* shown above, the upper bound is 32,767 and the lower bound is -32,767.

To use one of these value attributes, the type mark name is followed by the attribute desired. For example, this is the syntax to return the left bound of a type.

```
PROCESS(x)
   SUBTYPE smallreal IS REAL RANGE -1.0E6
      TO 1.0E6;
   VARIABLE q : real;
BEGIN
   q := smallreal'LEFT;
      -- use of 'left returns
      -- -1.0E6
END test;
```

In this example variable *q* is assigned the left bound of type *smallreal*. Variable *q* must have the same type as the bounds of the type for the assignment to occur (the assignment could also occur if variable *q* was cast into the appropriate type). After the assignment has occurred variable *q* will contain -1.0E6, which is the left bound of type *smallreal*.

In the next example all of the attributes are used to show what happens when a DOWNTO range is used for a type.

```
PROCESS(a)
   TYPE bit_range IS ARRAY(31 DOWNTO 0) OF BIT;
   VARIABLE left_range, right_range,
            uprange, lowrange : integer;
BEGIN
   left_range  := bit_range'LEFT;
   -- returns 31

   right_range := bit_range'RIGHT;
   -- returns 0
```

```
    uprange     := bit_range'HIGH;
    -- returns 31


    lowrange    := bit_range'LOW;
    -- returns 0
  END PROCESS;
```

This example shows how the different attributes can be used to return information about a type. When ranges of a type are defined using (a TO b) where $b > a$, the 'LEFT attribute will always equal the 'LOW attribute, but when a range specification using (b DOWNTO a) where $b > a$ is used the 'HIGH and 'LOW can be used to determine the upper and lower bounds of the type.

Value type attributes are not restricted to numeric types. These attributes can also be used with any scalar type. An example using enumerated types is shown below:

```
ARCHITECTURE b OF a IS
  TYPE color IS (blue, cyan, green,
                 yellow, red, magenta);
  SUBTYPE reverse_color IS
       color RANGE red DOWNTO green;
  SIGNAL color1, color2, color3,
         color4, color5, color6,
         color7, color8 : color;
BEGIN
  color1 <= color'LEFT;    -- returns blue
  color2 <= color'RIGHT;   -- returns magenta

  color3 <= color'HIGH;    -- returns magenta
  color4 <= color'LOW;     -- returns blue

  color5 <= reverse_color'LEFT;
  -- returns red

  color6 <= reverse_color'RIGHT;
  -- returns green

  color7 <= reverse_color'HIGH;
  -- returns red
```

```
    color8 <= reverse_color'LOW;
    -- returns green
  END b;
```

This example illustrates how value type attributes can be used with enumerated types to return information about the type. Signals *color1* and *color2* are assigned *blue* and *magenta,* respectively, the left and right bounds of the type. It is easy to see how these values are obtained by examining the declaration of the type. The left bound of the type is *blue* and the right bound is *magenta.* What will be returned for the 'HIGH and 'LOW attributes of an enumerated type? The answer relates to the position numbers of the type. For an integer and real type the position numbers of a value are equal to the value itself, but for an enumerated type the position numbers of a value are determined by the declaration of the type. Values declared earlier will have lower position numbers than values declared later. Value *blue* from the example above will have a position number of 0, because it is the first value of the type. Value *cyan* will have a position number 1, *green* has 2, etc. From these position numbers the high and low bounds of the type can be found.

Signals *color5* through *color8* are assigned attributes of the type *reverse_color.* This type has a DOWNTO range specification. Attributes 'HIGH and 'RIGHT will not return the same value because the range is reversed. Value *red* has a higher position number than value *green*, and therefore a DOWNTO is needed for the range specification.

6.1.2 Value Array Attributes

There is only one value array attribute, 'LENGTH. Given an array type, this attribute will return the total length of the array range specified. This attribute works with array ranges of any scalar type and with multidimensional arrays of scalar-type ranges. A simple example is shown below:

```
PROCESS(a)
  TYPE bit4 IS ARRAY(0 TO 3) of BIT;
  TYPE bit_strange IS ARRAY(10 TO 20) OF BIT;
  VARIABLE len1, len2 : INTEGER;
BEGIN
  len1 := bit4'LENGTH;          -- returns 4
```

```
    len2 := bit_strange'LENGTH; -- returns 11
  END PROCESS;
```

The assignment to *len1* will assign the value of the number of elements in array type *bit4*. The assignment to *len2* will assign the value of the number of elements of type *bit_strange*.

This attribute also works with enumerated-type ranges, as shown by the example below:

```
  PACKAGE p_4val IS
    TYPE t_4val IS ('x', '0', '1', 'z');
    TYPE t_4valX1 IS ARRAY(t_4val'LOW TO
            t_4val'HIGH) OF t_4val;

    TYPE t_4valX2 IS ARRAY(t_4val'LOW TO
            t_4val'HIGH) OF t_4valX1;

    TYPE t_4valmd IS ARRAY
       (t_4val'LOW TO t_4val'HIGH,
        t_4val'LOW TO t_4val'HIGH) OF t_4val;

    CONSTANT andsd : t_4valX2 :=
       (('x',      -- xx
         '0',      -- x0
         'x',      -- x1        (Notice this is an
         'x'),     -- xz        array of arrays.)
        ('0',      -- 0x
         '0',      -- 00
         '0',      -- 01
         '0'),     -- 0z
        ('x',      -- 1x
         '0',      -- 10
         '1',      -- 11
         'x'),     -- 1z
        ('x',      -- zx
         '0',      -- z0
         'x',      -- z1
         'x'));    -- zz

    CONSTANT andmd : t_4valmd :=
       (('x',      -- xx
         '0',      -- x0
         'x',      -- x1
```

```
          'x'),        -- xz      (Notice this example
         ('0',         -- 0x      is a multidimensional
          '0',         -- 00      array.)
          '0',         -- 01
          '0'),        -- 0z
         ('x',         -- 1x
          '0',         -- 10
          '1',         -- 11
          'x'),        -- 1z
         ('x',         -- zx
          '0',         -- z0
          'x',         -- z1
          'x'));       -- zz
END p_4val;
```

The two composite type constants, *andsd* and *andmd*, provide a lookup table for an AND function of type *t_4val*. The first constant, *andsd*, uses an array of array values, while the second constant, *andmd*, uses a multidimensional array to store the values. The initialization of both constants is specified by the same syntax. If the 'LENGTH attribute is applied to these types as shown below, the results shown in the VHDL comments are obtained.

```
PROCESS(a)
   VARIABLE len1, len2, len3, len4 : INTEGER;
BEGIN
   len1 := t_4valX1'LENGTH;         -- returns 4
   len2 := t_4valX2'LENGTH;         -- returns 4

   len3 := t_4valmd'LENGTH(1);      -- returns 4
   len4 := t_4valmd'LENGTH(2);      -- returns 4
END PROCESS;
```

Type *t_4valX1* is a four-element array of type *t_4val*. The range of the array is specified using the predefined attributes 'LOW and 'HIGH of the *t_4val* type. Assigning the length of type *t_4valX1* to *len1* will return the value 4, the number of elements in array type *t_4valX1*. The assignment to *len2* will also return the value 4, because the range of type *t_valX2* is from 'LOW to 'HIGH of element type *t_4valX1*.

The assignments to *len3* and *len4* make use of a multidimensional array type, *t_4valmd*. Since a multidimensional array has more than one range, an argument is used to specify a particular range. The range will default to the first range, if none is specified. In the type *t_4valmd* example, the designer can pick the first or second range, because there are only two to choose from. To pick a range, the argument passed to the attribute specifies the number of the range starting at 1. An argument value of 1 picks the first range, an argument value of 2 picks the second range, and so on.

The assignment to *len3* in the example above passed in the value 1 to pick the first range. The first range is from *t_4val*'LOW to *t_4val*'HIGH, or four entries. The second range is exactly the same as the first; therefore, both assignments will return 4 as the length of the array.

If the argument to 'LENGTH is not specified, it will default to 1. This was the case in the first examples of 'LENGTH, when no argument was specified. There was only one range, so the correct range was selected.

6.1.3 Value Block Attributes

There are two attributes that form the set of attributes that work with blocks and architectures. Attributes 'STRUCTURE and 'BEHAVIOR return information about how a block in a design is modeled. Attribute 'BEHAVIOR will return true if the block specified by the block label, or architecture specified by the architecture name, contains no component instantiation statements. Attribute 'STRUCTURE will return true if the block or architecture contains only component instantiation statements and/or passive processes.

Two examples shown below will illustrate how these attributes work. The first example contains only structural VHDL.

```
USE STD.std_logic.ALL;
ENTITY shifter IS
   PORT( clk, left : IN t_wlogic;
         right : OUT t_wlogic);
END shifter;

ARCHITECTURE structural OF shifter IS
   COMPONENT dff
      PORT( d, clk : IN t_wlogic;
            q : OUT t_wlogic);
   END COMPONENT;
```

```
      SIGNAL i1, i2, i3: t_wlogic;

   BEGIN
      u1: dff
         PORT MAP (d => left, clk => clk, q => i1);

      u2: dff
         PORT MAP (d => i1, clk => clk, q => i2);

      u3: dff
         PORT MAP (d => i2, clk => clk, q => i3);

      u4: dff
         PORT MAP (d => i3, clk => clk, q => right);

      checktime: PROCESS(clk)
         VARIABLE last_time : time := time'left;
      BEGIN
         ASSERT (NOW - last_time = 20 ns)
            REPORT "spike on clock"
            SEVERITY WARNING;
         last_time := now;
      END PROCESS checktime;
   END structural;
```

The example above is a shift register modeled using four *dff* components connected in series. A passive process statement exists in the architecture for entity *shifter*, used to detect spikes on the *clk* input. In the example below are shown the results of the attributes for the architecture *structural*.

- *structural*'BEHAVIOR: returns false
- *structural*'STRUCTURE: returns true

The passive process, *checktime*, will have no effect on the fact that the architecture is structural. If the process contained signal assignment statements, then the process would no longer be considered passive, and attribute 'STRUCTURE would also return false.

For any block or architecture that does not contain any component instantiation statements, attribute 'BEHAVIOR will be true, and attribute 'STRUCTURE will be false. For blocks or architectures that mix structure and behavior, both attributes will return false.

6.2 Function Kind Attributes

Function attributes return information to the designer about types, arrays, and signals. When a function kind attribute is used in an expression, a function call occurs that uses the value of the input argument to return a value. The value returned can be a position number of an enumerated value, an indication of whether a signal has changed this delta, or one of the bounds of an array.

Function attributes can be subdivided into three general classifications. These are:

- Function type attributes, which return type values
- Function array attributes, which return array bounds
- Function signal attributes, which return signal history information

6.2.1 Function Type Attributes

Function type attributes return particular information about a type. Given the position number of a value within a type, the value can be returned. Also values to the left or right of an input value of a particular type can be returned.

Function type attributes are one of the following:

- 'POS (value), which returns position number of value passed in
- 'VAL (value), which returns value from position number passed in
- 'SUCC (value), which returns next value in type after input value
- 'PRED (value), which returns previous value in type before input value
- 'LEFTOF (value), which returns value immediately to the left of the input value

- 'RIGHTOF (value), which returns value immediately to the right of the input value

A typical use of a function type attribute is to convert from an enumerated or physical type to an integer type. An example of conversion from a physical type to an integer type is shown below:

```
PACKAGE ohms_law IS
   TYPE current IS RANGE 0 TO 1000000
      UNITS
         ua;                  -- micro amps
         ma = 1000 ua;        -- milli amps
         a  = 1000 ma;        -- amps
      END UNITS;

   TYPE voltage IS RANGE 0 TO 1000000
      UNITS
         uv;                  -- micro volts
         mv = 1000 uv;        -- milli volts
         v  = 1000 mv;        -- volts
      END UNITS;

   TYPE resistance IS RANGE 0 TO 100000000
      UNITS
         ohm;                 -- ohms
         Kohm = 1000 ohm; -- kilo ohms
         Mohm = 1000 Kohm;-- mega ohms
      END UNITS;
END ohms_law;

use work.ohms_law.all;
ENTITY calc_resistance IS
   PORT( i : IN current; e : IN voltage;
         r : OUT resistance);
END calc_resistance;

ARCHITECTURE  behave OF calc_resistance IS
BEGIN
   ohm_proc: PROCESS( i, e )
      VARIABLE convi, conve, int_r : integer;
   BEGIN
      convi := current'POS(i); -- current in ua
      conve := voltage'POS(e); -- voltage in uv
```

```
        -- resistance in ohms
        int_r := conve / convi;

        r <= resistance'VAL(int_r);

        -- another way to write this example
        -- is shown below
        -- r <= resistance'VAL(current'POS(i)
        -- / voltage'POS(e));
    END PROCESS;
 END behave;
```

Package *ohms_law* declares three physical types used in this example. Types *current, voltage,* and *resistance* will be used to show how physical types can be converted to type INTEGER and back to a physical type.

Whenever ports *i* or *e* have an event occur on them, process *ohm_proc* is invoked and will calculate a new value of resistance (r) from the current (i) and the voltage (e). Variables *conve, convi,* and *int_r* were not necessary in this example but were added for ease of understanding. The commented-out assignment to output *r* shows an example where the internal variables are not needed.

The first statement of the process will assign the position number of the input value to variable *convi*. If the input value is 10 ua, then 10 will be assigned to variable *convi*.

The second statement will assign the position number of the value of input *e*, to variable *conve*. The base unit of type voltage is uv (microvolts); therefore the position number of any voltage value will be determined based on how many uv the input value is equal to.

The last line in the process converts the resistance value calculated from the previous line to the appropriate ohms value in type *resistance*. The 'VAL attribute is used to convert a position number to a physical type value of type *resistance*.

This example illustrated how 'POS and 'VAL worked, but not 'SUCC, 'PRED, 'RIGHTOF, and 'LEFTOF. A very simple example using these attributes is shown below:

```
PACKAGE p_color IS
  TYPE color IS ( red, yellow, green,
                  blue, purple, orange );

  SUBTYPE reverse_color is color RANGE
                 orange downto red ;

END p_color;
```

Assuming the types above, the following results are obtained:

- *color*'SUCC (blue), returns purple
- *color*'PRED (green), returns yellow
- *reverse_color*'SUCC (blue), returns green
- *reverse_color*'PRED (green), returns blue
- *color*'RIGHTOF (blue), returns purple
- *color*'LEFTOF (green), returns yellow
- *reverse_color*'RIGHTOF (blue), returns green
- *reverse_color*'LEFTOF (green), returns blue

For ascending ranges, the following is true:

- 'SUCC(x) = 'RIGHTOF(x);
- 'PRED(x) = 'LEFTOF(x);

For descending ranges, the opposite is true:

- 'SUCC(x) = 'LEFTOF(x);
- 'PRED(x) = 'RIGHTOF(x);

What happens if the value passed to 'SUCC, 'PRED, etc. is at the limit of the type? For instance, for type *color*, what is the value of the expression shown below?

```
y := red;
x := color'PRED(y);
```

The second expression above will cause a runtime error to be reported, because a range constraint has been violated.

6.2.2 Function Array Attributes

Function array attributes return the bounds of array types. An operation that requires accessing every location of an array can use these attributes to find the bounds of the array.

The four kinds of function array attributes are:

- array'LEFT (*n*), which returns the left bound of index range *n*
- array'RIGHT (*n*), which returns the right bound of index range *n*
- array'HIGH (*n*), which returns the upper bound of index range *n*
- array'LOW (*n*), which returns the lower bound of index range *n*

These attributes are exactly like the value type attributes that were discussed earlier, except that these attributes work with arrays.

For ascending ranges, the following is true:

- array'LEFT = array'LOW
- array'RIGHT = array'HIGH

For descending ranges, the opposite is true:

- array'LEFT = array'HIGH
- array'RIGHT = array'LOW

An example where these attributes are very useful is shown below:

```
PACKAGE p_ram IS
   TYPE t_ram_data IS ARRAY(0 TO 511)
        OF INTEGER;

   CONSTANT x_val : INTEGER := -1;
   CONSTANT z_val : INTEGER := -2;
END p_ram;

USE WORK.p_ram.ALL;
USE STD.std_logic.ALL;
```

```
ENTITY ram IS
   PORT( data_in : IN INTEGER;
         addr : IN INTEGER;
         data : OUT INTEGER;
         cs : IN t_wlogic;
         r_wb : in t_wlogic);
END ram;

ARCHITECTURE behave_ram OF ram IS
BEGIN
   main_proc: PROCESS( cs, addr, r_wb )
      VARIABLE ram_data : t_ram_data;
      VARIABLE ram_init : boolean := false;
   BEGIN
      IF NOT(ram_init) THEN
         FOR i IN ram_data'LOW TO
                     ram_data'HIGH LOOP
            ram_data(i) := 0;
         END LOOP;
         ram_init := TRUE;
      END IF;

      IF (cs = 'X') OR  (r_wb = 'X')THEN

         data <= x_val;
      ELSIF ( cs = '0' ) THEN
         data <= z_val;

      ELSIF (r_wb = '1') THEN
         IF (addr = x_val) OR (addr = z_val) THEN
            data <= x_val;
         ELSE
            data <= ram_data(addr);
         END IF;
      ELSE
         IF (addr = x_val) OR (addr = z_val) THEN
            ASSERT FALSE REPORT
               " writing to unknown address"
               SEVERITY ERROR;
            data <= x_val;
         ELSE
            ram_data(addr) := data_in;
```

```
            data <= ram_data(addr);
         END IF;
      END IF;
   END PROCESS;
END behave_ram;
```

This example implements an integer-based RAM device. There are 512 integer locations in the RAM, which is controlled by two control lines. The first is *cs* (chip select), and the second is *r_wb* (read/write bar). The model contains an IF statement that initializes the contents of the RAM to a known value. A boolean variable (*ram_init*) is declared to keep track of whether the RAM has been initialized or not. If this variable is false, the RAM has not yet been initialized. If true, initialization has been performed.

The first time the process is executed, variable *ram_init* will be false, and the IF statement will be executed. Inside the IF statement is a loop statement that will loop through every location of the RAM and set the location to a known value. This process is necessary because the starting value of type INTEGER is the value integer'LEFT, or -2,147,483,647. Notice the use of function array attributes 'LOW and 'HIGH to control the range of the initialization loop.

Once the loop has been executed and all RAM locations have been initialized, the *ram_init* variable is set to true. Setting the variable *ram_init* to true will prevent the initialization loop from executing again.

The rest of the model implements the read and write functions based on the values of *addr, data_in, r_wb*, and *cs.* This model performs a lot of error checking for unknown values on input ports. The model will try to intelligently handle these unknown input values.

6.2.3 Function Signal Attributes

Function signal attributes are used to return information about the behavior of signals. These attributes can be used to report whether a signal has just changed value, how much time has passed since the last event transition, or what the previous value of the signal was. There are five attributes that fall into this category, and a brief description is shown below:

- S'EVENT, which returns true if an event occurred during the current delta, and otherwise returns false
- S'ACTIVE, which returns true if a transaction occurred during the current delta, and otherwise returns false
- S'LAST_EVENT, which returns time elapsed since the previous event transistion of signal
- S'LAST_VALUE, which returns previous value of S before the last event
- S'LAST_ACTIVE, which returns time elapsed since the previous transaction of signal

6.2.4 Attributes 'EVENT and 'LAST_VALUE

Attribute 'EVENT is very useful for determining clock edges. By checking if a signal is at a particular value, and if the signal has just changed, it can be deduced that an edge has occurred on the signal. An example of a rising edge detector is shown below:

```
USE STD.std_logic.ALL;
ENTITY dff IS
   PORT( d, clk : IN t_wlogic;
         q : OUT t_wlogic);
END dff;

ARCHITECTURE dff OF dff IS
BEGIN
   PROCESS(clk)
   BEGIN
      IF ( clk = '1') AND ( clk'EVENT ) THEN
         q <= d;
      END IF;
   END PROCESS;
END dff;
```

This example shows a very simple *dff* model. The *clk* input is used to transfer the *d* input to the *q* output, on a rising edge of the *clk*. To detect the rising edge of the *clk* input, this model makes use of the 'EVENT attribute. If the value of the *clk* input is a '1', and the value has just changed, then a rising edge must have occurred.

What the example above ignores is the fact that an 'X' value to a '1' value will also look like a rising edge when it is not. The next example will show how to correct this problem using the 'LAST_VALUE attribute. The IF statement from the example above is rewritten as shown below:

```
IF ( clk = '1' ) AND ( clk'EVENT )
                 and ( clk'LAST_VALUE = '0') THEN
   q <= d;
END IF;
```

In this example, one more check is made to make certain that the last value of the *clk* input was a '0' before the new event occurred.

In both examples, the 'EVENT attribute was not really needed, because the process statement had only *clk* as its sensitivity list. The only way that the process statement could be executed would be because of an event on signal *clk*. This is a true statement, but it is a good modeling practice to check for the event anyway. Sometime in the future, the model may be modified to include an asynchronous preset or clear, and these signals will be added to the sensitivity list for the process statement. Now when an event occurs on any of the inputs, the process will be invoked. Using the 'EVENT attribute, the process can determine which input caused the process to be invoked.

6.2.5 Attribute 'LAST_EVENT

Attribute 'LAST_EVENT returns the time since the previous event occurred on the signal. This attribute is very useful for implementing timing checks, such as setup checks, hold checks, and pulse width checks. An example of a setup time and a hold time are shown in Figure 6-1.

The rising edge of signal *clk* is the reference edge to which all checks are performed. A setup time check will guarantee that the *data* input does not change during the setup time, and the hold time check will guarantee that the *data* input does not change during the time equal to the hold time after the reference edge. This will insure correct operation of the device.

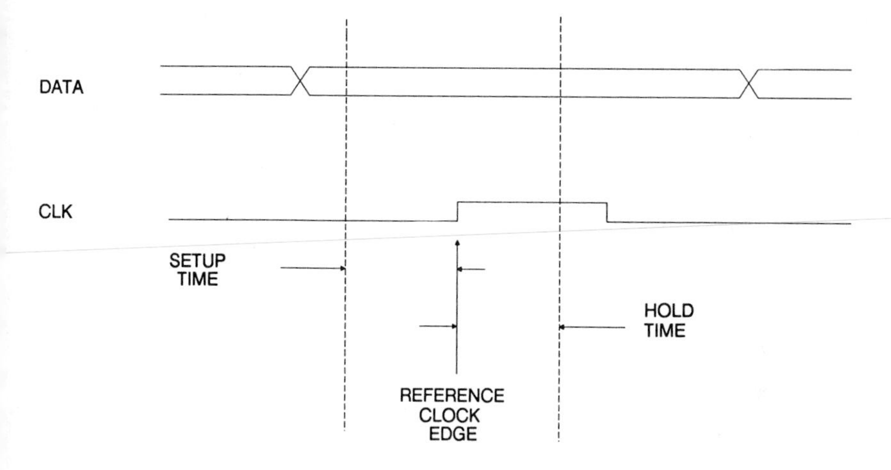

Figure 6-1

An example of the setup time check using the 'LAST_EVENT attribute is shown below:

```
USE STD.std_logic.ALL;
ENTITY dff IS
   GENERIC ( setup_time, hold_time : TIME );
   PORT( d, clk : IN t_wlogic;
         q : OUT t_wlogic);
BEGIN
   setup_check : PROCESS ( clk )
   BEGIN
      IF ( clk = F1 ) and ( clk'EVENT ) THEN
         ASSERT ( d'LAST_EVENT >= setup_time )
            REPORT "setup violation"
            SEVERITY ERROR;
      END IF;
   END PROCESS setup_check;
END dff;

ARCHITECTURE dff_behave OF dff IS
BEGIN
   dff_process : PROCESS ( clk )
   BEGIN
      IF ( clk = F1 ) AND ( clk'EVENT ) THEN
```

```
          q <= d;
        END IF;
      END PROCESS dff_process;
    END dff_behave;
```

The *setup_check* procedure is contained in a passive process in the entity for the *dff* model. The check could have been included in the architecture for the *dff* model but having the check in the entity allows the timing check to be shared among any architecture of the entity.

The passive process will execute for each event on signal *clk*. When the *clk* input has a rising edge, the ASSERT statement will be executed and perform the check for a setup violation.

The ASSERT statement will check to see that input *d* has not had an event during the setup time passed in by the generic *setup_time*. Attribute *d*'LAST_EVENT will return the time since the most recent event on signal *d*. If the time returned is less than the setup time, the assertion will fail and report a violation.

6.2.6 Attribute 'ACTIVE and 'LAST_ACTIVE

Attributes 'ACTIVE and 'LAST_ACTIVE trigger on transactions of the signal attached to and events. A transaction on a signal occurs when a model in or inout port has an event occur which triggers the execution of the model. The model is executed, but the result of the execution produces the same output values.

Attribute 'ACTIVE will return true when a transaction or event occurs on a signal, and attribute 'LAST_ACTIVE will return the time since a previous transaction or event occurred on the signal it is attached to. Both of these attributes are counterparts for attributes 'EVENT and 'LAST_EVENT, which provide the same behavior for events.

6.3 Signal Kind Attributes

Signal kind attributes are used to create special signals, based on other signals. These special signals return information to the designer about the signal that the attribute is attached to. The information returned is very similar to some of the functionality provided by some of the function attributes. The difference is that these special signals can be used anywhere that a normal signal can be used, including sensitivity lists.

Signal attributes return information such as whether a signal has been stable for a specified amount of time, when a transaction has occurred on a signal, and a delayed version of the signal can be created.

One restriction on the use of these attributes is that they cannot be used within a subprogram. A compiler error message will result if a signal kind attribute is used within a subprogram.

There are four attributes in the signal kind category. They are as follows:

- *s*'DELAYED [(time)], which creates a signal of the same type as the reference signal that follows the reference signal, delayed by the time of the optional time expression
- *s*'STABLE [(time)], which creates a boolean signal that is true whenever the reference signal has had no events for the time specified by the optional time expression
- *s*'QUIET [(time)], which creates a boolean signal that is true whenever the reference signal has had no transactions or events for the time specified by the optional time expression
- *s*'TRANSACTION, which creates a signal of type BIT that toggles its value for every transaction or event that occurs on *s*

6.3.1 Attribute 'DELAYED

Attribute 'DELAYED creates a delayed version of the signal that it is attached to. The same functionality can be obtained using a transport-delayed signal assignment. The difference between a transport delay assignment and the 'DELAYED attribute is that the designer has to do more bookkeeping with the transport signal assignment method. With a transport signal assignment a new signal must be declared.

Let's look at one use for the 'DELAYED attribute. One method for modeling ASIC devices is to place path-related delays on the input pins of the ASIC library part. An example of this method is shown in Figure 6-2.

Typically before the layout process, educated guesses are made for the delays of each input. After layout the real delay values are back-an-

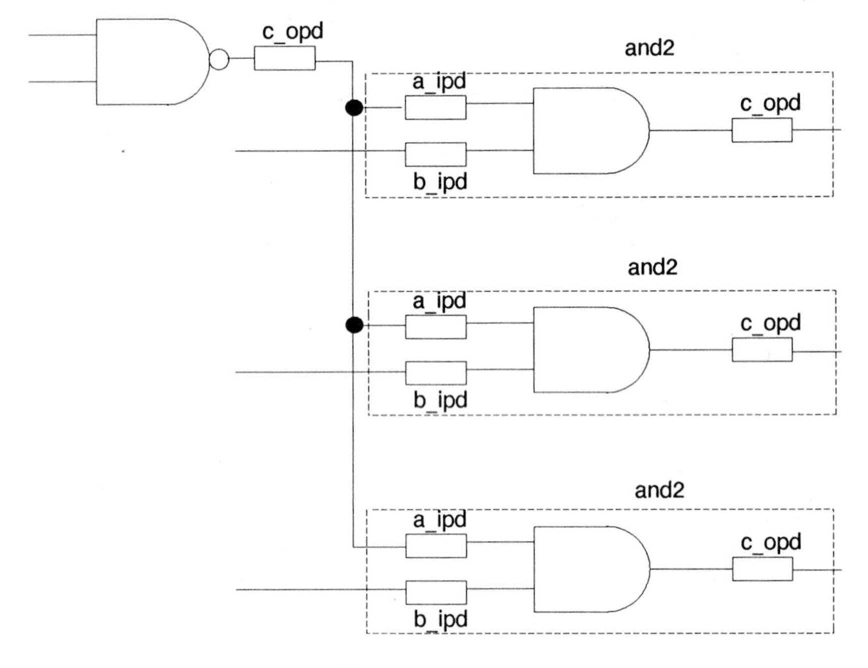

Figure 6-2

notated to the model, and the simulation is run again with the real delays. One method to provide for back annotation of the delay values is to use generic values specified in the configuration for the device (configurations are discussed in Chapter 7). A typical model for one of the *and2* gates shown in Figure 6-2 might look like this:

```
USE STD.std_logic.ALL;
USE STD.std_ttl.ALL;
ENTITY and2 IS
  GENERIC ( a_ipd, b_ipd, c_opd : TIME );
  PORT ( a, b : IN t_wlogic;
         c : OUT t_wlogic);
END and2;

ARCHITECTURE int_signals OF and2 IS
  SIGNAL inta, intb : t_wlogic;
BEGIN
  inta <= TRANSPORT a AFTER a_ipd;
  intb <= TRANSPORT b AFTER b_ipd;
```

```
   c <= inta AND intb AFTER c_opd;
END int_signals;

ARCHITECTURE attr OF and2 IS
BEGIN
   c <= a'DELAYED(a_ipd) AND b'DELAYED(b_ipd)
      AFTER c_opd;
END attr;
```

In the example above two architectures for entity *and2* show two different methods of delaying the input signals by the path delay. The first method uses transport-delayed internal signals to delay the input signals. These delayed signals are then ANDed together and assigned to output port *c*.

The second method makes use of the predefined signal attribute 'DELAYED. Input signals *a* and *b* are delayed by the path delay generic value *a_ipd* (a input path delay) and *b_ipd* (b input path delay). The values of the delayed signals are ANDed together and assigned to output port *c*.

If the optional time expression for attribute 'DELAYED is not specified, 0 ns is assumed. A signal delayed by 0 ns is delayed by one delta (delta delay is discussed in Chapter 2).

Another application for the 'DELAYED attribute is to perform a hold-check. Earlier in this chapter we discussed what setup and hold times were, and how to implement the setup check using 'LAST_EVENT. To implement the hold-check requires the use of a delayed version of the *clk* signal. The example shown before has been modified to include the hold-check function as shown below:

```
USE STD.std_logic.ALL;
ENTITY dff IS
   GENERIC ( setup_time, hold_time : TIME );
   PORT( d, clk : IN t_wlogic;
         q : OUT t_wlogic);
BEGIN
   setup_check : PROCESS ( clk )
   BEGIN
      IF ( clk = F1 ) and ( clk'EVENT ) THEN
         ASSERT ( d'LAST_EVENT <= setup_time )
```

```
            REPORT "setup violation"
            SEVERITY ERROR;
        END IF;
    END PROCESS setup_check;

    hold_check : PROCESS (clk'DELAYED(hold_time))
    BEGIN
        IF ( clk'DELAYED(hold_time) = F1 ) and
            ( clk'DELAYED(hold_time)'EVENT ) THEN

            ASSERT ( d'LAST_EVENT = 0 ns ) OR
                    ( d'LAST_EVENT < hold_time )
                REPORT "hold violation"
                SEVERITY ERROR;

        END IF;
    END PROCESS hold_check;
END dff;

ARCHITECTURE dff_behave OF dff IS
BEGIN
    dff_process : PROCESS ( clk )
    BEGIN

        IF ( clk = F1 ) AND ( clk'EVENT ) THEN
            q <= d;
        END IF;

    END PROCESS dff_process;
END dff_behave;
```

A delayed version of the *clk* input is used to trigger the hold-check. The *clk* input is delayed by the amount of the hold-check. If the *data* input changes within the hold time, *d*'LAST_EVENT will return a value that is less than the hold time. When *d* changes exactly at the same time as the delayed *clk* input, *d*'LAST_EVENT will return 0 ns. This is a special case, and is legal so it must be handled specially.

An alternative method for checking the hold time of a device is to trigger the hold-check process when the *d* input changes and then look back at the last change on the *clk* input. However, this is more complicated, and requires the designer to manually keep track of the last reference edge on the *clk* input.

Another interesting feature of attributes that this model pointed out is the cascading of attributes. In the example above, the delayed version of the *clk* signal was checked for an event. This necessitated the use of *clk*'DELAYED (hold_time) 'EVENT. The return value from this attribute will be true whenever the signal created by the 'DELAYED attribute has an event during the current delta time point. In general, attributes can be cascaded any level if the values returned from the previous attribute are appropriate for the next attribute.

6.3.2 Attribute 'STABLE

Attribute 'STABLE is used to determine the relative activity level of a signal. It can be used to determine if the signal just changed or has not changed in a specified period of time. The resulting value output is itself a signal that can be used to trigger other processes.

An example of how attribute 'STABLE works is shown below:

```
USE STD.std_logic.ALL;
ENTITY pulse_gen IS
   PORT( a : IN t_wlogic;
         b : OUT BOOLEAN);
END pulse_gen;

ARCHITECTURE pulse_gen OF pulse_gen IS
BEGIN
   b <= a'STABLE( 10 ns );
END pulse_gen;
```

Shown in Figure 6-3 is the resulting waveform *b* when waveform *a* is presented to the model.

At the first two changes in signal *a* (10 ns and 30 ns), signal *b* will immediately change to false (actually at the next delta). Then when signal *a* has been stable for 10 ns, signal *b* will change to true. At time 55 ns, signal *a* changes value again so signal *b* will change to false. Because signal *a* changes 5 ns later (60 ns), signal *a* will not have been stable long enough to allow output *b* to go to a true value. Only 10 ns after the last change on signal *a* (60 ns) will the input signal *a* have been stable long enough to allow signal *b* to change to true.

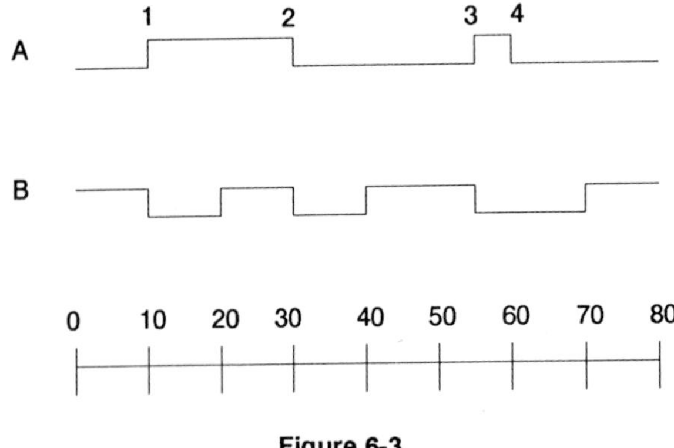

Figure 6-3

If the time value specified for the 'STABLE attribute is 0 ns, or not specified, then the 'STABLE attribute will be false for 1 delta whenever the signal that the attribute is attached to changes. An example of this scenario is shown in Figure 6-4.

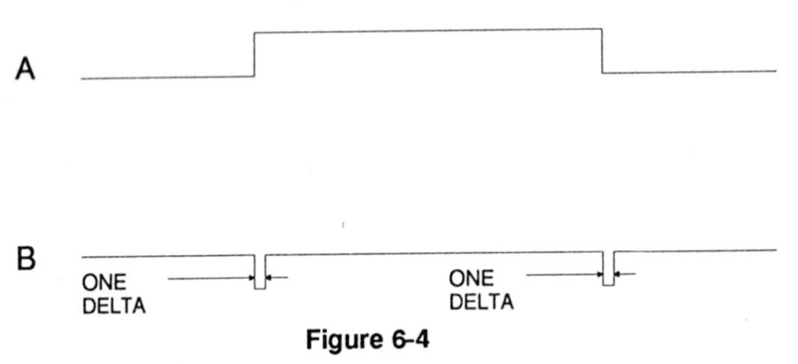

Figure 6-4

When used in this method, the resulting signal value has the same result as the function attribute 'EVENT. A statement to detect the rising edge of a clock could be written in two ways, as shown below:

```
IF (( clk'EVENT ) AND ( clk = '1' ) AND
              ( clk'LAST_VALUE = '0' )) THEN
    .
    .   -- DO PROCESSING
    .
END IF;
```

```
IF (( NOT( clk'STABLE) ) AND ( clk = '1' ) AND
                    ( clk'LAST_VALUE = '0' )) THEN
   .
   .   --- DO PROCESSING
   .
END IF;
```

In both cases, the IF statement will detect the rising edge, but the IF statement using 'EVENT will be more efficient in memory space and speed. The reason for this is that attribute 'STABLE creates an extra signal in the design which will use more memory to store, and whenever the value for the new signal needs to be updated it must be scheduled.

6.3.3 Attibute 'QUIET

Attribute 'QUIET has the same functionality as 'STABLE, except that 'QUIET is triggered by transactions on the signal that it is attached to in addition to events. Attribute 'QUIET will create a BOOLEAN signal that is true whenever the signal it is attached to has not had a transaction or event for the time expression specified.

Typically, models that deal with transactions involve complex models of devices at the switch level or the resolution of driver values. An interesting application using the attribute 'QUIET is shown below:

```
ARCHITECTURE test OF test IS
   TYPE t_int is (int1, int2, int3,
                  int4, int5 );

   SIGNAL int, intsig1, intsig2,
          intsig3 : t_int;

   SIGNAL lock_out : BOOLEAN;
BEGIN
   int1_proc: PROCESS
   BEGIN
      .
      .
      .
      WAIT ON trigger1; -- outside trigger signal
      WAIT UNTIL clk = '1';
      IF NOT(lock_out) THEN
         intsig1 <= int1;
```

```
      END IF;
   END PROCESS int1_proc;
   int2_proc: PROCESS
   BEGIN
      .
      .
      .
      WAIT ON trigger2;-- outside trigger signal
      WAIT UNTIL clk = '1';
      IF NOT(lock_out) THEN
         intsig2 <= int2;
      END IF;
   END PROCESS int2_proc;

   int3_proc: PROCESS
   BEGIN
      .
      .
      .
      WAIT ON trigger3;-- outside trigger signal
      WAIT UNTIL clk = '1';
      IF NOT(lock_out) THEN
         intsig3 <= int3;
      END IF;
   END PROCESS int3_proc;

   int <= intsig1 WHEN NOT(intsig1'QUIET) ELSE
          intsig2 WHEN NOT(intsig2'QUIET) ELSE
          intsig3 WHEN NOT(intsig3'QUIET) ELSE
          int;

   int_handle : PROCESS
   BEGIN
      WAIT ON int'TRANSACTION;-- described next
      lock_out <= TRUE;
      WAIT FOR 10 ns;
      CASE int IS
         WHEN int1 =>
            .
            .
         WHEN int2 =>
            .
```

```
                .
          WHEN int3 =>
                .
                .
          WHEN int4 =>
                .
                .
          WHEN int5 =>
                .
                .
        END CASE;
        lock_out <= false;
     END PROCESS;
  END test;
```

This example shows how a priority mechanism could be modeled for an interrupt handler. Process *int1_proc* has the highest priority, and process *int3_proc* has the lowest. Whenever one of the processes is triggered, the appropriate interrupt handler is placed on signal *int*, and the interrupt handler for that interrupt is called.

The model consists of three processes that drive the interrupt signal *int,* and another process to call the appropriate interrupt handling function. Signal *int* is not a resolved signal and therefore cannot have multiple drivers. If a resolution function is written for signal *int*, the order of the drivers cannot be used to determine priority. Therefore, the approach shown above was taken.

In this approach, three internal signals *intsig1, intsig2,* and *intsig3* are driven by each of the processes respectively. These signals are then combined, using a conditional signal assignment statement. The conditional signal assignment statement makes use of the predefined attribute 'QUIET to determine when a transaction has been assigned to a driver of a signal. It is required that transactions are detected on the internal signals, because the process will always assign the same value so an event will only occur on the first assignment.

The priority mechanism is controlled by the conditional signal assignment statement. When a transaction occurs on *intsig1, intsig2,* or *intsig3* the assignment statement will evaluate and assign the appropriate value to signal *int* based on the signal(s) that had a transaction. If a transaction occurred only on *intsig2*, *intsig2*'QUIET would be false, causing the conditional signal assignment statement to place the value of *intsig2* on signal *int*. But what happens if *intsig3* and *intsig2* occur at the same time? The conditional signal assignment statement will evaluate, and the first clause that has a WHEN expression return true will do the assignment and then exit the rest of the statement. For this example the value for *intsig2* will be returned, because it is first in the conditional signal assignment statement. The priority of the inputs is determined by the order of the WHEN clauses in the conditional signal assignment statement.

6.3.4 Attribute 'TRANSACTION

The process that implemented the interrupt handling for the previous example uses the 'TRANSACTION attribute in a WAIT statement. This attribute is another of the attributes that creates a signal where it is used. Attribute 'TRANSACTION creates a signal of type BIT that toggles from '1' or '0' for every transaction of the signal that it is attached to. This attribute is useful for invoking processes when transactions occur on signals.

In the example above the interrrupt handler process needs to be executed whenever a transaction occurs on signal *int*. This is true because the same interrupt could happen twice or more in sequence. If this occurred a transaction, not an event would be generated on signal *int*. Without the attribute 'TRANSACTION, WAIT statements are sensitive to events. By using the attribute 'TRANSACTION the value of *int*'TRANSACTION will toggle for every transaction causing an event to occur, thus activating the WAIT statement.

6.4 Type Kind Attributes

Type attributes return values of kind type. There is only one type attribute, and it must be used with another value or function type attribute. The only type attribute available in VHDL is the attribute

- t'BASE

This attribute will return the base type of a type or subtype. This attribute can only be used as the prefix of another attribute, as shown by the example below:

```
do_nothing : PROCESS(x)
   TYPE color IS (red, blue, green,
                  yellow, brown, black);
   SUBTYPE color_gun IS color RANGE
        red TO green;
   VARIABLE a : color;
BEGIN
   a := color_gun'BASE'RIGHT;          -- a = black
   a := color'BASE'LEFT;               -- a = red

   -- a = yellow
   a := color_gun'BASE'SUCC(green);

END PROCESS do_nothing;
```

In the first assignment to variable *a*, *color_gun*'BASE will return type *color*, the base type of *color_gun*. The statement *color*'RIGHT will then return the value *black*. In the second assignment statement, the base type of type *color* is type *color*. The statement *color*'LEFT will return the value *red*. In the last assignment *color_gun*'BASE returns type *color*, and *color*'SUCC(green) returns *yellow*.

6.5 Range Kind Attributes

The last two predefined attributes in VHDL return a value kind of range. These attributes work only with constrained array types and return the index range specified by the optional input parameter. The attribute notations are shown below:

- *a*'RANGE[(*n*)]
- *a*'REVERSE_RANGE[(*n*)]

Attributes 'RANGE will return the *n*th range denoted by the value of parameter *n*. Attribute 'RANGE will return the range in the order specified, and 'REVERSE_RANGE will will return the range in reverse order.

Attributes 'RANGE and 'REVERSE_RANGE can be used to control the number of times that a loop statement will loop. An example is shown below:

```
FUNCTION vector_to_int(vect: t_wlogic_vector)
      RETURN INTEGER IS
  VARIABLE result : INTEGER := 0;
BEGIN
  FOR i IN vect'RANGE LOOP

    result := result * 2;

    IF vect(i) = '1' THEN
      result := result + 1;
    END IF;

  END LOOP;
  RETURN result;
END vector_to_int;
```

This function converts an array of bits into an integer value. The number of times that the loop needs to be executed is determined by the number of bits in the input argument *vect*. When the function call is made, the input argument cannot be an unconstrained value; therefore, the attribute 'RANGE can be used to determine the range of the input vector. The range can then be used in the loop statement to determine the number of times to execute the loop and finish the conversion.

The 'REVERSE_RANGE attribute works similar to the 'RANGE attribute, except that the range will be returned in the reverse order. For a type shown below, the 'RANGE attribute will return 0 TO 15, and the 'REVERSE_RANGE attribute will return 15 DOWNTO 0.

```
TYPE array16 IS ARRAY(0 TO 15) OF BIT;
```

VHDL attributes extend the language to provide some very useful functionality. Attributes are used to return information about VHDL objects and types. In the next chapter we will examine configurations, the method of binding architectures to entities.

Chapter

7

Configurations

Configurations are a primary design unit used to bind component instances to entities. For structural models, configurations can be thought of as the parts list for the model. For component instances, the configuration will specify from many architectures for an entity which architecture to use for a specific instance. When the configuration for an entity-architecture combination is compiled into the library, a simulatable object is created.

Configurations can also be used to specify generic values for components instantiated in the architecture configured by the configuration. This mechanism, for example, provides a late-binding capability for delay values. Delay values calculated from a physical layout tool, such as a printed circuit board design system or a gate array layout system, can be inserted in a configuration to provide a simulation model with actual delays in the design.

If the designer wants to use a component in an architecture that has different port names from the architecture component declaration, the new component can have its ports mapped to the appropriate signals.

With this functionality, libraries of components can be mixed and matched easily.

The configuration can also be used to provide a very fast substitution capability. Multiple architectures can exist for a single entity. One architecture might be a behavioral model for the entity, while another architecture might be a structural model for the entity. The architecture used in the containing model can be selected by specifying which architecture to use in the configuration, and recompiling only the configuration. After compilation, the simulatable model will use the specified architecture.

7.1 Default Configurations

The simplest form of explicit configuration is the default configuration (the simplest configuration is none at all in which the last architecture compiled is used for an entity). This configuration can be used for models that do not contain any blocks or components to configure. The default configuration will specify the configuration name, the entity being configured, and the architecture to be used for the entity. An example of two default configurations are shown by configurations *big_count* and *small_count* below:

```
USE STD.std_logic.ALL;
ENTITY counter IS
   PORT(load, clear, clk : IN t_wlogic;
        data_in : IN INTEGER;
        data_out : OUT INTEGER);
END counter;

ARCHITECTURE count_255 OF counter IS
BEGIN
   PROCESS(clk)
      VARIABLE count : INTEGER := 0;
   BEGIN
      IF clear = '1' THEN
         count := 0;
      ELSIF load = '1' THEN
         count := data_in;
      ELSE
         IF (clk'EVENT) AND (clk = '1') AND
                   (clk'LAST_VALUE = '0') THEN
```

```
            IF (count = 255) THEN
               count := 0;
            ELSE
               count := count + 1;
            END IF;
         END IF;
      END IF;
      data_out <= count;
   END PROCESS;
END count_255;

ARCHITECTURE count_64k OF counter IS
BEGIN
   PROCESS(clk)
      VARIABLE count : INTEGER := 0;
   BEGIN
      IF clear = '1' THEN
         count := 0;
      ELSIF load = '1' THEN
         count := data_in;
      ELSE
         IF (clk'EVENT) AND (clk = '1') AND
                  (clk'LAST_VALUE = '0') THEN
            IF (count = 65535) THEN
               count := 0;
            ELSE
               count := count + 1;
            END IF;
         END IF;
      END IF;
      data_out <= count;
   END PROCESS;
END count_64k;

CONFIGURATION small_count OF counter IS
   FOR count_255
   END FOR;
END small_count;

CONFIGURATION big_count OF counter IS
   FOR count_64k
```

```
    END FOR;
  END big_count;
```

This example shows how two different architectures for a counter entity can be configured using two default configurations. The entity for the counter does not specify any bit width for the data to be loaded into the counter or data from the counter. The data type for the input and output data is INTEGER. With a data type of integer, multiple types of counters can be supported up to the integer representation limit of the host computer for the VHDL simulator.

The two architectures of entity counter specify two different-sized counters that can be used for the entity. The first architecture, *count_255*, specifies an 8-bit counter. The second architecture, *count_64k*, specifies a 16-bit counter. The architectures specify a synchronous counter with a synchronous load and clear. All operations for the device occur with respect to the clock.

Each of the two configurations for the entity specifies a different architecture for the *counter* entity. Let's examine the first configuration in more detail. The configuration design unit begins with the keyword CONFIGURATION and is followed by the name of the configuration. In this example the name of the configuration is *small_count*. The keyword OF precedes the name of the entity begin configured (*counter*). The next line of the configuration starts the block configuration section. The keyword FOR is followed by a name of the architecture to use for the entity being configured or the name of the block of the architecture that will be configured. Any component or block configuration information will then exist between the FOR ARCHITECTURE clause and the matching END FOR.

In this architecture, there are no blocks or components to configure; therefore the block configuration area from the FOR clause to the END FOR clause will be empty, and the default will be used. The configuration is called the default configuration, because the default will be used for all objects in the configuration.

The first configuration is called *small_count* and binds architecture *count_255* with entity *counter* to form a simulatable object. The second configuration binds architecture *count_64k* with entity *counter* and forms a simulatable object called *big_count*.

7.2 Component Configurations

In this section we will discuss how architectures that contain instantiated components can be configured. Architectures that contain other components are called structural architectures. These components are configured through component configuration statements.

Let's first look at some very simple examples of component configurations, and then at some progressively more complex examples. The first example is a simple 2-to-4 decoder device. Figure 7-1 shows the symbol for the decoder, and Figure 7-2 shows the schematic.

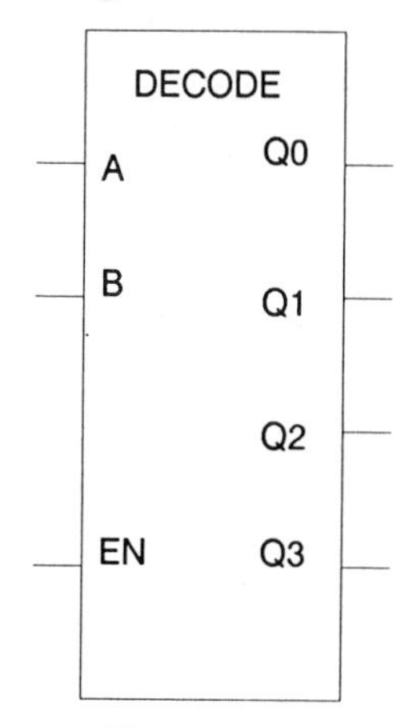

Figure 7-1

The components used in the design are defined using the VHDL description shown below:

```
USE STD.std_logic.ALL;
USE STD.std_ttl.ALL;
ENTITY inv IS
   PORT( a : IN t_wlogic;
         b : OUT t_wlogic);
END inv;

ARCHITECTURE behave OF inv IS
BEGIN
   b <= NOT(a) AFTER 5 ns;
END behave;
```

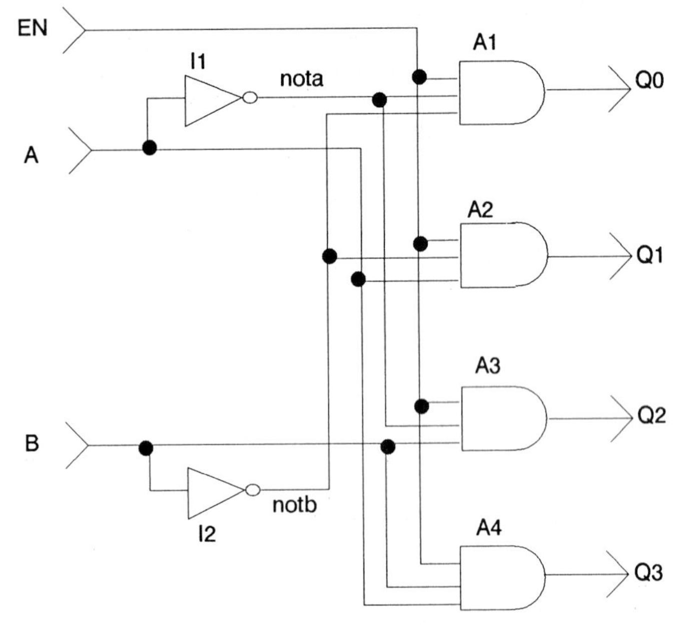

Figure 7-2

```
CONFIGURATION invcon OF inv IS
  FOR behave
  END FOR;
END invcon;

USE STD.std_logic.ALL;
USE STD.std_ttl.ALL;
ENTITY and3 IS
  PORT( a1, a2, a3 : IN t_wlogic;
        o1 : OUT t_wlogic);
END and3;

ARCHITECTURE behave OF and3 IS
BEGIN
  o1 <= a1 AND a2 AND a3 AFTER 5 ns;
END behave;

CONFIGURATION and3con OF and3 IS
  FOR behave
```

```
   END FOR;
END and3con;
```

Next, the entity and architecture for *decode* are shown below:

```
USE STD.std_logic.ALL;
ENTITY decode IS
   PORT( a, b, en : IN t_wlogic;
         q0, q1, q2, q3 : OUT t_wlogic);
END decode;

ARCHITECTURE structural OF decode IS
   COMPONENT inv
      PORT( a : IN t_wlogic;
            b : OUT t_wlogic);
   END COMPONENT;

   COMPONENT and3
      PORT( a1, a2, a3 : IN t_wlogic;
            o1 : OUT t_wlogic);
   END COMPONENT;

   SIGNAL nota, notb : t_wlogic;
BEGIN
   I1 : inv
      PORT MAP(a, nota);

   I2 : inv
      PORT MAP(b, notb);

   A1 : and3
      PORT MAP(nota, en, notb, Q0);

   A2 : and3
      PORT MAP(a, en, notb, Q1);

   A3 : and3
      PORT MAP(nota, en, b, Q2);

   A4 : and3
      PORT MAP(a, en, b, Q3);

END structural;
```

When all of the entities and architectures have been compiled into the working library, the circuit can be simulated. The simulator will use the last compiled architecture to build the executable design for the simulator because it is the default. Using the last compiled architecture for an entity to build the simulator will work fine in a typical system, until more than one architecture exists for an entity. Then it can become confusing as to which architecture was compiled last. A better method is to specify exactly which architecture to use for each entity. The component configuration binds architectures to entities.

Two different styles can be used for writing a component configuration for an entity. The lower-level configuration style specifies lower-level configurations for each component, and the entity-architecture style specifies entity-architecture pairs for each component. The word *style* is used to describe these two different configurations because there is no hard-and-fast rule about how to use them. Lower-level configurations can be mixed with entity-architecture pairs, creating a mixed-style configuration.

7.2.1 Lower-Level Configurations

Let's examine the configuration for the lower-level configuration style first. An example of such a configuration for the decode entity is shown below:

```
CONFIGURATION decode_llcon OF decode IS
   FOR structural
      FOR I1 : inv USE CONFIGURATION WORK.invcon;
      END FOR;

      FOR I2 : inv USE CONFIGURATION WORK.invcon;
      END FOR;
      FOR ALL : and3 USE CONFIGURATION
               WORK.and3con;
      END FOR;
   END FOR;
END decode_llcon;
```

This configuration specifies which configuration to use for each component in architecture *structural* of entity *decode*. The specified lower-level configuration must already exist in the library for the current configuration to compile. Each component being configured has a FOR clause to begin the configuration, and an END FOR clause to end the configuration specification for the component. Each component can be specified with the component instantiation label directly, as shown for component I1, or with an ALL or OTHERS clause as shown by the *and3* components.

Once the component is uniquely specified by label or otherwise, the USE CONFIGURATION clause specifies which configuration to use for this instance of the component. In the example above, the configuration specification for component I1 will use the configuration called *invcon*, from the working library. In order for configuration *decode_llcon* to compile, configuration *invcon* must have been already compiled into library WORK.

Notice that the names of the entities, architectures, and configurations reflect a naming convention. In general this is a good practice. It will help distinguish the different types of design units from one another when they all exist in a library.

The advantage of this style of configurations is that most configurations are easy to write and understand. The disadvantage is not being able to change the configuration of a lower-level component, without implementing a two-step or more process of recompilation when hierarchy levels increase.

7.2.2 Entity-Architecture Pair Configuration

The other style of component configurations is the entity-architecture pair style. An example of a configuration that uses the same entity and architectures as the previous example is shown below:

```
CONFIGURATION decode_eacon OF decode IS
  FOR structural
    FOR I1 : inv USE ENTITY WORK.inv(behave);
    END FOR;

    FOR OTHERS : inv USE ENTITY
                     WORK.inv(behave);
    END FOR;

    FOR A1 : and3 USE ENTITY WORK.and3(behave);
```

```
        END FOR;

        FOR OTHERS : and3 USE ENTITY
                          WORK.and3(behave);
        END FOR;

    END structural;
  END decode_eacon;
```

This configuration looks very similar to the lower-level configuration style except for the USE clause in the component specification. In the previous example a configuration was specified, but in this style, an entity-architecture pair is specified. The architecture is actually optional. If no architecture is specified, the last compiled architecture for the entity is used.

Let's take another look at the FOR clause for the first inverter, I1. In the example above the component is still specified by the label or by an ALL or OTHERS clause. In this example a USE ENTITY clause follows. This clause specifies the name of the entity to use for this component. The entity can have a completely different name than the component being specified. The component name comes from the component declaration in the architecture, while the entity name comes from the actual entity that has been compiled in the library specified. Following the entity is an optional architecture name that specifies which architecture to use for the entity.

Notice that the OTHERS clause is used for the second inverter in this example. The first inverter is configured from its label, I1, and all components that have not yet been configured will be configured by the OTHERS clause. This capability allows component I1 to use an architecture that is different from the other components to describe its behavior. This concept allows mixed-level modeling to exist. One component can be modeled at the switch or gate level, and the other can be modeled at the behavior level.

To change the architecture used for a component with the first configuration *decode_llcon* requires modifying the lower-level configuration and recompiling, then recompiling any higher-level configurations that depend on it. With the second configuration *decode_eacon*, to change the architecture for a component involves modifying configuration *decode_eacon* and recompiling. No other configurations need be recompiled.

7.2.3 Port Maps

In the last two examples of component configurations, default mapping of entity ports and component ports was used. When the port names for an entity being configured to a component match the component port names, no other mapping need take place. The default mapping will cause the ports to match. What happens when the component ports do not match the entity being mapped to the component instance? Without any further information the compiler cannot figure out which ports to map to which and will produce an error. However, more information can be passed to the compiler with the configuration port map clause.

The configuration port map clause looks exactly like the component instantiation port map clause used in an architecture. The configuration port map clause specifies which of the component ports map to the actual ports of the entity. If the port names are different, then the port map clause will specify the mapping.

Let's change the port names of the *inv* component used in the previous example and see what the effect will be in the configuration.

```
USE STD.std_logic.ALL;
USE STD.std_ttl.ALL;
ENTITY inv IS
   PORT( x : IN t_wlogic;
         y : OUT t_wlogic);
END inv;

ARCHITECTURE behave OF inv IS
BEGIN
   y <= NOT(x) AFTER 5 ns;
END behave;

CONFIGURATION invcon OF inv IS
   FOR behave
   END FOR;
END invcon;
```

The entity and architecture for *decode* will stay exactly the same, including the component declaration. The configuration, however, will need to add the port map clause, as shown in the example below:

```
CONFIGURATION decode_map_con OF decode IS
   FOR structural
      FOR I1 : inv USE ENTITY WORK.inv(behave);
         PORT MAP( a => x, b => y );
      END FOR;

      FOR I2 : inv USE ENTITY WORK.inv(behave);
         PORT MAP( a => x, b => y );
      END FOR;

      FOR ALL : and3 USE ENTITY
                     WORK.and3(behave);
      END FOR;

   END FOR;
END decode_map_con;
```

The port map clause will map the port names of the component declarations, called the *formal* ports, to the port names of the entities from the library. The term used for the ports of the entities from the library being mapped are *actuals*. The ports are mapped using named association. The rules for mapping ports using named association in the configuration port map clause are the same rules as used in the component instantiation port map clause.

In the example above, component declaration *inv*, port *a*, is mapped to entity *inv*, port *x*, of the actual entity. Component declaration *inv*, port *b*, is mapped to entity *inv*, port *y*, of the actual entity. Using the configuration port map clause can allow entities with completely different port names to be mapped into existing architectures.

7.3 Mapping Library Entities

Not only can the ports be mapped with the configuration statement, but entities from libraries can be mapped to components as well. This capability allows the names of components to differ from the actual entities being mapped to them. The designer can easily switch the entity used for each component in the architecture from one entity to another.

This feature allows the designer to map component instances to different entities.

Let's look again at the decode example from the beginning of this chapter. The inverter, *inv,* for the decoder could be modeled using NMOS transistors as shown in Figure 7-3:

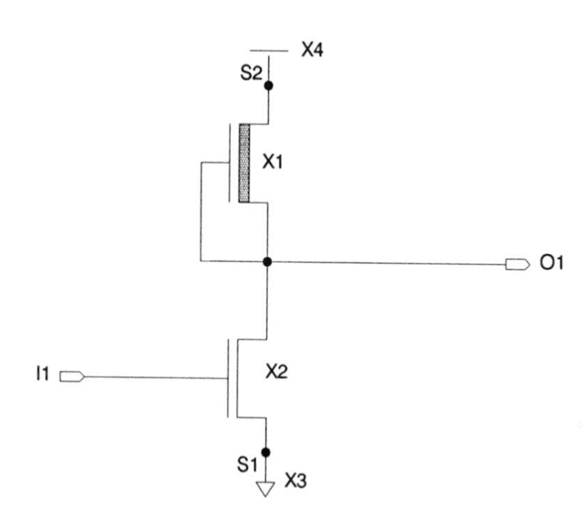

Figure 7-3

Component X1 is an NMOS depletion transistor, which for all intents and purposes in digital simulation acts like a resistor. Component X2 is a unidirectional pass transistor that transfers ground from the triangular-shaped component X3 to signal O1. Components X3 and X4 are ground and VCC, respectively. The model that represents this circuit is shown below:

```
USE STD.std_logic.ALL;
ENTITY ground IS
   PORT( x : OUT t_wlogic );
END ground;

ARCHITECTURE dirt OF ground IS
```

```
BEGIN
   X <= F0;
END dirt;

CONFIGURATION groundcon OF ground IS
   FOR dirt
   END FOR;
END groundcon;

USE STD.std_logic.ALL;
ENTITY vcc IS
   PORT( x : OUT t_wlogic);
END vcc;

ARCHITECTURE plus5 OF vcc IS
BEGIN
   x <= F1;
END plus5;

CONFIGURATION vcccon OF vcc IS
   FOR plus5
   END FOR;
END vcccon;
```

The two transistor devices are shown below:

```
USE STD.std_logic.ALL;
ENTITY dep IS
   PORT( top : IN t_wlogic;
         bottom : OUT t_wlogic);
END dep;

ARCHITECTURE behave OF dep IS
BEGIN
   bottom <= R1 WHEN top = F1 ELSE
             R0 WHEN top = F0 ELSE
             RX WHEN top = FX ELSE
             top;
END behave;

CONFIGURATION depcon OF dep IS
   FOR behave
   END FOR;
```

```
END depcon;

USE STD.std_logic.ALL;
ENTITY uxfr IS
   PORT( left, sw : IN t_wlogic;
         right : inout t_wlogic);
END uxfr;

ARCHITECTURE behave OF uxfr IS
BEGIN
   uxfr_proc: PROCESS(left, sw, right)
   BEGIN
      CASE f_state(sw) is
         WHEN '1' =>
            right <= left;
         WHEN '0' =>
            right <= f_convz(right);
         WHEN 'X' =>
            right <= FX;
      END CASE;
   END PROCESS uxfr_proc;
END behave;

CONFIGURATION uxfrcon OF uxfr IS
   FOR behave
   END FOR;
END uxfrcon;
```

These parts can be connected together, with the entity-architecture shown below, to form a structural representation of the inverter.

```
USE STD.std_logic.ALL;
ENTITY struc_inv IS
   PORT( I1 : IN t_wlogic;
         O1 : OUT t_wlogic);
END struc_inv;

ARCHITECTURE structural OF struc_inv IS
   COMPONENT ground
      PORT( X : OUT t_wlogic);
   END COMPONENT;

   COMPONENT vcc
```

```
      PORT( X : OUT t_wlogic);
   END COMPONENT;

   COMPONENT dep
      PORT( top : IN t_wlogic;
            bottom : OUT t_wlogic);
   END COMPONENT;

   COMPONENT uxfr
      PORT( left, sw : IN t_wlogic;
              right : OUT t_wlogic);
   END COMPONENT;

   SIGNAL s1, s2 : t_wlogic;

BEGIN

   x1 : dep
      PORT MAP( top => s2, bottom => O1 );

   x2 : uxfr
      PORT MAP( left => s1, sw => I1,
                right => O1 );

   x3 : ground
      PORT MAP( x => s1 );

   x4 : vcc
      PORT MAP( x => s2 );

END structural;
```

This architecture can then be configured with the following configuration:

```
CONFIGURATION inv_transcon OF struc_inv IS
   FOR x1 : dep USE CONFIGURATION WORK.depcon;
   END FOR;

   FOR x2 : uxfr USE CONFIGURATION WORK.uxfrcon;
   END FOR;

   FOR x3 : ground USE CONFIGURATION
```

```
                                WORK.groundcon;
      END FOR;

      FOR x4 : vcc USE CONFIGURATION WORK.vcccon;
      END FOR;
   END inv_transcon;
```

Now configuration *decode_map_con* of entity *decode*, described earlier, can be modified as shown below:

```
   CONFIGURATION decode_map_con OF decode IS
      FOR structural
         FOR I1 : inv USE ENTITY WORK.inv(behave);
            PORT MAP( a => x, b => y );
         END FOR;
         FOR I2 : struc_inv USE CONFIGURATION
                                 WORK.inv_transcon;
            PORT MAP( a => I1, b => O1 );
         END FOR;
         FOR ALL : and3 USE ENTITY
                            WORK.and3(behave);
         END FOR;

      END FOR;
   END decode_map_con;
```

This configuration maps the first inverter, I1, to entity *inv*, and the second inverter, I2, to the structural inverter, *struc_inv*. Also the I1 and O1 ports of *struc_inv* are mapped to ports *a* and *b* of the component declaration for component *inv*.

7.4 Generics in Configurations

Generics are parameters that are used to pass information into entities. Typical applications include passing in a generic value for the rise and fall delay of output signals of the entity. Other applications include passing in temperature, voltage, and loading to calculate delay values in the model (for modeling efficiency delay calculations should be done prior to simulation and the calculated delay values can then be passed back into the model through generics). A description of generics can be found in Chapter 3. This section will concentrate on how configurations can be used to specify the value of generics.

Generics can be declared in entities, but can have a value specified in a number of places.

- A default value can be specified in the generic declaration.
- A value can be mapped in the architecture, in the component instantiation.
- A default value can be specified in the component declaration.
- A value can be mapped in the configuration for the component.

Default values specified in the generic declaration, or the component declaration, can be overridden by mapped values in the architecture or configuration sections. If no overriding values are present, the default values will be used, but if a value is mapped to the generic with a generic map, the default value will be overridden.

To see an example of this, let's modify the decoder example, used previously in this chapter, to include two generics. The first will specify a timing mode to run the simulation, and the second is a composite type containing the delay values for the device. These two types are declared in the package *p_time_pack*, shown below:

```
USE STD.std_logic.ALL;
PACKAGE p_time_pack IS
   TYPE t_time_mode IS (minimum, typical,
                                      maximum);
   TYPE t_rise_fall IS
      RECORD
         rise : TIME;
         fall : TIME;
      END RECORD;

   TYPE t_time_rec IS ARRAY(t_time_mode'LOW TO
               t_time_mode'HIGH) OF t_rise_fall;

   FUNCTION calc_delay(
         newstate : IN t_wlogic;
         mode : IN t_time_mode;
         delay_tab : IN t_time_rec ) return time;
```

```
END p_time_pack;

PACKAGE BODY p_time_pack IS
   FUNCTION calc_delay(
         newstate : IN t_wlogic;
         mode : IN t_time_mode;
         delay_tab : IN t_time_rec )
         return time IS
   BEGIN
      CASE f_state(newstate) IS
         WHEN '0' =>
            RETURN delay_tab(mode).fall;
         WHEN '1' =>
            RETURN delay_tab(mode).rise;
         WHEN 'X' =>
            IF (delay_tab(mode).rise <=
                     delay_tab(mode).fall) THEN
               RETURN delay_tab(mode).rise;
            ELSE
               RETURN delay_tab(mode).fall;
            END IF;
      END CASE;
   END calc_delay;
END p_time_pack;
```

This package declares types *t_time_mode* and *t_time_rec*, which will be used for the generics of the inverter and three input AND gates. It also includes a new function, *calc_delay*, which will be used to retrieve the proper delay value from the delay table, depending on the type of transition occurring.

The *and3* and *inv* gates of the decoder example have been rewritten to include the generics discussed above, as well as the delay calculation function. The new models are shown below:

```
USE STD.std_logic.ALL;
USE STD.std_ttl.ALL;
USE WORK.p_time_pack.ALL;
ENTITY inv IS
   GENERIC( mode : t_time_mode;
         delay_tab : t_time_rec :=
            (( 1 ns, 2 ns),   -- min
             ( 2 ns, 3 ns),   -- typ
```

```
                  ( 3 ns, 4 ns)));-- max
      PORT( a : IN t_wlogic;
            b : OUT t_wlogic);
   END inv;

   ARCHITECTURE inv_gen OF inv IS
   BEGIN
      inv_proc : PROCESS(a)
         VARIABLE state : t_wlogic;
      BEGIN
         state := NOT(a);
         b <= state after calc_delay( state, mode,
                                        delay_tab);
      END PROCESS inv_proc;
   END inv_gen;

   USE STD.std_logic.ALL;
   USE STD.std_ttl.ALL;
   USE WORK.p_time_pack.ALL;
   ENTITY and3 IS
      GENERIC( mode : t_time_mode;
               delay_tab : t_time_rec :=
                    (( 2 ns, 3 ns),   -- min
                     ( 3 ns, 4 ns),   -- typ
                     ( 4 ns, 5 ns)));-- max
      PORT( a1, a2, a3 : IN t_wlogic;
            o1 : OUT t_wlogic);
   END and3;

   ARCHITECTURE and3_gen OF and3 IS
   BEGIN
      and3_proc : PROCESS( a1, a2, a3 )
         VARIABLE state : t_wlogic;
      BEGIN
         state := a1 AND a2 AND a3;
         o1 <= state after calc_delay( state, mode,
                                         delay_tab);
      END PROCESS and3_proc;
   END and3_gen;
```

After the entities and architectures for the gates have been defined, configurations that will provide specific values for the generics will be defined.

These models can have their generic values specified by two methods. The first method is to specify the generic values in the architecture where the components are being instantiated. The second method is to specify the generic values in the configuration for the model, where the components are instantiated.

7.5 Generic Value Specification in Architecture

Specifying the generic values in the architecture of an entity allows the designer to delay the specification of the generic values until the architecture of the entity is created. Different generic values can be specified for each instance of an entity allowing one entity to represent many different physical devices. An example of an architecture with the generic values specified in it is shown below:

```
ARCHITECTURE structural OF decode IS
   COMPONENT inv
      GENERIC( mode : t_time_mode;
               delay_tab : t_time_rec);
      PORT( a : IN t_wlogic;
            b : OUT t_wlogic);
   END COMPONENT;

   COMPONENT and3
      GENERIC( mode : t_time_mode;
               delay_tab : t_time_rec);
      PORT( a1, a2, a3 : IN t_wlogic;
            o1 : OUT t_wlogic);
   END COMPONENT;

   SIGNAL nota, notb : t_wlogic;
BEGIN
   I1 : inv
      GENERIC MAP( mode => maximum,
         delay_tab => ((1.3 ns, 1.9 ns),
                       (2.1 ns, 2.9 ns),
                       (3.2 ns, 4.1 ns)))
      PORT MAP( a, nota );

   I2 : inv
      GENERIC MAP( mode => minimum,
         delay_tab => ((1.3 ns, 1.9 ns),
```

```
                       (2.1 ns, 2.9 ns),
                       (3.2 ns, 4.1 ns)))
      PORT MAP( b, notb );

   A1 : and3
      GENERIC MAP( mode => typical,
         delay_tab => ((1.3 ns, 1.9 ns),
                       (2.1 ns, 2.9 ns),
                       (3.2 ns, 4.1 ns)))
      PORT MAP( nota, en, notb, q0 );

   A2 : and3
      GENERIC MAP( mode => minimum,
         delay_tab => ((1.3 ns, 1.9 ns),
                      (2.1 ns, 2.9 ns),
                      (3.2 ns, 4.1 ns)))
      PORT MAP( a, en, notb, q1 );

   A3 : and3
      GENERIC MAP( mode => maximum,
         delay_tab => ((1.3 ns, 1.9 ns),
                      (2.1 ns, 2.9 ns),
                      (3.2 ns, 4.1 ns)))
      PORT MAP( nota, en, b, q2 );

   A4 : and3
      GENERIC MAP( mode => maximum,
         delay_tab => ((2.3 ns, 2.9 ns),
                      (3.1 ns, 3.9 ns),
                      (4.2 ns, 5.1 ns)))
      PORT MAP( a, en, b, q3 );
END structural;
```

Generics are treated in the same manner as ports with respect to how they are mapped. If a component port in a component declaration has a different name than the actual entity compiled into the library, then a port map clause is needed in the configuration specification, for the containing entity. The same is true for a generic. If a generic declaration in a component declaration has a different name than the actual generic for the component, then a generic map clause is needed to make the appropriate mapping.

In the example above the generic names are the same in the entity declaration and the component declaration, and therefore the default mapping will provide the appropriate connection between the two.

The configuration for the example above needs only to specify which actual entities will be used for the component instantiations in the architecture. No generic information needs to be provided, because the generics have been mapped in the architecture. The configuration can be specified as below:

```
CONFIGURATION decode_gen_con2 OF decode IS
   FOR structural
      FOR i1, i2 : inv USE ENTITY
                              WORK.inv(inv_gen);
      END FOR;

      FOR a1, a2, a3, a4 : and3 USE ENTITY
                              WORK.and3(and3_gen);
      END FOR;
   END FOR;
END decode_gen_con2;
```

The lower-level configuration cannot specify values for the generics if the architecture has mapped values to the generics in the architecture.

7.6 Generic Specifications in Configurations

The method of specifying generic values with the most flexibility is to specify generic values in the configuration for the entity. This method allows the latest binding of all the methods for specifying the values for generics. Usually, the later the values are specified, the better. Late binding allows back annotation of path delay generics to occur in the configuration.

For instance there are a number of steps involved in the design of an ASIC.

- Create the logic design model of a device.
- Simulate the model.
- Add estimated delays to device model.
- Simulate model.

- Create physical layout of the model.
- Calulate physical delays from the layout.
- Feed back physical delays to the device model.
- Resimulate using actual delays.

The process of feeding back the physical delays into the model can be accomplished by modifying the architecture or by creating a configuration to map the delays back to the model. Modifying the architecture would involve changing the values in all of the generic map clauses used to map the delays in the architecture. This method has a big drawback. Modifying the architecture that contains the component instantiation statements requires recompilation of the architecture and the configuration for the design unit. This can be an expensive proposition in a very large design.

The second method, which creates a configuration that maps all of the delays to the generics of the entity, is much more efficient. A configuration of this type would contain a generic map value for each generic to be specified in the configuration. Any generics not specified in the configuration would be mapped in the architecture or defaulted.

Let's use the decoder example again but now assume that it represents part of an ASIC that will have delays back annotated to it. The *inv* and *and3* devices will have an intrinsic propagation delay through the device that is based on the internal characteristics of the device, and these devices will have an external delay that is dependent on the driver path and device loading. The intrinsic and external delays will be passed into the model as generic values. The intrinsic delay is passed into the model to allow a single model to be used for model processes. The external delay is passed to the model, because it may vary for every instance, as loading may be different for each instance (a more accurate model of delays is obtained using input delays).

The entity and architecture for the *inv* and *and3* gates look like this:

```
USE STD.std_logic.ALL;
USE STD.std_logic.ALL;
ENTITY inv IS
   GENERIC(int_rise, int_fall, ext_rise,
           ext_fall : time);
```

```
   PORT( a: IN t_wlogic;
         b: OUT t_wlogic);
END inv;

ARCHITECTURE inv_gen1 OF inv IS
BEGIN
   inv_proc : PROCESS(a)
      VARIABLE state : t_wlogic;
   BEGIN
      state := NOT(a);
      IF state = '1' THEN
         b <= state AFTER (int_rise + ext_rise);
      ELSIF state = '0' THEN
         b <= state AFTER (int_fall + ext_fall);
      ELSE
         b <= state AFTER (int_fall + ext_fall);
      END IF;
   END PROCESS inv_proc;
END inv_gen1;
----------------------------------------------------
USE STD.std_logic.ALL;
USE STD.std_ttl.ALL;
ENTITY and3 IS
   GENERIC(int_rise, int_fall, ext_rise,
           ext_fall : time);
   PORT( a1, a2, a3: IN t_wlogic;
         o1: OUT t_wlogic);
END and3;

ARCHITECTURE and3_gen1 OF and3 IS
BEGIN
   and3_proc : PROCESS(a1, a2, a3)
      VARIABLE state : t_wlogic;
   BEGIN
      state := a1 AND a2 AND a3;

      IF state = '1' THEN
         o1 <= state AFTER (int_rise + ext_rise);
      ELSIF state = '0' THEN
         o1 <= state AFTER (int_fall + ext_fall);
      ELSE
         o1 <= state AFTER (int_fall + ext_fall);
```

```
        END IF;

    END PROCESS and3_proc;
  END and3_gen1;
```

There are no local configurations specified at this level in the design because this has nearly the same effect of mapping the generic values in the architecture. Instead a full configuration for entity *decode* will be specified that will map the generics at all levels of the decoder. The entity and architecture for the decoder, as shown below, are very similar to the original example used earlier.

```
USE STD.std_logic.ALL;
ENTITY decode IS
  PORT( a, b, en : IN t_wlogic;
        q0, q1, q2, q3 : OUT t_wlogic);
END decode;

ARCHITECTURE structural OF decode IS
  COMPONENT inv
    PORT( a : IN t_wlogic;
          b : OUT t_wlogic);
  END COMPONENT;

  COMPONENT and3
    PORT( a1, a2, a3 : IN t_wlogic;
          o1 : OUT t_wlogic);
  END COMPONENT;

  SIGNAL nota, notb : t_wlogic;
BEGIN
  I1 : inv
    PORT MAP( a, nota);

  I2 : inv
    PORT MAP( b, notb);

  AN1 : and3
    PORT MAP( nota, en, notb, q0);

  AN2 : and3
    PORT MAP( a, en, notb, q1);
```

```
    AN3 : and3
      PORT MAP( nota, en, b, q2);

    AN4 : and3
      PORT MAP( a, en, b, q3);
  END structural;
```

Notice that the component declarations for components *inv* and *and3* in the architecture declaration section do not contain the generics declared in the entity declarations for entities *inv* and *and3*. Since the generics are not being mapped in the architecture there is no need to declare the generics for the components in the architecture.

The configuration to bind all of these parts together into an executable model is shown below:

```
CONFIGURATION decode_gen1_con OF decode IS
  FOR structural
    FOR I1 : inv USE ENTITY WORK.inv(inv_gen1)
      GENERIC MAP( int_rise => 1.2 ns,
                   int_fall => 1.7 ns,
                   ext_rise => 2.6 ns,
                   ext_fall => 2.5 ns);
    END FOR;

    FOR I2 : inv USE ENTITY WORK.inv(inv_gen1)
      GENERIC MAP( int_rise => 1.3 ns,
                   int_fall => 1.4 ns,
                   ext_rise => 2.8 ns,
                   ext_fall => 2.9 ns);
    END FOR;

    FOR AN1 : and3 USE ENTITY
                  WORK.and3(and3_gen1)
      GENERIC MAP( int_rise => 2.2 ns,
                   int_fall => 2.7 ns,
                   ext_rise => 3.6 ns,
                   ext_fall => 3.5 ns);
    END FOR;

    FOR AN2 : and3 USE ENTITY
                  WORK.and3(and3_gen1)
      GENERIC MAP( int_rise => 2.2 ns,
```

```
                          int_fall => 2.7 ns,
                          ext_rise => 3.1 ns,
                          ext_fall => 3.2 ns);
      END FOR;

      FOR AN3 : and3 USE ENTITY
                        WORK.and3(and3_gen1)
        GENERIC MAP( int_rise => 2.2 ns,
                          int_fall => 2.7 ns,
                          ext_rise => 3.3 ns,
                          ext_fall => 3.4 ns);
      END FOR;

      FOR AN4 : and3 USE ENTITY
                        WORK.and3(and3_gen1)
        GENERIC MAP( int_rise => 2.2 ns,
                         int_fall => 2.7 ns,
                         ext_rise => 3.0 ns,
                         ext_fall => 3.1 ns);
      END FOR;
    END FOR;
  END decode_gen1_con;
```

Each component instance is configured to the correct entity and architecture, and the generics of the entity are mapped with a generic map clause. Using this type of configuration allows each instance to have unique delay characteristics. Of course, the generics passed into the device can represent any type of data that the designer wishes, but typically the generics are used to represent delay information.

The power of this type of configuration is realized when the delay values are updated. For instance, in the ASIC example, the estimated delays are included in the configuration initially, but after the ASIC device has been through the physical layout process, the actual delay information can be determined. This information can be fed back into the configuration so that the configuration has the actual delay information calculated from the layout tool. To build a new simulatable device, including the new delay information, requires only a recompile of the configuration. The entities and architectures do not need to be recompiled.

If the delay information was included in the architecture for the device, then a lot more of the model would need to be recompiled in order to build the simulatable entity. All of the architectures that included the generics would need to be recompiled, and so would the configuration for the entity. A lot of extra code would be recompiled unneccessarily.

The information in this section on generics can be summarized by the charts shown in Figures 7-4 and 7-5 (these charts were originally created by Paul Krol).

These charts shows the effect of the declarations and mapping of generics on the values actually obtained in the model. The first four columns of Figure 7-4 describe where a particular generic, G, can be declared, and mapped to a value. The next column describes the error/warning number returned from a particular combination of declaration and mapping. The next two columns describe the values obtained by the generic, G, and any other generics for the entity for a particular declaration and mapping combination. At the bottom of Figure 7-4 and in Figure 7-5 are the tables of translations used to translate the character values used to the appropriate action taken.

7.7 Board-Socket-Chip Analogy

A good analogy for describing how entity declarations, architectures, component declarations, and configuration specifications all interact is the board-socket-chip analogy (this analogy was originally presented to the author by Dr. Alec Stanculescu). In this analogy the architecture of the top -level entity represents the board being modeled. The component instance represents a socket on the board, and the lower-level entity being instantiated in the architecture represents the chip.

This analogy helps describe how the ports and generics are mapped at each level. At the board (architecture) level component socket pins are interconnected with signals. The chip pins are then connected to socket pins when the chip is plugged into the socket. An example of how this works is shown below:

```
USE STD.std_logic.ALL;
ENTITY board IS
   GENERIC (qdelay, qbdelay : time);
   PORT( clk, reset, data_in : IN t_wlogic;
```

Declaration		Mapping		Error/ Warning	Generic Values	
Entity	Component	Instance	Config- uration		Same	Other
D	D	A			I	E
D	N	A			I	E
D	N		A		C	E
N	D	A			I	M
N	D		A		C	M
X	D/N		A	1		
X	D/N			2		
X	D/N	A		2		
D/N	X	A		3		
D/N	X		A		C	E
		A	A	4		
		X	X	5		

Declarations/Mapping

D → Declared, with default value

N → Declared, with no default value

X → Not declared

A → Actual mapped

Figure 7-4

Errors / Warnings

1 → Can only map generic in configuration if declared in the entity

2 → Generic declared in component but not in entity, hence is not used

3 → Can only map generic in component instance if declared in component declarations

4 → Can't map a generic in the component instance and the configuration

5 → Must map at least one generic to get the default value for other generics

Values Assigned To Generics

E → Default taken from entity

M → Default taken from configuration

I → Actual taken from component instance

C → Actual taken from configuration

Figure 7-5

```
         data_out : OUT t_wlogic);
END board;

ARCHITECTURE structural OF board IS
   COMPONENT dff
      GENERIC( g1, g2 : time);
      PORT( p1, p2, p3, p4 : IN t_wlogic;
            p5, p6 : OUT t_wlogic);
   END COMPONENT;

   SIGNAL ground : t_wlogic := F1;
   SIGNAL int1, nc : t_wlogic;
BEGIN
   U1 : dff
      GENERIC MAP( g1 => qdelay,
                   g2 => qbdelay)
      PORT MAP( p1 => clk,
                p2 => data_in,
```

```
                    p3 => reset,
                    p4 => ground,
                    p5 => int1,
                    p6 => nc);


    U2 : dff
      GENERIC MAP( g1 => qdelay,
                   g2 => qbdelay)
      PORT MAP( p1 => clk,
                p2 => int1,
                p3 => reset,
                p4 => ground,
                p5 => data_out,
                p6 => nc);
END structural;
```

The entity and architecture shown are a simple 2-bit shift register made from two D flip-flop (DFF) component instantiations. This example, though relatively simple, will show how ports and generics are mapped at different levels.

The component instance for component DFF in the architecture statement part acts like a *socket* in the architecture for the board. When a component instance is placed in the architecture, signals are used to connect the component to the board, which is the architecture. The actual chip is not connected to the socket until a configuration is specified for the board entity. If all of the names of the socket ports and generics match the names of the actual entity being used, then no mapping is needed. The default mapping will connect the chip to the socket. If the names are different, or the number of ports are not the same, for the component instantiation and the actual entity, then a mapping between the socket (component instantiation) and the chip (actual entity) is needed.

The actual chip to be mapped is described by the entity and architecture shown below:

```
USE STD.std_logic.ALL;
USE STD.std_ttl.ALL;
ENTITY dff IS
  GENERIC( q_out, qb_out : time);
```

```
    PORT( preset, clear, din,
          clock : IN t_wlogic;
          q, qb : OUT t_wlogic);
END dff;

ARCHITECTURE behave OF dff IS
BEGIN
   dff_proc : PROCESS(preset, clear, clock)
      VARIABLE int_q : t_wlogic;
   BEGIN
      IF preset = '0' and clear = '0' THEN
         IF (clock'EVENT) AND (clock = '1') THEN
            int_q := din;
         END IF;

      ELSIF preset = '1' AND clear = '0' THEN
         int_q := f_ttl('1');

      ELSIF clear = '1' AND preset = '0' THEN
         int_q := f_ttl('0');

      ELSE
         int_q := f_ttl('X');

      END IF;

      q <= int_q after q_out;

      int_q := not(int_q);
      qb <= int_q after qb_out;

   END PROCESS dff_proc;
END behave;
```

The names of the ports and generics are completely different than the component declaration; therefore mapping is required. A configuration that will place the actual chip in the socket (map the ports and generics) is shown below:

```
CONFIGURATION board_con OF board IS
   FOR structural
      FOR U1,U2: dff USE WORK.dff(behave)
         GENERIC MAP( q_out => g1, qb_out => g2)
```

```
            PORT MAP( preset => ground, clear => p3,
                      din => p2, clock => p1,
                      q => p5, qb => p6);
        END FOR;
    END FOR;
END board_con;
```

7.8 Block Configurations

When an architecture contains block statements, the configuration must reflect this fact (block statements are discussed in Chapter 2). Blocks act like another level of hierarchy between the containing architecture and any components being configured. The configuration must specify which block of a configuration is being configured when the architecture is being configured.

Below is shown an architecture fragment that contains three blocks:

```
USE STD.std_logic.ALL;
ENTITY cpu IS
   PORT( clock : IN t_wlogic;
         addr  : OUT t_wlogic_vector(0 to 3);
         data  : INOUT t_wlogic_vector(0 to 3);
         interrupt : IN t_wlogic;
         reset : IN t_wlogic);
END cpu;

ARCHITECTURE fragment OF cpu IS
   COMPONENT int_reg
      PORT( data : IN t_wlogic;
            regclock : IN t_wlogic;
            data_out : OUT t_wlogic);
   END COMPONENT;

   COMPONENT alu
      PORT( a, b : IN t_wlogic;
            c, carry : OUT t_wlogic);
   END COMPONENT;
   SIGNAL a, c, carry : t_wlogic_vector(0 TO 3);
BEGIN
   reg_array : BLOCK
   BEGIN
      R1 : int_reg
```

```
         PORT MAP( data(0), clock,
                   data(0));

      R2 : int_reg
         PORT MAP( data(1), clock,
                   data(1));
      R3 : int_reg
         PORT MAP( data(2), clock,
                   data(2));

      R4 : int_reg
         PORT MAP( data(3), clock,
                   data(3));

   END BLOCK reg_array;

   shifter : BLOCK
   BEGIN
      A1 : alu
         PORT MAP( a(0), data(0), c(0),
            carry(0));

      A2 : alu
         PORT MAP( a(1), data(1), c(1),
            carry(1));

      A3 : alu
         PORT MAP( a(2), data(2), c(2),
            carry(2));

      A4 : alu
         PORT MAP( a(3), data(3), c(3),
            carry(3));

      shift_reg : BLOCK
      BEGIN
         R1 : int_reg
            PORT MAP( data, shft_clk, data_out);

      END BLOCK shift_reg;
   END BLOCK shifter;
END fragment;
```

The architecture consists of three blocks, which each contain component instantiations. The first block contains four *int_reg* components, and the second contains an *alu* component, plus another BLOCK statement. The last block contains a single *int_reg* component.

The configuration for this architecture must take into account the fact that BLOCK statements exist in the architecture. A simple configuration for the architecture is shown below:

```
CONFIGURATION cpu_con OF cpu IS
   FOR fragment
      FOR reg_array
         FOR ALL: int_reg USE CONFIGURATION
                                  WORK.int_reg_con;
         END FOR;
      END FOR;
      FOR shifter
         FOR A1  : alu USE CONFIGURATION
                                  WORK.alu_con;
         END FOR;
         FOR shift_reg
            FOR R1  : int_reg USE CONFIGURATION
                                  WORK.int_reg_con;
            END FOR;
         END FOR;
      END FOR;
   END FOR;
END cpu_con;
```

In the configuration *cpu_con* of entity *cpu*, architecture *fragment* will be used for the entity. Inside of block *reg_array*, all (R1-R4) of the *int_reg* components will use configuration *int_reg_con*. In block *shifter*, the *alu* component (A1) will use configuration *alu_con*. For block *shift_reg* inside of block *shifter*, the *int_reg* component will use configuration *int_reg_con*.

7.9 Architecture Configurations

The last type of configuration that will be discussed is the architecture configuration. This configuration exists in the architecture declarative region and specifies the configurations of parts used in the architecture.

If this type of configuration is used, a separate configuration declaration is not needed to configure the components used in the architecture.

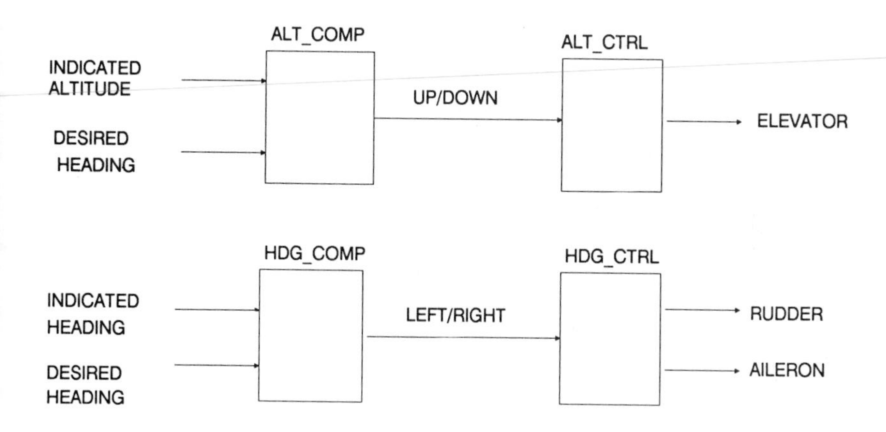

Figure 7-6

The example configuration shown will be for a very high level description of an autopilot. The autopilot block diagram is shown in Figure 7-6. An example of this type of configuration is shown below:

```
PACKAGE ap IS
  TYPE alt IS INTEGER RANGE 0 TO 50000;
  TYPE hdg IS INTEGER RANGE 0 TO 359;
  TYPE vdir IS INTEGER RANGE 0 TO 9;
  TYPE hdir IS INTEGER RANGE 0 TO 9;
  TYPE control IS INTEGER RANGE 0 TO 9;
END ap;

USE WORK.ap.ALL;
ENTITY autopilot IS
  PORT( altitude : IN alt;
        altitude_set : IN alt;
        heading : IN hdg;
        heading_set : IN hdg;
        rudder : OUT control;
```

```
        aileron : OUT control;
        elevator : OUT control);
END autopilot;

ARCHITECTURE block_level OF autopilot IS
  COMPONENT alt_compare
    PORT( alt_ref : IN alt;
          alt_ind : IN alt;
          up_down : OUT vdir);
  END COMPONENT;

  COMPONENT hdg_compare
    PORT( hdg_ref : IN hdg;
          hdg_ind : IN hdg;
          left_right : OUT hdir);
  END COMPONENT;

  COMPONENT hdg_ctrl
    PORT( left_right : IN hdir;
          rdr : OUT control;
          alrn : OUT control);
  END COMPONENT;

  COMPONENT alt_ctrl
    PORT( up_down : IN vdir;
          elevator : OUT control);
  END COMPONENT;

  SIGNAL up_down : vdir;
  SIGNAL left_right : hdir;

  FOR M1 : alt_compare USE CONFIGURATION
    WORK.alt_comp_con;

  FOR M2 : hdg_compare USE CONFIGURATION
    WORK.hdg_comp_con;

  FOR M3 : hdg_ctrl USE ENTITY
    WORK.hdg_ctrl(behave);

  FOR M4 : alt_ctrl USE ENTITY
    WORK.alt_ctrl(behave);
```

```
BEGIN
   M1 : alt_compare
      PORT MAP( alt_ref => altitude,
                alt_ind => alt_set,
                up_down => up_down);

   M2 : hdg_compare
      PORT MAP( hdg_ref => heading,
                hdg_ind => hdg_set,
                left_right => left_right);

   M3 : hdg_ctrl
      PORT MAP( left_right => left_right,
                rdr => rudder,
                alrn => aileron);

   M4 : alt_ctrl
      PORT MAP( up_down => up_down,
                elevator => elevator);

END block_level;
```

This model is a top-level description of an autopilot. There are four instantiated components that provide the necessary functionality of the autopilot. This model demonstrates how component instantiations can be configured in the architecture declaration section of an architecture. Notice that after the component declarations in the architecture declaration section of architecture *block_level*, there are four statements similar to the one shown below:

```
FOR M1 : alt_compare USE CONFIGURATION
   WORK.alt_comp_con;
```

These statements allow the designer to specify either the configuration or the entity-architecture pair to use for a particular component type. This type of configuration does not provide the same flexibility to the designer as the separate configuration declaration, but it is useful for small designs.

Configurations are a useful tool for managing large designs. With proper use of configurations a top-down design approach can be implemented that allows all levels of description of the design to be used for the most efficient model needed at any point in the design process.

The reader has now been introduced to the basic features of VHDL. In the next chapter we will examine some of the more esoteric but useful features that exist in VHDL.

Chapter

8

Advanced Topics

In this chapter some of the more esoteric features of VHDL will be discussed. Some of the features may be useful for certain types of designs, and not for others. Typical usage examples will be presented to show how these features might be taken advantage of.

Some of the features discussed will be overloading, qualified expressions, user-defined attributes, generate statements, and TextIO. All of these features provide the user with an advanced environment with which to do modeling.

8.1 Overloading

Overloading allows the designer to write much more readable code. An object is overloaded when the same object name exists for multiple subprograms or type values. The VHDL compiler will select the appropriate object to use in each instance.

In VHDL a number of types of overloading are possible. Subprograms can be overloaded, operators can be overloaded, and enumeration types can be overloaded. Overloading subprograms allows subprograms to operate on objects of different types. Overloading an operator allows the operator to perform the same operation on multiple types. Overloading frees the designer from the necessity of generating countless unique names for subprograms that do virtually the same operation. The result of using overloaded subprograms and operators is models that are easier to read and maintain.

8.1.1 Subprogram Overloading

Subprogram overloading allows the designer to write multiple subprograms with the same name, but the number of arguments, the type of arguments, and return value (if any) can be different. The VHDL compiler, at compile time, will select the subprogram that matches the subprogram call. If no subprogram matches the call, an error is generated.

The example below illustrates how a subprogram can be overloaded by the argument type.

```
USE STD.std_logic.ALL;
PACKAGE p_shift IS
   TYPE s_int IS RANGE 0 TO 255;
   TYPE s_array IS ARRAY(0 TO 7) OF t_wlogic;

   FUNCTION shiftr( a : s_array) return s_array;
   FUNCTION shiftr( a : s_int) return s_int;
END p_shift;

PACKAGE BODY p_shift IS
   FUNCTION shiftr( a : s_array)
                              return s_array IS
      VARIABLE result : s_array;
   BEGIN
      FOR i IN a'RANGE LOOP
         IF i = a'HIGH THEN
            result(i) := F0;
         ELSE
            result(i) := a(i + 1);
         END IF;
      END LOOP;

      RETURN result;
   END shiftr;
```

```
    FUNCTION shiftr( a : s_int) return s_int IS
    BEGIN
      RETURN (a/2);
    END shiftr;
  END p_shift;
```

The package *p_shift* contains two functions both named *shiftr*. Both functions provide a right-shift capability, but each function operates on a specific type. One function works only with type *s_int*, and the other works only with type *s_array*. The compiler will pick the appropriate function, based on the calling argument(s) and return argument.

In the example below different types of function calls are shown, and the results obtained with each call.

```
USE WORK.p_shift.ALL;
ENTITY shift_example IS
END shift_example;

ARCHITECTURE test OF shift_example IS
  SIGNAL int_signal : s_int;
  SIGNAL array_signal : s_array;
BEGIN
  -- picks function that works with s_int type
  int_signal <= shiftr(int_signal);

  -- picks function that works with
  -- s_array type
  array_signal <= shiftr(array_signal);

  -- produces error because no function
  -- will match
  array_signal <= shiftr(int_signal);
END test;
```

The architecture *test* contains three calls to function *shiftr*. The first calls *shiftr* with an argument type of *s_int*, and a return type of *s_int*. This call will use the second function described in package body *p_shift*, the function with input arguments, and return type of *s_int*.

The second call to *shiftr* uses the array type *s_array*, and therefore will pick the first function defined in package *p_shift*. Both the input argument(s) type(s) and return type must match in order for the function to match the call.

The third call to function *shiftr* shows an example of a call where the input argument matches the *s_int* type function, but the return type of the function does not match the target signal. With the functions currently described in package *p_shift,* no function matches exactly, and therefore the compilation of the third line will produce an error.

To make the third call legal, all that is needed is to define a function that matches the types of the third call. An example of the function declaration is shown below. The function body for this function is left as an exercise for the reader.

```
FUNCTION shiftr( a : s_int) return s_array;
```

8.1.1.1 Overloading Subprogram Argument Types

In order to overload argument types, the base type of the subprogram parameters or return value must differ. For example, base types do not differ when two subtypes are of the same type. Two functions that try to overload these subtypes will produce a compile error. An example is shown below:

```
PACKAGE type_error IS
   SUBTYPE log4 IS BIT_VECTOR( 0 TO 3);
   SUBTYPE log8 IS BIT_VECTOR( 0 TO 7);

   -- this function is Ok
   FUNCTION not( a : log4) return integer;

   -- this function declaration will cause an
   -- error
   FUNCTION not( a : log8) return integer;

END type_error;
```

This package declares two subtypes, *log4* and *log8*, of the unconstrained BIT_VECTOR type. Two functions named *not* are then declared using these subtypes. The first function declaration is legal, but the second function declaration will cause an error. The error is that two functions have been declared for the same base type. The two types *log4* and *log8* are not distinct, because they both belong to the same base type.

All of the examples shown so far have been overloading of functions. Overloading of procedures works in the same manner.

8.1.1.2 Subprogram Parameter Overloading

Two or more subprograms with the same name can have a different number of parameters. The types of the parameters could be the same, but the number of parameters can be different. This is shown by the example below:

```
USE STD.std_logic.ALL;
PACKAGE p_addr_convert IS
   FUNCTION convert_addr(a0, a1 : t_wlogic)
      return integer;

   FUNCTION convert_addr(a0, a1, a2 : t_wlogic)
      return integer;

   FUNCTION convert_addr(a0, a1, a2,
      a3 : t_wlogic) return integer;

END p_addr_convert;

PACKAGE BODY p_addr_convert IS
   FUNCTION convert_addr(a0, a1 : t_wlogic)
               RETURN INTEGER IS
      VARIABLE result : INTEGER := 0;
   BEGIN
      IF (a0 = '1') THEN
         result := result + 1;
      END IF;

      IF (a1 = '1') THEN
         result := result + 2;
      END IF;

      RETURN result;
   END convert_addr;

   FUNCTION convert_addr(a0, a1, a2 : t_wlogic)
               RETURN INTEGER IS
```

```
      VARIABLE result : INTEGER := 0;
    BEGIN

      result := convert_addr(a0, a1);

      IF (a2 = '1') THEN
        result := result + 4;
      END IF;
      RETURN result;
    END convert_addr;

    FUNCTION convert_addr(a0, a1, a2,
              a3 : t_wlogic) RETURN INTEGER IS
      VARIABLE result : INTEGER := 0;
    BEGIN

      result := convert_addr(a0, a1, a2);

      IF (a3 = '1') THEN
        result := result + 8;
      END IF;
      RETURN result;
    END convert_addr;
  END p_addr_convert;
```

This package declares three functions that convert 2, 3, or 4 input bits into integer representation. Each function is named the same, but the appropriate function will be called depending on the number of input arguments that are passed to the function. If 2 bits are passed to the function, then the function with two arguments is called. If 3 bits are passed, the function with three arguments is called, and so on.

An example using these functions is shown below:

```
USE STD.std_logic.ALL;
USE WORK.p_addr_convert.ALL;
ENTITY test IS
  PORT(i0, i1, i2, i3 : in t_wlogic);
END test;

ARCHITECTURE test1 OF test IS
  SIGNAL int1, int2, int3 : INTEGER;
BEGIN
```

```
      -- uses first function
      int1 <= convert_addr(i0, i1);

      -- uses second function
      int2 <= convert_addr(i0, i1, i2);

      -- uses third function
      int3 <= convert_addr(i0, i1, i2, i3);
   END test1;
```

The first call to the *convert_addr* function has only two arguments in the argument list, and therefore the first function in package *p_addr_convert* will be used. The second call has three arguments in its argument list, and will call the second function. The last call matches the third function from package *p_addr_convert*.

8.1.2 Overloading Operators

One of the most useful applications of overloading is the overloading of operators. The need for overloading operators arises because the operators supplied in VHDL only work with specific types. For instance, the + operator only works with integer, real, and physical types, while the & (concatenation) operator only works with array types. If a designer wants to use a particular operator on a user-defined type, then the operator must be overloaded to handle the user type. A complete listing of the operators and the types supported by them can be found in Chapter 7 of the LRM.

An example of a typical overloaded operator is the + operator. The + operator is defined for the numeric types, but if the designer wants to add two BIT_VECTOR objects, the + operator will not work. The designer must write a function that overloads the operator to accomplish this operation. The package below shows an overloaded function for operator + that will allow addition of two objects of BIT_VECTOR types.

```
PACKAGE math IS
   FUNCTION "+"( l,r : BIT_VECTOR)
      RETURN INTEGER;
END math;

PACKAGE BODY math IS
```

```
  FUNCTION vector_to_int( S : BIT_VECTOR)
             RETURN INTEGER IS
    VARIABLE result : INTEGER := 0;
    VARIABLE prod : INTEGER:= 1;
  BEGIN
    FOR i IN s'RANGE LOOP
      IF s(i) = '1' THEN
         result := result + prod;
      END IF;
      prod := prod * 2;
    END LOOP;

    RETURN result;
  END vector_to_int;

  FUNCTION "+"(l,r : BIT_VECTOR)
             RETURN INTEGER IS
  BEGIN
    RETURN ( vector_to_int(l) +
      vector_to_int(r));
  END;
END math;
```

Whenever the + operator is used in an expression, the compiler will call the + operator function that matches the types of the operands. When the operands are of type INTEGER, the built-in + operator function will be called. If the operands are of type BIT_VECTOR, then the function from package *math* will be called. The example below shows uses for both functions:

```
USE WORK.math.ALL;
ENTITY adder IS
  PORT( a, b : IN BIT_VECTOR(0 TO 7);
        c : IN INTEGER;
        dout : OUT INTEGER);
END adder;

ARCHITECTURE test OF adder IS
  SIGNAL internal : INTEGER;
BEGIN
  internal <= a + b;
  dout <= c + internal;
END test;
```

This example illustrates how overloading can be used to make very readable models. The value assigned to signal *internal* is the sum of inputs *a* and *b*. Since *a* and *b* are of type BIT_VECTOR, the overloaded operator function that has two BIT_VECTOR arguments is called. This function will add the values of *a* and *b* together and return an integer value to be assigned to signal *internal*.

The second addition uses the standard built-in addition function that is standard in VHDL because both operands are of type INTEGER. This model could have been written as shown below, but would still function in the same manner.

```
PACKAGE math IS
   FUNCTION addvec( l,r : bit_vector)
      RETURN INTEGER;
END math;

PACKAGE BODY math IS
   FUNCTION vector_to_int( S : bit_vector)
                  RETURN INTEGER IS
      VARIABLE result : INTEGER := 0;
      VARIABLE prod : INTEGER:= 1;
   BEGIN
      FOR i IN s'RANGE LOOP
         IF s(i) = '1' THEN
            result := result + prod;
         END IF;
         prod := prod * 2;
      END LOOP;
      RETURN result;
   END vector_to_int;

   FUNCTION addvec(l,r : bit_vector)
                  RETURN INTEGER IS
   BEGIN
      RETURN ( vector_to_int(l) +
         vector_to_int(r));
   END;
END math;

USE WORK.math.ALL;
ENTITY adder IS
```

```
    PORT( a, b : IN BIT_VECTOR(0 TO 7);
          c : IN INTEGER;
          dout : OUT INTEGER);
END adder;

ARCHITECTURE test2 OF adder IS
    SIGNAL internal : INTEGER;
BEGIN
    internal <= addvec(a,b);
    dout <= c + internal;
END test2;
```

In this example a function called *advec* is used to add *a* and *b*. Both coding styles give exactly the same results, but the first example using the overloaded + operator is much more readable, and easier to maintain. If another person besides the designer of a model takes over the maintenance of the model, it will be much easier for the new person to understand the model if overloading was used.

8.1.2.1 Operator Argument Type Overloading

Arguments to overloaded operator functions do not have to be of the same type, as the previous two examples have shown. The parameters to an overloaded operator function can be of any type. In some cases it is preferrable to write two functions so that the order of the arguments is not important.

Let's examine the functions for an overloaded logical operator that mixes signals of type BIT, and signals of a nine-state value system.

```
PACKAGE p_logic_pack IS
    TYPE t_nine_val IS (Z0, Z1, ZX,
                        R0, R1, RX,
                        F0, F1, FX);

    FUNCTION "AND"( l, r : t_nine_val)
        RETURN BIT;

    FUNCTION "AND"( l : BIT; r : t_nine_val)
        RETURN BIT;

    FUNCTION "AND"( l : t_nine_val; r : BIT)
        RETURN BIT;
```

```
END p_logic_pack;

PACKAGE BODY p_logic_pack IS
   FUNCTION nine_val_2_bit( t : IN t_nine_val)
                     RETURN BIT IS
      TYPE t_nine_val_conv IS
               ARRAY(t_nine_val) OF BIT;
      CONSTANT nine_2_bit : t_nine_val_conv :=
         ('0',    -- Z0
          '1',    -- Z1
          '1',    -- ZX
          '0',    -- R0
          '1',    -- R1
          '1',    -- RX
          '0',    -- F0
          '1',    -- F1
          '1');   -- FX
   BEGIN
      RETURN nine_2_bit(t);
   END nine_val_2_bit;

   FUNCTION "AND"(l,r : t_nine_val)
                            RETURN BIT IS
   BEGIN
      RETURN (nine_val_2_bit(l)
         AND nine_val_2_bit(r));
   END;

   FUNCTION "AND"(l :BIT; r : t_nine_val)
                              RETURN BIT IS
   BEGIN
      RETURN ( l AND nine_val_2_bit(r));
   END;

   FUNCTION "AND"(l : t_nine_val; r : BIT)
                              RETURN BIT IS
   BEGIN
      RETURN (nine_val_2_bit(l) AND r);
   END;
END p_logic_pack;
```

The package *p_logic_pack* declares three overloaded functions for the AND operator. In one function, both input types are type *t_nine_val*. In the other two functions, only one input is type *t_nine_val*, and the other input is type BIT. All functions return a result of type BIT. Notice that to overload the AND operator, the syntax is the same as overloading the + operator from the previous example.

When the AND operator is used in a model, the appropriate function will be called based on the types of the operands. In the code fragments shown below, we can see the differences.

```
SIGNAL a, b : t_nine_val;
SIGNAL c,e  : bit;

e <= a AND b;
-- calls first function

e <= a AND c;
-- calls third function

e <= c AND b;
-- calls second function
```

By having three functions called AND, we do not need to worry about which side of the operator an expression resides on. All of the possible combinations of operator order will be covered with three functions, because the function for two inputs of type BIT are built in.

8.2 Qualified Expressions

One of the side effects of overloading is that multiple functions or procedures may match in a particular instance because the types are ambiguous. In order for the compiler to figure out which subprogram to use, a qualified expression may be required. A qualified expression states the exact type that the expression should attain. For instance, when evaluating an expression containing a mixture of overloaded subprograms and constant values, the designer may need to qualify an expression to produce correct results. An example of such a situation is shown below:

```
PACKAGE p_qual IS
  TYPE int_vector IS ARRAY(NATURAL RANGE <>)
    OF INTEGER;
```

```
    FUNCTION average( a : int_vector)
      RETURN INTEGER;

    FUNCTION average( a : int_vector)
      RETURN REAL;

  END p_qual;

  USE WORK.p_qual.ALL;
  ENTITY normalize IS
    PORT( factor : IN REAL;
          points : IN int_vector;
          result : OUT REAL);
  END normalize;

  ARCHITECTURE qual_exp OF normalize IS
  BEGIN
    result <= REAL'(average(points)) * factor;
  END qual_exp;
```

Package *p_qual* defines two overloaded functions named *average* and an unconstrained type, *int_vector*. The package body is left as an exercise for the reader.

Architecture *qual_exp* has a single concurrent signal assignment statement that calls function *average*. Since there are two functions named *average*, there are two possible functions that can be used by this call. In order to clarify which function to use, the expression has been qualified to return a REAL type. The keyword REAL followed by a ' mark specifies that the expression inside the parentheses will return a type REAL.

The expression was qualified to make sure that the *average* function returning a REAL number was called instead of the *average* function that returns an INTEGER. In this example the expression required a qualified expression to allow the architecture to compile. The compiler will not make any random guesses about which function to use. The designer must specify exactly which one to use in cases where more than one function can match, otherwise an error is generated.

Another use for a qualified expression is to build the source value for an assignment statement. Based on the type of the signal assignment target the source value can be built. An example is shown below:

```
PACKAGE p_qual_2 IS
   TYPE vector8 IS ARRAY( 0 TO 7) OF BIT;
END p_qual_2;

USE WORK.p_qual_2.ALL;
ENTITY latch IS
   PORT( reset, clock : IN BIT;
         data_in : IN vector8;
         data_out : OUT vector8);
END latch;

ARCHITECTURE behave OF latch IS
BEGIN
   PROCESS(clock)
   BEGIN
      IF (clock = '1') THEN
         IF (reset = '1') THEN
            data_out <= vector8'(others => '0');
         ELSE
            data_out <= data_in;
         END IF;
      END IF;
   END PROCESS;
END behave;
```

This example is an 8-bit transparent latch, with a reset line to set the latch to zero. When the *clock* input is a '1' value, the latch is transparent, and input values are reflected on the output. When the *clock* input is '0', the *data_in* value is latched. When *reset* is a '1' value while *clock* input is a '1', the latch will be reset. This is accomplished by assigning all '0's to *data_out*. One method to assign all '0's to *data_out* is to use an aggregate assignment. Since *data_out* is 8 bits, the aggregate assignment shown below will set *data_out* to all '0's.

```
data_out <= ('0', '0', '0', '0',
             '0', '0', '0', '0');
```

This aggregate will work fine unless the type of *data_out* changes. If the type of output *data_out* was suddenly changed to 16 bits instead of 8, the aggregate could no longer be used.

Another method to accomplish the assignment to output *data_out* is to use a qualified expression. The assignment to *data_out* when *reset* = *'1'* in the above example shows how this might be done. The expression

```
(others => '0')
```

can be qualified with the type of the target signal (*data_out*). This allows the compiler to determine how large the target signal is and how large to make the source being assigned to the signal. Now whenever the target signal type is changed, the source will change to match.

8.3 User-Defined Attributes

VHDL user-defined attributes are a mechanism for attaching data to VHDL objects. The data attached can be used during simulation or by another tool that reads the VHDL description. Data such as the disk file name of the model, loading information, driving capability, resistance, capacitance, physical location, etc. can be attached to objects. The type and value of the data is completely user-definable. The value once specified is constant throughout the simulation.

User-defined attributes can behave similar to entity generic values, with one exception. Generics are only legal on entities, but user-defined attributes can be assigned to the following list of objects.

- Entity
- Architecture
- Configuration
- Procedure
- Function
- Package
- Type and Subtype
- Constant

- Signal
- Variable
- Component
- Label

To see how user-defined attributes operate, let's examine the following description:

```
PACKAGE p_attr IS
  TYPE t_package_type IS ( leadless,
                           pin_grid,
                           dip);

  ATTRIBUTE package_type : t_package_type;
  ATTRIBUTE location : INTEGER;

END p_attr;

USE WORK.p_attr.ALL;
ENTITY board IS
  PORT(
         .
         .
         .
             );
END board;

ARCHITECTURE cpu_board OF board IS
  COMPONENT mc68040
    GENERIC(  ...... );
    PORT(
           .
           .
           .
               );
  END COMPONENT;
  SIGNAL a : INTEGER;
  SIGNAL b : t_package_type;

  ATTRIBUTE package_type OF mc68040 :
       COMPONENT IS pin_grid;
```

```
    ATTRIBUTE location OF mc68040 :
         COMPONENT IS 20;
BEGIN
    a <= mc68040'location;
    -- returns 20

    b <= mc68040'package_type;
    -- returns pin_grid

END cpu_board;
```

This is a very simple example of how attributes can be attached to objects. Much more complicated types and attributes can be created. What this example shows is a code fragment of a CPU board design in which the package type and location information are specified as attributes of the single microprocessor used in the design.

The *package_type* attribute is used to hold the kind of packaging used for the microprocessor. Attributes that have values specified do not have to be used in the simulation. Other tools such as physical layout tools or fault simulation can make use of attributes that a logic simulator cannot.

In this example a physical layout tool could read the package type information from the *package_type* attribute and, based on the value assigned to the attribute, fill in the value for the location attribute.

The package *p_attr* defines the type used for one of the attributes and contains the attribute declarations for two attributes. The attribute declarations make the name and type of the attribute visible to any object for use if needed.

In the architecture *cpu_board* of entity *board* are the attribute specifications. The attribute specification describes the attribute name to be used, the name of the object to which the attribute is attached, the object kind, and finally the value of the attribute.

To access the value of a user-defined attribute, use the same syntax for a predefined attribute. In the signal assignment statements of architecture *cpu_board*, the attribute value is retrieved by specifying the name of the object, followed by a ', and finally the attribute name.

8.4 Generate Statements

Generate statements provide the designer the capability of creating replicated structures, or selecting between multiple representations of a model. Generate statements can contain IF-THEN and looping constructs, nested to any level, that will create concurrent statements.

Typical applications include memory arrays, registers, etc. Another application is to emulate a conditional compilation mechanism found in other languages such as C.

A simple example showing the basics of generate statements is shown below:

```
USE STD.std_logic.ALL;
ENTITY shift IS
   PORT( a, clk : IN t_wlogic;
         b :  OUT t_wlogic);
END shift;

ARCHITECTURE gen_shift OF shift IS
   COMPONENT dff
      PORT( d, clk : IN t_wlogic;
              q : OUT t_wlogic);
   END COMPONENT;

   SIGNAL z : t_wlogic_vector( 0 TO 4 );
BEGIN
   z(0) <= a;

   g1 : FOR i IN 0 TO 3 GENERATE
      dffx : dff PORT MAP( z(i), clk, z(i + 1));
   END GENERATE;

   b <= z(4);
END gen_shift;
```

This example represents the behavior for a 4-bit shift register. Port *a* is the input to the shift register, and port *b* is the output. Port *clk* will shift the data from *a* to *b*.

Architecture *gen_shift* of entity *shift* contains two concurrent signal assignment statements, and one GENERATE statement. The signal assignment statements connect the internal signal *z* to input port *a* and output port *b*. The generate statement in this example uses a FOR scheme to generate four DFF components. The resultant schematic for this architecture is shown in Figure 8-1.

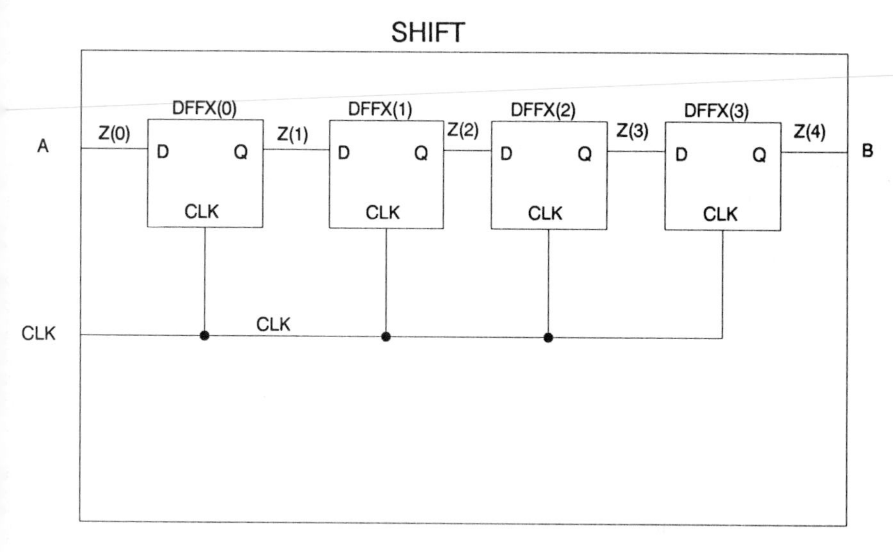

Figure 8-1

The FOR in the generate statement acts exactly like the FOR loop sequential statement in that variable *i* need not be declared previously, *i* is not visible outside the generate statement, and *i* cannot be assigned inside the generate statement.

The result of the generate statement is functionally equivalent to the following architecture:

```
ARCHITECTURE long_way_shift OF shift IS
   COMPONENT dff
      PORT( d, clk : IN t_wlogic;
            q : OUT t_wlogic);
   END COMPONENT;

   SIGNAL z : t_wlogic_vector( 0 TO 4 );
BEGIN
   z(0) <= a;
```

```
    dff1: dff PORT MAP( z(0), clk, z(1) );
    dff2: dff PORT MAP( z(1), clk, z(2) );
    dff3: dff PORT MAP( z(2), clk, z(3) );
    dff4: dff PORT MAP( z(3), clk, z(4) );

    b <= z(4);
  END long_way_shift;
```

The difference between the two architectures is that architecture *gen_shift* could be specified with generic parameters such that different size shift registers could be generated based on the value of the generic parameters. Architecture *long_way_shift* is fixed in size and cannot be changed.

8.4.1 Irregular Generate Statement

The last example showed how a regular structure could be generated, but in practice most structures are not completely regular. Most regular structures have irregularities at the edges. This is shown by Figure 8-2.

In the last example the irregularities were handled by the two concurrent signal assignment statements. Another way to handle the irregularities is shown by the example below:

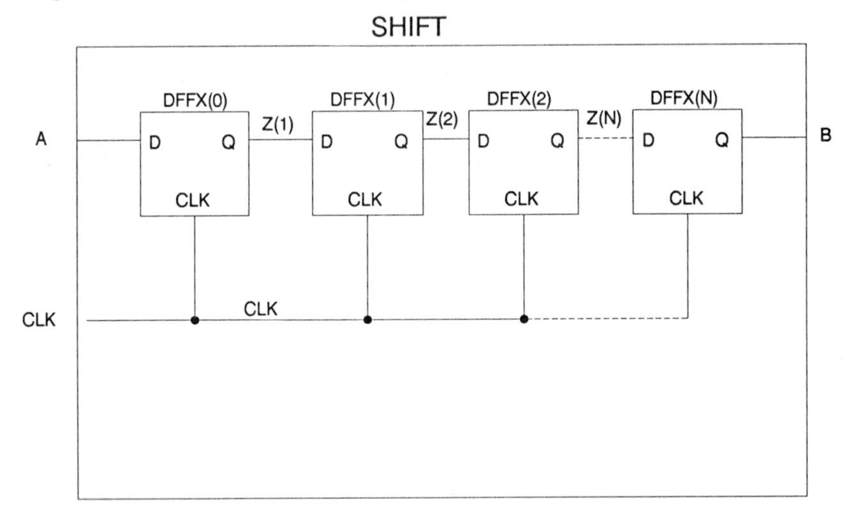

Figure 8-2

```
USE STD.std_logic.ALL;
ENTITY shift IS
   GENERIC ( len : INTEGER);
   PORT( a, clk : IN t_wlogic;
         b : OUT t_wlogic);
END shift;

ARCHITECTURE if_shift OF shift IS
   COMPONENT dff
      PORT( d, clk : IN t_wlogic;
            q : OUT t_wlogic);
   END COMPONENT;

   SIGNAL z : t_wlogic_vector( 1 TO (len -1) );
BEGIN
   g1 : FOR i IN 0 TO (len -1) GENERATE
      IF i = 0 GENERATE
         dffx : dff PORT MAP( a, clk, z(i + 1));
      END GENERATE;

      IF i = (len -1) GENERATE
         dffx : PORT MAP( z(i), clk, b );
      END GENERATE;

      IF (i > 0) AND i < (len -1) GENERATE
         dffx : PORT MAP( z(i), clk, Z(i + 1) );
      END GENERATE;

   END GENERATE;
END if_shift;
```

This example uses a shift register that has a configurable size. Generic *len* passed in specifies the length of the shift register (generic *len* must be at least 2 for the shift register to work properly). Generic *len* is used in the specification of the length of signal array *z*. This type of array is known as a generically constrained array because the size of the array is specified through one or more generics.

The FOR clause of the generate also uses generic *len* to specify the maximum number of DFF components to be generated. Notice that this generate statement uses the conditional form of the generate statement.

If the condition is true, the concurrent statements inside the generate statement are generated; otherwise nothing is generated.

The first IF-THEN condition checks for the first flip-flop in the shift register. If this is the first flip-flop, notice that the port map clause will map the input signal *a* directly to the flip-flop instead of through an intermediate signal. The same is true of the next IF-THEN condition. It checks for the last flip-flop of the shift register and maps the last output to output port *b*. Any other flip-flops in the shift register are generated by the third conditional generate statement.

Another interesting example using the conditional generate statement is shown below:

```
PACKAGE gen_cond IS
  TYPE t_checks IS ( onn, off);
END gen_cond;

USE WORK.gen_cond.ALL;
USE STD.std_logic.ALL;
ENTITY dff IS
  GENERIC( timing_checks : t_checks;
           setup, qrise, qfall,
           qbrise, qbfall : time);
  PORT( din, clk : IN t_wlogic;
        q, qb : OUT t_wlogic);
END dff;

ARCHITECTURE condition OF dff IS
BEGIN
  G1 : IF (timing_checks = onn) GENERATE
    ASSERT ( din'LAST_EVENT > setup)
      REPORT "setup violation"
      SEVERITY ERROR;
  END GENERATE;

  PROCESS(clk)
    VARIABLE int_qb : t_wlogic;
  BEGIN
    IF (clk = '1') AND (clk'EVENT) AND
          (clk'LAST_VALUE = '0') THEN

      int_qb := not din;
```

```
        q <= din AFTER
                f_delay( din, qrise, qfall);

        qb <= int_qb AFTER
                f_delay( int_qb, qbrise, qbfall);
      END IF;
    END PROCESS;
  END condition;
```

In this example, a DFF component is modeled using a generate statement to control whether or not a timing check statement is generated for the architecture. The generic, *timing_checks*, can be passed a value of *onn* or *off* (we cannot use a value of on because it is a reserved word). If the value is *onn*, then the generate statement will generate a concurrent assertion statement. If the value of generic *timing_checks* is *off*, then no assertion statement is generated. This functionality emulates the conditional compilation capability of some programming languages, such as C and Pascal.

8.5 TextIO

One of the predefined packages that is supplied with VHDL is the Textual Input and Output (TextIO) package. The TextIO package contains procedures and functions that allow the designer the capability of reading from, and writing to formatted text files. These text files are ASCII files of any format that the designer desires (VHDL does not impose any limits of format, but the host machine might impose limits). TextIO treats these ASCII files as files of lines, where a line is a string, terminated by a carriage return. There are procedures to read a line, write a line, and a function that checks for end of file.

The TextIO package also declares a number of types that are used while processing text files. Type *line* is declared in the TextIO package and is used to hold a line to write to a file or a line that has just been read from the file. The *line* structure is the basic unit upon which all TextIO operations are performed. For instance, when reading from a file, the first step is to read in a line from the file into a structure of type *line*. Then the *line* structure is processed field by field.

The opposite is true for writing to a file. First the *line* structure is built field by field in a temporary line data structure, then the *line* is written to the file.

A very simple example of a TextIO behavior is shown below:

```
USE STD.TEXTIO.ALL;
ENTITY square IS
  PORT( go : IN t_wlogic);
END square;

ARCHITECTURE simple OF square IS
BEGIN
  PROCESS(go)
    FILE infile : TEXT IS
            IN "/doug/test/example1";

    FILE outfile : TEXT IS
            OUT "/doug/test/outfile1";

    VARIABLE out_line, my_line : LINE;
    VARIABLE int_val : INTEGER;
  BEGIN
    WHILE NOT( ENDFILE(infile)) LOOP
      -- read a line from the input file
      READLINE( infile, my_line);

      -- read a value from the line
      READ( my_line, int_val);

      -- square the value
      int_val := int_val **2;

      -- write the squared value to the line
      WRITE( out_line, int_val);

      -- write the line to the output file
      WRITELINE( outfile, out_line);
    END LOOP;
  END PROCESS;
END simple;
```

This example shows how to read a single integer value from a line, square the value, and write the squared value to another file. It illustrates how TextIO can be used to read values from files and write values to files.

The process statement is executed whenever signal *go* has an event occur. The process will then loop until an end-of-file condition occurs on the input file *infile*. The READLINE statement reads a line from the file and places the line in variable *my_line*. The next executable line contains a READ procedure call that will read a single integer value from *my_line* into variable *int_val*. Procedure READ is an overloaded procedure that will read different type values from the line, depending on the type of the argument passed to it.

Once the value from the file has been read into variable *int_val*, the variable is squared, and the squared value is written to another variable of type *line*, called *out_line*. Procedure WRITE is also an overloaded procedure that will write a number of different value types, depending on the type of the argument passed to it.

The last TextIO procedure call made is the WRITELINE procedure call. This procedure will write out the line variable *out_line* to the output file *outfile*.

If the input file shown below is used as input to this architecture, the second file shown will reflect the output generated.

```
10
20
50
16#A#                <-- hex input
1_2_3                <-- underscores ignored
87          52       <-- second argument ignored
```

The output from the input file would look like this:

```
100
400
2500
100
15129
7569
```

The first value in the input file is 10. It is squared to result in 100 and written to the output file. The same is true for the values 20 and 50. The next value in the file is specified in hexadecimal notation. A hexadecimal A value is 10 base ten, which squared results in 100.

The next example in the file shows a number with embedded underscore characters. The underscores are used to separate fields of a number and are ignored in the value of the number. The number 1_2_3 is the same as 123.

The last entry in the input file shows a line with two input values on the line. When the line is read into the *my_line* variable, both values will exist in the line, but because there is only one READ procedure call, only the first value will be read from the line.

More than one data item can be read from a single line, as well as data items of any types. For instance a TextIO file could be a list of instructions for a microprocessor. The input file could contain the type of instruction, a source address, and a destination address. This is shown by the simple example below:

```
USE STD.TEXTIO.ALL;
PACKAGE p_cpu IS
  TYPE t_instr IS (jump, load,
                   store, addd,
                   subb, test, noop);

  FUNCTION convertstring( s : STRING)
    RETURN t_instr;

END p_cpu;

PACKAGE BODY p_cpu IS
  FUNCTION convertstring( s : STRING)
      RETURN t_instr IS
    SUBTYPE twochar IS string(1 to 2);
    VARIABLE val : twochar;
  BEGIN
    val := s(1 to 2);
    CASE val IS
```

```
         WHEN "ju" =>
            RETURN jump;
         WHEN "lo" =>
            RETURN load;
         WHEN "st" =>
            RETURN store;
         WHEN "ad" =>
            RETURN addd;
         WHEN "su" =>
            RETURN subb;
         WHEN "te" =>
            RETURN test;
         WHEN "no" =>
            RETURN noop;
         WHEN others =>
            RETURN noop;
      END CASE;
   END convertstring;
END p_cpu;

USE WORK.p_cpu.ALL;
USE STD.TEXTIO.ALL;
ENTITY cpu_driver IS
   PORT( next_instr : IN BOOLEAN;
         instr : OUT t_instr;
         src : OUT INTEGER;
         dst : OUT INTEGER);
END cpu_driver;

ARCHITECTURE a_cpu_driver OF cpu_driver IS
   FILE instr_file : TEXT IS IN "instfile";
BEGIN
   read_instr : PROCESS( next_instr)
      VARIABLE aline : LINE;
      VARIABLE a_instr : STRING(1 to 4);
      VARIABLE asrc, adst : INTEGER;
   BEGIN
      IF next_instr THEN
         IF ENDFILE(instr_file) THEN
            ASSERT FALSE
               REPORT "end of instructions"
```

```
                SEVERITY WARNING;
          ELSE
             READLINE( instr_file, aline);
             READ( aline, a_instr);
             READ( aline, asrc);
             READ( aline, adst);
          END IF;

          instr <= convertstring(a_instr);
          src <= asrc;
          dst <= adst;

       END IF;
    END PROCESS read_instr;
END a_cpu_driver;
```

Package *p_cpu* defines type *t_instr*, the enumerated type that represents CPU instructions to be executed. The package also defines a function, *convert_string,* that will be used to convert the string value read in using TextIO procedures into a *t_instr* type. The conversion is necessary because the TextIO package does not contain any procedures for reading in user-defined types (however, a designer can write a user-defined overloaded procedure that has the same basic interface as the procedures in the TextIO package). This process is usually very straightforward, as seen by the *convert_string* procedure.

Entity *cpu_driver* is the entity that will be reading in the file of instructions. It has a single input port called *next_instr* which is used to signal the entity to read in the next instruction. When a true event occurs on input port *next_instr,* process *read_instr* will execute. If the file is at the end already, the assert statement will be called, and a warning message will be issued. If we are not at the end of the file, the process will read in a line from the file into variable *aline*.

Successive reads on variable *aline* will retrieve the appropriate fields from the line. All of the reads return the value into internal variables, but variables *asrc* and *adst* were not really needed because there exists a TextIO procedure for reading integer values. Variable *ainstr* was used to allow the string read in to be converted into the enumerated type *t_instr* before being assigned to the output port *instr*.

This chapter showed some of the more esoteric features of VHDL. This chapter concludes the discussion of VHDL features. The next chapter will concentrate on some of the decisions required when the modeling process is in the early stages. The next few chapters will then guide the reader through a top-down description of a device.

Chapter

9

Modeling Considerations

In all of the previous chapters, VHDL language features have been introduced and explained in some detail. This chapter will begin the process of actually describing how real systems can be described. The first task in modeling a device is to define the basic logic value system that will be used throughout the modeling process. This logic value system is akin to the basic data structures that are used to describe a new program.

The value system used in this book for most of the examples is a strength/value system of forty-six states. This value system makes use of interval notation to provide smarter unknown handling. So why does a designer using VHDL need forty-six states to represent the values that a signal can attain? Most likely the designer will never need to use all of the values, but having forty-six values allows the designer to

- Mix technologies – ECL, TTL, CMOS, etc.
- Model to the bidirectional switch level
- Handle unknown conditions less pessimistically

Before we discuss what the forty-six states are and how they work, let's see how hardware technology, along with simulator technology has evolved to forty-six state values.

9.1 Two-State Value System

Originally simulators used a two-state value system, representing a logical '1' or true value, and a logical '0' or false value. Signals could only obtain one of these two values. A VHDL-type declaration for this type of system would be the BIT type.

```
TYPE BIT IS ('0', '1');
```

For simple systems where signals only have one source, this value system will work well. However, for real-world simulations two states are not nearly enough. Whenever a signal has multiple sources driving conflicting values of the same strength, the two-state system breaks down and can no longer represent the output value. Figure 9-1 shows two NAND gates with their outputs wired together. In some technologies this might work fine, but in others it probably will be a design error. With only two states, the designer cannot represent an error condition on the output signal.

Another condition that cannot be modeled with a two-state value system is the value a signal should start with upon start up. Assuming a

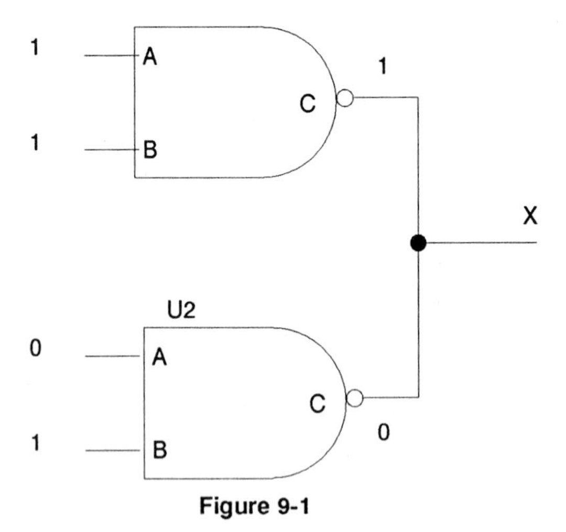

Figure 9-1

'1' or a '0' value for a startup value can cause overly optimistic results. Nodes in the simulation will be assumed to start up at a known value when in reality they will not.

9.2 Three-State Value System

To solve some of the problems in a two-value system, simulator designers realized that they needed to add a new state to the value system. The next value added was the unknown value. This value is usually represented by the 'X' or 'U' character. For our purposes the 'X' character will be used to represent the unknown state. The unknown state represents a '1' or a '0' value but we do not know which. A typical type declaration for a three-state value system is shown below:

```
TYPE threestate IS ('X', '0', '1');
```

The unknown state value can represent many different behaviors to different people. For instance, some designers think of the unknown state as a voltage value between 0v and 5v. Others think of the unknown value as oscillating between a '1' and a '0' value. For our purposes the unknown value will be either a '1' value or a '0' value, but we are not sure which.

Where does the value 'X' come from in the simulation of a design? The first cause of an 'X' value is the initialization value of a signal. All signals receive the value 'X' on startup. This value may be overwritten by the value of a circuit element later, but the 'X' value on the signal emulates the value of the signal during a startup sequence. When the simulation first starts, every signal in the design is assigned the value X'. The external input values are then applied to the circuit inputs. The external input values will propagate throughout the circuit, overwriting the X startup values. Only the circuit elements affected by the external input values and the circuit elements that these elements drive will overwrite the X values that were received during initialization.

Another cause of 'X' values in a simulation is caused by connecting more than one output signal together and driving opposite logical values. An example is shown in Figure 9-2.

The NAND gate labeled U1 will drive the output signal with a '1' value, while NAND gate U2 will drive the output signal with a '0' value. Without

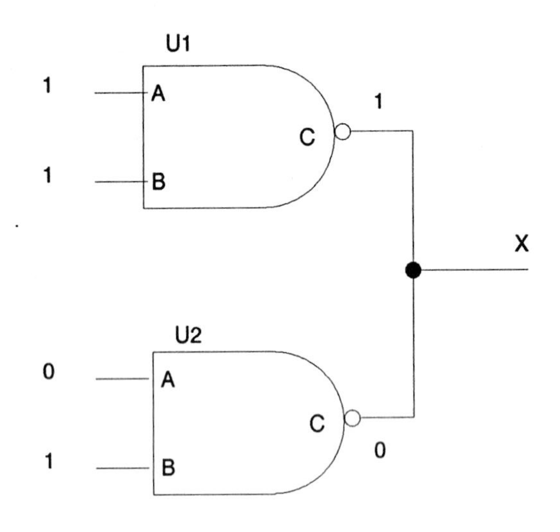

Figure 9-2

knowing what technology is being used for the NAND gates, the simulator assumes that the strengths of the '1' and '0' values are the same. The resultant value of the two outputs tied together will be an 'X'.

Connecting two output values together may have been intentional and the design is not behaving as expected. The connection of the two outputs together may have also been a design error. In either case the simulator has to correctly predict the output value. In this example, without more information about the relative strengths of the two outputs the simulator cannot assume a '1' or '0' for the output value and must return an 'X' value.

9.3 Four-State Value System

So far we have discussed two-value systems with the values { '0', '1' } and three value systems with the values { '0', '1', 'X' }. Neither of these value systems is very useful for modeling typical hardware systems with bidirectional data busses in them. Neither value system can handle a memory data bus efficiently because an open-collector or high-impedance condition cannot be modeled with just two- or three-state values. The open-collector or high-impedance condition allows the designer to implement sharing of busses and bidirectional data busses, etc.

Representing an open-collector or high-impedance effect requires the addition of yet another state, called 'Z'. A VHDL type describing this system is shown below:

```
TYPE fourstate IS ('X', '0', '1', 'Z');
```

The Z state represents the condition of the output of a tristate device when the output enable pin is turned off (set to a 0) or the output transistor of an open-collector device is turned off (not conducting). Examples of both cases are illustrated in Figures 9-3 and 9-4.

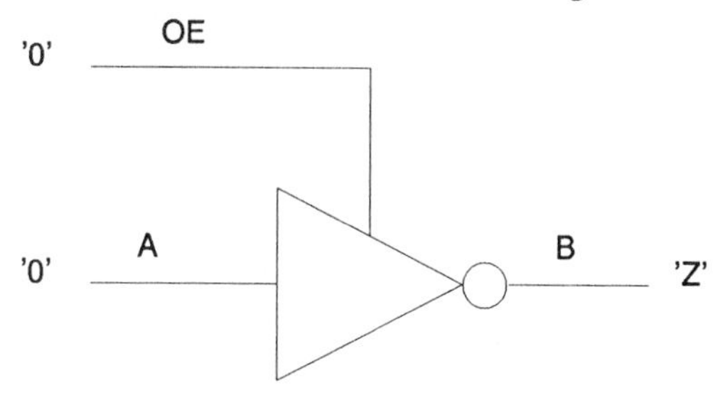

Figure 9-3

In Figure 9-3 is a tristate inverter with the output enable turned off. It makes no difference what the input value on pin A is, when the OE pin is at a '0' value the output on pin B will be 'Z'.

The example in Figure 9-4 shows the output stage of a TTL open-collector device. When the base of the transistor is a 1 value, the transistor will pull the output signal to a ground value (which is 0). When the base of the transistor is a 0 level, the transistor will not conduct and the output signal will float to an indeterminate value, unless driven by another source (the usual case). For the purposes of simulation, this floating value is represented by the value Z. If another source is connected to the output signal and is driving a 1 or a 0 value, then the Z value is overdriven and the signal will assume the 1 or 0 value from the other source.

9.3.1 Bidirectional Buses

These effects allow multiple sources on a signal, bidirectional buses, etc. By allowing only one source at a time to drive a signal, data can flow in

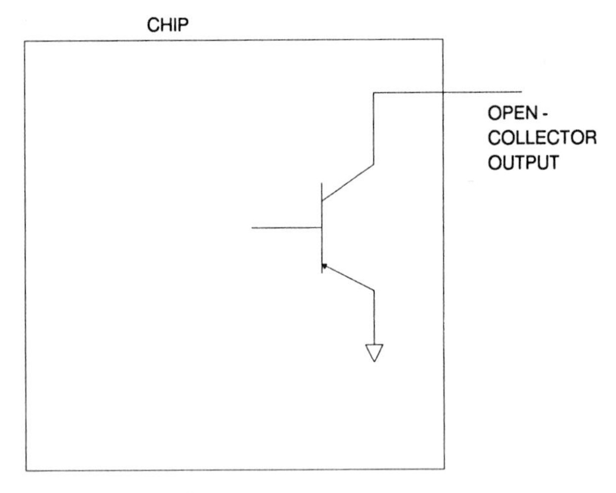

Figure 9-4

both directions on a signal. This is demonstrated by the example in Figure 9-5 . This example is a bidirectional bus using tristate drivers.

Assume the input value to U1 is a '1' and the input value to U4 is a '0'. When EN1 is a '1', U1 will drive a '1' on to the bus. If EN2 is a '0' then U4 will be driving a 'Z' value onto the bus. The bus will have two inputs, one which is a '1' and the other which is a 'Z'. The resolution of these two values is a '1' because any '1', '0', or 'X' is stronger than a 'Z'. The direction of data flow will be from left to right.

If EN1 is a '0' and EN2 is a '1', then U4 will be driving a '0' onto the bus and U1 will be driving a 'Z' onto the bus. The resulting value, a 'Z' and a '0' will be the value '0'. The direction of data flow will be from right to left.

But what happens if both EN1 and EN2 are '1' values? U1 will be driving a '1' onto the bus and U4 will be driving a '0' onto the bus. The resulting value on the bus will be 'X', because neither value is stronger than the other.

Figure 9-6 shows a table that can be used to resolve the values on a bus using a four-state { '0', '1', 'X', 'Z' } value system. For instance, from the table it can be seen that the resolution of values {'1', 'Z'} will result in

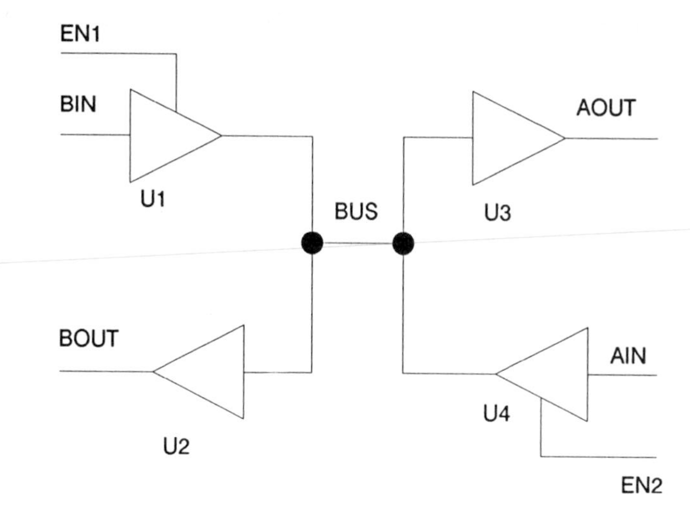

Figure 9-5

the value '1'. Also the resolution of {'Z', '0'} will result in the value '0'. The resolution of {'1', '0'}, will result in the value 'X'.

The table only shows what would happen with two inputs driving a bus. What happens if more than two sources are driving a bus? Because the table is commutative and associative, the table can be used on pairs of values at a time to calculate intermediate results. These intermediate

	0	1	X	Z
0	0	X	X	0
1	X	1	X	1
X	X	X	X	X
Z	0	1	X	Z

Figure 9-6

results can be used to calculate the final result. An example showing three sources is shown in Figure 9-7:

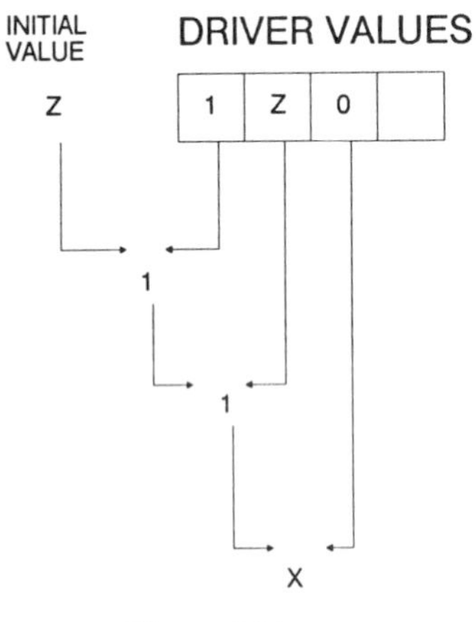

Figure 9-7

The initial value and first driver produce a '1' value. Now applying the table again with the first result and the next driver ('Z') produces the value '1'. Finally the previous result ('1') with the last driver ('0') produces the value 'X'. As long as the table is commutative and associative, this method will work for any number of drivers.

9.4 Nine-State Value System

With a four-state value system we can model TTL devices (including tristate, but not open-collector with pull-up resistors) with fair accuracy. However, with the advent of MOS technology four states were not enough. In MOS technology, the '1' and '0' values have different strengths. In NMOS the '0' value is stronger than the '1' value, and in PMOS the '1' value is stronger than the '0' value. Also in NMOS and PMOS when a node is tristated, charge is stored and the logical value of the node is maintained, for a period of time.

To represent all of these conditions the value system designers developed a nine-state value system. The value system consists of three strengths and three logical values. The three strengths are the values Z for high impedance or stored charge, R for resistive, and F for a forcing

		Logical Value		
		0	1	X
Strength	Z	Z0	Z1	ZX
	R	R0	R1	RX
	F	F0	F1	FX

Figure 9-8

strength. The nine states that are representable with this value system are shown in Figure 9-8. These states are represented by the enumerated type shown below.

```
TYPE ninestate IS (Z0, Z1, ZX,
                   R0, R1, RX,
                   F0, F1, FX);
```

These states represent the following conditions:

- Z0 – high-impedance strength, logical 0
- Z1 – high-impedance strength, logical 1
- ZX – high-impedance strength, logical X
- R0 – resistive strength, logical 0
- R1 – resistive strength, logical 1
- RX – resistive strength, logical X
- F0 – forcing strength, logical 0
- F1 – forcing strength, logical 1
- FX – forcing strength, logical X

The forcing states F0, F1, FX are very similar to the '0', '1', 'X' values that were discussed in the three-state value system. The main difference is that now a strength value has been attached. The value Z that was discussed in the four-valued system has been expanded into three separate states (Z0, Z1, ZX) to represent the logical values that a stored charge can attain. Three resistive strength values have been added to handle cases of the NMOS weaker '1' value and the PMOS weaker '0' value.

The forcing strength is the strongest of the three strengths and can be equivalent to a power supply. The resistive strength is weaker than the forcing strength and can be generated by passing a forcing strength through a resistor as shown in Figure 9-9.

F0 R0

Figure 9-9

The resistive strength is equivalent to the strength generated by a pull-up resistor. Finally the high-impedance strength is the weakest of all and is equivalent to the amount of charge stored in the capacitance of an NMOS, or PMOS, or CMOS device when the gate is turned off.

An example of a stored charge is shown by the circuit shown in Figure 9-10. When the gate is at a '0' or off state, signal B has nothing driving it. However, there will be stored charge trapped on the gate of device U2. The logical value of this stored charge will remain at the value that was last driven on this signal for a period of time.

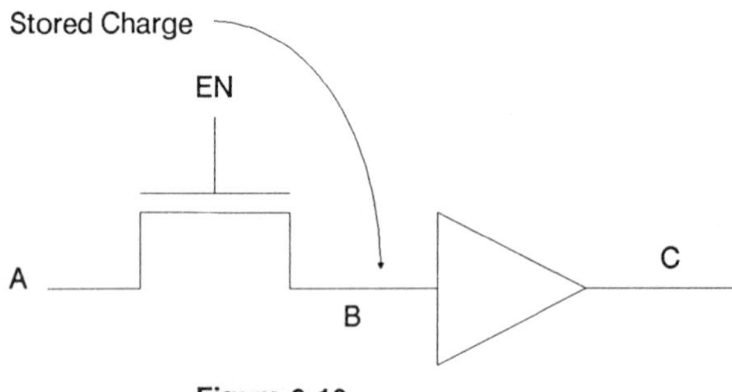

Figure 9-10

Next let's look at how the resistive strengths are used in modeling NMOS and PMOS type circuits. In Figure 9-11 is shown an NMOS inverter. It consists of two transistor devices, X1 and X2. Device X2 is a standard enhancment type NMOS switch device. Device X1 is a depletion type device. It acts like a resistor that has a resistance that changes with respect to the voltage across it. For our purposes we will just consider it a resistor.

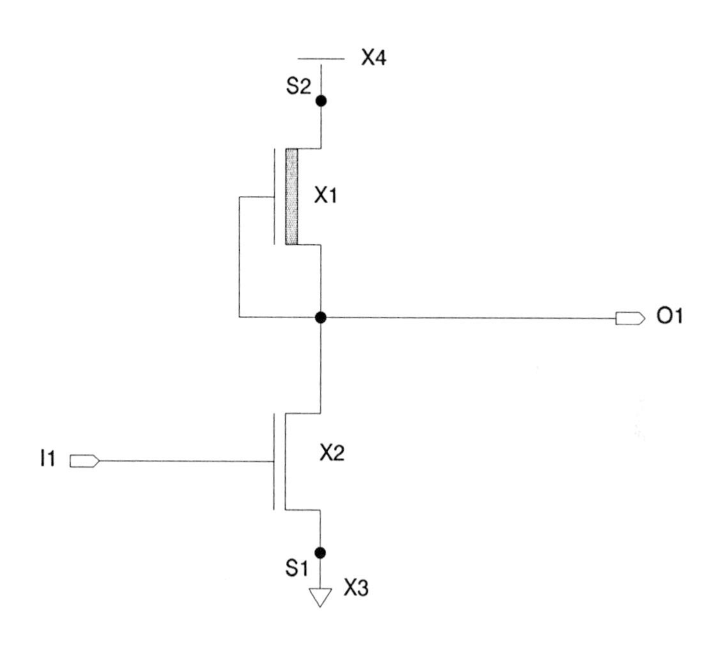

Figure 9-11

When input I1 has a '1' level on it, device X2 will conduct and signal O1 will be pulled to ground level (F0). Device X1 will conduct also but with a much higher resistance. The output of the inverter will be an F0. When input I1 is at a '0' level device X2 will not conduct and will be at a very high resistance. Device X1 will be at a medium resistance level and therefore output O1 will be driven to a '1' level by device X1. The strength of the output level will not be forcing, however, because device

X1 has a medium resistance level. The output strength will be an R1 (resistive 1) because device X1 acts like a resistor. Device X2 will output a high impedance of whatever the previous value was when its gate input is at a '0' level. This value will be overdriven by the R1 value output from device X1. A truth table for the inverter is shown in Figure 9-12.

IN	OUT
0	R1
1	F0
X	FX

Figure 9-12

Why have we chosen FX for the value to output when the input is an X? We have to look at both cases to determine what the output value should be. If the input X value is a '0' then the output will be R1. If the input value is a '1' then the output value will be a F0. If we assume the worst case because the output logical value changes for each case we have to assume that the output logical value will be X. Also since the worst case strength is forcing, we have to assume this strength.

Let's look again at the NMOS switch. Figure 9-13 shows another circuit using an NMOS transfer or pass gate. As we discussed previously, device U2 acts like a switch. When EN is a '1' value the value on signal C will be the value on signal B. When EN is a '0' value, signal C will store charge representing its previous logical value. The charge will be stored on the combination of gate and wire capacitance of device U3 and signal C.

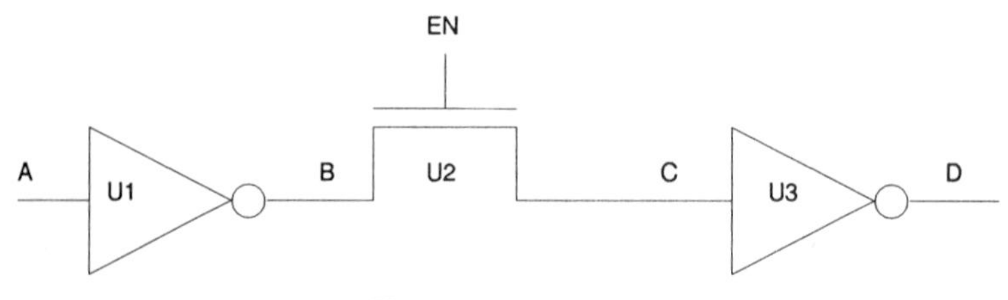

Figure 9-13

The truth table for the switch is shown in Figure 9-14. Looking at the truth table for the switch device, the gate = X case is interesting. In the nine-state value system, there is no good value to represent the condition of the output for certain cases. Assume the case represented by the switch in Figure 9-15.

GATE	OUTPUT
0	PREVIOUS VALUE + Z STRENGTH
1	OUTPUT = INPUT

X	IF (LOGICAL VALUE = PREVIOUS LOGICAL VALUE) THEN
	    OUTPUT = LOGICAL VALUE + INPUT STRENGTH
	ELSE
	    OUTPUT = X + INPUT STRENGTH

Figure 9-14

The source input has a stable F0 value on it. The drain has a stored Z1 value on it, and the gate has a 0 value. This is a steady-state condition and no values will change. If the gate now changes to a value of 'X', then what should the new value of the output be? With an 'X' value on the

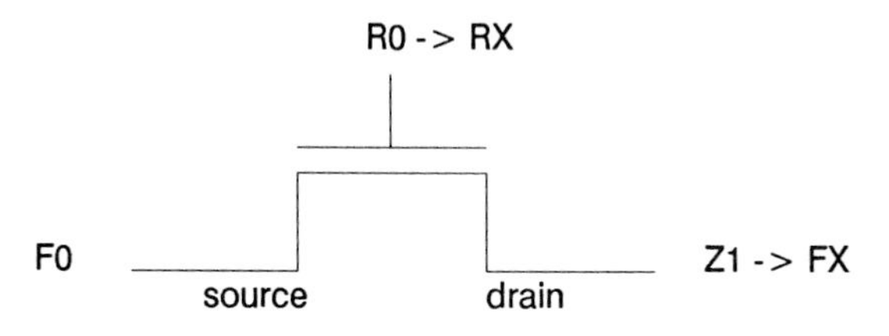

Figure 9-15

gate of device U2, there are two possible output values, depending on whether the X value is really a '0' or a '1'.

If the 'X' value is a 0, the output of device U2 will continue at Z1. If the 'X' value is a '1', the output of device U2 will then change to F0. Grouping both of these values as a pair yields the following result, { F0, Z1 }. In examining the pair of states we find that the strengths of each state are different as well as the logical value. We cannot assume that the output will be of a known strength or logical value. The worst-case value must be output. The worst-case strength is forcing, and the worst-case value is 'X'.

9.5 Twelve-State Value System

The problem with putting out 'X' values is that they propagate throughout the circuit. This causes overly pessimistic results. In a lot of cases the pessimistic results could have been prevented. A first attempt at trying to solve the problem of pessimistic results is to add another strength to the value system. If we add a new strength U, the value system looks as in Figure 9-16.

	0	1	X
Z	Z0	Z1	ZX
R	R0	R1	RX
F	F0	F1	FX
U	U0	U1	UX

Figure 9-16

The U strength represents an R, Z, or F strength but we do not know which. It's much like the 'X' representing a '1' or a '0' but we do not know which. The U is useful for representing the strength of a switch device with the gate at an 'X' value.

With the extra strength added, the value system becomes twelve different states. There are three logical values and four strengths. The product of these two provides twelve state values.

This is represented by the type declaration shown below.

```
TYPE twelvestate IS (Z0, Z1, ZX,
                     R0, R1, RX,
                     F0, F1, FX,
                     U0, U1, UX);
```

What kind of a circuit will generate a value with a 'U' strength? An example circuit is shown below in Figure 9-17.

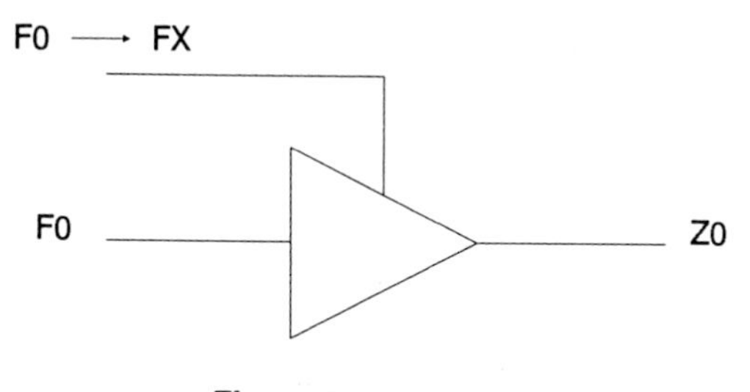

Figure 9-17

The circuit shown is a tristate buffer with a '0' value on the input, a Z0 currently stored on the output, and the switch making a transition from '0' to 'X'. The tristate buffer is a TTL technology device and will put out forcing strength values on its output when enabled.

If the switch input remains at a '0' then the output value will remain at a Z0. If the switch is a '1' then the current value of the output will be an F0. Since the switch input is an 'X', the pair of possible output values will be in the set { F0, Z0 }. The logical value will be a '0' because both states predict a '0' logical value. The strength of the output will be between F and Z. To represent this condition, the strength value U was created. The output value assigned will be a U0.

With twelve states there are still a number of trivial circuit examples that do not work. These cases are not the norm, but happen during initialization or error conditions. In the case of a CMOS RS flip-flop made of NAND gates, the circuit will never initialize. One way around it is to put initialization values at strategic signals in the circuit. This is a very tedious process and one which very few designers will favor. A very simple example of the type of circuit that exhibits overly pessimistic behavior is shown in Figure 9-18.

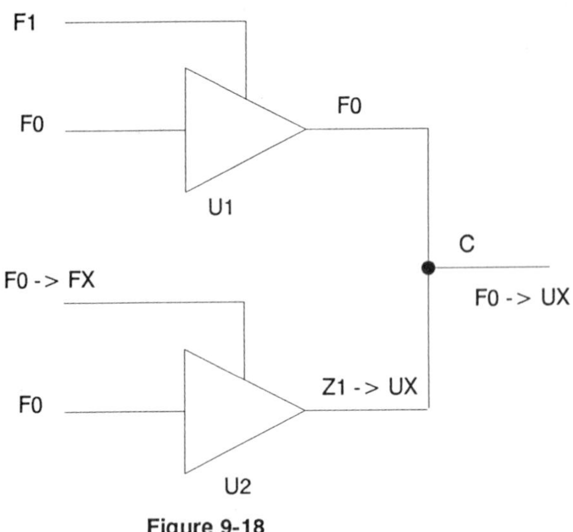

Figure 9-18

This is an example of two tristate buffers trying to drive a signal. In normal operation, both drivers will never be trying to drive the signal at the same time. However, during initialization a condition such as shown in this example can occur.

With a twelve-state value system, device U1 will predict its contribution to the value of signal C to be an F0, because all of its input values are of a known value. Device U2 does not have all of its inputs as known values and will predict an output value of UX. The output strength will be U because of the 'X' value on the gate of device U2. The output logical value will be X because the input value and the current output value do not agree.

A resolution function will be called to resolve the value of signal C. Device U1 is predicting an F0 for the value of signal C. Device U2 is predicting a UX for the value of signal C. The resolution of these two values will result in an FX for the value of signal C. This is definitely not the result wanted, but with the information currently available in the value system it is the best that can be done.

FX is not the correct value in this circuit. Both tristate inverters have an F0 on their respective inputs and therefore whether the switch input on U2 is a '1' or a '0' is of no consequence. The correct output on signal C should be an F0.

If this condition only happens during initialization, why all the fuss? A signal that goes to unknown during initialization may cause other signals to go unknown, which may cause others to go unknown, and so on. The end result is that the circuit does not initialize properly.

9.6 Forty-Six-State Value System

To solve these kinds of problems more information must be kept about the state of each signal. This is how the quantum leap from twelve states to the forty-six-state value system we will be using is made. Each signal value will be represented by what is called *interval notation*. By using interval notation, we can maintain and use more information about what the current and predicted values are during resolution.

Interval notation is a very compact and straightforward method of representing the range of values that a signal can attain. The simple ranges are the values themselves. For instance, a signal that is currently F0 can be represented by the range from F0 to F0. The other ranges are the most interesting and useful in solving our problems, however. Examine the chart shown in Figure 9-19.

Notice the range that spans the values from Z0 to Z1. This range is called ZX. This state can have any of the values from Z0 to Z1 and any state in between. The same holds true for WX, RX, and FX.

The top of this chart holds the basic state values available for use. You will notice that most of the values are familiar, but three values have been added. The new values are W0, W1, and D. The W values are just another strength value called weak resistive added between the resistive and high-impedance strengths. This strength is useful for modeling memories, weak pull-up resistors, etc.

The value D is a new concept. It represents the value of a node that has no capacitance and therefore cannot store a charge value. Another

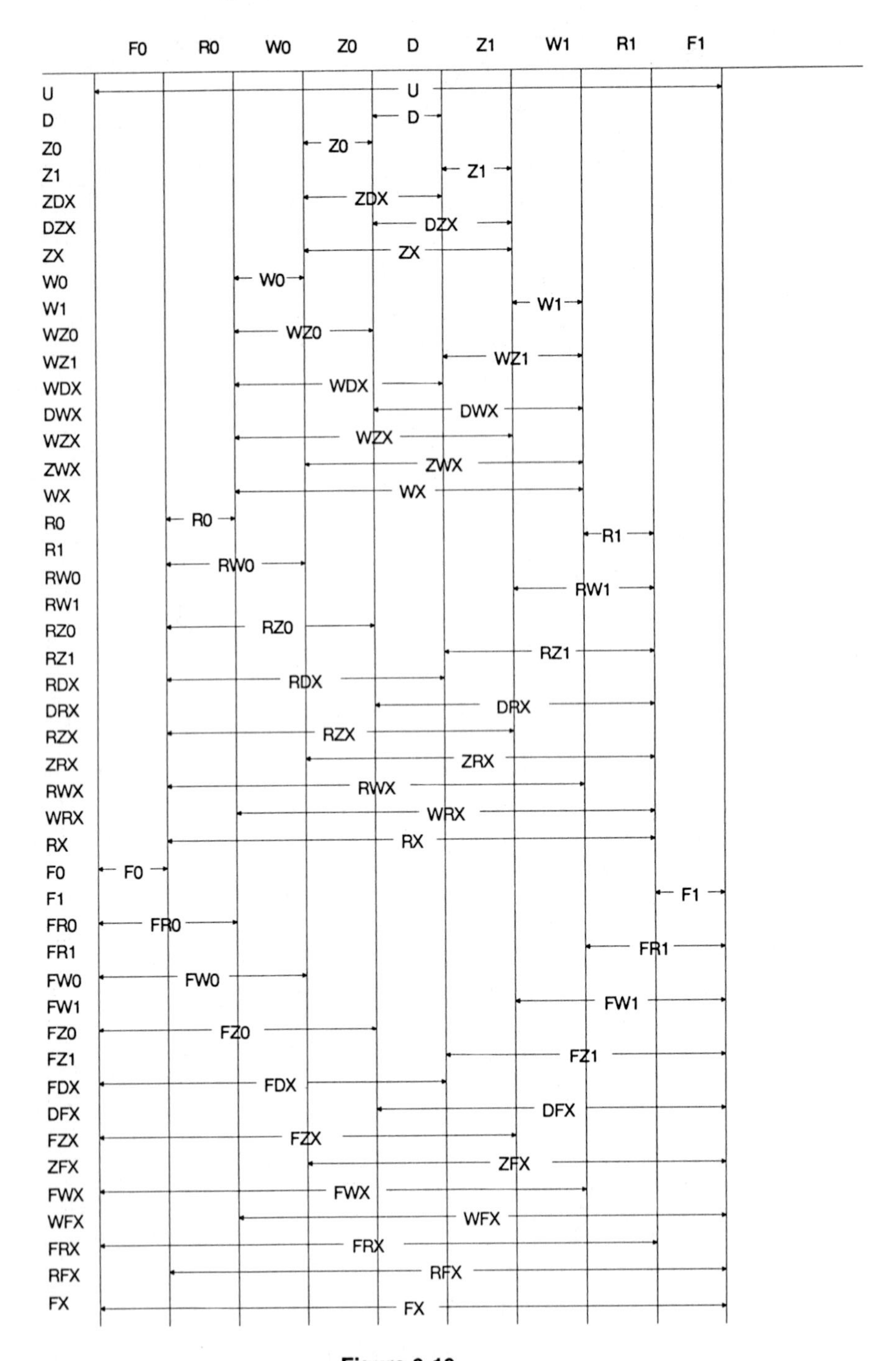
F0
R0
W0
Z0
D
Z1
W1
R1
F1
U
D
Z0
Z1
ZDX
DZX
ZX
W0
W1
WZ0
WZ1
WDX
DWX
WZX
ZWX
WX
R0
R1
RW0
RW1
RZ0
RZ1
RDX
DRX
RZX
ZRX
RWX
WRX
RX
F0
F1
FR0
FR1
FW0
FW1
FZ0
FZ1
FDX
DFX
FZX
ZFX
FWX
WFX
FRX
RFX
FX

Figure 9-19

description that some designers use is that the value D represents a disconnected net.

In Appendix A the STD_LOGIC package is presented. This package implements the forty-six-state logic system, described in this section. The package includes the basic forty-six-state type, a resolution function, a forty-six-state resolved type, and a number of useful modeling functions.

Let's look at some of the most useful values in the forty-six-state value system. In Figure 9-20 is shown the example of the two tristate buffers with their outputs connected together.

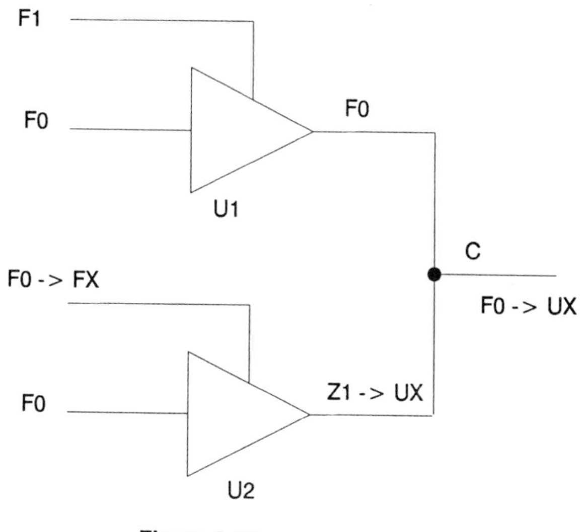

Figure 9-20

Device U1 will perform exactly as before. The contribution of U1 to the output signal C will be an F0. Device U2 will not behave as before. In the interval notation, much more information about the condition of the node can be passed on to the resolution function. With the interval notation the contribution of device U2 can be represented as a range of values. If the output enable of device U2 (which is at an 'X' value) is assumed to be a '0' value, then the output contribution will remain at a Z1 value. However, if the output enable is assumed to be a '1' value, then the output contribution will be an F0.

This condition can be represented by a state that is the range from F0 to Z1. The name of this state from Figure 9-19 is FZX. The first F character represents the strength of the '0' logical value, the Z character represents the strength of the '1' logical value, and the X represents the fact that the range crosses the center of the '1' and '0' values. If the range remains on just the logical '1' value side or the logical '0' value side then the logical value will be a '1' or a '0' respectively. However when the range is partly in the '1' range and partly in the '0' range the logical value is 'X'.

The FZX state conveys to the resolution function that the strongest strength that this state can have is a forcing and that when forcing the logical value will be a '0'. It also conveys that the strongest '1' value that can be attained is a Z strength. Armed with this information the resolution function will look at the two contributions affecting the output signal. This is shown graphically in Figure 9-21.

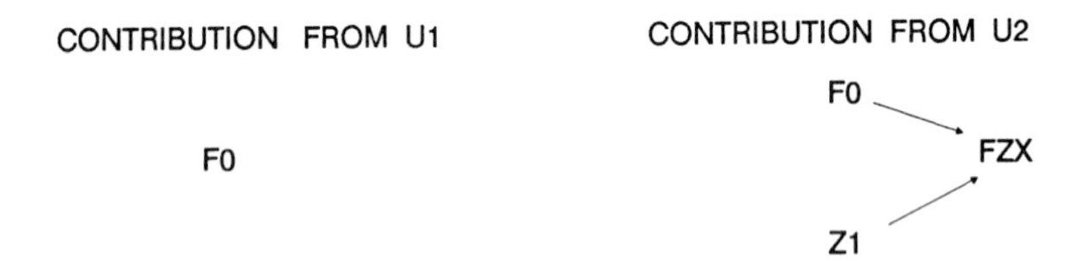

Figure 9-21

In one case of the contribution from U2, the value of U1 will supercede the value of U2, and in the other case the two values agree. What will happen in this example is that the resolution function will predict state F0 for signal C. This is the state that the designer expects to see. This state will also stop the proliferation of unneeded 'X' values in the circuit.

A few more of the interesting ranges are shown below.

- FZ0 – range from F0 to Z0, in which logical value is 0 because both range values are on the 0 side
- ZFX – range from Z0 to F1, in which logical value is X because range crosses over center of 0 and 1

- ZDX – range from Z0 to D, in which logical value is X because range extends out of the range of 0

This is the essence of the interval notation: to provide a way to pass more information about the state of a node to the resolution function, and to allow smarter handling of unknown conditions. With nine basic values, when all of the possible combinations are added up the following number of states results.

$$9 + 8 + 7 + 6 + 5 + 4 + 3 + 2 + 1 = 45$$

Where does the forty-sixth value come from? It was decided during the course of the value system creation that a useful state to have would be a state that represented the value of a node that had never been assigned a value. A signal that has never had a value assigned would have a value U. This state represents the uninitialized signal value and therefore the rationalization for the symbol U.

With forty-six states almost any logical condition can be represented. But most designers do not want to worry about designing with forty-six states. The value system also supports subsets that allow the designer to think in terms of technology, and ignore the fact that there are really forty-six different states in the value system. The value system currently supports five different types of technology, but adding a new technology is a trivial task.

The five different types of technology supported are TTL, CMOS, NMOS, ECL, and TTLOC. With TTL technology a '1' logical value is represented by an F1 and a '0' logical value is represented by an F0. Tables for each technology are shown in Figure 9-22.

Each of the technologies has the values listed for a '0', '1', and 'X' value from the technology. For instance the technologies with symmetrical '1' value and '0' value strengths, the 'X' output value is the '0' strength, with an 'X' logical value. The two technologies that exhibit this fact are the TTL and CMOS technologies.

Technologies that have nonsymmetrical strengths for '1' and '0' values have interval output values when the logical value output is to be 'X'. Examples are ECL, NMOS, and TTLOC.

	TTL	ECL	NMOS	CMOS	TTLOC
0	F0	R0	F0	F0	F0
1	F1	F1	R1	F1	ZX
X	FX	RFX	FRX	FX	FZX

Figure 9-22

In this chapter we have examined a number of value systems and the reasons for each. In the next few chapters we will start to apply all of the language features and modeling insight with a design example described in a top-down manner.

Chapter

10

Top-Level System Design

In the last few chapters we have discussed VHDL language features and how to develop a value system. In the next few chapters we will tie all of these ideas together by developing a top-down design for a vending machine controller. We will start at the system level and continue to break the design down until we reach a level where the design can be built with standard off-the-shelf parts or can be synthesized with synthesis tools.

10.1 Vending Machine Controller

The vending machine controller we will describe is very similar to the ones that control machines that exist in cafeterias. There are a number of items in the machine that can be purchased by inserting the correct amount of money and then selecting the appropriate button to dispense the item. If more money was entered than was needed to purchase the item, the controller will return the correct amount of change.

The controller also has to manage some other functions that may or may not be obvious. For instance, when the money entered is enough to purchase the item with the maximum price, then no more money needs to be entered. The vending machine will activate a signal to the mechanical device that receives coins to reject any further coins.

The vending machine also has to keep track of how many of each item has been dispensed. When all of a particular item has been dispensed, a light on the front of the machine lights up, signifying that the machine has no more of that particular item.

The controller also has to keep track of how much change has been given out to a customer so that when a customer enters too much money for an item, the machine has enough change internally to return the correct amount. If the machine does not have enough change, then a light on the front of the machine will light up to signal that the machine needs exact change only.

To save writing of a lot of redundant VHDL code, we will use a vending machine that supports only four items for this example. The four items and their cost will be

- Pretzels, 50 cents
- Chips, 45 cents
- Cookies, 55 cents
- Doughnuts, 60 cents

The basic stock of each item is 5, but the machine can be configured to hold more of each.

The kinds of coins that can be input to the machine are as follows:

- Nickel
- Dime
- Quarter
- Half Dollar

The first step in the controller description will be to describe a package that contains descriptions of the above items.

10.2 Top-Level Package

The first step in describing the system from the top down is to describe all of the object types that will be used in the design. At the very beginning of the design process it is usually advantageous to use as much of the abstract modeling capability of VHDL as possible. This includes using as much of the abstract types, such as enumerated types, composite types, etc., as possible. This will make writing the VHDL description easier and make the model more efficient in runtime (if done correctly). When the design is correct, the abstract types can be replaced with concrete types, and the design can be produced.

Using the description of the objects from the previous section, the top-level package can be described with the following.

```
PACKAGE p_vending IS
   TYPE t_coin IS ( no_coin, nickel, dime,
                    quarter, half_dollar);

   TYPE t_item IS ( no_item, pretzels, chips,
                    cookies, doughnut);

   -- used later for controlling a multiplexer
   TYPE t_mux_sel IS (val0, val1, val2);

   SUBTYPE t_value IS INTEGER;

   FUNCTION coin_to_int( coin : IN t_coin)
      RETURN t_value;

   FUNCTION int_to_coin( val : IN t_value)
      RETURN t_coin;

   CONSTANT zero : t_value := 0;
END p_vending;

PACKAGE BODY p_vending IS
   FUNCTION int_to_coin( val : IN t_value)
      RETURN t_coin IS
   BEGIN
      IF (val = 5) THEN
         RETURN nickel;
```

```
      ELSIF (val = 10) THEN
         RETURN dime;
      ELSIF (val = 25) THEN
         RETURN quarter;
      ELSIF (val = 50) THEN
         RETURN half_dollar;
      ELSE
         RETURN no_coin;
      END IF;
   END int_to_coin;

   FUNCTION coin_to_int( coin : IN t_coin)
      RETURN t_value IS
   BEGIN
      CASE coin IS
         WHEN no_coin =>
             RETURN 0;
         WHEN nickel =>
             RETURN 5;
         WHEN dime =>
             RETURN 10;
         WHEN quarter =>
             RETURN 25;
         WHEN half_dollar =>
             RETURN 50;
      END CASE;
   END coin_to_int;
END p_vending;
```

Two types, *t_coin* and *t_item*, describe the objects that will be used in the controller. Type *t_coin* is an enumerated type that describes the possible coin values to be input. Type *t_item* describes all of the possible items that can be purchased.

Type *t_mux_sel* will be described later, as it is used for some parts that will be used to build the design. Subtype *t_value* will be used for all of the numeric values used in the design, such as how much money has been entered, how much change needs to be returned, etc. The type specified initially is INTEGER, to make use of the built-in mathematical functions, but when the description is defined down to the component level, this type will need to be updated with the number of bits that will be used in the computations.

Two functions are also included in the top-level package. These functions make it possible to convert from the coins entered into a mathematical value for these coins, and back again. This will facilitate keeping track of how much money has been entered and how much change to return.

10.3 Top-Level Entity

The next step in any top-down design description is to describe the system interface at the top level. As shown in Figure 10-1 the system interface consists of input signals, output signals, any inout signals, and any parameters that need to be passed into the top level. Along with the direction of the signals, the type of the signals also need to be described.

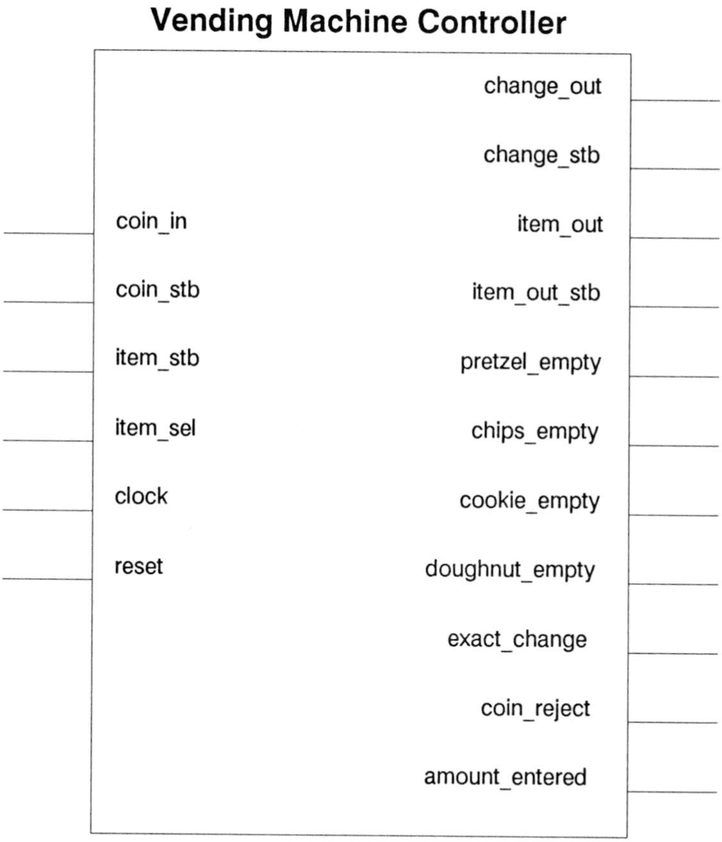

Figure 10-1

The system interface in VHDL is described by the entity. The first step in the system level description will be to create the top-level entity. The top-level entity will describe the inputs and outputs of the system and any parameters that need to be passed into the system.

A top-level entity can be created from the symbol shown in Figure 10-1, using the types described by the top-level package, *p_vending*. This entity is shown below:

```
USE STD.std_logic.ALL;
USE WORK.p_vending.ALL;
ENTITY vend_control IS
  GENERIC( p_price : t_value := 50;
           ch_price : t_value := 45;
           c_price : t_value := 55;
           d_price : t_value := 60;
           p_total : t_value := 5;
           ch_total : t_value := 5;
           c_total : t_value := 5;
           d_total : t_value := 5;
           num_nickels : t_value := 25;
           num_dimes : t_value := 25;
           max_price : t_value := 60);
  PORT( coin_in : IN t_coin;
        coin_stb : IN t_wlogic;
        item_stb : IN t_wlogic;
        item_sel : IN t_item;
        clock : IN t_wlogic;
        reset : IN t_wlogic;
        change_out : OUT t_coin;
        change_stb : OUT t_wlogic;
        item_out : OUT t_item;
        item_out_stb : OUT t_wlogic;
        pretzel_empty : OUT t_wlogic;
        chips_empty : OUT t_wlogic;
        cookie_empty : OUT t_wlogic;
        doughnut_empty : OUT t_wlogic;
        exact_change : OUT t_wlogic;
        coin_reject : OUT t_wlogic;
        amount_entered : OUT t_value);
END vend_control;
```

10.3.1 Generics

The entity begins with the generics used to control the price of an item, the number of items in the machine, and the number of coins kept for change. Generic *p_price* is the price of pretzels, *ch_price* is the price of chips, etc. In the same fashion generic *p_total* relates how many pretzel items exist in the machine when it is stocked. The other generics with a total in their names describe the total items stocked for these items as well.

Generics *num_nickels*, and *num_dimes* determine how many of each coin are kept in the machine to give out as change. Generic *max_price*, is used to determine when enough money has been entered into the machine to buy the most expensive item. This generic affects when the machine will no longer accept any more coins.

10.3.2 Ports

The ports described by the port clause are only input and output ports. There are no ports which are inout. Port *reset* is used to initialize the controller to a known state. It is active high, and when equal to '1', the system will initialize itself.

Port *clock* is used to synchronize all of the activity of the controller. All of the output signals will be a variation of the *clock* signal.

Ports *coin_in* and *coin_stb* act together to allow coins to be entered into the system. To enter a coin into the controller, the driving device will put the coin value on the *coin_in* port and then strobe the value into the controller by submitting a rising edge on the *coin_stb* port.

Ports *item_sel* and *item_stb* work the same way as the coin ports. Port *item_sel* is the item value input, and *item_stb* is the strobe line to enter the value into the controller.

Ports *change_out*, *change_stb*, *item_out*, and *item_out_stb* work the same way as the coin and item input ports, except that these ports are output ports. The change lines are used to drive the change dispensing device in the vending machine. When a change value is output, the type of change will be output on the *change_out* port and then a rising edge will be driven from port *change_stb*. The same is true of the item ports, *item_out* and *item_out_stb*.

The *pretzel_empty, chips_empty*, etc. ports are output ports used to drive lights on the front panel of the vending machine. If the machine is out of cookies, then the *cookie_empty* will be a '1' value; otherwise it will be a '0' value.

The *exact_change* port is used to tell the potential customer of the vending machine that the machine does not have enough change to output, so the customer should only enter correct change. It is a '1' value when the machine is low on change, and a '0' value otherwise.

Port *coin_reject* is not seen externally directly by the customer. When the customer has entered enough money to buy the most expensive item no more money needs to be entered to buy any item. Therefore the machine should reject any new coins. The *coin_reject* port will cause the coin entry mechanism to reject any new coins when the maximum price has been reached. Coins will be rejected when the *coin_reject* value is '1' and not rejected when the value is '0'.

The last port is the *amount_entered* port. This port is used to display the amount of money currently entered by the customer. It will drive a display on the front of the machine.

Now that the interface to the controller has been specified, the input port to output port behavior can be specified by a behavioral architecture for the controller.

10.4 Top-Level Architecture

The top-level architecture for the vending machine controller will be written at a very high level so that the concept of the controller can be verified before a lot of time and effort go into the actual construction of the controller. This top-level architecture can be thought of as the system specification for the design. Together with the top-level entity, the complete behavior of the design will be documented.

The architecture of the top level has been expressed as a single process to facilitate the transfer of information from the various pieces of the architecture. With a single process, variables are global to all parts of the architecture. The various pieces of the behavioral description are activated by using the 'EVENT attribute of the input signals in an IF statement.

The behavioral architecture for the top-level design is shown below:

```
ARCHITECTURE a_vend_control OF vend_control IS
BEGIN
   coin_proc : PROCESS
      VARIABLE current_total : t_value;
      VARIABLE p_sold, ch_sold, c_sold,
               d_sold : INTEGER;
      VARIABLE dime_out,
               nickel_out : INTEGER := 0;

   BEGIN
      IF reset = '1' THEN
         current_total := 0;
         p_sold := 0;
         ch_sold := 0;
         c_sold := 0;
         d_sold := 0;
         dime_out := 0;
         nickel_out := 0;

      ELSIF (coin_stb = '1') AND
                  (coin_stb'EVENT) THEN
         IF current_total >= max_price THEN
            coin_reject <= F1;
         ELSE
            coin_reject <= F0;
            CASE coin_in IS
               WHEN nickel =>
                  current_total :=
                     current_total + 5;

               WHEN dime =>
                  current_total :=
                     current_total + 10;

               WHEN quarter =>
                  current_total :=
                     current_total + 25;
```

```
            WHEN half_dollar =>
               current_total :=
                  current_total + 50;

            WHEN no_coin =>
               null;
         END CASE;
      END IF;
   ELSIF (item_stb = '1') AND
                 (item_stb'EVENT) THEN
      CASE item_sel IS
         WHEN pretzels =>
            IF current_total >= p_price THEN
               IF p_sold < p_total THEN
                  item_out <= pretzels;
                  p_sold := p_sold + 1;
                  current_total :=
                     current_total - p_price;

                  IF p_sold < p_total THEN
                     pretzel_empty <= F0;
                  ELSE
                     pretzel_empty <= F1;
                  END IF;
               ELSE
                  pretzel_empty <= F1;
               END IF;
            END IF;
         WHEN  cookies =>
            IF current_total >= c_price THEN
               IF c_sold < c_total THEN
                  item_out <= cookies;
                  c_sold := c_sold + 1;
                  current_total :=
                     current_total - c_price;

                  IF c_sold < c_total THEN
                     cookie_empty <= F0;
                  ELSE
                     cookie_empty <= F1;
                  END IF;
               ELSE
```

```
            cookie_empty <= F1;
         END IF;
      END IF;
   WHEN  chips =>
      IF current_total = ch_price THEN
         IF ch_sold < ch_total THEN
            item_out <= chips;
            ch_sold := ch_sold + 1;
            current_total :=
               current_total - ch_price;

            IF ch_sold < ch_total THEN
               chips_empty <= F0;
            ELSE
               chips_empty <= F1;
            END IF;
         ELSE
            chips_empty <= F1;
         END IF;
      END IF;

   WHEN  doughnut =>
      IF current_total = d_price THEN
         IF d_sold < d_total THEN
            item_out <= doughnut;
            d_sold := d_sold + 1;
            current_total :=
               current_total - d_price;

            IF d_sold < d_total THEN
               doughnut_empty <= F0;
            ELSE
               doughnut_empty <= F1;
            END IF;
         ELSE
            doughnut_empty <= F1;
         END IF;
      END IF;
   WHEN no_item =>
      null;
END CASE;
```

```
          item_out_stb <= F1;
          WAIT UNTIL clock = '1';
          item_out_stb <= F0;

          WHILE current_total > 0 LOOP
             IF (current_total > 5) THEN
                change_out <= dime;
                change_stb <= F1;
                current_total :=
                   current_total - 10;
                dime_out := dime_out + 1;
                ASSERT dime_out <= num_dimes
                   REPORT "out of dimes"
                   SEVERITY ERROR;
             ELSE
                change_out <= nickel;
                change_stb <= F1;
                current_total :=
                   current_total - 5;
                nickel_out := nickel_out + 1;
                ASSERT nickel_out <= num_nickels
                   REPORT "out of nickels"
                   SEVERITY ERROR;
             END IF;

             IF ((num_dimes - dime_out) < 5) OR
                ((num_nickels - nickel_out) < 5)
             THEN
                exact_change <= F1;
             ELSE
                exact_change <= F0;
             END IF;

             WAIT UNTIL clock = '1';
             change_stb <= F0;
          END LOOP;
       END IF;
       WAIT ON  coin_stb, item_stb, reset;
    END PROCESS;
 END a_vend_control;
```

The main process, *coin_proc*, has been implemented using WAIT statements inside the process. Therefore the process statement cannot have a sensitivity list. However, at the end of the process, a WAIT statement exists that makes the process sensitive to *coin_stb, item_stb,* and *reset*.

When *reset* changes, process *coin_proc* will be invoked. If *reset* is a '1', then the first IF statement will be satisfied, and all internal variables of the process will be initialized. This allows the vending machine to be reset to a known state.

The other two inputs that can cause process *coin_proc* to be invoked are *item_stb* and *coin_stb.* When an event occurs on *coin_stb,* process *coin_proc* will be invoked, and if a rising edge has occurred on *coin_stb,* the first ELSIF statement of the first IF statement will be satisfied. Execution of the process will then proceed to the IF statement that checks to make sure that the amount of money entered cannot buy the most expensive item. If the most expensive item can already be bought, then no more money needs to be entered; otherwise it will be returned as change. If the most expensive item can be bought, then the *coin_reject* signal is set to a '1' value (forcing strength); otherwise the *coin_reject* signal is set to a '0' (forcing strength) value.

If the coin is not rejected, then execution continues with the CASE statement. The CASE statement will add the amount of the coin to the *current_total* variable, based on the kind of the coin entered. The *current_total* variable keeps track of the total amount of money entered into the vending machine. This variable is used to determine whether enough money has been entered into the vending machine to buy an item or if coins should be rejected.

If the *item_stb* port has a rising edge occur, then the second ELSIF statement (shown below) will be satisfied.

```
ELSIF (item_stb = '1') AND
   (item_stb'EVENT) THEN
```

The VHDL statements following this statement will handle the processing needed to purchase an item. These statements will update the total money in the vending machine, update the number of items sold, and place the appropriate item on the *item_out* port.

A case statement selects the appropriate statements to execute based on the type of item being purchased.

```
CASE item_sel IS
```

The next check makes sure that enough money has been entered into the vending machine to purchase the item.

```
IF current_total >= p_price THEN
```

Another check is then performed to make sure that at least one item is available for purchase.

```
IF p_sold < p_total THEN
```

If execution proceeds to this point, then the item can be purchased. The item_out port receives the value of the item.

```
item_out <= pretzels;
```

Next the appropriate counter is updated to reflect the fact that an item was sold.

```
p_sold := p_sold + 1;
```

Now that an item has been sold, the purchase price of the item must be subtracted from the total money that has been entered.

```
current_total := current_total - p_price;
```

Finally a check needs to be made, to ensure that the current sale did not exhaust the vending machine of a particular item.

```
IF p_sold < p_total THEN
  pretzel_empty <= F0;
ELSE
  pretzel_empty <= F1;
END IF;
```

If it did, then the empty light for that particular item needs to be lit; otherwise keep it turned off.

The description above showed how the statements for the pretzel item worked. The other items in the vending machine work the same way.

Next let's examine the statements that provide the output strobe for the item and the change. These statements begin at the end of the CASE statement just described, with the line shown below:

```
item_out_stb <= F1;
```

This first statement will schedule the *item_out_stb* to a '1' value (forcing strength). The next statement will cause this process to suspend until an event whose value is '1' is detected on the clock signal.

```
WAIT UNTIL clock = '1';
item_out_stb <= F0;
```

These three statements will create a strobe pulse on the *item_out_stb* port that is at least one clock pulse long. The WAIT statement causes the process to suspend until the next rising edge of the clock signal. Then the *item_out_stb* signal is set to a '0' value (forcing strength).

The next operation for the vending machine controller is to output change from the purchase, if required. Since change is returned one coin at a time, a loop will be used to provide the necessary return mechanism. The change return loop starts with the statement shown below:

```
WHILE current_total > 0 LOOP
```

If variable *current_total* is equal to 0, then the purchase completely exhausted the money entered into the vending machine, and no change need be returned. However, if *current_total* is nonzero and positive, the amount of change to be returned is the value of *current_total.* If *current_total* is greater than a nickel value, then at least one dime needs to be returned.

```
IF (current_total > 5) THEN
```

Otherwise, just one nickel can be returned. The appropriate coin is placed on the *change_out* port, and the *change_stb* port is set to a '1' value. Then the change value needs to be subtracted from the *current_total.*

```
current_total := current_total - 10;
```

The counter for the change that was given out has to be updated to reflect the number of each type of coins that were given out.

```
dime_out := dime_out + 1;
```

The model also contains error-checking code to report when a particular type of change coin has been exhausted.

```
ASSERT dime_out <= num_dimes
   REPORT "out of dimes"
   SEVERITY ERROR;
```

Finally, the *exact_change* light needs to be illuminated when the amount of change drops below a predefined value. In this example, when there are more than four of each type of coin left, the *exact_change* light is unlit, but when the amount of either of the two types of change drops below 5, the *exact_change* light will be lit. At the end of the IF statement, inside the change loop, is another WAIT statement that will allow the *change_stb* signal to last at least one clock.

When *current_total* drops to zero as change is given, the loop will terminate, and the process will resume waiting for events on the *coin_stb, item_stb,* or *reset* ports.

10.5 Vending Machine Configuration

The configuration *c_vend_control* for entity *vend_control* is shown below, and represents a default configuration for *vend_control.* Architecture *a_vend_control* contains no component instantiations, or blocks, and therefore this configuration only need bind the architecture to the entity.

```
CONFIGURATION c_vend_control OF vend_control IS
  FOR a_vend_control
  END FOR;
END c_vend_control;
```

This configuration is not required if architecture *a_vend_control* has just been compiled into the working library. However, when more than one architecture exists for entity *vend_control,* the architecture will need to be uniquely specified.

Now that we have the top-level description of the vending machine, we can verify that the design works at the behavioral level. This level of description can become the system-level specification that will be used to drive the lower-level specifications. At some point it will be possible for this description to generate the lower levels of abstraction automatically through a process called *synthesis*. At the time of this writing, the synthesis tools were not quite able to handle this level of abstraction.

In the next few chapters, this design will be refined to lower and lower levels of abstraction, until the device could possibly be built.

Chapter

11

Vending Machine : First Decomposition

In this chapter we will use the system-level specification from the last chapter as a guide to further break down the description of the vending machine controller. By looking at how the statements are grouped together, we can see that there are three logical pieces that the controller can be broken into.

- Coin handler
- Item processor
- Change maker

The coin handler accepts coins and keeps track of the total amount of money in the vending machine. The item dispenser accepts purchase requests and determines if the money entered is enough to purchase an item. If so, the item dispenser outputs the item. The change maker outputs change, if needed, following a purchase.

Figure 11-1 shows how these components are wired together with signals to form a vending machine controller.

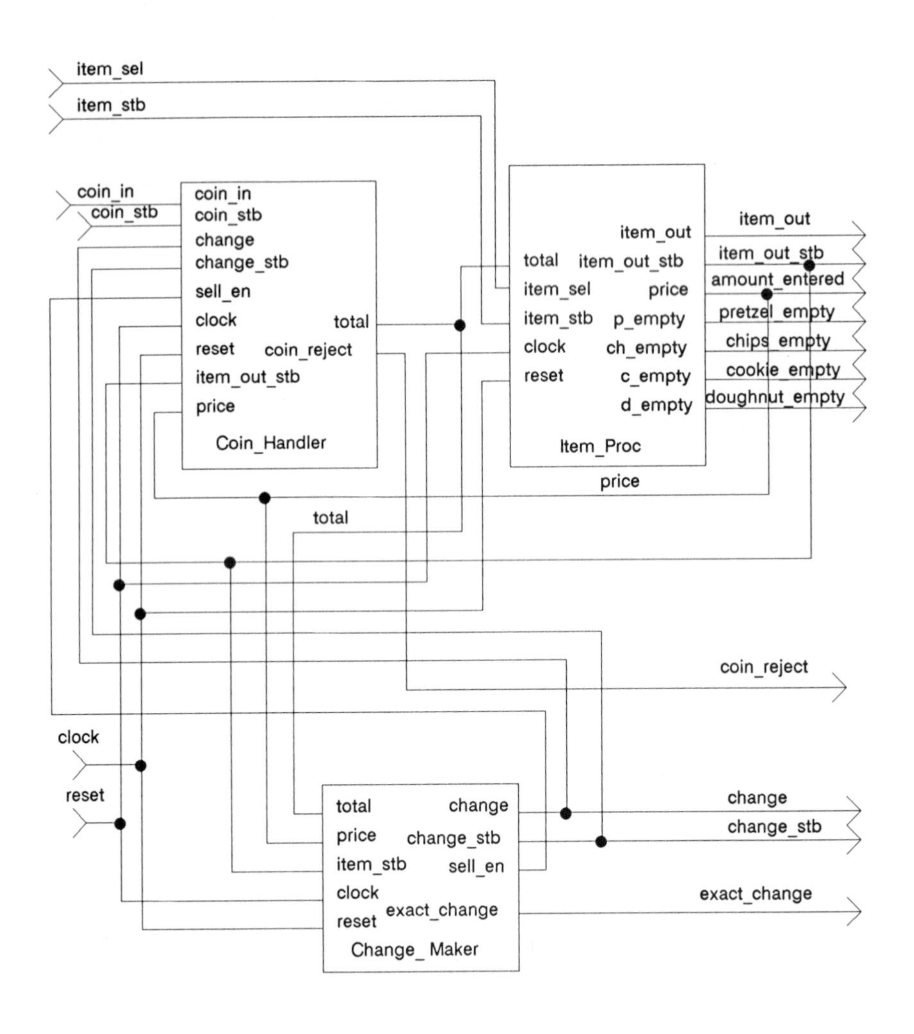
item_sel
item_stb
coin_in
coin_stb
coin_in
coin_stb
change
change_stb
sell_en
clock
total
reset
coin_reject
item_out_stb
price
Coin_Handler
item_out
total
item_out_stb
item_sel
price
item_stb
p_empty
clock
ch_empty
reset
c_empty
d_empty
Item_Proc
item_out
item_out_stb
amount_entered
pretzel_empty
chips_empty
cookie_empty
doughnut_empty
price
total
coin_reject
clock
reset
total
change
price
change_stb
item_stb
sell_en
clock
exact_change
reset
Change_ Maker
change
change_stb
exact_change

Figure 11-1

11.1 Coin Handler

The *coin_handler* component is used to maintain the total amount of money currently held in the vending machine. The symbol shown in Figure 11-2 shows the inputs and output signals to the *coin_handler*. An entity and architecture that implement the function of the *coin_handler* are shown later.

There are only two ouput ports from the *coin_handler*. The total money in the vending machine at any time is output on port *total*. Port *coin_reject* is a '1' when the money entered into the machine can buy the most expensive item, or if input *sell_en* is a '0' value.

Ports *coin_in* and *coin_stb* are used to enter coin values into the *coin_handler*. The coin value is placed on port *coin_in*, and then strobed into the *coin_handler* component, with a rising edge on signal *coin_stb*.

Ports *item_out_stb* and *price* are used to subtract the price of an item from the total when an item has been purchased. The price of the item purchased is placed on signal *price* and strobed into component *coin_handler* with a rising edge on signal *item_out_stb*.

Ports *change* and *change_stb* are used to subtract change given out after a purchase from the total. The change value is placed on the change signal

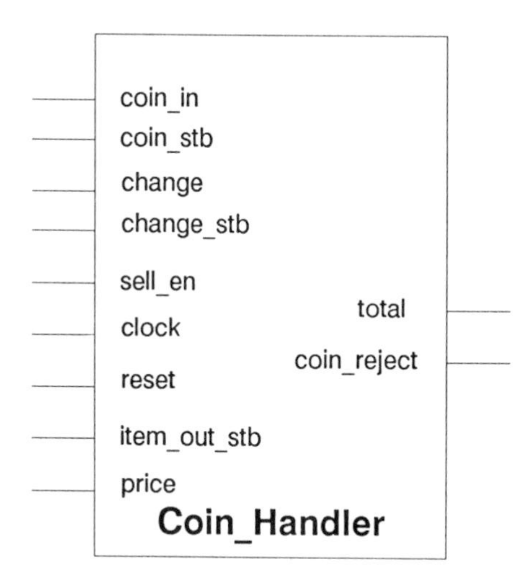

Figure 11-2

and strobed into the *coin_handler* component, with a rising edge on *change_stb*.

Signal *sell_en* is used to control the input of coins. When *sell_en* is equal to a '1' value, coin values can be entered into the *coin_handler*. When *sell_en* is equal to a '0', coins will be rejected from the vending machine. The only time that *sell_en* is equal to '0' is when the *change_maker* is making change.

11.2 Item Processor

The *item_proc* component is used to dispense a purchased item. Ports *item_sel* and *item_stb* are used to select an item to be purchased. The rising edge of *item_stb* will trigger the *item_proc* component to check the *total* signal and make sure that enough money has been entered into the machine to buy the requested item.

If an item can be purchased, the item is sent out on the *item_out* signal and strobed by the *item_out_stb* signal. Signal *price* is used to communicate to the *coin_handler* and *change_maker* components the value of the purchase price of the item.

The last function of the *item_proc* component is to output the correct status of the *item_empty* signals, where *item* is one of the four items in the vending machine. These signals tell the customer whether the supply of an item has been exhausted or not.

A symbol for the *item_proc* component is shown in Figure 11-3. This symbol shows the input and output signals of the component. An entity and architecture that match the symbol are shown later.

11.3 Change Maker

The *change_maker* component is used to output the correct change when an item has been purchased. The *item_stb_out* signal is used to alert the *change_maker* that an item has been purchased. The *change_maker* component will then look at the *price* and *total* inputs to determine how much change needs to be returned. A symbol for the *change_maker* component is shown in Figure 11-4.

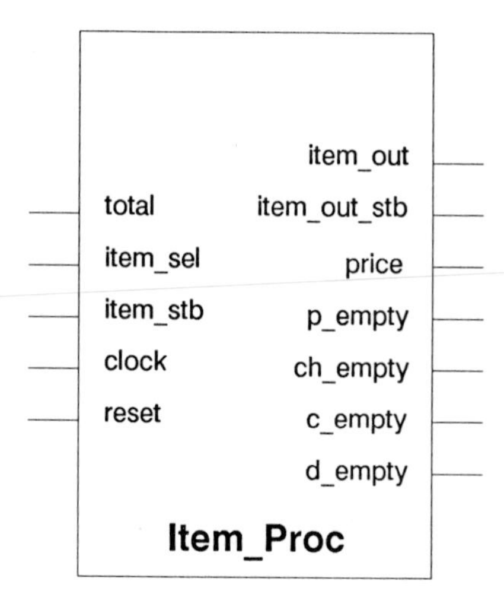

Figure 11-3

The change is returned a single coin at a time from the *change* and *change_stb* signals. The *change* signal contains the coin to be returned, and the *change_stb* signal is used to strobe the coin out.

The *clock* signal is used to synchronize the operation of the *change_maker* component with all of the other components. The *reset* signal will initialize the *change_maker* component to a known state.

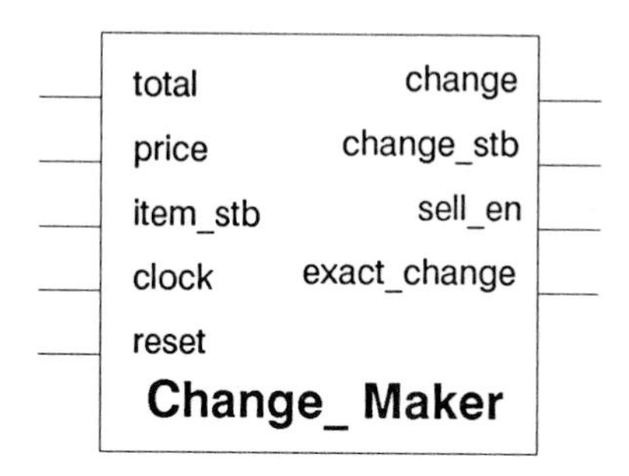

Figure 11-4

The *exact_change* signal will be a '1' value whenever the change available to return to the customer drops below a preset limit, for each type of coin returned. In this design, whenever the change drops below five units of either dimes or nickels, the *exact_change* signal will illuminate.

The *sell_en* signal is used to inhibit coins from being entered, while change is being returned to the customer. This signal will be '0' while change is being made, and '1' otherwise.

11.4 Structural Architecture

A structural architecture that defines the three components and instantiates them is shown below:

```
ARCHITECTURE first_level OF vend_control IS
   COMPONENT coin_handler
      GENERIC( max_price : t_value);
      PORT( change_in : IN t_coin;
            change_stb : IN t_wlogic;
            coin_in : IN t_coin;
            coin_stb : IN t_wlogic;
            clock : IN t_wlogic;
            reset : IN t_wlogic;
            sell_en : IN t_wlogic;
            price : IN t_value;
            item_out_stb : IN t_wlogic;
            total : OUT t_value;
            coin_reject : OUT t_wlogic);
   END COMPONENT;

   COMPONENT change_maker
      GENERIC( num_dimes, num_nickels : t_value);
      PORT( total : IN t_value;
            price : IN t_value;
            item_stb : IN t_wlogic;
            clock : IN t_wlogic;
            reset : IN t_wlogic;
            exact_change : OUT t_wlogic;
            change : OUT t_coin;
            change_stb : OUT t_wlogic;
            sell_en : OUT t_wlogic);
```

```
END COMPONENT;

COMPONENT item_proc
   GENERIC( p_price, ch_price, c_price,
            d_price, p_total, ch_total,
            c_total, d_total : t_value);
   PORT( total : IN t_value;
         item_sel : IN t_item;
         item_stb : IN t_wlogic;
         item_out : OUT t_item;
         item_out_stb : OUT t_wlogic;
         clock : IN t_wlogic;
         reset : IN t_wlogic;
         price : OUT t_value;
         p_empty, ch_empty, c_empty,
         d_empty : OUT t_wlogic);
END COMPONENT;

SIGNAL total, price : t_value;
SIGNAL sell_en : t_wlogic;
SIGNAL change_int : t_coin;
SIGNAL change_stb_int,
      item_stb_int : t_wlogic;

BEGIN

   U1 : coin_handler GENERIC MAP( max_price)
      PORT MAP( change_in => change_int,
                change_stb => change_stb_int,
                coin_in => coin_in,
                coin_stb => coin_stb,
                clock => clock,
                reset => reset,
                sell_en => sell_en,
                price => price,
                item_out_stb => item_stb_int,
                total => total,
                coin_reject => coin_reject);

   U2 : change_maker GENERIC MAP( num_dimes,
                                  num_nickels)
      PORT MAP( total => total,
```

```
                      price => price,
                      item_stb => item_stb_int,
                      exact_change => exact_change,
                      change => change_int,
                      change_stb => change_stb_int,
                      clock => clock,
                      reset => reset,
                      sell_en => sell_en);

         U3 : item_proc GENERIC MAP(
                      p_price, ch_price,
                      c_price, d_price,
                      p_total, ch_total,
                      c_total, d_total)
           PORT MAP( total => total,
                      item_sel => item_sel,
                      item_stb => item_stb,
                      item_out => item_out,
                      item_out_stb => item_stb_int,
                      clock => clock,
                      reset => reset,
                      price => price,
                      p_empty => pretzel_empty,
                      ch_empty => chips_empty,
                      c_empty => cookie_empty,
                      d_empty => doughnut_empty);

      change_out <= change_int;
      change_stb <= change_stb_int;
      item_out_stb <= item_stb_int;
      amount_entered <= total;

    END first_level;
```

Notice that the same entity is used for the interface signals as was used for the behavioral architecture. Now instead of behavioral statements being used to define the behavior of the vending machine, three components will be used.

The architecture declaration contains the component declarations for the three components and the local signals that will be used to tie the components together. In the architecture statement part are the three component instantiations.

Also in the architecture statement part are four concurrent signal assignment statements as shown below:

```
change_out <= change_int;
change_stb <= change_stb_int;
item_out_stb <= item_stb_int;
amount_entered <= total;
```

These statements are necessary because the signals that drive these ports are also used internally. In VHDL an output port (e.g. *change_out*) cannot have its value read inside the architecture that drives the port. Since the value of this output port is needed internally, as well as externally, an internal signal (e.g. *change_int*) is used to drive the output port, and also the ports internally where the value is needed. The internal signal is also assigned to the external port.

Another method to solve this problem is to buffer the output signals with an actual buffer component. This was not done because the buffer component is not needed in the final design. Another alternative is to use a port type of BUFFER on the output ports instead of type OUT. Ports of type BUFFER can be assigned to and read from, but can have only one driver.

Next let's examine the VHDL descriptions for the three components instantiated in the structural architecture. For each component an entity, architecture, and configuration will be presented that describes the next level of the hierarchy.

11.4.1 Coin Handler

The entity for the *coin_handler* component uses the *std_logic* package and the *p_vending* packages to access the types and functions provided by each. The entity contains one generic which specifies to the *coin_handler* the price of the most expensive item. When the money collected reaches this price, the *coin_handler* can reject any further coins.

```
USE STD.std_logic.ALL;
USE WORK.p_vending.ALL;
ENTITY coin_handler IS
```

```
    GENERIC( max_price : t_value);
    PORT( change_in : IN t_coin;
          change_stb : IN t_wlogic;
          coin_in : IN t_coin;
          coin_stb : IN t_wlogic;
          clock : IN t_wlogic;
          reset : IN t_wlogic;
          sell_en : IN t_wlogic;
          price : IN t_value;
          item_out_stb : IN t_wlogic;
          total : OUT t_value;
          coin_reject : OUT t_wlogic);
  END coin_handler;
```

The *coin_handler* entity matches the architecture component declaration exactly in terms of port names and types. This is not necessary, but it will make the configuration simpler.

The architecture for the *coin_handler* described in this chapter will be a behavioral one. It is shown below:

```
ARCHITECTURE behave OF coin_handler IS
BEGIN
   change_proc : PROCESS( coin_stb, change_stb,
                          item_out_stb, reset)

      VARIABLE local_change : INTEGER := 0;
      VARIABLE int_total : INTEGER := 0;
   BEGIN
      IF reset = '1' THEN
         int_total := 0;
         total <= 0;
      ELSE
         IF sell_en = '1' THEN
            IF (coin_stb = '1') AND
                     ( coin_stb'EVENT) THEN
               IF int_total >= max_price THEN
                  coin_reject <= F1;
               ELSE
                  coin_reject  <= F0;
                  int_total := int_total +
                     coin_to_int(coin_in);

                  total <= int_total;
```

```
         END IF;
      END IF;
   END IF;
   IF ( change_stb = '1') AND
               ( change_stb'EVENT) THEN
      local_change :=
               coin_to_int( change_in);

      IF ( int_total >= local_change )THEN
         int_total :=
                int_total - local_change;

         total <= int_total;
         IF int_total >= max_price THEN
            coin_reject <= F1;
         ELSE
            coin_reject <= F0;
         END IF;
      ELSE
         ASSERT FALSE REPORT
            "error: change too large"
            SEVERITY ERROR;
      END IF;
   END IF;
   IF ( item_out_stb = '1') AND
               ( item_out_stb'EVENT) THEN
      IF ( int_total >= price )THEN
         int_total := int_total - price;
         total <= int_total;
         IF int_total >= max_price THEN
            coin_reject <= F1;
         ELSE
            coin_reject <= F0;
         END IF;
      ELSE
         ASSERT FALSE REPORT
            "error: price too large"
            SEVERITY ERROR;
      END IF;
   END IF;
END IF;
```

```
    END PROCESS change_proc;
  END behave;
```

The *coin_handler* architecture consists of a single process sensitive to the following three strobe signals:

- *coin_stb*
- *change_stb*
- *item_out_stb*

and the *reset* line. When the *reset* signal changes to the value '1', the *coin_handler* is initialized so that the vending machine contains no money. If the *reset* line is not a '1' value, then execution will start with the IF statement shown below:

```
  IF sell_en = '1' THEN
```

This statement will be true if the *change_maker* is not currently making change. If the *change_maker* is making change, then this signal will be '0' and no coins can be entered.

If signal *sell_en* is '1' then the next IF statement will check for a rising edge on the *coin_stb* port. A rising edge will signify that a coin has been entered. If the total money in the vending machine is already greater than or equal to *max_price*, then *coin_reject* will be activated.

If the maximum price has not been reached, then the coin from the *coin_in* port is converted to type *t_value* and added to the internal total. The internal total value in variable *int_total* is then assigned to output port *total*, where it will be communicated to the other components in the design. If *sell_en* is not equal to '1', then change is being returned from the *change_maker*, so any coins entered will be rejected.

If an event occurs on the *change_stb* port, the *change_maker* is sending change. The change that is sent out needs to be subtracted from the total. The coin being sent out is first converted to type *t_value* so that the integer subtract operation can be performed. The change value is also range-checked to make sure that the value is not too large.

When an event occurs on the *item_out_stb*, an item has been purchased. The price of the item will be subtracted from the total.

The *coin_handler* has only one behavioral architecture, with no blocks or components instantiated. Therefore the default configuration shown below is enough to specify the configuration for the entity. Currently this configuration is not needed, but it may be useful later when more than one architecture exists for component *coin_handler.*

```
CONFIGURATION coin_handle_con OF coin_handler IS
   FOR behave
   END FOR;
END coin_handle_con;
```

11.4.2 Item Processor

The *item_proc* component can also be described by an entity, architecture, and configuration. The entity for the item processor is shown below:

```
USE STD.std_logic.ALL;
USE WORK.p_vending.ALL;
ENTITY item_proc IS
   GENERIC( p_price, ch_price,
        c_price, d_price,
        p_total, ch_total,
        c_total, d_total : t_value);
   PORT( total : IN t_value;
         item_sel : IN t_item;
         item_stb : IN t_wlogic;
         item_out : OUT t_item;
         item_out_stb : OUT t_wlogic;
         clock : IN t_wlogic;
         reset : IN t_wlogic;
         price : OUT t_value;
         p_empty : OUT t_wlogic;
         ch_empty : OUT t_wlogic;
         c_empty : OUT t_wlogic;
         d_empty : OUT t_wlogic);
END item_proc;
```

The entity for the *item_proc* component passes eight of the generic values from the vending machine entity into the *item_proc* entity. Four of these generics, *p_price, ch_price, c_price,* and *d_price*, are used to pass the prices of the items to purchase to the *item_proc* entity. The other four generics, *p_total, ch_total, c_total,* and *d_total,* are used to specify how many of each item were loaded into the vending machine when it was stocked.

Port *total* is used to pass in the current amount of money entered into the vending machine. Entity *item_proc* will compare the value on signal total with the price of an item being purchased to determine if the purchase can be made.

Ports *item_stb* and *item_sel* are used to purchase an item. Port *clock* is used to synchronize the components, and port *reset* is used to initialize the *item_proc* model.

The outputs generated are

- *item_out*: the item purchased
- *item_out_stb*: strobe for the item out
- *price*: the cost of the item purchased
- *p_empty*: empty indicator for pretzels
- *ch_empty*: empty indicator for chips
- *c_empty*: empty indicator for cookies
- *d_empty*: empty indicator for doughnuts

The architecture for the *item_proc* model is shown below:

```
ARCHITECTURE behave OF item_proc IS
BEGIN
  item_process : PROCESS

    VARIABLE p_sold, ch_sold,
             c_sold, d_sold : t_value;

  BEGIN
    IF ( reset = '1') THEN
      p_sold  := 0;
      ch_sold  := 0;
      c_sold  := 0;
      d_sold  := 0;
    END IF;

    IF ( item_stb = '1') AND
                        ( item_stb'EVENT) THEN
```

```
CASE item_sel IS
   WHEN pretzels =>
      IF p_sold  < p_total THEN
         IF total >= p_price THEN
            item_out <= pretzels;
            price <= p_price;
            p_sold := p_sold + 1;
            IF p_sold >= p_total THEN
               p_empty <= F1;
            ELSE
               p_empty <= F0;
            END IF;
         END IF;
      END IF;
   WHEN chips =>
      IF ch_sold < ch_total THEN
         IF total >= ch_price THEN
            item_out <= chips;
            price <= ch_price;
            ch_sold := ch_sold + 1;
            IF ch_sold >= ch_total THEN
               ch_empty  <= F1;
            ELSE
               ch_empty <= F0;
            END IF;
         END IF;
      END IF;
   WHEN cookies  =>
      IF c_sold < c_total THEN
         IF total >= c_price THEN
            item_out <= cookies;
            price <= c_price;
            c_sold := c_sold + 1;
            IF c_sold >= c_total THEN
               c_empty <= F1;
            ELSE
               c_empty <= F0;
            END IF;
         END IF;
      END IF;
   WHEN doughnut  =>
```

```
            IF d_sold < d_total THEN
               IF total >= d_price THEN
                  item_out <= doughnut;
                  price  <= d_price;
                  d_sold := d_sold + 1;
                  IF d_sold >= d_total THEN
                     d_empty <= F1;
                  ELSE
                     p_empty <= F0;
                  END IF;
               END IF;
            END IF;
         WHEN OTHERS =>
            ASSERT FALSE REPORT
               "illegal item selected"
               SEVERITY ERROR;
      END CASE;

      item_out_stb <= F1;
      WAIT UNTIL clock = '1';

      item_out_stb <= F0;
    END IF;

    WAIT ON item_stb, reset;

  END PROCESS item_process;
END behave;
```

Architecture *behave* of *item_proc* has four local variables, *p_sold, ch_sold, c_sold,* and *d_sold,* that track how many of each item have been purchased. These variables are initialized to zero whenever signal *reset* is a '1'.

If the *item_stb* input has a rising edge, then the IF statement shown below will be satisfied and the CASE statement will execute.

```
IF ( item_stb = '1') AND
                  ( item_stb'EVENT) THEN
```

The CASE statement will execute the appropriate statements based on the value of the *item_sel* port. Let's examine what will happen if the input item is *chips.*

The CASE statement alternative shown below will match, and execution will begin on the statement following this statement.

```
WHEN chips =>
```

The first step is to make sure that all of the chip items have not already been sold. If there is an item to purchase, then the next check makes sure that enough money has been entered, by checking the value of signal total versus the price of the chips item.

If both of these tests pass, then the item can be purchased. The *item_out* port is assigned the value chips, and the sold counter for chips, *ch_sold,* is incremented to reflect the sale. The sold counter is checked one more time to make sure that the current sale did not exhaust the vending machine of this item.

After the CASE statement alternative code has been executed, the statements below are executed.

```
item_out_stb <= F1;
WAIT UNTIL clock = '1';

item_out_stb <= F0;
```

These statements will strobe the item from the *item_proc* device to the mechanical device that dispenses the item to cause the item to be dispensed. These statements make sure that the output signal on *item_out_stb* is at least one clock cycle wide.

Since the architecture of the *item_proc* entity also does not instantiate any components or contain any blocks, the default configuration shown below will configure this entity. Again, this configuration is not needed currently.

```
CONFIGURATION item_proc_con OF item_proc IS
   FOR behave
   END FOR;
END item_proc_con;
```

11.4.3 Change Maker

This section will examine the entity, architecture, and configuration for the *change_maker* component. The entity for the *change_maker* is shown below.

```
USE STD.std_logic.ALL;
USE WORK.p_vending.ALL;
ENTITY change_maker IS
   GENERIC( num_dimes, num_nickels : t_value);
   PORT( total : IN t_value;
         price : IN t_value;
         item_stb : IN t_wlogic;
         clock : IN t_wlogic;
         reset : IN t_wlogic;
         exact_change : OUT t_wlogic;
         change : OUT t_coin;
         change_stb : OUT t_wlogic;
         sell_en : OUT t_wlogic);
END change_maker;
```

The generics *num_nickels* and *num_dimes* are used to communicate to the *change_maker* model how many of each type of coin used to make change were entered into the vending machine.

Ports *total* and *price* are used by the model to determine how much change to return. The difference between these two signal values is the change that needs to be returned.

Port *item_stb* alerts the *change_maker* that an item has been sold and that the *change_maker* needs to act on this event. Ports *clock* and *reset* are used in the same way as in components *item_proc* and *coin_handler*. Port *exact_change* communicates to the customer of the vending machine that the amount of change held internally has dropped below a specified level. The *change* and *change_stb* ports are used to output the coin as change.

The *sell_en* port is used to disable the vending machine from accepting coins while change is being made.

The architecture for the *change_maker* is a behavioral architecture, and is shown below:

```
ARCHITECTURE behave OF change_maker IS
BEGIN
   change_mak_proc : PROCESS
      VARIABLE int_change : t_value;
      VARIABLE dime_out : t_value := num_dimes;
      VARIABLE nickel_out : t_value
```

```
         := num_nickels;
BEGIN

   IF reset = '1' THEN
      dime_out := num_dimes;
      nickel_out := num_nickels;
   ELSIF ( item_stb = '1') AND
            ( item_stb'EVENT) THEN

      IF ( total > price) THEN
         int_change := total - price;
         sell_en <= F0;
         WHILE ( int_change > 0) LOOP
            IF ( int_change >= 10) THEN
               change <= dime;
               int_change := int_change - 10;
               dime_out := dime_out -1;
            ELSE
               change <= nickel;
               int_change := int_change - 5;
               nickel_out := nickel_out -1;
            END IF;

            IF (dime_out < 5) OR
                     (nickel_out < 5) THEN

               exact_change <= F1;
            ELSE
               exact_change  <= F0;
           END IF;

            change_stb <= F1;
            WAIT UNTIL clock = '1';

            change_stb <= F0;
         END LOOP;
      END IF;
   END IF;

   sell_en <= F1;
   WAIT ON item_stb;
```

```
    END PROCESS change_mak_proc;
  END behave;
```

This architecture keeps track of two internal variables, *dime_out* and *nickel_out,* to record how many of each coin has been given out as change. When port *reset* is a '1', these two internal variables are set to the amount of each type of change that is stocked in the vending machine. These values are passed in through the two generic values, *num_dimes*, and *num_nickels*.

If an item is sold, the *item_stb* port will receive an event that will kick off *change_maker* processing. The *change_maker* first makes sure that *total* is greater than *price.* If *total* is equal to *price*, no change needs to be given. If *total* is less than *price*, an internal error has occurred.

Next an internal variable, *int_change*, is set to the amount of change that needs to be returned; which is, the total money in the machine minus the price of the item sold. The *sell_en* port is now set to '0' (forcing strength) to prevent any more money from entering the vending machine while change is being made.

The architecture contains a LOOP statement that will continue to loop as long as the *int_change* value is not 0, or less than 0. The LOOP statement allows change to be given sequentially, one coin at a time. Inside the loop, the change is checked for greater than or equal to 10. If true, a dime will be returned as change. If not, a single nickel will be returned as change.

If a dime is to be returned, the *change_out* port is set to the value of a dime, and the *dime_out* counter is decremented by 1. Then the *int_change* value has a dime, 10, in change subtracted from it. For a nickel change value, the processing is the same using different values for the change.

The loop will continue to output dimes and a nickel, until the *int_change* value is zero. Once this happens the loop will terminate.

When the loop terminates, the change counters will be checked to determine if the *exact_change* indicator needs to be illuminated.

At the end of this processing, the *sell_en* port will be set to an F1 value again, and the process will wait for the next item to be purchased.

The configuration for the *change_maker* is a simple default configuration like all the other components, as shown below:

```
CONFIGURATION change_mak_con OF change_maker IS
   FOR behave
   END FOR;
END change_mak_con;
```

11.5 Next-Level Configuration

Now that the three components that make up the vending machine have been described, and instantiated, the configuration that binds these components to the respective entities needs to be described. A typical configuration is shown below:

```
CONFIGURATION first_level_con OF
      vend_control IS
   FOR first_level
      FOR U1 : coin_handler
         USE CONFIGURATION WORK.coin_handle_con;
      END FOR;
      FOR U2 : change_maker
         USE CONFIGURATION WORK.change_mak_con;
      END FOR;
      FOR U3 : item_proc
         USE CONFIGURATION WORK.item_proc_con;
      END FOR;
   END FOR;
END first_level_con;
```

Each of the component instances is paired with a configuration for the lower-level entity that will be used for each instance. This configuration will allow the vending machine simulation to execute using behavioral models for the three lower-level components.

11.6 Group Configurations

When a design has been broken down to this level of abstraction, the entity-architecture pair of the lower-level components act as the specification for the next level of the design. Each of the lower-level components can be designed and tested independently of the other components, but tested in the system level by using the proper configurations.

The specification for the current level of the design contains three behavioral components connected together by a higher-level structural architecture. This is shown pictorially in Figure 11-5.

Configuration *c_vend_control* configures the vending machine at the top level with a behavioral architecture. Configuration *first_level_con* configures the vending machine at the next level down, where the design now consists of three subcomponents.

Each of these three subcomponents can now be handed off to different design teams to complete the lower-level design. Each design team can use a behavioral version of the components that they are not working on and the structural version of the component being designed. For instance, let's look at a possible design hierarchy for the design team working on a structural description of the *item_proc* component. This is shown in Figure 11-6.

The *item_proc* design team is using a structural architecture for component *item_proc*, but a behavioral architecture for components *change_maker* and *coin_handler*.

The design team working on the *coin_handler* would have the design hierarchy shown in Figure 11-7.

This design team would have behavioral architectures for the *change_maker* and *item_proc* components and a structural architecture for the *coin_handler*.

11.7 Team Configurations

To split the design in such a manner, the designers can make use of configurations. A configuration for the *item_proc* design team is shown below:

```
CONFIGURATION item_design_team OF
      vend_control IS
   FOR first_level

      -- behavioral architecture
      FOR U1 : coin_handler
```

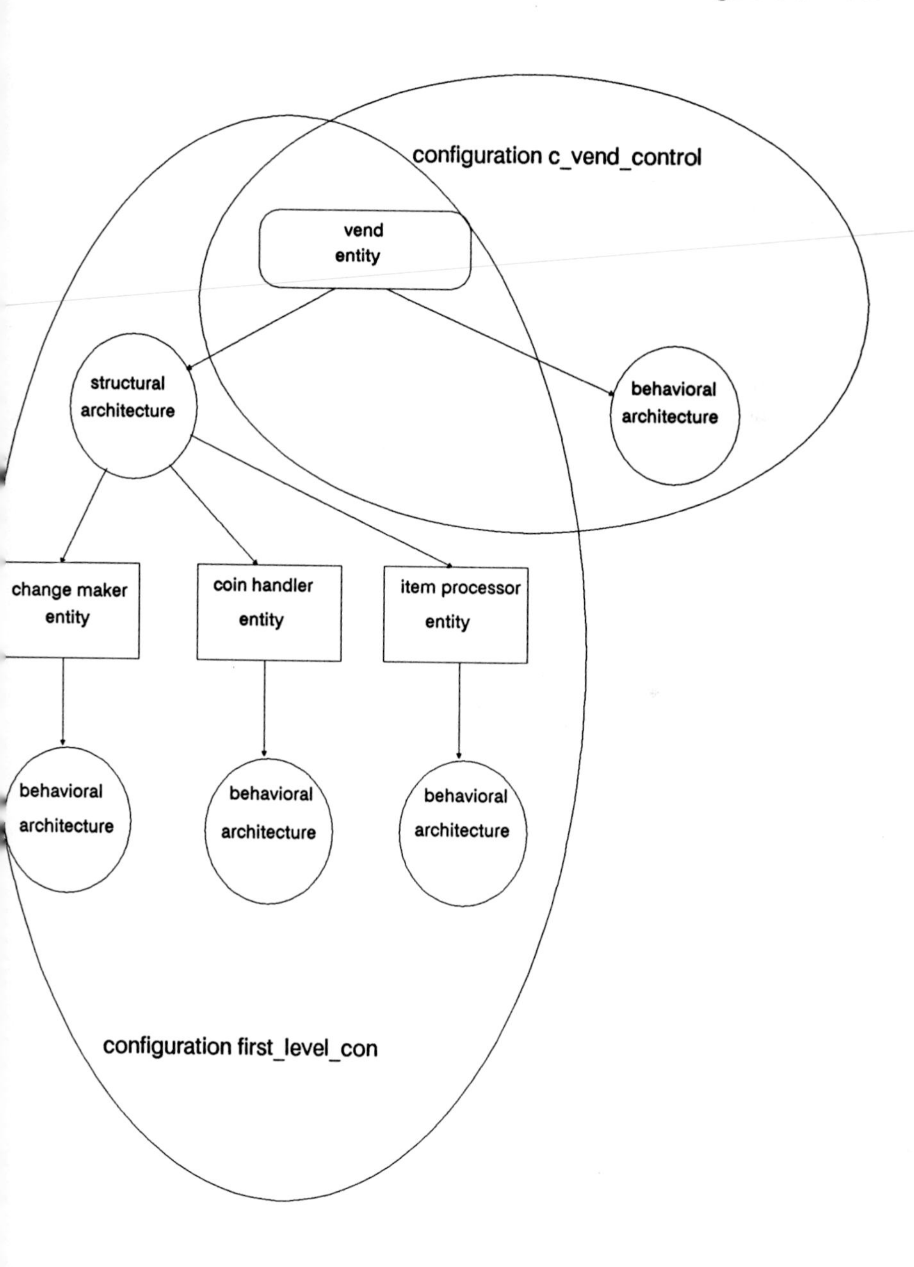
configuration c_vend_control
vend
entity
structural
architecture
behavioral
architecture
change maker
entity
coin handler
entity
item processor
entity
behavioral
architecture
behavioral
architecture
behavioral
architecture
configuration first_level_con

Figure 11-5

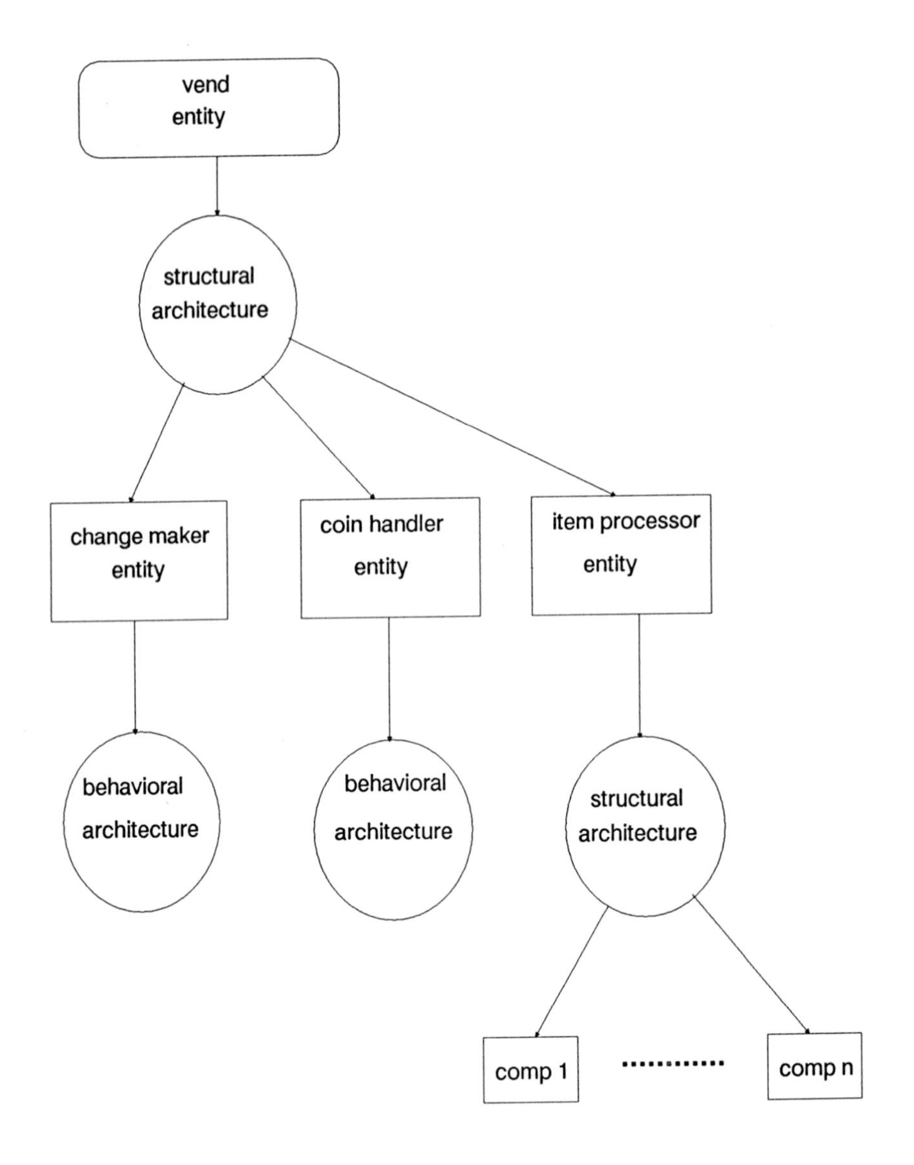
vend
entity
structural
architecture
change maker
entity
coin handler
entity
item processor
entity
behavioral
architecture
behavioral
architecture
structural
architecture
comp 1
....
comp n

Figure 11-6

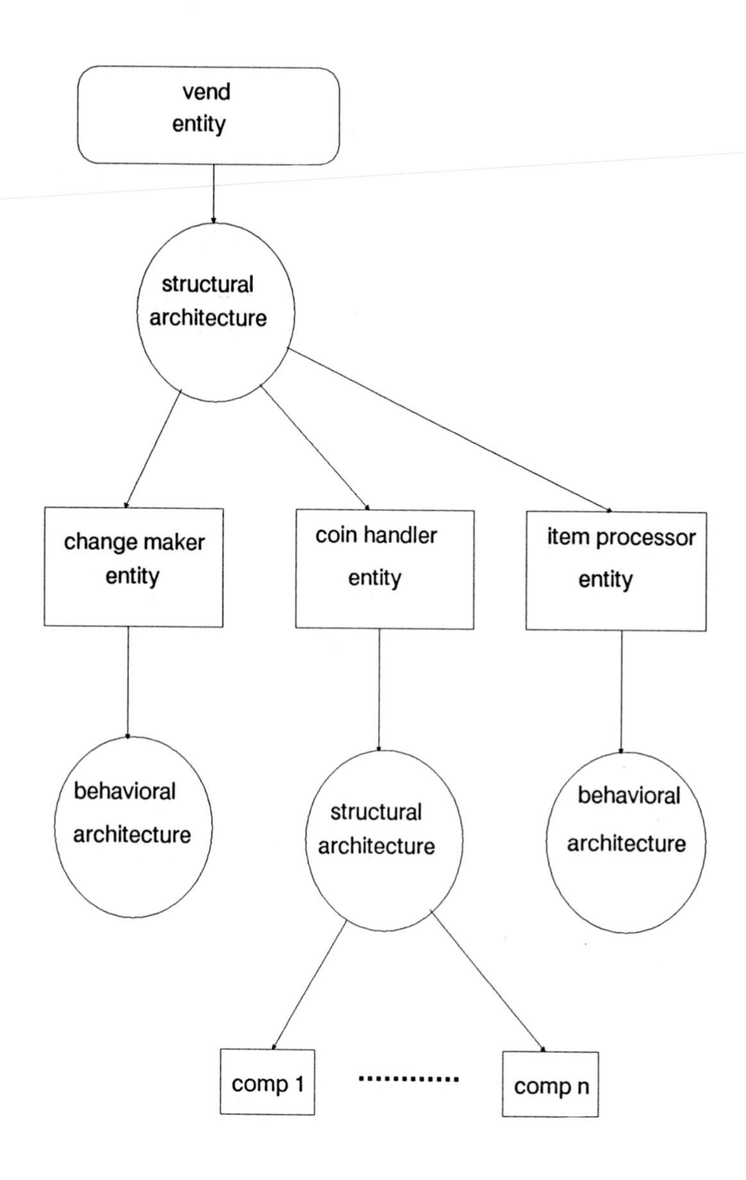
vend
entity
structural
architecture
change maker
entity
coin handler
entity
item processor
entity
behavioral
architecture
structural
architecture
behavioral
architecture
comp 1
comp n

Figure 11-7

```
      USE CONFIGURATION WORK.coin_handle_con;
    END FOR;

    -- behavioral architecture
    FOR U2 : change_maker
      USE CONFIGURATION WORK.change_mak_con;
    END FOR;

    -- structural architecture
    FOR U3 : item_proc
      USE CONFIGURATION WORK.item_struc_con;
  END FOR;

  END FOR;
END item_design_team;
```

Notice that this configuration specifies all the same configuration items for components U1 and U2 as configuration *first_level_con*, but that for component U3, a structural version of the *item_proc* component is selected. Components U1 and U2 of the design will use their behavioral versions, while component U3 can be refined to whatever level the design team chooses.

In this chapter the behavioral vending machine description was further decomposed into a structural description of three behavioral components. The behavior of each of the components was then presented and described. In the next chapter, each of the three components used to make up the structural description will be described at a structural level to further decompose the design to a lower level.

Chapter

12

Vending Machine : Second Decomposition

In this chapter the vending machine will be decomposed another level lower in the design hierarchy. The three components used to describe the vending machine in the first decomposition will be described by lower-level components. These lower-level components will be connected with signals to form a structural architecture for each of the three components, the *coin_handler*, the *change_maker*, and the *item_proc*.

The easiest method to describe the next level of the hierarchy is to create the basic architecture of the component using lower-level components and use one or more behavioral type components to generate the timing and control signals. The behavioral components can then be easily broken down into the next level of hierarchy to specific parts from the implementing technology. This methodology will be used for all three components.

12.1 Coin Handler

Let's begin our discussion with a description of the *coin_handler* component at a structural level. A block diagram of the *coin_handler* is shown in Figure 12-1.

The diagram shows 11 components used to describe the structural architecture. The components are as follows:

- U1, *convert*: converts coin values to integer values
- U2, *coin_mux*: multiplexes three different money values
- U3, *adder*: adds new coins, subtracts change and item prices from current total
- U4, *negate*: changes incoming change value to a negative value for subtraction
- U5, *negate*: changes incoming price to a negative value for subtraction
- U6, *convert*: converts change value to an integer value
- U7, *reg*: holds value of money in vending machine
- U8, *comp*: compares current total with *max_price*
- U9, *coin_tim_ctrl*: generates control signals for *coin_handler*
- U10, *inv*: inverts comparator output
- U11, *nand2*: generates *coin_reject* signal

All of these components are described in greater detail in the next chapter, but a discussion of how these components work together to produce the *coin_handler* behavior is presented now.

Components U3 (*adder*) and U7 (*reg*) form the basic accumulator function. Component U3 adds the previous value (*a1* input) with the new value on the *a2* input, and the resulting value is loaded into *reg* U7. These two components will accumulate the total amount of money in the vending machine. New values are added or subtracted depending on the arithmetic signs of the input values.

Component U2 (*mux*) is used to select an input value from the three possible money inputs, to be added or subtracted from the current total.

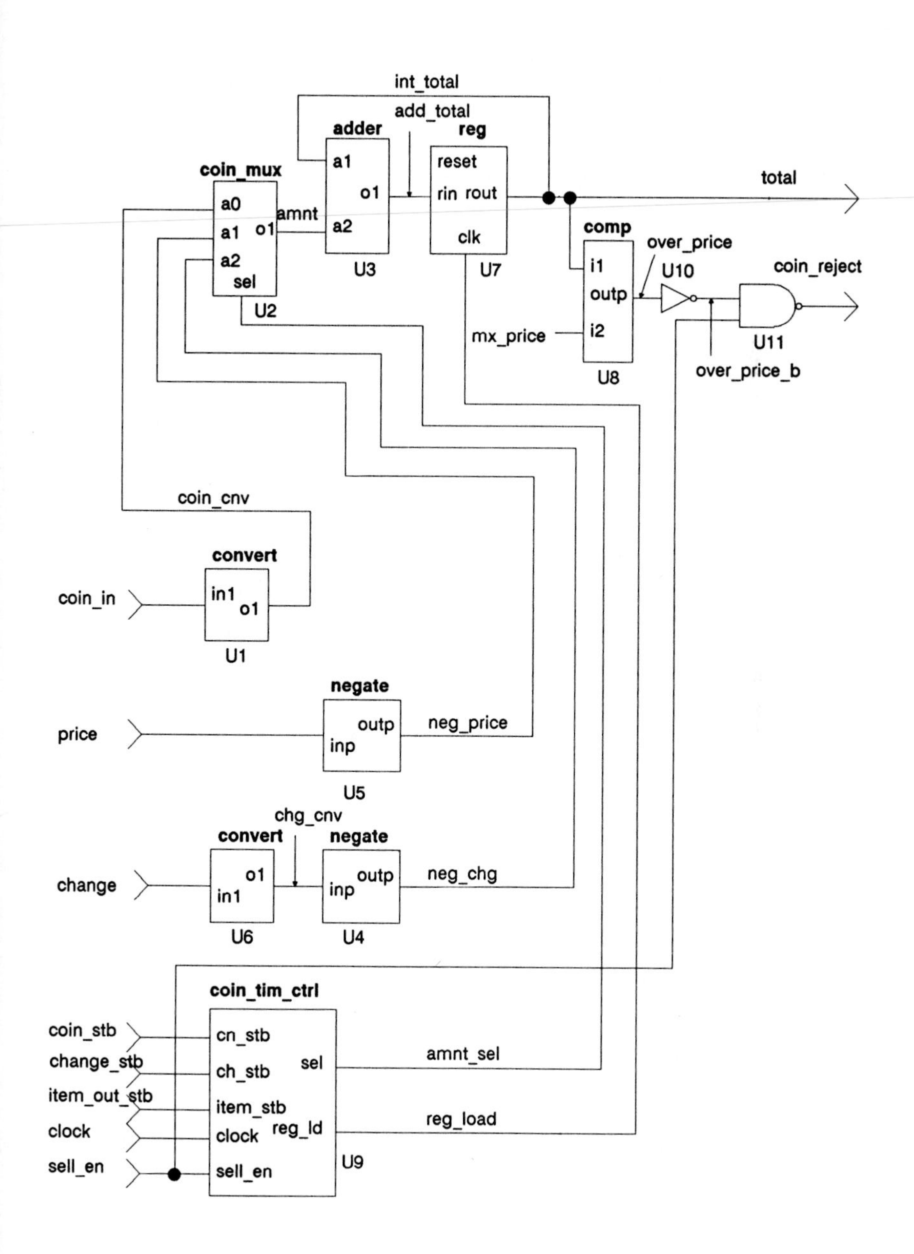
int_total
add_total
adder
reg
coin_mux
a1
o1
reset
rin rout
total
a0
amnt
a1 o1
a2
clk
a2
sel
U3
U7
comp
over_price
i1
U10
coin_reject
outp
U2
mx_price
i2
U11
U8
over_price_b
coin_cnv
convert
coin_in
in1
o1
U1
negate
price
outp
inp
neg_price
U5
chg_cnv
convert
negate
change
o1
in1
outp
inp
neg_chg
U6
U4
coin_tim_ctrl
coin_stb
cn_stb
change_stb
ch_stb
sel
amnt_sel
item_out_stb
item_stb
reg_load
clock
clock
reg_ld
sell_en
sell_en
U9

Figure 12-1

If input *a0* is selected, a new coin value will be added to signal *int_total.* If input *a1* is selected, an item has been purchased, and the purchase price will be subtracted from signal *int_total.* Finally if input *a2* is selected, change is being returned, and the change value must be subtracted from signal *int_total.*

Components U4 and U5 translate the input values to the opposite sign. Component U4 converts the change value, which will be a positive value equal to a coin value, to a negative value so that a subtraction operation is performed when the *neg_chg* signal is added to the *int_total* signal. The same is true of component U5. This component converts the price of the item sold to a negative value so that it can be subtracted from the total money in the vending machine.

Component U8 is a comparator component that will output a '1' (forcing strength) value on its output, whenever input *i1* is greater than or equal to input *i2.* In this instance, whenever the money in the vending machine is greater than or equal to *max_price*, signal *over_price* will be a '1' (forcing strength), indicating that coins should be rejected.

Component U9, *coin_tim_ctrl*, provides all of the timing and control signals for the *coin_handler* entity. All of the strobe signals, *clock*, and *sell_en* are input to this component. Component U9 generates output signals *reg_ld*, for loading the total register, and the *amnt_sel* signal, used to control which value is added or subtracted from the total.

If *item_out_stb* has a rising edge, component U9 will be alerted to an item purchase occurrence. Component U9 will then apply the correct value on the *amnt_sel* signal to select a price from component U2, the *coin_mux* component. After the adder (U3) computes the new total value with the item price subtracted, signal *reg_ld* is strobed to clock the new total into component U7.

When the *change_stb* signal has a rising edge, a similar operation occurs. The difference is that component U2 selects the *a2* input, the change value, to subtract from the total. Signal *reg_ld* is then strobed to load in the new total value, with the change value subtracted.

If *sell_en* is a '1', when a rising edge occurs on *coin_stb*, the coin value is added to the total. Component U9 will select input *a0* when a rising edge occurs on the *coin_stb* input. The coin value will be added to the total money in the vending machine, and *reg_ld* will then strobe the result into component U7.

Components U10 and U11 will provide the logic needed to generate the *coin_reject* signal from the two inputs, *over_price*, and *sell_en*. Signal *over_price* is the output of component U8, a comparator, and *sell_en* is an input signal.

A structural architecture that connects the components as shown in Figure 12-1 is outlined below:

```
ARCHITECTURE structural OF coin_handler IS
   COMPONENT convert
      PORT( in1 : IN t_coin;
            o1 : OUT t_value);
   END COMPONENT;

   COMPONENT coin_mux
      PORT( a0, a1, a2 : IN t_value;
            sel : IN t_mux_sel;
            o1 : OUT t_value);
   END COMPONENT;

   COMPONENT adder
      PORT( a1, a2 : IN t_value;
            o1 : OUT t_value);
   END COMPONENT;

   COMPONENT negate
      PORT( inp : IN t_value;
            outp : OUT t_value);
   END COMPONENT;

   COMPONENT reg
      PORT( rin : IN t_value;
            reset : IN t_wlogic;
            clk : IN t_wlogic;
            rout : OUT t_value);
   END COMPONENT;

   COMPONENT comp
      PORT( i1, i2 : IN t_value;
            outp : OUT t_wlogic);
```

```
    END COMPONENT;

    COMPONENT coin_tim_ctrl
      PORT( cn_stb, ch_stb, item_stb,
            clock, sell_en : IN t_wlogic;
            sel : OUT t_mux_sel;
            reg_ld : OUT t_wlogic);
    END COMPONENT;

    COMPONENT nand2
      PORT( in1, in2 : IN t_wlogic;
            o1 : OUT t_wlogic);
    END COMPONENT;

    COMPONENT inv
      PORT( in1 : IN t_wlogic;
            o1 : OUT t_wlogic);
    END COMPONENT;

    SIGNAL neg_price, neg_chg, coin_cnv, amnt,
           add_total, chg_cnv : t_value;

    SIGNAL reg_load, over_price,
           over_price_b : t_wlogic;

    SIGNAL amnt_sel : t_mux_sel;
    SIGNAL int_total : t_value;
    SIGNAL mx_price : t_value := max_price;

  BEGIN
    U1 : convert
      PORT MAP( in1 => coin_in,
                o1 => coin_cnv);

    U2 : coin_mux
      PORT MAP( a0 => coin_cnv,
                a1 => neg_price,
                a2 => neg_chg,
                sel => amnt_sel,
                o1 => amnt);

    U3 : adder
```

```
    PORT MAP( a1 => int_total,
              a2 => amnt,
              o1 => add_total);

U4 : negate
    PORT MAP( inp => chg_cnv,
              outp => neg_chg);

U5 : negate
    PORT MAP( inp => price,
              outp => neg_price);

U6 : convert
    PORT MAP( in1 => change_in,
              o1 => chg_cnv);

U7 : reg
    PORT MAP( rin => add_total,
              reset => reset,
              clk => reg_load,
              rout => int_total);

U8 : comp
    PORT MAP( i1 => int_total,
              i2 => mx_price,
              outp => over_price);

U9 : coin_tim_ctrl
    PORT MAP( cn_stb => coin_stb,
              ch_stb => change_stb,
              item_stb => item_out_stb,
              clock => clock,
              sell_en => sell_en,
              sel => amnt_sel,
              reg_ld => reg_load);

U10 : inv
    PORT MAP( in1 => over_price,
              o1 => over_price_b);

U11 : nand2
    PORT MAP( in1 => over_price_b,
```

```
                    in2 => sell_en,
                    o1 => coin_reject);

    total <= int_total;

  END structural;
```

Since this architecture instantiates 11 components, the configuration shown below can be used to specify the configurations for each of the components.

```
CONFIGURATION coin_struc_con OF coin_handler IS
  FOR structural

    FOR U1 : convert
      USE CONFIGURATION WORK.conv_con;
    END FOR;

    FOR U2 : coin_mux
      USE CONFIGURATION WORK.coin_mux_con;
    END FOR;

    FOR U3 : adder
      USE CONFIGURATION WORK.addercon;
    END FOR;

    FOR U4 : negate
      USE CONFIGURATION WORK.negcon;
    END FOR;

    FOR U5 : negate
      USE CONFIGURATION WORK.negcon;
    END FOR;

    FOR U6 : convert
      USE CONFIGURATION WORK.conv_con;
    END FOR;

    FOR U7 : reg
      USE CONFIGURATION WORK.regcon;
    END FOR;
```

```
      FOR U8 : comp
        USE CONFIGURATION WORK.compcon;
      END FOR;

      FOR U9 : coin_tim_ctrl
        USE CONFIGURATION
            WORK.timing_control_con;
      END FOR;

      FOR U10 : inv
        USE CONFIGURATION WORK.invcon;
      END FOR;

      FOR U11 : nand2
        USE CONFIGURATION WORK.nand2con;
      END FOR;

    END FOR;
  END coin_struc_con;
```

12.2 Item Processor

The next component of the three top-level components is the *item_proc* component. A block diagram of the *item_proc* structural description is shown in Figure 12-2.

There are 10 components used to describe the *item_proc* component, as follows:

- U1, *item_reg*: holds the item selected for purchase
- U2, *mux4*: selects item price
- U3, *comp*: compares total with item price
- U4, *item_reg*: holds item purchased
- U5, *select4*: selects which item count to decrement
- U6, *count*: counter for pretzels sold
- U7, *count*: counter for chips sold
- U8, *count*: counter for cookies sold
- U9, *count*: counter for doughnuts sold

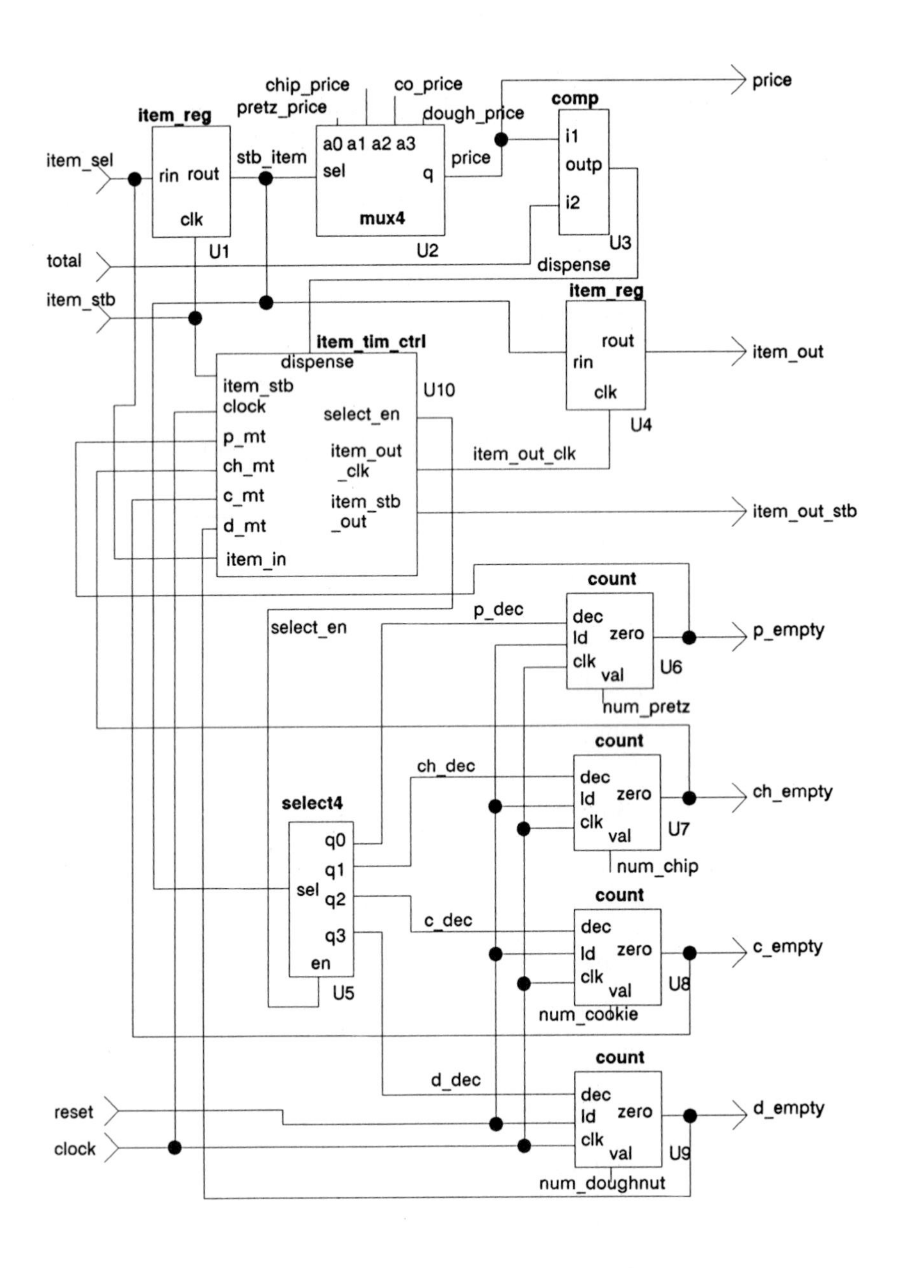

chip_price
co_price
price
pretz_price
item_reg
dough_price
comp
item_sel
a0 a1 a2 a3
i1
stb_item
price
rin rout
sel
q
outp
clk
mux4
i2
U1
U2
U3
total
dispense
item_stb
item_reg
item_tim_ctrl
rout
item_out
dispense
rin
item_stb
U10
clk
clock
select_en
U4
p_mt
item_out
_clk
item_out_clk
ch_mt
c_mt
item_stb
_out
item_out_stb
d_mt
item_in
count
p_dec
select_en
dec
ld
zero
p_empty
clk
U6
val
num_pretz
count
ch_dec
dec
select4
ld
zero
ch_empty
clk
q0
val
U7
q1
num_chip
sel
q2
count
c_dec
dec
q3
ld
zero
c_empty
en
clk
val
U8
U5
num_cookie
count
d_dec
dec
reset
ld
zero
d_empty
clock
clk
val
U9
num_doughnut

Figure 12-2

- U10, *item_tim_ctrl*: controls timing and control signals for item processor

Once again the complete component descriptions are given in Chapter 13, but the description below shows how the components of the design work together to produce the desired behavior.

The main function of the *item_proc* component is to determine if an item can be purchased with the money available in the vending machine. Secondarily, the vending machine counts how many of each item is sold, and illuminates the *item_empty* lights if necessary.

Component U1 stores the item selected with signal *item_sel* upon a rising edge on signal *item_stb*. Based on the item stored in *reg* U1, component U2 will select one of the four prices on its inputs. If the item input is *pretzels*, component U2 will output the price for pretzels. If the item input is *chips*, component U2 will output the price for chips. Component U3 compares the selected price from U2, with the total money in the vending machine, the value of signal *total*. If the money entered in the machine is greater than or equal to the price of the item, then the dispense signal will be set to '1' (forcing strength). If there is not enough money in the vending machine to buy the selected item, the dispense signal will be '0'.

The four item counters, components U6 to U9, are used to indicate when a particular item has been sold out. These counters are loaded when the *ld* input, connected to the *reset* signal, is a '1'. The counters will be loaded with the value specified on the *val* input port. The values specified for the *val* input port are the total number of each item in the vending machine. Each *clk* rising edge, along with the *dec* input set to a '1' value, will cause the counter to decrement by 1. When the counter reaches zero, the *zero* output is set to a '1', indicating that the item has been sold out.

Component U10, the control block for the *item_proc* component, is alerted to a purchase by a rising edge on the *item_stb* input. If the *dispense* signal transitions to a '1' one clock later, then an item purchase occurs. Component U10 will output the necessary signals to load the item into component U4 (*reg*) for output. After component U4 has been loaded with the item purchased, one clock later the *item_stb_out* signal will strobe the item purchased out.

Component U10 will then set the *select_en* signal to a '1' value. This signal enables one of the item sold counters to count down by one value. Component U5 selects the appropriate counter based on the item selected. For instance, if the item selected is *chips*, then the *ch_dec* signal will be set to a '1' and component U7 will decrement by 1.

Component U10 also examines the empty lines from the four item counters, to determine if an item can be dispensed. Based on the item selected, component U10 makes sure that the *item_empty* line is '0' before an item is dispensed.

A structural architecture that connects the components as shown in Figure 12-2 is outlined below:

```
ARCHITECTURE structural OF item_proc IS
   COMPONENT item_reg
      PORT( rin : IN t_item;
            clk : IN t_wlogic;
            rout : OUT t_item);
   END COMPONENT;

   COMPONENT mux4
      PORT( sel : IN t_item;
            a0, a1, a2, a3 : in t_value;
            q : OUT t_value);
   END COMPONENT;

   COMPONENT comp
      PORT( i1, i2 : IN t_value;
            outp : OUT t_wlogic);
   END COMPONENT;

   COMPONENT select4
      PORT( sel : IN t_item;
            en : IN t_wlogic;
            q0, q1, q2, q3 : OUT t_wlogic);
   END COMPONENT;

   COMPONENT count
      PORT( dec, ld, clk : IN t_wlogic;
```

```
            val : IN t_value;
            zero : OUT t_wlogic);
    END COMPONENT;

    COMPONENT item_tim_ctrl
        PORT( dispense : IN t_wlogic;
              item_stb : IN t_wlogic;
              clock : IN t_wlogic;
              item_out_clk : OUT t_wlogic;
              select_en : OUT t_wlogic;
              item_stb_out : OUT t_wlogic);
    END COMPONENT;

    SIGNAL stb_item : t_item;
    SIGNAL int_price : t_value;
    SIGNAL dispense, select_item,
           item_out_clk : t_wlogic;

    SIGNAL pretz_price : t_value := p_price;
    SIGNAL chip_price : t_value := ch_price;
    SIGNAL co_price : t_value := c_price;
    SIGNAL dough_price : t_value := d_price;

    SIGNAL num_pretz : t_value := p_total;
    SIGNAL num_chip : t_value := ch_total;
    SIGNAL num_cookie : t_value := c_total;
    SIGNAL num_doughnut : t_value := d_total;

    SIGNAL select_en, p_dec, ch_dec,
              c_dec, d_dec : t_wlogic;
BEGIN

    U1 : item_reg
        PORT MAP( rin => item_sel,
                  clk => item_stb,
                  rout => stb_item);

    U2 : mux4
        PORT MAP( sel => stb_item,
                  a0 => pretz_price,
                  a1 => chip_price,
                  a2 => co_price,
```

```
                a3 => dough_price,
                q => int_price);

      U3 : comp
         PORT MAP( i1 => total,
                   i2 => int_price,
                   outp => dispense);

      U4 : item_reg
         PORT MAP( rin => stb_item,
                   clk => item_out_clk,
                   rout => item_out);

      U5 : select4
         PORT MAP( sel => stb_item,
                   en => select_en,
                   q0 => p_dec,
                   q1 => ch_dec,
                   q2 => c_dec,
                   q3 => d_dec);

      U6 : count
         PORT MAP( dec => p_dec,
                   ld => reset,
                   clk => clock,
                   val => num_pretz,
                   zero => p_empty);

      U7 : count
         PORT MAP( dec => ch_dec,
                   ld => reset,
                   clk => clock,
                   val => num_chip,
                   zero => ch_empty);

      U8 : count
         PORT MAP( dec => c_dec,
                   ld => reset,
                   clk => clock,
                   val => num_cookie,
                   zero => c_empty);
```

```
  U9 : count
     PORT MAP( dec => d_dec,
               ld => reset,
               clk => clock,
               val => num_doughnut,
               zero => d_empty);

  U10 : item_tim_ctrl
     PORT MAP( dispense => dispense,
               item_stb => item_stb,
               clock => clock,
               item_out_clk => item_out_clk,
               select_en => select_en,
               item_stb_out => item_out_stb);
  price <= int_price;
END structural;
```

A configuration to specify which architectures to use for each of the 10 components in the *item_proc* entity is shown below:

```
CONFIGURATION item_struc_con OF item_proc IS
  FOR structural

    FOR U1 : item_reg
      USE CONFIGURATION WORK.item_regcon;
    END FOR;

    FOR U2 : mux4
      USE CONFIGURATION WORK.mux4con;
    END FOR;

    FOR U3 : comp
      USE CONFIGURATION WORK.compcon;
    END FOR;

    FOR U4 : item_reg
      USE CONFIGURATION WORK.item_regcon;
    END FOR;

    FOR U5 : select4
      USE CONFIGURATION WORK.select4con;
    END FOR;
```

```
      FOR U6 : count
        USE CONFIGURATION WORK.countcon;
      END FOR;

      FOR U7 : count
        USE CONFIGURATION WORK.countcon;
      END FOR;

      FOR U8 : count
        USE CONFIGURATION WORK.countcon;
      END FOR;

      FOR U9 : count
        USE CONFIGURATION WORK.countcon;
      END FOR;

      FOR U10 : item_tim_ctrl
        USE CONFIGURATION WORK.item_ctrl_con;
      END FOR;

    END FOR;
  END item_struc_con;
```

12.3 Change Maker

The last top-level component that needs to be described is the *change_maker* component. This component is used to output the correct change when an item has been purchased. A block diagram of a structural description of the *change_maker* is shown in Figure 12-3.

There are 12 components used to make up the design, as shown below:

- U1, *sub*: subtracts price from total
- U2, *reg*: holds change value
- U3, *mux*: selects new change value or current change being made
- U4, *reg*: holds intermediate change being made
- U5, *comp*: compares change amount for > = 5
- U6, *comp*: compares change amount for > = 10

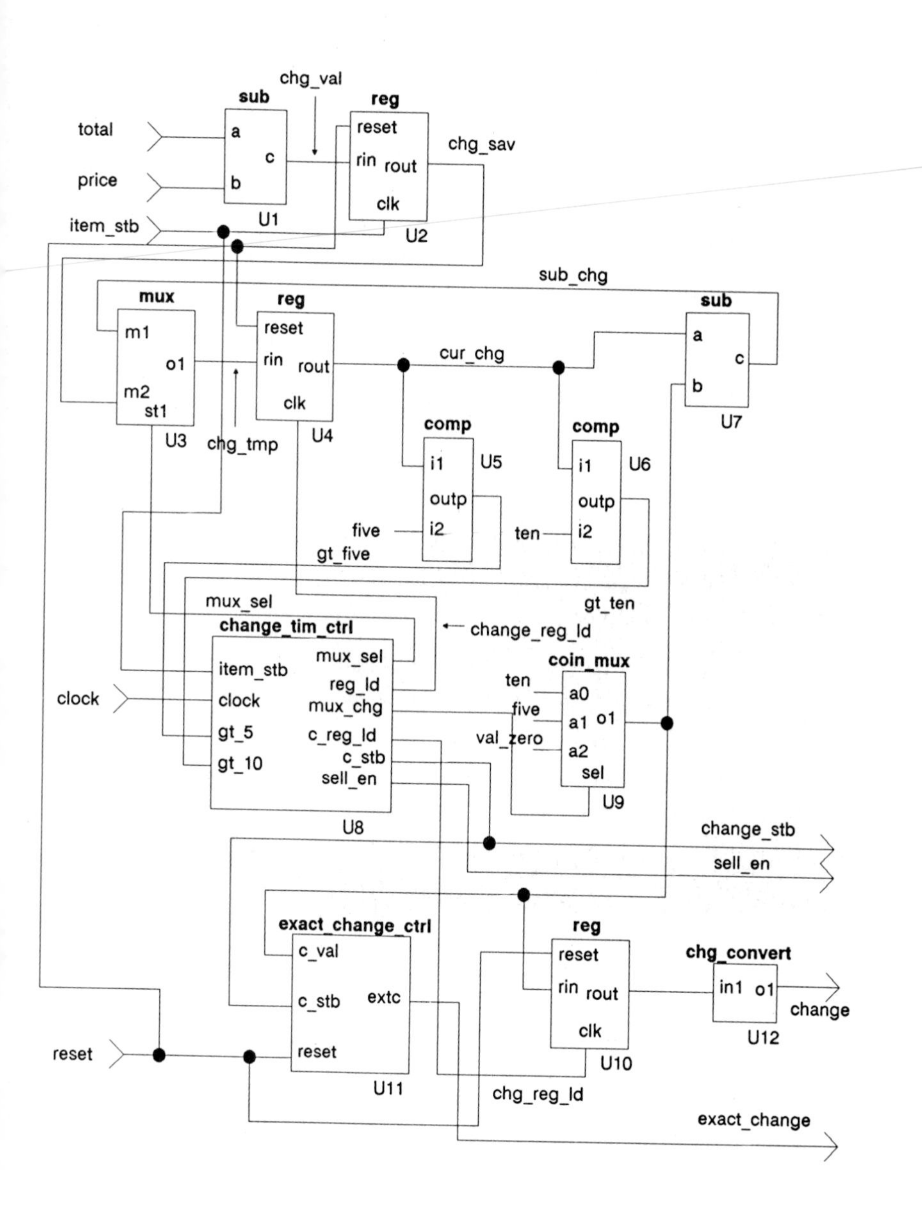
chg_val
sub
reg
total
a
reset
c
chg_sav
rin
rout
price
b
clk
item_stb
U1
U2
sub_chg
mux
reg
sub
m1
reset
a
o1
rin
rout
cur_chg
c
m2
b
st1
clk
U3
chg_tmp
U4
U7
comp
comp
i1
U5
i1
U6
outp
outp
five
i2
ten
i2
gt_five
mux_sel
gt_ten
change_tim_ctrl
change_reg_ld
mux_sel
coin_mux
item_stb
reg_ld
ten
a0
clock
clock
mux_chg
five
a1
o1
gt_5
c_reg_ld
val_zero
a2
gt_10
c_stb
sel
sell_en
U9
U8
change_stb
sell_en
exact_change_ctrl
reg
c_val
reset
chg_convert
rin
rout
in1
o1
c_stb
extc
change
clk
U12
reset
reset
U10
U11
chg_reg_ld
exact_change

Figure 12-3

- U7, *sub*: subtracts change given out from change left to give
- U8, *change_tim_ctrl*: generates control signals for *change_maker*
- U9, *coin_mux*: selects change value to give out
- U10, *reg*: holds change being output
- U11, *exact_change_ctrl*: maintains change coin totals and illuminates exact change light
- U12, *chg_convert*: converts the change value to a coin value

A full description of all of the components is given in Chapter 13. The description that follows will describe how all of these components work together to provide the *change_maker* functionality.

Component U1 is used to find the amount of change that needs to be returned to the customer. The price of the item is subtracted from the total money in the vending machine. The resulting value is then clocked into component U2, a register used to hold the intermediate change value, with a rising edge on input signal *item_stb*.

The rising edge on the *item_stb* input will also trigger component U8, the *change_tim_ctrl* component, to begin making change. First the change value in *reg* U2 will be transferred to register U4 through component U3, the *mux* component. This process occurs as component U8 generates the appropriate select value on signal *mux_sel* to select input *m2*. The change value is then strobed into component U4 with the *change_reg_ld* signal.

Now that the register has been loaded with the amount of change to return, component U8 will examine the two comparator outputs to determine the next step. If the *gt_ten* signal is a '1', then a dime needs to be returned as change. Component U8 will output the appropriate value on signal *mux_chg* to select input *a0* of *mux* U9. Input *a0* has the value of a *dime* as its input. Component U9 will drive the change value onto signal *sel_chg* to components U7 and U10. Component U7, a subtractor, will subtract the change value from the change to be given, held in *reg* U4. The result will be passed through *mux* U3, and clocked into *reg* U4.

If signal *gt_5* is a '1' and signal *gt_10* is a '0', then only a nickel value needs to be returned as change. Component U8 will select input *a1* of *mux* U9. The nickel value will be subtracted, and the resulting value placed in *reg* U4. When both signal *gt_5* and *gt_10* are '0', the change-making process will conclude.

Component U10 is used to hold the change value, while the *change_stb* signal strobes the change value out. The change value is converted to a *t_coin* value by component U12. A *t_coin* value is needed for the mechanical interface, while a numeric value is needed internally for the adder-subtractor components.

Finally component U11 will provide the operation of the *exact_change* signal. Whenever a coin is sent to the customer as change, the *exact_change_ctrl* component will decrement the number of coins available for that particular type of coin. When the amount of either type of coin falls below 5, the *exact_change* signal is set to true, indicating that correct change may not be given for any subsequent purchases.

The *change_tim_ctrl* component also provides the control necessary for the *sell_en* output. When the *change_maker* is making change, signal *sell_en* is set to '0'. When the *change_maker* is not making change, signal *sell_en* is set to '1'.

A structural architecture that implements the block diagram for the *change_maker* is shown below:

```
ARCHITECTURE structural OF change_maker IS
   COMPONENT sub
      PORT( a, b : IN t_value;
            c : OUT t_value);
   END COMPONENT;

   COMPONENT reg
      PORT( rin : IN t_value;
            reset : IN t_wlogic;
            clk : IN t_wlogic;
            rout : OUT t_value);
   END COMPONENT;

   COMPONENT mux
      PORT( m1, m2 : IN t_value;
```

```
            st1 : IN t_wlogic;
            o1 : OUT t_value);
    END COMPONENT;

    COMPONENT comp
        PORT( i1, i2 : IN t_value;
            outp : OUT t_wlogic);
    END COMPONENT;

    COMPONENT coin_mux
        PORT( a0, a1, a2 : IN t_value;
            sel : IN t_mux_sel;
            o1 : OUT t_value);
    END COMPONENT;

    COMPONENT change_tim_ctrl
        PORT( item_stb : IN t_wlogic;
            clock : IN t_wlogic;
            reset : IN t_wlogic;
            gt_5 : IN t_wlogic;
            gt_10 : IN t_wlogic;
            mux_sel : OUT t_wlogic;
            reg_ld : OUT t_wlogic;
            mux_chg : OUT t_mux_sel;
            c_reg_ld : OUT t_wlogic;
            c_stb : OUT t_wlogic;
            sell_en : OUT t_wlogic);
    END COMPONENT;

    COMPONENT exact_change_ctrl
        GENERIC( num_dimes, num_nickels : t_value);
        PORT( c_val : IN t_value;
            c_stb : IN t_wlogic;
            reset : IN t_wlogic;
            extc : OUT t_wlogic);
    END COMPONENT;

    COMPONENT chg_convert
        PORT( in1 : IN t_value;
            o1 : OUT t_coin);
    END COMPONENT;
```

```
   SIGNAL sub_chg, cur_chg, chg_tmp,
         chg_sav, chg_val, sel_chg : t_value;

   SIGNAL mux_sel, change_reg_ld, chg_reg_ld,
         gt_five, gt_ten : t_wlogic;

   SIGNAL mux_chg : t_mux_sel;
   SIGNAL val_zero : t_value := 0;

   SIGNAL ten : t_value := 10;
   SIGNAL five : t_value := 5;
   SIGNAL zero : t_wlogic := F0;

   SIGNAL change_int : t_value;
   SIGNAL change_stb_int : t_wlogic;
BEGIN

   U1 : sub
      PORT MAP( a => total,
               b => price,
               c => chg_val);

   U2 : reg
      PORT MAP( rin => chg_val,
               reset => reset,
               clk => item_stb,
               rout => chg_sav);

   U3 : mux
      PORT MAP( m1 => sub_chg,
               m2 => chg_sav,
               st1 => mux_sel,
               o1 => chg_tmp);

   U4 : reg
      PORT MAP( rin => chg_tmp,
               reset => reset,
               clk => change_reg_ld,
               rout => cur_chg);

   U5 : comp
      PORT MAP( i1 => cur_chg,
```

```
                    i2 => five,
                    outp => gt_five);

    U6 : comp
       PORT MAP( i1 => cur_chg,
                 i2 => ten,
                 outp => gt_ten);

    U7 : sub
       PORT MAP( a => cur_chg,
                 b => sel_chg,
                 c => sub_chg);

    U8 : change_tim_ctrl
       PORT MAP( item_stb => item_stb,
                 clock => clock,
                 reset => reset,
                 gt_5 => gt_five,
                 gt_10 => gt_ten,
                 mux_sel => mux_sel,
                 reg_ld => change_reg_ld,
                 mux_chg => mux_chg,
                 c_reg_ld => chg_reg_ld,
                 c_stb => change_stb_int,
                 sell_en => sell_en);

    U9 : coin_mux
       PORT MAP( a0 => ten,
                 a1 => five,
                 a2 => val_zero,
                 sel => mux_chg,
                 o1 => sel_chg);

    U10 : reg
       PORT MAP( rin => sel_chg,
                 reset => reset,
                 clk => chg_reg_ld,
                 rout => change_int);

    U11 : exact_change_ctrl
       GENERIC MAP( num_dimes => num_dimes,
                    num_nickels => num_nickels)
```

```
      PORT MAP( c_val => sel_chg,
                c_stb => change_stb_int,
                reset => reset,
                extc => exact_change);

   U12 : chg_convert
      PORT MAP( in1 => change_int,
                o1 => change);

   change_stb <= change_stb_int;

END structural;
```

A configuration that specifies the architecture to use for each component in the design is shown below:

```
CONFIGURATION change_struc_con OF
     change_maker IS
   FOR structural

      FOR U1 : sub
        USE CONFIGURATION WORK.subcon;
      END FOR;

      FOR U2 : reg
        USE CONFIGURATION WORK.regcon;
      END FOR;

      FOR U3 : mux
        USE CONFIGURATION WORK.muxcon;
      END FOR;

      FOR U4 : reg
        USE CONFIGURATION WORK.regcon;
      END FOR;

      FOR U5 : comp
        USE CONFIGURATION WORK.compcon;
      END FOR;

      FOR U6 : comp
        USE CONFIGURATION WORK.compcon;
      END FOR;
```

```
      FOR U7 : sub
        USE CONFIGURATION WORK.subcon;
      END FOR;

      FOR U8 : change_tim_ctrl
        USE CONFIGURATION WORK.chg_ctrl_con;
      END FOR;

      FOR U9 : coin_mux
        USE CONFIGURATION WORK.coin_mux_con;
      END FOR;

      FOR U10 : reg
        USE CONFIGURATION WORK.regcon;
      END FOR;

      FOR U11 : exact_change_ctrl
        USE CONFIGURATION WORK.exact_chg_con;
      END FOR;

      FOR U12 : chg_convert
        USE CONFIGURATION WORK.chg_conv_con;
      END FOR;
    END FOR;
  END change_struc_con;
```

12.4 Second-Level Configuration

The structural architectures for components *coin_handler*, *item_proc*, and *change_maker* need to be specified for each component. Configurations *coin_struc_con, item_struc_con,* and *change_struc_con* specify the structural architecture for each of the three components, respectively. These configurations can be specified for the three components, as shown in the configuration below:

```
  CONFIGURATION second_level_con OF
      vend_control IS
    FOR first_level

      FOR u1 : coin_handler
        USE CONFIGURATION WORK.coin_struc_con;
      END FOR;
```

```
        FOR u2 : change_maker
          USE CONFIGURATION WORK.change_struc_con;
        END FOR;

        FOR u3 : item_proc
          USE CONFIGURATION WORK.item_struc_con;
        END FOR;

    END FOR;
  END second_level_con;
```

A second-level configuration, *second_level_con* of entity *vend_control*, specifies the three structural configurations for each of the three components.

In this chapter we examined the next level of hierarchy of the vending machine description. In the next chapter, we will examine the component descriptions of each of the components used to model the *coin_handler*, *item_proc*, and *change_maker* components.

Chapter

13

Vending Machine Components

In this chapter the nineteen different components used to make up the structural architectures for the *coin_handler, item_proc,* and *change_maker* components will be discussed. An entity, architecture, and configuration will be shown for each component.

13.1 Negate

The first component to be discussed is the *negate* component. The negate component is used to change the sign of the input value from negative to positive, or from positive to negative. In the vending machine it is mainly used to change the sign of an input value to a negative amount. The amount can then be subtracted with an adder.

The symbol used to represent the negate component in the schematic is shown in Figure 13-1. The entity and architecture for the negate component are shown below:

```
USE WORK.p_vending.ALL;
ENTITY negate IS
```

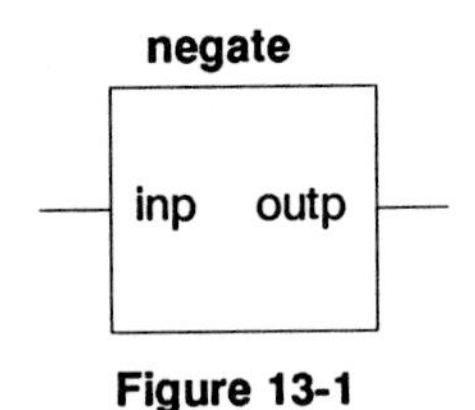

Figure 13-1

```
    PORT( inp : IN t_value;
          outp : OUT t_value);
END negate;

ARCHITECTURE behave OF negate IS
BEGIN
   -- since type t_value is a subtype of integer
   -- we can use the built in negation operator
   -- for the integer type
   outp <= -( inp);
END behave;
```

The architecture simply performs an integer negate on the input value and assigns this value to the output port.

13.2 Mux

The second component is the *mux* component. Based on the value of a select input, one of two inputs is transferred to the output. This device was used to allow the accumulator functionality of the *coin_handler* to be loaded.

The symbol for the the mux component is shown in Figure 13-2. The entity and architecture for the mux are shown below:

```
USE WORK.p_vending.ALL;
USE STD.std_logic.ALL;
ENTITY mux IS
   PORT( m1, m2 : IN t_value;
         st1 : IN t_wlogic;
         o1 : OUT t_value);
END mux;

ARCHITECTURE behave OF mux IS
```

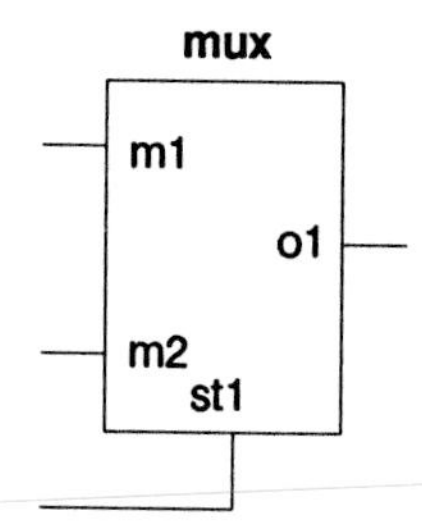

Figure 13-2

```
BEGIN
   mux_proc : PROCESS( m1, m2, st1)
   BEGIN
      IF ( st1 = '1') THEN
         o1 <= m1;
      ELSE
         o1 <= m2;
      END IF;
   END PROCESS mux_proc;
END behave;
```

13.3 Adder

The next component described is the *adder.* This component adds the values of its two inputs, and outputs a single value. This adder contains no carry in or carry out for simplicity, and in the vending machine example there was no need for the extra inputs or outputs. This device was used to form the accumulator functionality in the *coin_handler.*

The symbol used in the schematic for the adder is shown in Figure 13-3. The entity and architecture that match the symbol are shown below:

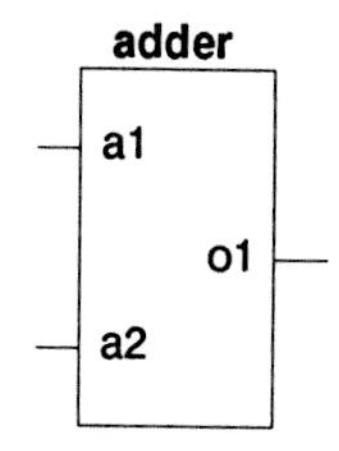

Figure 13-3

```
USE WORK.p_vending.ALL;
ENTITY adder IS
   PORT( a1, a2 : IN t_value;
         o1 : OUT t_value);
END adder;

ARCHITECTURE behave OF adder IS
BEGIN
      -- since type t_value is of type integer
      -- we can use the built in add operation
      -- for type integer

      o1 <= a1 + a2;
END behave;
```

The architecture consists of a single addition operation of inputs *a1* and *a2*. The result of this operation is assigned to the output *o1*.

13.4 Reg

The *reg* component forms the basic element used to model register operations in the vending machine controller. This device is similar to a D flip-flop except that the inputs are of type *t_value*, which currently is an integer type.

The reg component synchronously loads the input value on a rising edge of the input *clock*, but has an asynchronous *reset* input to clear the device.

The symbol for the reg component is shown in Figure 13-4.

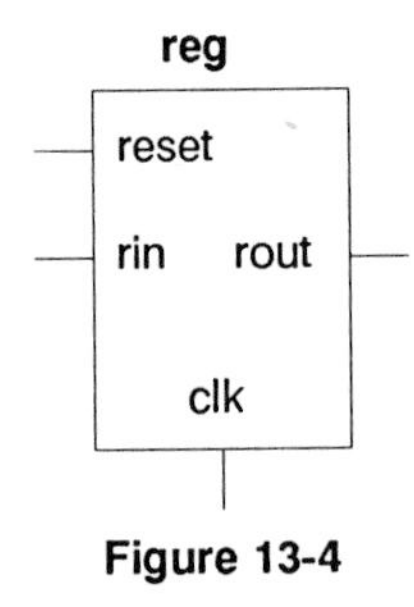

Figure 13-4

The entity and architecture that implement this functionality are shown below:

```
USE WORK.p_vending.ALL;
USE STD.std_logic.ALL;
ENTITY reg IS
   PORT( rin : IN t_value;
         reset : IN t_wlogic;
         clk : IN t_wlogic;
         rout : OUT t_value);
END reg;

ARCHITECTURE behave OF reg IS
BEGIN
   reg_proc : PROCESS( reset, clk)
   BEGIN
      IF ( reset = '1') THEN
         rout <= 0;
      ELSIF ( clk = '1') AND ( clk'EVENT) THEN
         rout <= rin;
      END IF;
   END PROCESS reg_proc;
END behave;
```

13.5 Comp

The next component in the list is the *comp* component. The comp component is used to perform comparison operations in the vending machine controller. This device is used to determine if enough money has been entered into the vending machine to purchase an item or if enough change has been given out.

The symbol for the comp component is shown in Figure 13-5. The entity and architecture describing this component are shown below:

```
USE WORK.p_vending.ALL;
USE STD.std_logic.ALL;
ENTITY comp IS
   PORT( i1, i2 : IN t_value;
         outp   : OUT t_wlogic);
END comp;

ARCHITECTURE behave OF comp IS
```

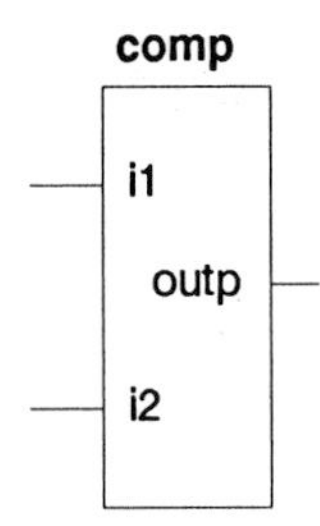

Figure 13-6

```
BEGIN
   comp_proc : PROCESS( i1, i2)
   BEGIN
      IF ( i1 >= i2) THEN
         outp <= F1;
      ELSE
         outp <= F0;
      END IF;
   END PROCESS comp_proc;
END behave;
```

13.6 Nand2

The next component is the *nand2* gate. This component will provide the NAND logical function on two input signals. It is used to generate the *coin_reject* function of the *coin_handler* block.

The symbol for the *nand2* is shown in Figure 13-6.

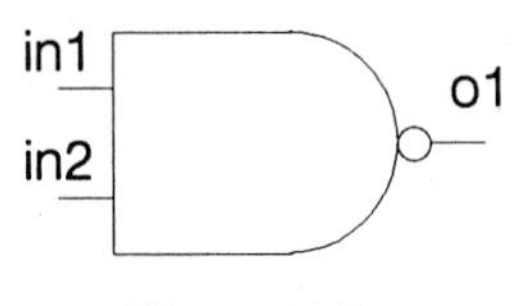

Figure 13-5

The entity and architecture for the device are shown below:

```
USE STD.std_logic.ALL;
USE STD.std_ttl.ALL;
ENTITY nand2 IS
   PORT( in1, in2 : IN t_wlogic;
```

```
        o1 : OUT t_wlogic);
END nand2;

ARCHITECTURE behave OF nand2 IS
BEGIN
   nand_proc : PROCESS( in1, in2)
   BEGIN
      o1 <= not(in1 AND in2);
   END PROCESS nand_proc;
END behave;
```

13.7 Inv

The next component described is the *inv* component. This component inverts the value of the input. If the input is a '1', the output will be a '0'. If the input is a '0', the output will be a '1'. It is used in the logic to generate the *coin_reject* signal.

A symbol of the inverter is shown in Figure 13-7.

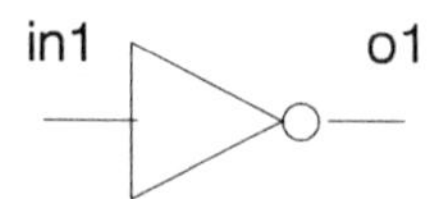

Figure 13-7

The entity and architecture of the inverter are shown below:

```
USE STD.std_logic.ALL;
USE STD.std_ttl.ALL;
ENTITY inv IS
   PORT( in1 : IN t_wlogic;
        o1 : OUT t_wlogic);
END inv;

ARCHITECTURE behave OF inv IS
BEGIN
   inv_proc : PROCESS( in1)
   BEGIN
      o1 <= NOT(in1);
   END PROCESS inv_proc;
END behave;
```

13.8 Item_reg

The *item_reg* component is used to perform a register operation for data of type *t_item.* Because of strong VHDL type checking, the register component described earlier cannot be used with types *t_value* and *t_item*. (If types *t_value* and *t_item* were subtypes of the same base type a single register model would be possible. In this example this is not case). The types of the ports of the entity determine what type can be connected to the entity. For the *item_reg*, the types of the ports are *t_item*. That is the major difference between the *item_reg* and the reg component described above. The only other difference is that the *item_reg* has no *reset* input.

The symbol for the *item_reg* component is shown in Figure 13-8.

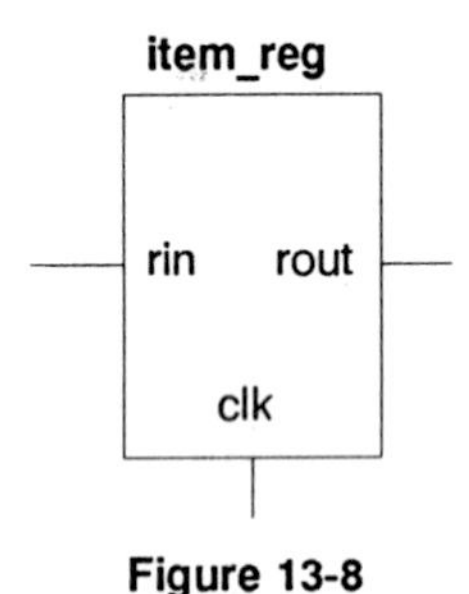

Figure 13-8

The entity and architecture that match the *item_reg* are shown below:

```
USE STD.std_logic.ALL;
USE WORK.p_vending.ALL;
ENTITY item_reg IS
   PORT( rin : IN t_item;
         clk : IN t_wlogic;
         rout : OUT t_item);
END item_reg;

ARCHITECTURE behave OF item_reg IS
BEGIN
   item_reg_proc : PROCESS( clk)
   BEGIN
      IF ( clk = '1') AND ( clk'EVENT) THEN
         rout <= rin;
```

```
      END IF;
   END PROCESS item_reg_proc;
END behave;
```

Whenever a rising edge is detected on the *clk* input, the value of the *rin* input port is assigned to the output port *rout*.

13.9 Mux4

The *mux4* component is used to multiplex four input values of type *t_value*. Based on the type of item passed to the multiplexer select input *sel*, the mux4 component will select one of the four inputs. This component is used to select the appropriate price for an item being purchased. The value of input *sel* selects the appropriate input from component *mux4* that contains the price of the input item.

The symbol of the mux4 component is shown in Figure 13-9.

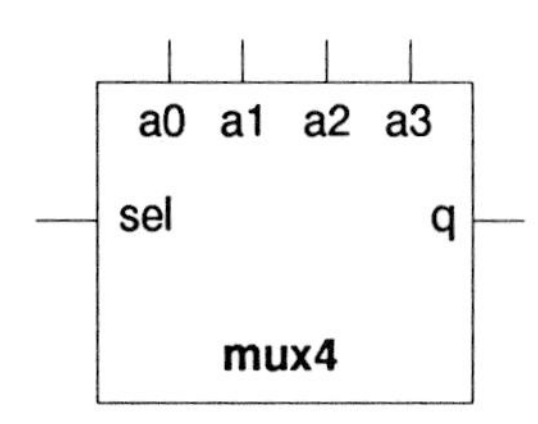

Figure 13-9

The model of the mux4 component, including entity and architecture are shown below:

```
USE STD.std_logic.ALL;
USE WORK.p_vending.ALL;
ENTITY mux4 IS
   PORT (sel : IN t_item;
         a0, a1, a2, a3 : IN t_value;
         q : OUT t_value);
END mux4;

ARCHITECTURE behave OF mux4 IS
BEGIN
   mux4_proc : PROCESS( a0, a1, a2, a3, sel)
   BEGIN
      CASE sel IS
```

```
            WHEN pretzels =>
               q <= a0;
            WHEN chips =>
               q <= a1;
            WHEN cookies =>
               q <= a2;
            WHEN doughnut =>
               q <= a3;
            WHEN OTHERS =>
               ASSERT FALSE REPORT "bad item"
               SEVERITY ERROR;
         END CASE;
      END PROCESS mux4_proc;
   END behave;
```

A single process is used to model the device and is sensitive to the four input values *a0, a1, a2, a3* and the *sel* input. When any of these inputs change, the process will execute. For this design, the *a0* to *a3* inputs will never change, so these inputs could have been left out of the sensitivity list, but in general this is not a good practice and will make the component harder to reuse later in another design.

The process contains a single CASE statement that will assign the appropriate input value to the output port, based on the value of input *sel*.

13.10 Select4

The *select4* component is used to decode an input item value into four output control signals. Based on the value of an input of type *t_item,* one of the four output signals will be assigned a '1' value. This component is used to enable the decrementing of the appropriate item counter when an item is sold.

The symbol for the select4 component is shown in Figure 13-10. The model that describes the behavior of the select4 component is shown below:

```
USE STD.std_logic.ALL;
USE WORK.p_vending.ALL;
ENTITY select4 IS
   PORT (sel : in t_item;
         en : in t_wlogic;
```

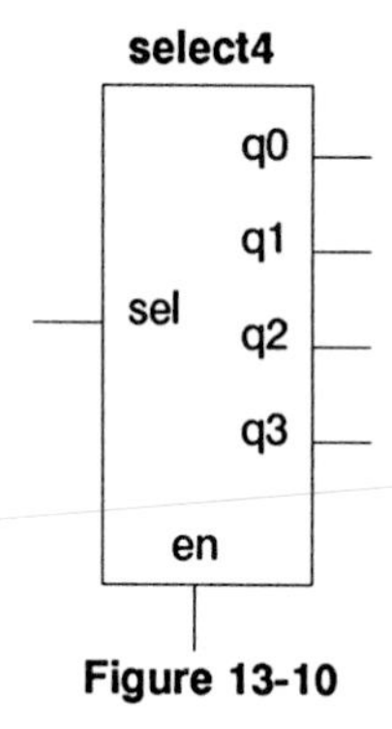

Figure 13-10

```
        q0, q1, q2, q3 : OUT t_wlogic);
END select4;

ARCHITECTURE behave OF select4 IS
BEGIN
   q0 <= F1 WHEN (( sel = pretzels)
               AND ( en = '1')) ELSE
        F0;

   q1 <= F1 WHEN (( sel = chips)
               AND ( en = '1')) ELSE
        F0;

   q2 <= F1 WHEN (( sel = cookies)
               AND ( en = '1')) ELSE
        F0;

   q3 <= F1 WHEN (( sel = doughnut)
               AND ( en = '1')) ELSE
        F0;
END behave;
```

The model makes use of four conditional signal assignment statements. When the appropriate item value is entered, and the *en* input port has the value '1', one of the output ports will be assigned '1' (forcing strength).

13.11 Count

The *count* component counts down to a zero value, and will then output a signal when zero is reached. It is used to keep track of how many of a particular vending machine item are still present in the machine. The symbol for the count component is shown in Figure 13-11.

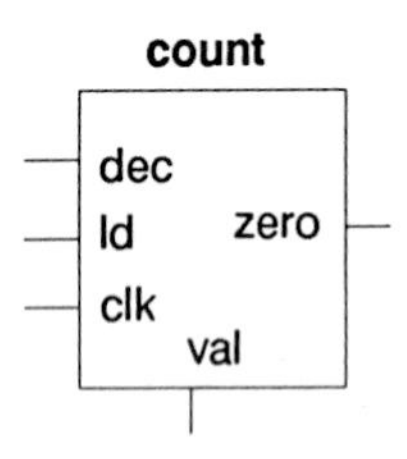

Figure 13-11

To implement the function of the count component, the entity and architecture shown below are used.

```
USE STD.std_logic.ALL;
USE WORK.p_vending.ALL;
ENTITY count IS
   PORT (dec, ld, clk : IN t_wlogic;
         val : IN t_value;
         zero : OUT t_wlogic);
END count;

ARCHITECTURE behave OF count IS
BEGIN
   count_proc : PROCESS( clk)
      VARIABLE count_int : t_value;
   BEGIN
      IF (ld = '1') THEN
         count_int := val;
         zero <= F0;
      ELSIF (clk = '1') AND (clk'EVENT)
                        AND (dec = '1') THEN
         IF ( count_int = 1) THEN
            count_int := 0;
            zero <= F1;
         ELSIF ( count_int = 0) THEN
```

```
            ASSERT FALSE REPORT
               " decrement below zero"
               SEVERITY WARNING;
         ELSE
            count_int := count_int -1;
         END IF;
      END IF;
   END PROCESS count_proc;
END behave;
```

The architecture first checks to see if the *ld* input port is a '1' value. If so, the counter is being loaded with a value from the *val* input port. The internal variable *count_int* is used to keep track of the internal value of the counter.

If the *ld* input is not a '1' value, then the counter may be able to count down. To enable the counter to count down, the *dec* input must be a '1' value and the *clk* input has to have a rising edge occur. The ELSIF part of the initial IF statement checks for all of these conditions and will allow the counter to count down if these conditions are met.

If the counter value is at the value 1, then the counter will be at zero after another transition on the *clk* input. The *zero* output is set to a '1' value to indicate that the counter is currently at 0.

If the counter value is at 0 and a decrement operation is performed, an ASSERT message will inform the designer that the counter is already at 0. If neither of these two cases exist, the counter is decremented normally.

13.12 Sub

The *sub* component is the opposite of the adder component. Given two input values, the sub component will subtract one from the other and return the result. The sub component is used to subtract change from the total change, as change is being given out. The symbol for the sub component is shown in Figure 13-12.

The entity and architecture of the sub component are shown below:

```
USE STD.std_logic.ALL;
USE WORK.p_vending.ALL;
ENTITY sub IS
```

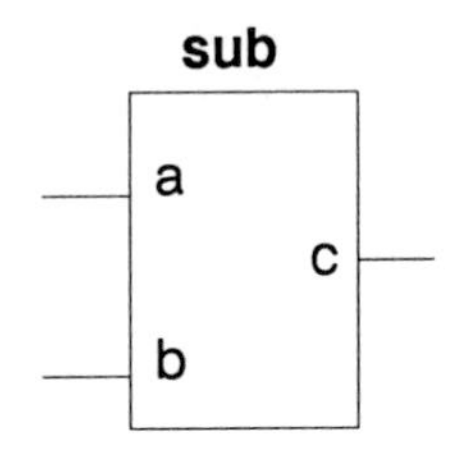

Figure 13-13

```
   PORT( a, b : IN t_value;
         c : OUT t_value);
END sub;

ARCHITECTURE a_sub OF sub IS
BEGIN
   c <= a - b;
END a_sub;
```

13.13 Convert

The *convert* component is used to convert an input value of type *t_coin* into an output value of type *t_value*. Values of type *t_coin* are discrete enumerated type values that each represent a type of coin. These values are not appropriate for arithmetic operations until they have been converted into arithmetic values. The convert component accomplishes this operation. The symbol for the convert component is shown in Figure 13-13.

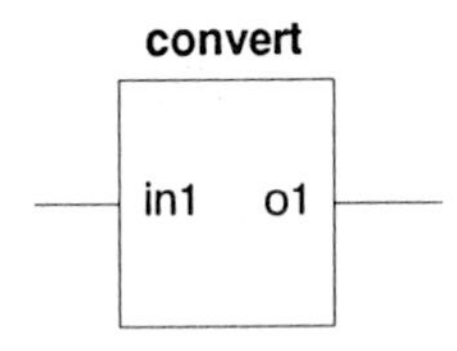

Figure 13-12

The entity and architecture for the convert component are shown below:

```
USE WORK.p_vending.ALL;
ENTITY convert IS
   PORT( in1 : IN t_coin;
         o1 : OUT t_value);
END convert;

ARCHITECTURE behave OF convert IS
BEGIN
   conv_proc: PROCESS( in1)
   BEGIN
      CASE in1 IS
         WHEN nickel =>
            o1 <= 5;
         WHEN dime =>
            o1 <= 10;
         WHEN quarter =>
            o1 <= 25;
         WHEN half_dollar =>
            o1 <= 50;
         WHEN OTHERS =>
            o1 <= 0;
      END CASE;
   END PROCESS conv_proc;
END behave;
```

13.14 Chg_convert

The *chg_convert* component is used to convert from arithmetic values, to coin values. Arithmetic values passed in must match the arithmetic value of a coin exactly for a coin type to be returned. The symbol for the chg_convert component is shown in Figure 13-14.

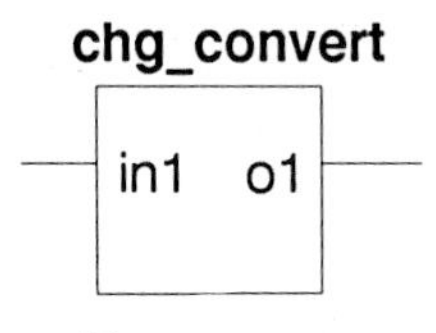

Figure 13-14

The entity and architecture for the chg_convert component are shown below:

```
USE WORK.p_vending.ALL;
ENTITY chg_convert IS
   PORT( in1 : IN t_value;
         o1 : OUT t_coin);
END chg_convert;

ARCHITECTURE behave OF chg_convert IS
BEGIN
   chg_conv_proc: PROCESS( in1)
   BEGIN
      CASE in1 IS
         WHEN 5 =>
            o1 <= nickel;
         WHEN 10 =>
            o1 <= dime;
         WHEN 25 =>
            o1 <= quarter;
         WHEN 50 =>
            o1 <= half_dollar;
         WHEN OTHERS =>
            o1 <= no_coin;
      END CASE;
   END PROCESS chg_conv_proc;
END behave;
```

13.15 Coin_mux

The *coin_mux* is used to select among three different inputs, based on the value of the *sel* input. This mux is different from the mux4 component, again because VHDL type checking forces it. The mux4 component had a *sel* input that was of type *t_item*. For component *coin_mux*, the *t_item* type does not make sense to use to choose among the input values, therefore the *coin_mux* has a *t_mux_sel* type for the *sel* input. In all cases of the *coin_mux*, only three inputs were needed. The symbol for the *coin_mux* is shown in Figure 13-15.

The entity and architecture for the *coin_mux* are shown below:

```
USE WORK.p_vending.ALL;
USE STD.std_logic.ALL;
```

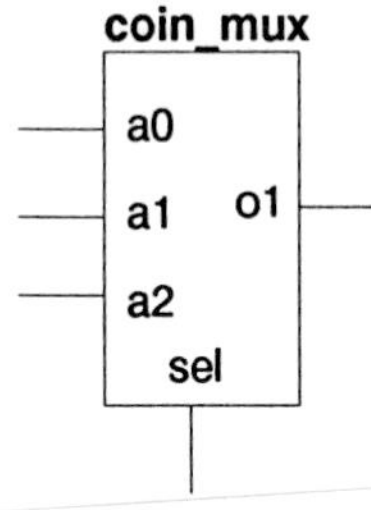

Figure 13-15

```
ENTITY coin_mux IS
  PORT( a0, a1, a2 : IN t_value;
        sel : IN t_mux_sel;
        o1 : OUT t_value);
END coin_mux;

ARCHITECTURE behave OF coin_mux IS
BEGIN
  cmxproc : PROCESS( a0, a1, a2, sel)
  BEGIN
    CASE sel IS
      WHEN val0 =>
        o1 <= a0;
      WHEN val1 =>
        o1 <= a1;
      WHEN val2 =>
        o1 <= a2;
    END CASE;
  END PROCESS cmxproc;
END behave;
```

13.16 Coin_tim_ctrl

The *coin_tim_ctrl* component is used to generate the control signals for the *coin_handler* component and control the timing of the *coin_handler* component output signals. The *coin_tim_ctrl* component is triggered by the *cn_stb, ch_stb*, or *item_stb* inputs. When one of these three inputs has a rising edge occur, the appropriate value is output on the *sel* output. For instance, when the *cn_stb* input has a rising edge occur, a coin has been entered into the vending machine that needs to be added to the total.

The *sel* output is assigned the value *val0*, which will allow the coin value to be added to the total money in the vending machine.

Then the *coin_tim_ctrl* will wait one clock cycle for the value to be added and hold the control signals for one clock cycle more to allow the next component time to make use of the signals. Similar operations happen for the other two input strobe signals, *ch_stb* and *item_stb*. The symbol for the *coin_tim_ctrl* component is shown in Figure 13-16.

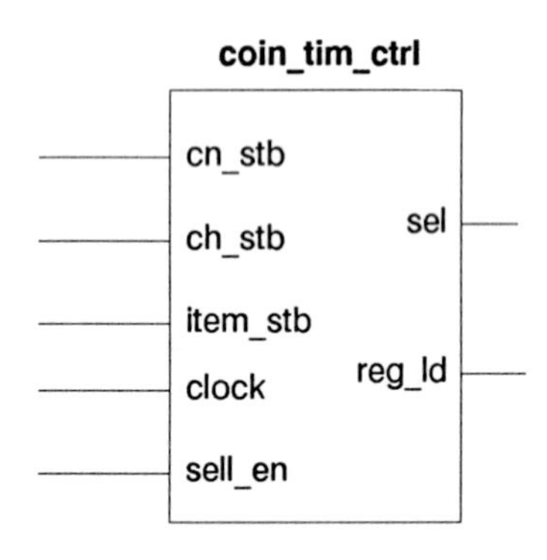

Figure 13-16

The entity and architecture for the *coin_tim_ctrl* component are shown below:

```
USE WORK.p_vending.ALL;
USE STD.std_logic.ALL;
ENTITY coin_tim_ctrl IS
   PORT( cn_stb, ch_stb, item_stb,
         clock, sell_en : IN t_wlogic;
         sel : OUT t_mux_sel;
         reg_ld : OUT t_wlogic);
END coin_tim_ctrl;

ARCHITECTURE behave OF coin_tim_ctrl IS
BEGIN
   ctrlproc : PROCESS
   BEGIN
      IF (cn_stb = '1') AND (cn_stb'EVENT) THEN
         IF (sell_en = '1') THEN
```

```
          sel <= val0;
        END IF;

      ELSIF (ch_stb = '1') AND (ch_stb'EVENT)
          THEN
        sel <= val2;

      ELSIF (item_stb = '1') AND
            (item_stb'EVENT) THEN
        sel <= val1;

      END IF;

      WAIT UNTIL clock = '1';
      reg_ld <= F1;

      WAIT UNTIL clock = '1';
      reg_ld <= F0;

      WAIT UNTIL (cn_stb = '1') OR
        (ch_stb = '1') OR (item_stb = '1');

    END PROCESS ctrlproc;
  END behave;
```

The architecture waits until one of the strobe signals has a '1' event occur on it. The IF statement will then determine which input caused the process to invoke. The appropriate *sel* value is assigned based on the input that changed, and then the process outputs the *reg_ld* signal, synchronized to the *clock* input.

13.17 Item_tim_ctrl

The *item_tim_ctrl* component is used to generate control signals for the *item_proc* component. Whenever an item is purchased, this component will control the completion of the transaction. The *item_tim_ctrl* component will be triggered whenever a rising edge occurs on the *item_stb* signal. The *item_tim_ctrl* component will make sure that enough money has been entered to buy an item, and that the item is not sold out. If these checks pass, the *item_tim_ctrl* component will cause the item to be dispensed. The symbol for the *item_tim_ctrl* component is shown in Figure 13-17.

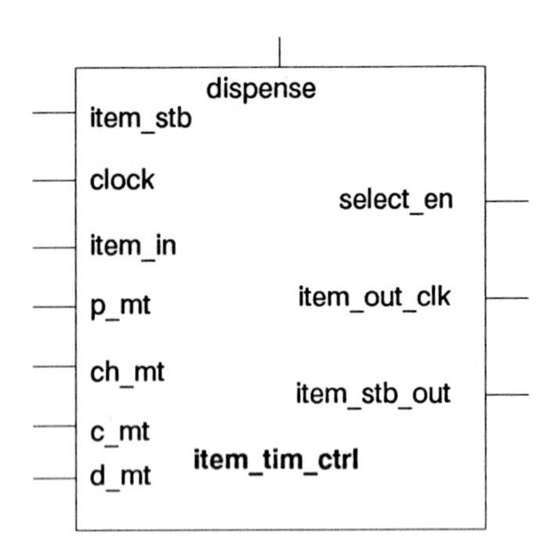

Figure 13-17

The entity and architecture of the *item_tim_ctrl* component are shown below:

```
USE WORK.p_vending.ALL;
USE STD.std_logic.ALL;
ENTITY item_tim_ctrl IS
   PORT( dispense : IN t_wlogic;
         item_stb : IN t_wlogic;
         clock : IN t_wlogic;
         item_in : t_item;
         p_mt, ch_mt, c_mt, d_mt : in t_wlogic;
         item_out_clk : OUT t_wlogic;
         select_en : OUT t_wlogic;
         item_stb_out : OUT t_wlogic);
END item_tim_ctrl;

ARCHITECTURE behave OF item_tim_ctrl IS
BEGIN
   itemproc : PROCESS
      VARIABLE sold : BOOLEAN := FALSE;
   BEGIN
      IF ( item_stb = '1') AND
           ( item_stb'EVENT) THEN

         WAIT UNTIL clock = '1';
```

```
   sold := FALSE;

   IF ( dispense = '1') THEN
      CASE item_in IS
         WHEN pretzels =>
            IF p_mt = '0' THEN
               sold := TRUE;
            END IF;

         WHEN chips =>
            IF ch_mt = '0' THEN
               sold := TRUE;
            END IF;
         WHEN cookies =>
            IF c_mt = '0' THEN
               sold := TRUE;
            END IF;

         WHEN doughnut =>
            IF d_mt = '0' THEN
               sold := TRUE;
            END IF;
      END CASE;

      IF sold THEN
         item_out_clk <= F1;
         select_en <= F1;
         WAIT UNTIL clock = '1';

         item_out_clk <= F0;
         select_en <= F0;
         item_stb_out <= F1;
         WAIT UNTIL clock = '1';

         item_stb_out <= F0;
      END IF;
   END IF;
END IF;

WAIT ON item_stb;
```

```
    END PROCESS itemproc;
  END behave;
```

When an event occurs on the *item_stb* input, the *itemproc* process will begin executing. If the triggering event was a rising edge, the first IF statement in the process will be satisfied and the process will wait for a rising edge on the *clk* input. This delay is used to allow the sub components enough time to determine if enough money has been entered to buy the selected item. If so, the *dispense* signal will be a '1' value, and the next step is to make sure that at least one item of the correct type exists in the vending machine. If so, the *item_out_clk* signal is used to clock the item value into the output register. Also, the *item_stb_out* signal is generated to strobe the item to the mechanical device that dispenses the item. The *select_en* signal is strobed to decrement the appropriate item counter by 1, signaling that the sale has been made.

13.18 Change_tim_ctrl

The *change_maker* component is controlled by the *change_tim_ctrl* component. This component is used to generate the appropriate change when an item is sold. Signal *item_stb* is used to trigger the *change_tim_ctrl* component into action. The *change_tim_ctrl* component will load the difference between the sale price and the money entered in the vending machine into a register, and this value will be decremented as change is being made, until no more change needs to be returned. The symbol for the *change_tim_ctrl* component is shown in Figure 13-18.

The entity and architecture for the *change_tim_ctrl* component are shown below:

```
USE WORK.p_vending.ALL;
USE STD.std_logic.ALL;
ENTITY change_tim_ctrl IS
   PORT( item_stb : IN t_wlogic;
         clock : IN t_wlogic;
         reset : IN t_wlogic;
         gt_5 : IN t_wlogic;
         gt_10 : IN t_wlogic;
         mux_sel : OUT t_wlogic;
         reg_ld : OUT t_wlogic;
         mux_chg : OUT t_mux_sel;
         c_reg_ld : OUT t_wlogic;
```

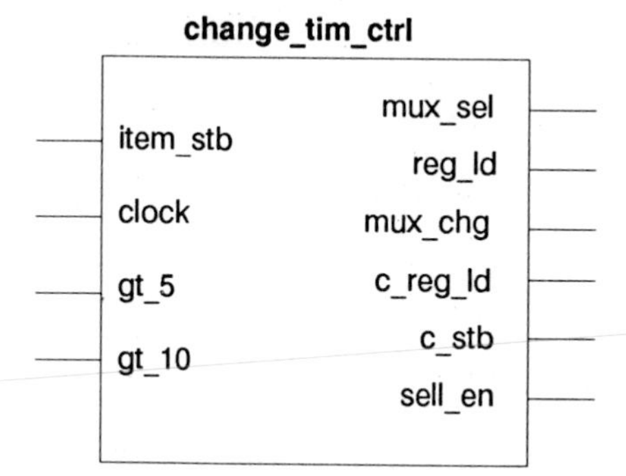

Figure 13-18

```
        c_stb : OUT t_wlogic;
        sell_en : OUT t_wlogic);
END change_tim_ctrl;

ARCHITECTURE behave OF change_tim_ctrl IS
BEGIN
   changeproc : PROCESS
   BEGIN
      IF (item_stb ='1')AND(item_stb'EVENT) THEN
         mux_sel <= F0;
         sell_en <= F0;
         WAIT UNTIL clock = '1';

         reg_ld <= F1;
         WAIT UNTIL clock = '1';

         mux_sel <= F1;
         reg_ld <= F0;
         WHILE (gt_5 = '1') OR (gt_10 = '1') LOOP
            IF (gt_10 = '1') THEN
               mux_chg <= val0;
               WAIT UNTIL clock = '1';

               reg_ld <= F1;
               c_reg_ld <= F1;
               WAIT UNTIL clock = '1';

               c_stb <= F1;
```

```
                    reg_ld <= F0;
                    c_reg_ld <= F0;
                    WAIT UNTIL clock = '1';

                    c_stb <= F0;

                 ELSIF (gt_5 = '1') THEN
                    mux_chg <= val1;
                    WAIT UNTIL clock = '1';

                    reg_ld <= F1;
                    c_reg_ld <= F1;
                    WAIT UNTIL clock = '1';

                    c_stb <= F1;
                    reg_ld <= F0;
                    c_reg_ld <= F0;
                    WAIT UNTIL clock = '1';

                    c_stb <= F0;
                 END IF;
              END LOOP;
              sell_en <= F1;
           END IF;
        END PROCESS changeproc;
     END behave;
```

The architecture waits for a rising edge on signal *item_stb* to begin execution. When a rising edge occurs, signal *sell_en* is set to false, indicating that a sale is in progress. Also signal *mux_sel* is set to a '1' (forcing strength) to cause the change value to be loaded into the register that holds the current amount of change to be given. This is component U4 of the *change_maker* structural architecture. After a delay to allow the change value to propagate through the mux, the change value is loaded into register U4 with the *reg_ld* signal.

Once the value is loaded into the register, a looping process begins, which will loop until no more change needs to be given. The two comparator output signals, *gt_5* and *gt_10*, are used to determine when no more change needs to be given. If both signals are '0', then the change value to be returned is 0, and the change loop can be exited. Otherwise, change is given by selecting the appropriate value from the mux4 component, with signal *mux_chg*, and strobing the value out, by transitions on output port *c_stb*. The change value is also subtracted from the current value of change to be given and loaded back into the register. Signal *reg_ld* loads the register, and signal *c_reg_ld* is used to strobe the value of change given, to the mechanical device that dispenses the change.

13.19 Exact_change_ctrl

The *exact_change_ctrl* component is used to determine when the amount of coins available in the vending machine to provide change to a customer has dropped below a predetermined limit. This component will maintain a count of each coin given out as change, and when the amount of coins of either type has dropped below the limit, signal *exact_change* will be set to '1' (forcing strength). The symbol for the *exact_change_ctrl* component is shown in Figure 13-19.

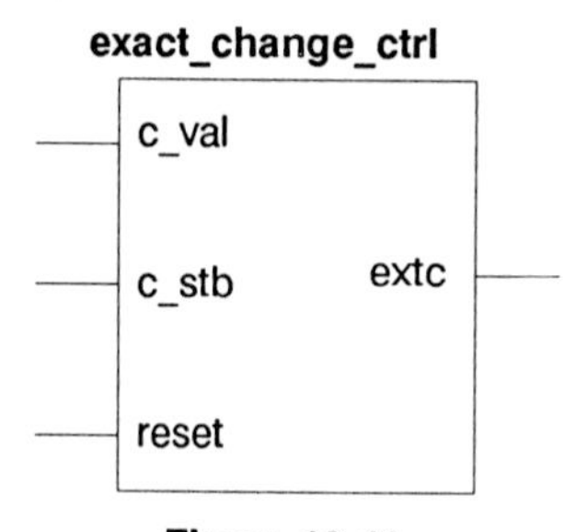

Figure 13-19

The entity and architecture for the component are shown below:

```
USE WORK.p_vending.ALL;
USE STD.std_logic.ALL;
ENTITY exact_change_ctrl IS
   GENERIC( num_dimes, num_nickels : t_value);
   PORT( c_val : IN t_value;
         c_stb : IN t_wlogic;
         reset : IN t_wlogic;
         extc : OUT t_wlogic);
END exact_change_ctrl;
```

```
ARCHITECTURE behave OF exact_change_ctrl IS
BEGIN
  extcproc : PROCESS( c_stb, reset)
    VARIABLE coin : t_coin;
    VARIABLE dimes_left : t_value;
    VARIABLE nickels_left : t_value;
  BEGIN
    IF ( c_stb = '1') AND ( c_stb'EVENT) THEN
      coin := int_to_coin(c_val);
      IF ( coin = nickel) THEN
        IF (nickels_left <= 0) THEN
          ASSERT FALSE
            REPORT "out of nickels"
            SEVERITY WARNING;
        ELSE
          nickels_left := nickels_left - 1;
        END IF;

      ELSIF ( coin = dime) THEN
        IF (dimes_left <= 0) THEN
          ASSERT FALSE REPORT "out of dimes"
          SEVERITY WARNING;
        ELSE
          dimes_left := dimes_left - 1;
        END IF;
      ELSE
        ASSERT FALSE REPORT "bad coin"
        SEVERITY ERROR;
      END IF;

      IF (( dimes_left < 3) OR
           (nickels_left < 3)) THEN
        extc <= F1;
      ELSE
        extc <= F0;
      END IF;
    END IF;

    IF (reset = '1') THEN
      dimes_left := num_dimes;
      nickels_left := num_nickels;
```

```
      END IF;
    END PROCESS extcproc;
  END behave;
```

The *extcproc* process is triggered whenever a rising edge occurs on the *c_stb* input port. This port is connected to the *coin_stb* signal, used to strobe out the change coins. The process will check which type of coin is being given out and then decrement the appropriate counter, *nickels_left* or *dimes_left*. If the counter is already at zero, a warning message is issued that the machine is out of the particular coin.

Next the number of each coin available is checked against the predetermined limit. In this example, the limit is set at 4 for each type of coin. When the number of either coin drops below 4, the *exact_change* signal will be set to '1'.

In this chapter we examined the parts used to build the second-level decomposition of the vending machine. In the next chapter, we will look at how the design can be decomposed further, to allow closer approximation with the real design.

Chapter

14

Low-Level Description

In the last few chapters, the vending machine description has been taken from a very high level specification to one that consists of a number of components interconnected by signals. The types of signals are still at an abstract level, and some of the components are still described at a behavioral level. In this chapter, the signal types will be described by types closer to the actual hardware, and some of the components will be modified to show how to take advantage of the new types.

The types used to describe the vending machine are declared in package *p_vending* described in Chapter 10. The types that we are concerned with from this package are *t_coin, t_item, t_mux_sel,* and *t_value*. The first three types are enumerated types, and the last type, *t_value*, is actually a subtype of INTEGER. These types are shown below:

```
PACKAGE p_vending IS
   TYPE t_coin IS ( no_coin, nickel, dime,
                    quarter, half_dollar);

   TYPE t_item IS ( no_item, pretzels, chips,
                    cookies, doughnut);
```

```
    TYPE t_mux_sel IS (val0, val1, val2);

    SUBTYPE t_value IS INTEGER;
        .
        .
        .
        .
END p_vending;
```

To be able to build the vending machine controller from gates, flip-flops, etc. these types must be decomposed to types that closer represent the physical operation of the vending machine controller. For instance an INTEGER value cannot be directly represented in digital circuitry by a single signal. The current subtype used to represent the money values in the vending machine is a subtype of INTEGER. To physically build the signal representation for the *t_value* subtype would require more than one signal.

Subtype *t_value* can be represented as an array of signal values, whose combined value represents the value of the money in the vending machine. The number of bits of the array will determine the range of values that can be represented by the type. For our purposes, 8 bits of representation will be enough. No item to be purchased is over 60 cents. With 8 bits, the values from -128 to +127 can be represented. The new subtype of type *t_value* is shown below:

```
SUBTYPE t_value IS t_wlogic_vector( 0 to 7);
```

This subtype creates a *t_wlogic_vector* type that is 8 bits wide. (Type *t_wlogic_vector* is an unconstrained array of the *t_wlogic* type. It is defined in Appendix A). The eight separate signals of the array type can be used to represent the value of the money currently entered into the vending machine.

Enumerated types also need a hardware counterpart to be able to implement the values of the enumerated type in physical hardware. To represent typical enumerated type values requires one or more signals and some constant values. This methodology will allow changes in the underlying type without a rewrite of the model for a lot of cases. For instance, type *t_coin* can be represented as shown below:

```
TYPE t_coin IS t_wlogic_vector( 0 TO 2);

CONSTANT no_coin      : t_coin := (F0, F0, F0);
CONSTANT nickel       : t_coin := (F0, F0, F1);
CONSTANT dime         : t_coin := (F0, F1, F0);
CONSTANT quarter      : t_coin := (F0, F1, F1);
CONSTANT half_dollar  : t_coin := (F1, F0, F0);
```

The type definition defines an array of three signals that will be used to represent the possible enumerated values. However, the enumerated values are now constants, of type *t_coin*. By defining constants, the enumerated type values already in the models do not have to be replaced by actual values. A simple recompile is all that is needed to replace the enumeration values by the constant values.

There are components, however, that will require more than a simple recompile to work properly. For instance, addition and subtraction operations are defined for integer types but not for *t_wlogic_vector* types. Any model that uses the addition of *t_wlogic_vector* types will need to be modified for the new type. An alternative approach is to overload the + operator to handle *t_wlogic_vector* types.

14.1 Structural Description of Reg Component

Because the input port types are now closer to the physical hardware implementation, the physical gates to be used to build the device can be entered. For instance, the reg component consists of 8 register components. Each register component is connected to one of the input port bits, and all registers are clocked with a common clock. An example implementation is shown below:

```
PACKAGE p_struct IS
   SUBTYPE t_value IS t_wlogic_vector( 0 to 7);

   TYPE t_coin IS t_wlogic_vector( 0 TO 2);
   CONSTANT no_coin     : t_coin := (F0, F0, F0);
   CONSTANT nickel      : t_coin := (F0, F0, F1);
   CONSTANT dime        : t_coin := (F0, F1, F0);
   CONSTANT quarter     : t_coin := (F0, F1, F1);
   CONSTANT half_dollar: t_coin := (F1, F0, F0);
```

```
    TYPE t_mux_sel IS t_wlogic_vector( 0 TO 1);
    CONSTANT val0        : t_mux_sel := (F0, F0);
    CONSTANT val1        : t_mux_sel := (F0, F1);
    CONSTANT val2        : t_mux_sel := (F1, F0);

    TYPE t_item IS t_wlogic_vector( 0 TO 2);
    CONSTANT no_item  : t_item := (F0, F0, F0);
    CONSTANT pretzels : t_item := (F0, F0, F1);
    CONSTANT chips    : t_item := (F0, F1, F0);
    CONSTANT cookies  : t_item := (F0, F1, F1);
    CONSTANT doughnut : t_item := (F1, F0, F0);
END p_struct;

USE WORK.p_struct.ALL;
ENTITY reg IS
    PORT( rin : in t_value;
          reset : in t_wlogic;
          clk : in t_wlogic;
          rout : out t_value);
END reg;

ARCHITECTURE struct OF reg IS
    COMPONENT dff
        PORT( din : IN t_wlogic;
              clk : IN t_wlogic;
              clear : IN t_wlogic;
              q : OUT t_wlogic);
    END COMPONENT;
BEGIN
    U0 : dff
        PORT MAP( din => rin(0),
                  clk => clk,
                  clear => reset,
                  q => rout(0));

    U1 : dff
        PORT MAP( din => rin(1),
                  clk => clk,
                  clear => reset,
                  q => rout(1));

    U2 : dff
```

```
      PORT MAP( din => rin(2),
                clk => clk,
                clear => reset,
                q => rout(2));

   U3 : dff
      PORT MAP( din => rin(3),
                clk => clk,
                clear => reset,
                q => rout(3));

   U4 : dff
      PORT MAP( din => rin(4),
                clk => clk,
                clear => reset,
                q => rout(4));

   U5 : dff
      PORT MAP( din => rin(5),
                clk => clk,
                clear => reset,
                q => rout(5));

   U6 : dff
      PORT MAP( din => rin(6),
                clk => clk,
                clear => reset,
                q => rout(6));

   U7 : dff
      PORT MAP( din => rin(7),
                clk => clk,
                clear => reset,
                q => rout(7));
END struct;
```

Notice that the entity requires no coding change, only a recompile to reflect the new type definitions. However, the architecture now consists of 8 *dff* components, connected to form a structural architecture for the reg component. Each *dff* component is connected to one input bit of *rin*, and one output bit of *rout*.

14.2 Structural Description of Mux Component

Figure 14-1 shows the schematic for the *mux* component.

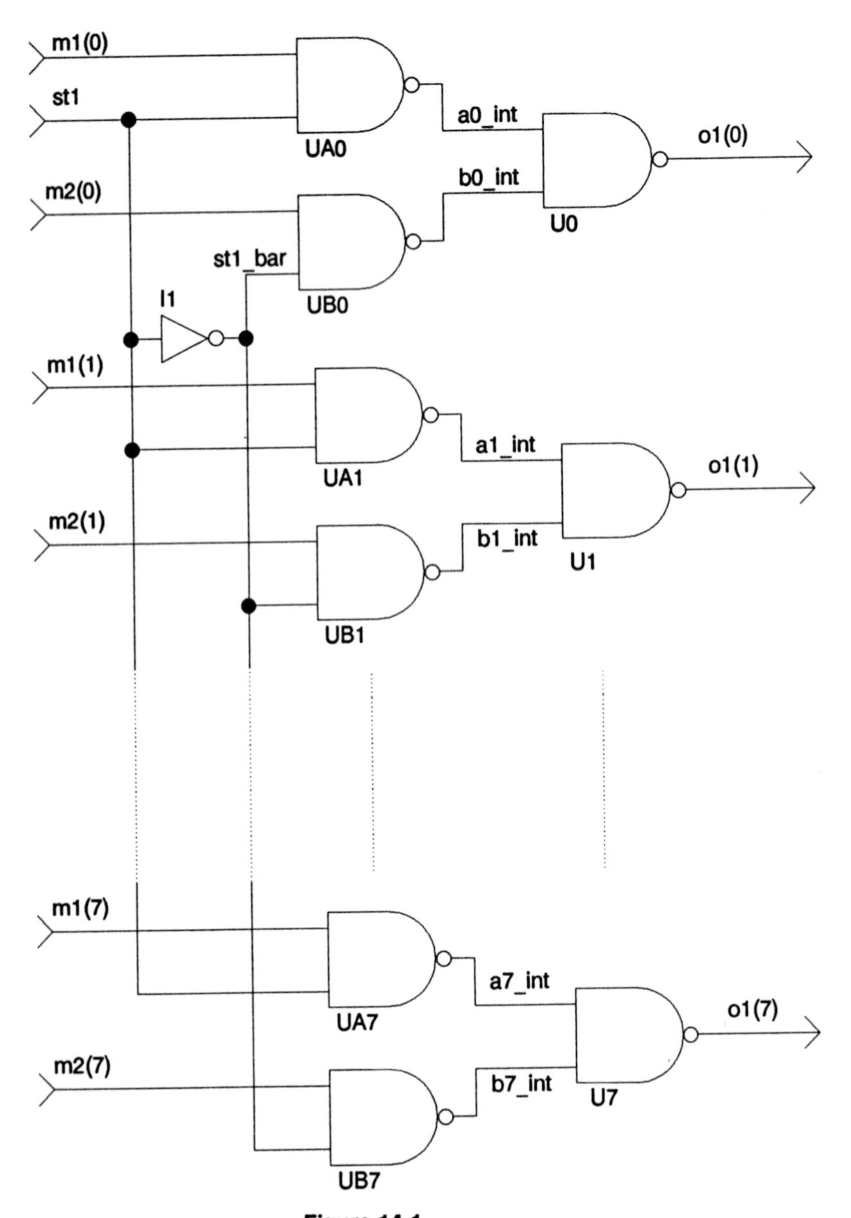

Figure 14-1

The architecture that implements this schematic is shown below:

```
USE STD.std_logic.ALL;
ENTITY mux IS
   PORT( m1, m2 : IN t_value;
         st1 : IN t_wlogic;
         o1 : OUT t_value);
END mux;

ARCHITECTURE struct OF mux IS
   COMPONENT nand2
      GENERIC( rise, fall : time);
      PORT( a, b : IN t_wlogic;
            c : OUT t_wlogic);
   END COMPONENT;

   COMPONENT inv
      GENERIC( rise, fall : time);
      PORT( a : IN t_wlogic;
            b : OUT t_wlogic);
   END COMPONENT;

   SIGNAL a0_int, a1_int, a2_int,
          a3_int, a4_int, a5_int,
          a6_int, a7_int : t_wlogic;

   SIGNAL b0_int, b1_int, b2_int,
          b3_int, b4_int, b5_int,
          b6_int, b7_int : t_wlogic;

   SIGNAL st1_bar : t_wlogic;

BEGIN

   I1 : inv
      GENERIC MAP( 1.5 ns, 2.0 ns)
      PORT MAP( a => st1, b => st1_bar);

   UA0 : nand2
      GENERIC MAP( 2.5 ns, 3.5 ns)
      PORT MAP( a => m1(0),
                b => st1,
```

```
                c => a0_int);

      UB0 : nand2
        GENERIC MAP( 2.5 ns, 3.5 ns)
        PORT MAP( a => m2(0),
                  b => st1_bar,
                  c => b0_int);

      U0 : nand2
        GENERIC MAP( 2.5 ns, 3.5 ns)
        PORT MAP( a => a0_int,
                  b => b0_int,
                  c => o1(0));

      UA1 : nand2
        GENERIC MAP( 2.5 ns, 3.5 ns)
        PORT MAP( a => m1(1),
                  b => st1,
                  c => a1_int);

      UB1 : nand2
        GENERIC MAP( 2.5 ns, 3.5 ns)
        PORT MAP( a => m2(1),
                  b => st1_bar,
                  c => b1_int);

      U1 : nand2
        GENERIC MAP( 2.5 ns, 3.5 ns)
        PORT MAP( a => a1_int,
                  b => b1_int,
                  c => o1(1));

      UA2 : nand2
        GENERIC MAP( 2.5 ns, 3.5 ns)
        PORT MAP( a => m1(2),
                  b => st1,
                  c => a2_int);

      UB2 : nand2
        GENERIC MAP( 2.5 ns, 3.5 ns)
        PORT MAP( a => m2(2),
                  b => st1_bar,
```

```
                c => b2_int);

    U2 : nand2
       GENERIC MAP( 2.5 ns, 3.5 ns)
       PORT MAP( a => a2_int,
                b => b2_int,
                c => o1(2));

    UA3 : nand2
       GENERIC MAP( 2.5 ns, 3.5 ns)
       PORT MAP( a => m1(3),
                b => st1,
                c => a3_int);

    UB3 : nand2
       GENERIC MAP( 2.5 ns, 3.5 ns)
       PORT MAP( a => m2(3),
                b => st1_bar,
                c => b3_int);

    U3 : nand2
       GENERIC MAP( 2.5 ns, 3.5 ns)
       PORT MAP( a => a3_int,
                b => b3_int,
                c => o1(3));

    UA4 : nand2
       GENERIC MAP( 2.5 ns, 3.5 ns)
       PORT MAP( a => m1(4),
                b => st1,
                c => a4_int);

    UB4 : nand2
       GENERIC MAP( 2.5 ns, 3.5 ns)
       PORT MAP( a => m2(4),
                b => st1_bar,
                c => b4_int);

    U4 : nand2
       GENERIC MAP( 2.5 ns, 3.5 ns)
       PORT MAP( a => a4_int,
                b => b4_int,
```

```
               c => o1(4));

     UA5 : nand2
        GENERIC MAP( 2.5 ns, 3.5 ns)
        PORT MAP( a => m1(5),
                  b => st1,
                  c => a5_int);

     UB5 : nand2
        GENERIC MAP( 2.5 ns, 3.5 ns)
        PORT MAP( a => m2(5),
                  b => st1_bar,
                  c => b5_int);

     U5 : nand2
        GENERIC MAP( 2.5 ns, 3.5 ns)
        PORT MAP( a => a5_int,
                  b => b5_int,
                  c => o1(5));

     UA6 : nand2
        GENERIC MAP( 2.5 ns, 3.5 ns)
        PORT MAP( a => m1(6),
                  b => st1,
                  c => a6_int);

     UB6 : nand2
        GENERIC MAP( 2.5 ns, 3.5 ns)
        PORT MAP( a => m2(6),
                  b => st1_bar,
                  c => b6_int);

     U6 : nand2
        GENERIC MAP( 2.5 ns, 3.5 ns)
        PORT MAP( a => a6_int,
                  b => b6_int,
                  c => o1(6));

     UA7 : nand2
        GENERIC MAP( 2.5 ns, 3.5 ns)
        PORT MAP( a => m1(7),
                  b => st1,
```

```
                  c => a7_int);

      UB7 : nand2
         GENERIC MAP( 2.5 ns, 3.5 ns)
         PORT MAP( a => m2(7),
                  b => st1_bar,
                  c => b7_int);

      U7 : nand2
         GENERIC MAP( 2.5 ns, 3.5 ns)
         PORT MAP( a => a7_int,
                  b => b7_int,
                  c => o1(7));
   END struct;
```

Notice that the entity for the component is the same, but the architecture is now built from NAND gates instead of behavioral statements.

Each group of three NAND gates handles one bit of the input and output ports. Input port *st1* and signal *st1_bar* will control which of the two input signals is gated through by enabling one or the other of the NAND gates controlling the input signals. The output of these two NAND gates is then gated by a third NAND gate to provide the output value.

14.3 Item_tim_ctrl Structural Description

The final component described at a structural level is the *item_tim_ctrl* component. This component has not been fully decomposed to the component level yet. In Figure 14-2 is shown component *item_tim_ctrl* decomposed to the component level.

Signal *item_stb* is strobed into flip-flop U1 by the *clk* input. If the *dispense* signal is a '1' value, then enough money has been entered into the vending machine to purchase an item. This will cause a '1' value to be strobed into component U3. Signal *select_en* will also receive a '1' value, allowing the appropriate item counter to be decremented.

The output of component U3 drives output port *item_out_clk*, allowing the item selected to be transferred to the output register for output. Finally, component U4 will strobe the output value.

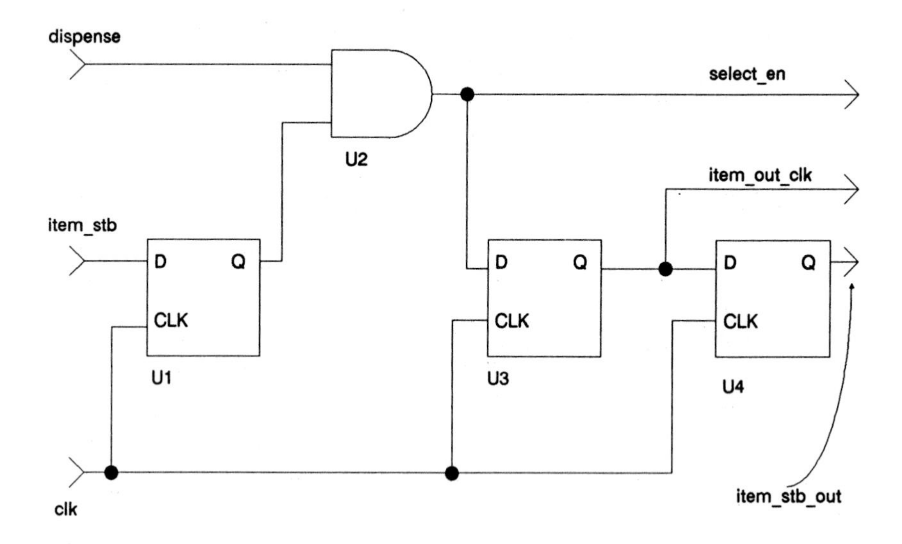

Figure 14-2

The following structural architecture will describe the schematc just presented:

```
USE STD.std_logic.ALL;
ENTITY item_tim_ctrl IS
   PORT( dispense : IN t_wlogic;
         item_stb : IN t_wlogic;
         clock : IN t_wlogic;
         item_out_clk : OUT t_wlogic;
         item_stb_out : OUT t_wlogic);
END item_tim_ctrl;

ARCHITECTURE struct OF item_tim_ctrl IS
   COMPONENT and2
      PORT( in1, in2 : IN t_wlogic;
            o1 : OUT t_wlogic);
   END COMPONENT;

   COMPONENT dff
      PORT( d, clk : IN t_wlogic;
            q : OUT t_wlogic);
   END COMPONENT;
```

```
    SIGNAL stb_out, select_int,
           item_clk_int : t_wlogic;

BEGIN

    U1 : dff
       PORT MAP( d => item_stb,
                 clk => clk,
                 q => stb_out);

    U2 : and2
       PORT MAP( in1 => dispense,
                 in2 => stb_out,
                 o1 => select_int);

    U3 : dff
       PORT MAP( d => select_int,
                 clk => clk,
                 q => item_clk_int);

    U4 : dff
       PORT MAP( d => item_clk_int,
                 clk => clk,
                 q => item_stb_out);
END struct;
```

All of the other components can be decomposed in the same manner, until they are at a level where the device can be built, using the target technology. For instance if the target technology is a CMOS gate array, then the design will need to be refined down to the gate array macros allowed in the CMOS array being used.

14.4 Synthesis

An alternative to decomposing the design down to the lowest level is to take advantage of the synthesis tools available, at the time of this writing. These tools accept a register transfer level (RTL) description and generate the lower-level gate representation, to a target technology. Using an RTL description allows the designer to maintain a high-level, very readable, and maintainable description for the design, and let an automatic process take care of the mundane chore of conversion to the target technology.

So what does an RTL description in VHDL look like, and how do we go about generating this description? With a VHDL RTL level description, not all of the functionality of VHDL can be used, because some of the language features do not map into the RTL paradigm. Typically, the features that will not be supported by synthesis tools are the features that do not relate to how the actual hardware will be built. Examples are as follows:

- *Access types*. Access types are used to build dynamic structures, that is, structures that grow and shrink. This feature of the language is usually used for programming language types of operations.
- 'LAST_EVENT, 'ACTIVE, 'TRANSACTION, etc. These attributes do not relate to the hardware being built. They are used to provide information about events scheduled in the simulation.

There is a larger class of constructs, however, that are supported by synthesis tools, and can be used to create RTL descriptions of devices.

The features typically supported will include those features that can easily be mapped to hardware and a set that with some restrictions, can also be mapped to hardware. Examples are shown below:

- IF THEN ELSE *statement*: typically mapped to a multiplexor, or logic that implements a multiplexor function
- WAIT *statement*: typically restricted to synchronous clock signals; provides a registering mechanism
- *Boolean expression assignment*: creates appropriate boolean function in gates and drives signal being assigned
- *Signal assignment statement*: appropriate wiring is generated

The most powerful features of the VHDL synthesis capabilities are the automatic generation of synchronous logic and the optimization features. While the logic is being synthesized, the synthesis tools can try a number of different possible implementations to see which circuit matches the goals of the designer. If the goals are the smallest possible circuit, then the synthesis tools will optimize for the smallest area. If the goals are for the fastest possible design, then the synthesis tools will pick an implementation that meets the speed goals of the designer.

Let's look at a couple of examples, and the logic that results. The first example will be an IF statement.

```
PACKAGE synth_pack IS
   SUBTYPE bit4 IS BIT_VECTOR( 0 TO 3);
END synth_pack;

USE WORK.synth_pack.ALL;
ENTITY mux IS
   PORT( a, b : IN bit4;
         sel : IN BIT;
         c : OUT bit4);
END mux;

ARCHITECTURE synth OF mux IS
BEGIN
   synth_proc : PROCESS( a, b, sel)
   BEGIN
      IF sel = '0' THEN
         c <= a;
      ELSE
         c <= b;
      END IF;
   END PROCESS synth_proc;
END synth;
```

The logic generated from the VHDL description will depend on the gates, macros, and components available in the target library. One example implementation is shown in Figure 14-3.

To generate a register using the VHDL synthesis approach, the use of the 'STABLE or 'EVENT attribute is required. These attributes, in combination with an IF statement or a WAIT statement, can be used to specify clock edges unambiguously. Knowing which signals are the *clock* inputs is very important in determining how to connect a register in the circuit.

The example below shows how a register might be described in VHDL, as input for a synthesis tool.

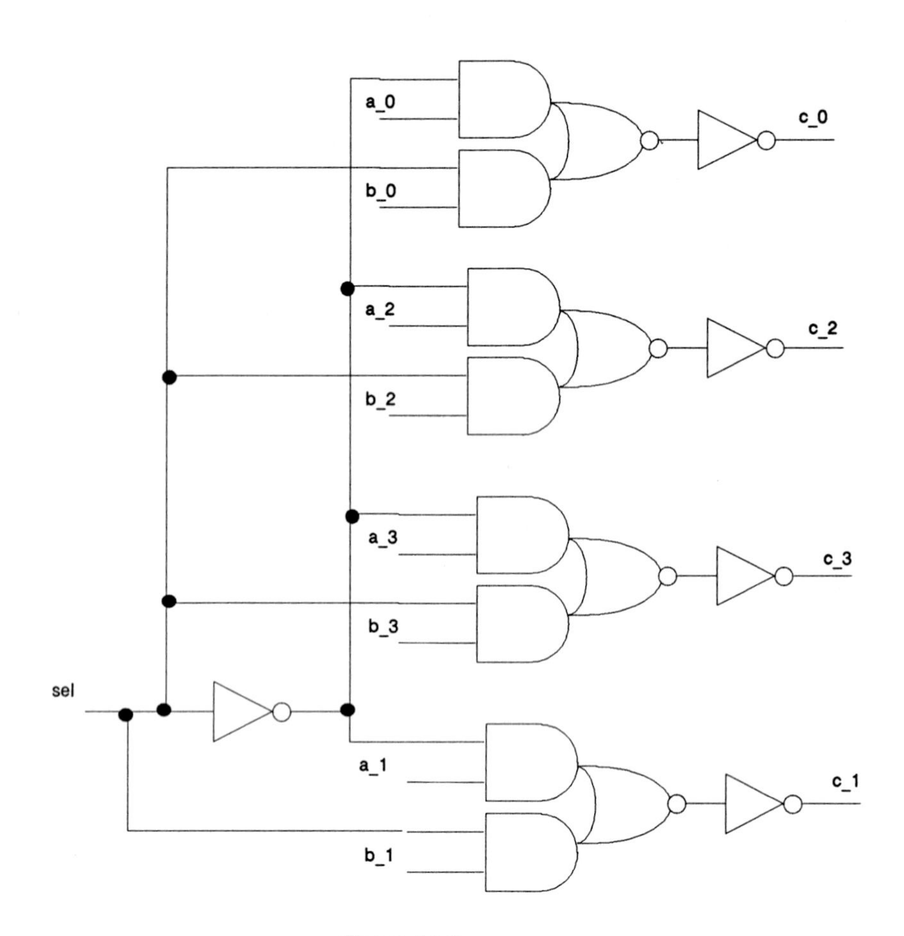

Figure 14-3

```
PACKAGE buspack IS
  SUBTYPE bit8 is BIT_VECTOR( 7 DOWNTO 0);
END buspack;

USE WORK.buspack.ALL;
ENTITY reg IS
  PORT( rin : IN bit8;
        clk : IN BIT;
        rout : OUT bit8);
END reg;
```

```
ARCHITECTURE synth OF reg IS
BEGIN
   synth_proc : PROCESS
   BEGIN
      WAIT UNTIL (clk'EVENT) AND (clk = '1');
      rout <= rin;
   END PROCESS synth_proc;
END synth;
```

This example will generate an 8-bit register, as shown in Figure 14-4.

If the register has a synchronous reset capability, then the VHDL description would look as below:

```
USE WORK.buspack.ALL;
ENTITY reg_w_clr IS
   PORT( rin : IN bit8;
         clk : IN bit;
         clr : IN bit;
         rout : OUT bit8);
END reg_w_clr;

ARCHITECTURE synth OF reg_w_clr IS
BEGIN
   synth_proc : PROCESS
   BEGIN
      WAIT UNTIL (clk'EVENT) AND (clk = '1');

      IF clr = '0' THEN
         rout <= rin;
      ELSE
         rout <= "00000000";
      END IF;
   END PROCESS synth_proc;
END synth;
```

This architecture will generate the logic shown in Figure 14-5.

In this chapter we have examined two ways to decompose a behavioral, or RTL, description to the point where it can be built. The first involved using a manual method of breaking the VHDL description to gates, and the second involved using a new class of synthesis tools. The manual method is very tedious and error-prone, while the synthesis tools show great promise for the future.

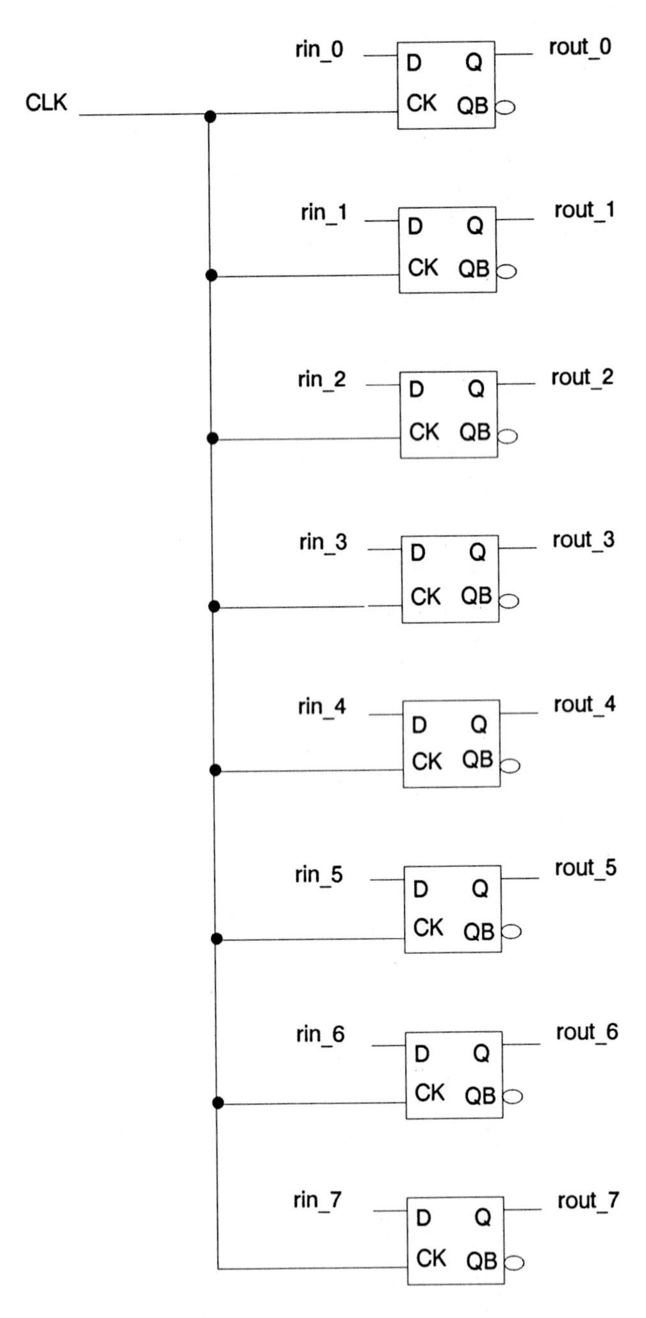
CLK
rin_0
D
Q
CK
QB
rout_0
rin_1
D
Q
CK
QB
rout_1
rin_2
D
Q
CK
QB
rout_2
rin_3
D
Q
CK
QB
rout_3
rin_4
D
Q
CK
QB
rout_4
rin_5
D
Q
CK
QB
rout_5
rin_6
D
Q
CK
QB
rout_6
rin_7
D
Q
CK
QB
rout_7

Figure 14-4

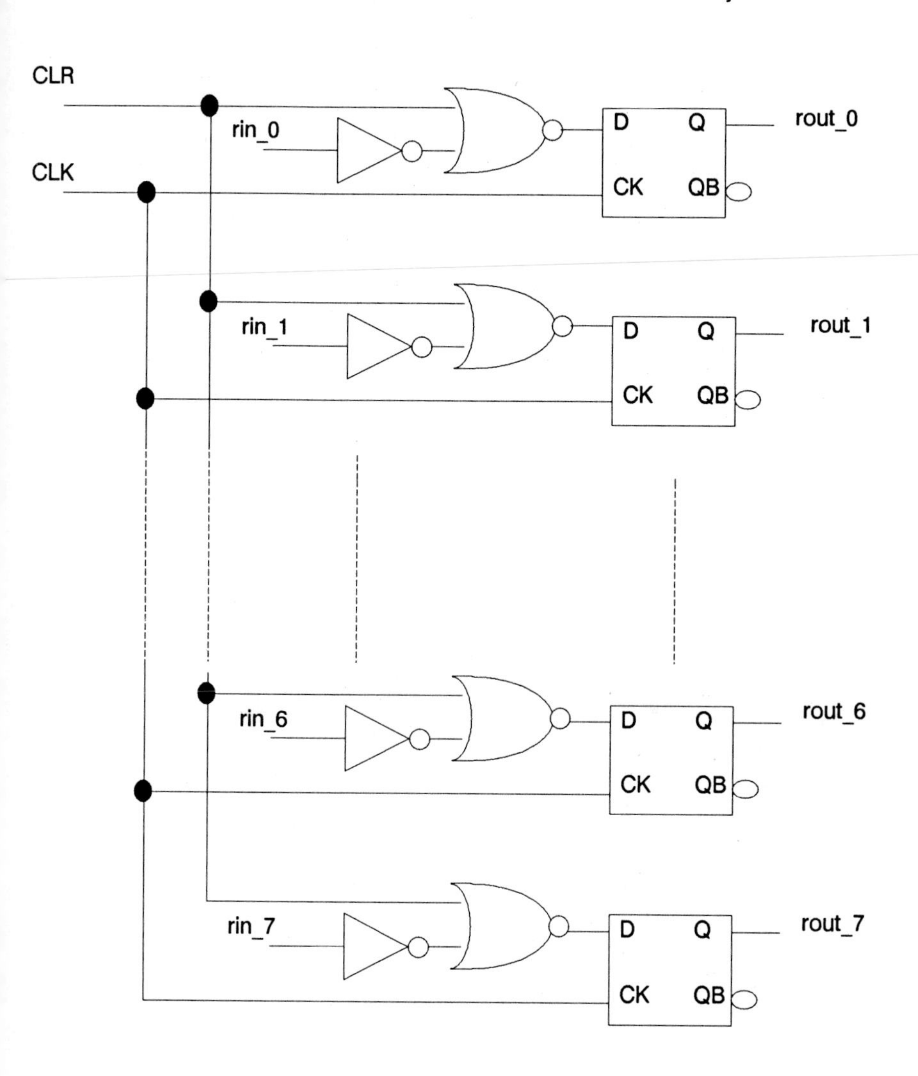
CLR
CLK
rin_0
D
Q
rout_0
CK
QB
rin_1
D
Q
rout_1
CK
QB
rin_6
D
Q
rout_6
CK
QB
rin_7
D
Q
rout_7
CK
QB

Figure 14-5

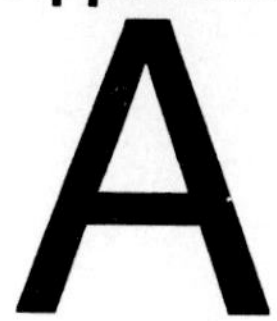

Appendix A

STD_LOGIC Package

This appendix will present a subset of the STD_LOGIC package provided in the public domain by Vantage Analysis Systems Inc. The complete package can be obtained in magnetic format from Vantage.

This package is provided as an example of typical requirements of a package needed for simulation of models. This package includes type definitions for standard types, a resolution function for the standard types, and a number of functions and procedures that ease the modeling task.

The package will be presented, and each of the types, functions, etc. in the package will be discussed.

```
---------------------------------------------
--              copyright 1988
--              Vantage Analysis Systems, Inc.
--              all rights reserved
--
--    File name :  std_logic.vhdl
--    Title     :  STD_LOGIC package VHDL source
--    Subsystem :  analyzer
--    Module    :  VHDL source
```

```
--
--    Purpose     :  source for STD_LOGIC package
--
--    Author(s) :  dlp,kes,drc,ast
--
--    Revision    :  1/14/89
--                   1/20/89
--
--    Remarks     :  Defines the TYPEs for the
--                   standard logic value
--                   system and also some FUNCTIONs
--                   and arrays to access parts
--                   of a standard logic value. Also
--                   provided are standard logic
--                   FUNCTIONs on these logic
--                   values.
--
-----------------------------------------------
PACKAGE std_logic IS
--$ !VANTAGE_METACOMMENTS_ON
--$ !VANTAGE_DNA_ON
```

The package starts with a declaration of type *t_logic.* This type declares an enumerated type with 46 different values. The values of this type describe the possible states available in a 46-state value system, as described in Chapter 9.

```
TYPE t_logic IS
   (U,
    D,
    Z0, Z1, ZDX, DZX, ZX,
    W0, W1, WZ0, WZ1, WDX, DWX, WZX, ZWX, WX,
    R0, R1, RW0, RW1, RZ0, RZ1, RDX, DRX, RZX,
    ZRX, RWX, WRX, RX,
    F0, F1, FR0, FR1, FW0, FW1, FZ0, FZ1, FDX,
    DFX, FZX, ZFX, FWX, WFX, FRX, RFX, FX);
```

Next, type *t_logic_vector* is declared. This type is needed for the resolution function of *t_logic*. This type will be used to represent a driver array for signals with a *t_logic* type.

```
TYPE t_logic_vector IS
     ARRAY(NATURAL RANGE <>) OF t_logic;
```

Function *f_logic_bus* is the resolution function to be used with the *t_logic* type. Given an unconstrained array input of all of the drivers of a signal, the resolution function will calculate the resolved value.

```
FUNCTION f_logic_bus( s : t_logic_vector )
     RETURN t_logic;
```

Now that the *t_logic* type has been defined and a resolution function has been declared, a resolved type using this resolution function can be declared. This resolved type is shown below as subtype *t_wlogic*.

```
SUBTYPE t_wlogic IS f_logic_bus t_logic;
```

Type *t_wlogic_vector* declares an unconstrained array of the subtype *t_wlogic*, to be used in functions described later.

```
TYPE t_wlogic_vector IS
     ARRAY(NATURAL RANGE <>) OF t_wlogic;
```

Type *t_state*, shown below, represents the logical values available in the 46-state value system. Declaring type *t_state* allows the designer to use these logical values in the model, instead of one or more of the 46-state values. For instance, the value '1' from the *t_state* type can match the Z1, W1, R1, and F1 values of type *t_wlogic* when the comparison operator is overloaded.

```
TYPE t_state IS ( '0', '1', 'X' );
```

Type *t_strength* represents the strength values of the 46-state value system. These strength values allow the designer to use one of the strength values, to determine the relative strength of a state. For instance, the value R will match the strength of values R0, R1, and RX.

```
TYPE t_strength IS ( 'U', 'Z', 'W', 'R', 'F' );
```

Type *t_technology* defines the technologies that are supported by the STD_LOGIC package. These values are passed to table *f_tech* (described later) to determine the final output state of a logical value.

```
TYPE t_technology IS ( ecl, cmos, nmos,
                       ttl, ttloc );
```

The type declarations shown next are used to facilitate the creation of look-up tables in the package. Look-up tables are the fastest method of retrieving a value. For instance, type *f_state_t* is used by table (constant) *f_state*, to return the logical value for a 46-state value. Type F_2_X_1 is used to create logical functions of two inputs. This type is an array of an array and defines a two-dimensional matrix that can be filled with *t_state* values. The text following is all comments in the package used to describe the function of each of the tables.

```
-- Internal Types:  Types for look-up tables:
--
-- f_state_T : Takes t_logic value,
--             RETURNs t_state.
--
-- f_strength_T : Takes t_logic value,
--                RETURNs the t_strength.
--
-- f_logic_T    : Takes t_logic value,
--                converts to different t_logic.
--
-- F_1_X_1   : Takes t_state,
--             converts to a different t_state.
--             (ie, f_convz, f_not)
--
-- F_2_X_1   : Takes 2 t_state values,
--             converts to new t_state.
--             (ie, f_and, f_or, f_nand,
--              f_nor, f_xor)
```

```
--
-- f_str      : Used IN f_log_con_t.
--
-- f_log_con_t : Takes t_state and t_strength,
--                RETURNs t_logic.
--
-- f_tech_con  : Used IN f_tech_T.
--
-- f_tech_T : Takes t_state and t_technology,
--             RETURNs t_logic.
--
-- f_specific_T  : Takes t_state,
--            RETURNs t_logic based on technology.
--
-- f_boolean_T  : Takes t_logic,
--                 RETURNs boolean.
--
TYPE f_state_T IS
   ARRAY (t_logic'low to t_logic'high) OF t_state;

TYPE f_strength_T IS
   ARRAY (t_logic'low to t_logic'high)
   OF t_strength;

TYPE f_logic_T IS
   ARRAY (t_logic'low to t_logic'high) OF t_logic;

TYPE F_1_X_1 IS
   ARRAY (t_state'low to t_state'high) OF t_state;

TYPE F_2_X_1 IS
   ARRAY (t_state'low to t_state'high) OF F_1_X_1;

TYPE f_str IS
   ARRAY (t_strength'low to t_strength'high)
   OF t_logic;

TYPE f_log_con_T IS
   ARRAY (t_state'low to t_state'high) OF f_str;

TYPE f_logs_con_t IS
   ARRAY (t_strength'LOW TO t_strength'HIGH)
```

```
   OF f_str;

TYPE f_tech_con IS
   ARRAY (t_technology'low to t_technology'high)
   OF t_logic;

TYPE f_tech_T IS
   ARRAY (t_state'low to t_state'high)
   OF f_tech_con;

TYPE f_specific_t IS
   array( t_state'low to t_state'high ) of t_logic;

TYPE f_boolean_t IS
   array( t_logic'low to t_logic'high ) of boolean;
```

The next set of declarations are overloaded-operator declarations. These functions overload the logical operators so that *t_state* types and *t_wlogic, t_logic* types can be intermixed for comparisons. For instance, with the overloaded operators, both of the following IF statements are legal. (This code is not in the STD_LOGIC package.)

```
Signal x : t_wlogic;

   IF ( x = '1') THEN
      -- some statements
   END IF;

   IF ( '1' = x) THEN
      -- some statements
   END IF;
```

Notice that signal *x* has a *t_wlogic* type, while the value '1' is a *t_state* type value.

```
FUNCTION "="  ( l : t_logic;  r : t_state )
   RETURN boolean;

FUNCTION "="  ( l : t_state;  r : t_logic )
   RETURN boolean;
```

```
FUNCTION "/=" ( l : t_logic;  r : t_state )
   RETURN boolean;

FUNCTION "/=" ( l : t_state;  r : t_logic )
   RETURN boolean;

FUNCTION ">"  ( l : t_logic;  r : t_state )
   RETURN boolean;

FUNCTION ">"  ( l : t_state;  r : t_logic )
   RETURN boolean;

FUNCTION ">=" ( l : t_logic;  r : t_state )
   RETURN boolean;

FUNCTION ">=" ( l : t_state;  r : t_logic )
RETURN boolean;

FUNCTION "<"  ( l : t_logic;  r : t_state )
  RETURN boolean;

FUNCTION "<"  ( l : t_state;  r : t_logic )
   RETURN boolean;

FUNCTION "<=" ( l : t_logic;  r : t_state )
   RETURN boolean;
FUNCTION "<=" ( l : t_state;  r : t_logic )
   RETURN boolean;
```

The next set of function declarations overloads the logical operators, so that special functions will not have to be called when logical operations are required for values of 46-state types. With these overloaded functions, the following statements are legal. (This code is not in the package.)

```
SIGNAL x, y : t_wlogic;
SIGNAL z : t_state;

z <= x AND y;
z <= '1' XOR x;
z <= x OR '0';
```

The overloaded operators will be called because the operands of the logical functions are of mixed types. Notice that the functions overload operands of type *t_logic*, but not of type *t_wlogic*. Values of type *t_wlogic* can be passed to these functions, because *t_wlogic* is a subtype of *t_logic*.

```
FUNCTION "and" ( l : t_logic;  r : t_logic )
   RETURN t_state;

FUNCTION "and" ( l : t_state;  r : t_logic )
   RETURN t_state;

FUNCTION "and" ( l : t_logic;  r : t_state )
   RETURN t_state;

FUNCTION "and" ( l : t_state;  r : t_state )
   RETURN t_state;

FUNCTION "or" ( l : t_logic;  r : t_logic )
   RETURN t_state;

FUNCTION "or" ( l : t_state;  r : t_logic )
   RETURN t_state;

FUNCTION "or" ( l : t_logic;  r : t_state )
   RETURN t_state;

FUNCTION "or" ( l : t_state;  r : t_state )
   RETURN t_state;

FUNCTION "nand" ( l : t_logic;  r : t_logic )
   RETURN t_state;

FUNCTION "nand" ( l : t_state;  r : t_logic )
   RETURN t_state;

FUNCTION "nand" ( l : t_logic;  r : t_state )
   RETURN t_state;

FUNCTION "nand" ( l : t_state;  r : t_state )
   RETURN t_state;

FUNCTION "nor" ( l : t_logic;  r : t_logic )
```

```
   RETURN t_state;

FUNCTION "nor" ( l : t_state;  r : t_logic )
   RETURN t_state;

FUNCTION "nor" ( l : t_logic;  r : t_state )
   RETURN t_state;

FUNCTION "nor" ( l : t_state;  r : t_state )
   RETURN t_state;

FUNCTION "xor" ( l : t_logic;  r : t_logic )
   RETURN t_state;

FUNCTION "xor" ( l : t_state;  r : t_logic )
   RETURN t_state;

FUNCTION "xor" ( l : t_logic;  r : t_state )
   RETURN t_state;

FUNCTION "xor" ( l : t_state;  r : t_state )
   RETURN t_state;
```

The next declaration in the package is a constant declaration used to convert between types. This constant is used to convert values of type *t_wlogic* or *t_logic* into type *t_state*. What this table does is remove the strength from a state and return the logical value. Given a 46-state value such as R1, this constant will return '1'. A '0' value will be returned from the value Z0.

```
CONSTANT f_state : f_state_t := (
   'X', -- U
   'X', -- D
   '0', -- Z0
   '1', -- Z1
   'X', -- ZDX
   'X', -- DZX
   'X', -- ZX
   '0', -- W0
   '1', -- W1
   '0', -- WZ0
   '1', -- WZ1
   'X', -- WDX
```

```
   'X',  -- DWX
   'X',  -- WZX
   'X',  -- ZWX
   'X',  -- WX
   '0',  -- R0
   '1',  -- R1
   '0',  -- RW0
   '1',  -- RW1
   '0',  -- RZ0
   '1',  -- RZ1
   'X',  -- RDX
   'X',  -- DRX
   'X',  -- RZX
   'X',  -- ZRX
   'X',  -- RWX
   'X',  -- WRX
   'X',  -- RX
   '0',  -- F0
   '1',  -- F1
   '0',  -- FR0
   '1',  -- FR1
   '0',  -- FW0
   '1',  -- FW1
   '0',  -- FZ0
   '1',  -- FZ1
   'X',  -- FDX
   'X',  -- DFX
   'X',  -- FZX
   'X',  -- ZFX
   'X',  -- FWX
   'X',  -- WFX
   'X',  -- FRX
   'X',  -- RFX
   'X'   -- FX     );
```

The next constant is another look-up table, but this table is used to retrieve the strength value from a state. Given a 46-state value such as F0, this constant will return 'F'.

```
CONSTANT f_strength : f_strength_t := (
   'F',  -- U
   'U',  -- D
   'Z',  -- Z0
```

```
'Z', -- Z1
'Z', -- ZDX
'Z', -- DZX
'Z', -- ZX
'W', -- W0
'W', -- W1
'W', -- WZ0
'W', -- WZ1
'W', -- WDX
'W', -- DWX
'W', -- WZX
'W', -- ZWX
'W', -- WX
'R', -- R0
'R', -- R1
'R', -- RW0
'R', -- RW1
'R', -- RZ0
'R', -- RZ1
'R', -- RDX
'R', -- DRX
'R', -- RZX
'R', -- ZRX
'R', -- RWX
'R', -- WRX
'R', -- RX
'F', -- F0
'F', -- F1
'F', -- FR0
'F', -- FR1
'F', -- FW0
'F', -- FW1
'F', -- FZ0
'F', -- FZ1
'F', -- FDX
'F', -- DFX
'F', -- FZX
'F', -- ZFX
'F', -- FWX
'F', -- WFX
'F', -- FRX
```

```
    'F',   -- RFX
    'F'    -- FX     );
```

The next constant declaration is for a constant to build 46-state values, from logical values and strength values. Given a logical value, such as '0', and a strength, such as F, this constant will result in F0. This constant is basically the reverse operation of the *f_state* and *f_strength* constants.

Since this constant is an array of arrays, the syntax for use is not the same as a function call. The arguments to the constant are separated by more parentheses than would be expected with a function call. An example of a use is shown below. (This code is not in the package.)

```
x <= f_logic ('0')('F');
```

Signal *x* would receive the value F0 after assignment.

```
CONSTANT f_logic : f_log_con_t := (
    ( D ,        -- '0', 'U'
      Z0,        -- '0', 'Z'
      W0,        -- '0', 'W'
      R0,        -- '0', 'R'
      F0 ),      -- '0', 'F'
    ( D ,        -- '1', 'U'
      Z1,        -- '1', 'Z'
      W1,        -- '1', 'W'
      R1,        -- '1', 'R'
      F1 ),      -- '1', 'F'
    ( D ,        -- 'X', 'U'
      ZX,        -- 'X', 'Z'
      WX,        -- 'X', 'W'
      RX,        -- 'X', 'R'
      FX )       -- 'X', 'F'    );
```

The next set of constant declarations in the package allow the designer to find the correct 46-state value for a given technology, given the logical value. Each of these constants will return the appropriate 46-state value when applied to a logical value (type *t_state*). There are five constants, one for each technology type supported. To use the constant, simply apply the constant to a logical value, and the state for that technology will result. An example for CMOS technology is shown below.(This code is not in the package.)

```
x <= f_cmos('1');
```

This assignment will cause the value F1 to be assigned to signal *x*.

```
CONSTANT f_ecl : f_specific_t :=
   ( R0,        -- '0'
     F1,        -- '1'
     RFX        -- 'X' );

CONSTANT f_cmos : f_specific_t :=
   ( F0,        -- '0'
     F1,        -- '1'
     FX         -- 'X' );

CONSTANT f_nmos : f_specific_t :=
   ( F0,        -- '0'
     R1,        -- '1'
     FRX        -- 'X' );

CONSTANT f_ttl : f_specific_t :=
   ( F0,        -- '0'
     F1,        -- '1'
     FX         -- 'X' );

CONSTANT f_ttloc : f_specific_t :=
   ( F0,        -- '0'
     ZX,        -- '1'
     FZX        -- 'X' );
```

The other method of generating 46-state values based on the technology is the constant *f_tech*. This constant is of type *f_tech_t*, which is an array of array type. Passing the logical value as one array index and the technology as the other, will return the appropriate 46-state value. The following statement will return the 46-state value for technology TTL, with a logical value of '0'. (This statement is not in the package.)

```
x <= f_tech('0')(ttl);
```

The value F0 will be assigned to signal x.

```
CONSTANT f_tech : f_tech_t := (
   ( R0,        -- '0', ecl
     F0,        -- '0', cmos
     F0,        -- '0', nmos
     F0,        -- '0', ttl
     F0 ),      -- '0', ttloc
   ( F1,        -- '1', ecl
     F1,        -- '1', cmos
     R1,        -- '1', nmos
     F1,        -- '1', ttl
     ZX ),      -- '1', ttloc
   ( RFX,       -- 'X', ecl
     FX,        -- 'X', cmos
     FRX,       -- 'X', nmos
     FX,        -- 'X', ttl
     FZX )      -- 'X', ttloc );
```

The next constant is used to return value of a tristate gate when the enable is off. For instance, if the value of a tristate device was an F1 before the enable was turned off, then after the enable was turned off the output value would be a Z1. The same logical value is maintained, but the strength is transformed to high impedance (Z).

```
CONSTANT f_convz : f_logic_t := (
  ZX, -- U
  D, -- D
  Z0, -- Z0
  Z1, -- Z1
  ZDX, -- ZDX
  DZX, -- DZX
  ZX, -- ZX
  Z0, -- W0
  Z1, -- W1
  Z0, -- WZ0
  Z1, -- WZ1
  ZDX, -- WDX
  DZX, -- DWX
  ZX, -- WZX
  ZX, -- ZWX
  ZX, -- WX
  Z0, -- R0
```

```
Z1,  -- R1
Z0,  -- RW0
Z1,  -- RW1
Z0,  -- RZ0
Z1,  -- RZ1
ZDX,  -- RDX
DZX,  -- DRX
ZX,  -- RZX
ZX,  -- ZRX
ZX,  -- RWX
ZX,  -- WRX
ZX,  -- RX
Z0,  -- F0
Z1,  -- F1
Z0,  -- FR0
Z1,  -- FR1
Z0,  -- FW0
Z1,  -- FW1
Z0,  -- FZ0
Z1,  -- FZ1
ZDX,  -- FDX
DZX,  -- DFX
ZX,  -- FZX
ZX,  -- ZFX
ZX,  -- FWX
ZX,  -- WFX
ZX,  -- FRX
ZX,  -- RFX
ZX   -- FX     );
```

The next function is also used for tristate devices. This function, *f_convu*, is used to return the appropriate interval state value when the enable of a tristate device is at an indeterminate state (see the 46-state value system description in Chapter 9). This function will calculate the new output value for a tristate device, based on the current output value, the new input value, and the technology of the device.

If the current output value is an F0, and the new input logical value to the device is a '0', then the output value will remain at a '0' logical value, plus a strength determined by the technology of the device.

An example that shows how *f_convz* and *f_convu* can be put to use is shown in the tristate device model below. (This code is not in the package.)

```
USE STD.std_logic.ALL;
ENTITY tristate IS
  GENERIC( tech : t_technology);
  PORT( inval, enable : IN t_wlogic;
        outval : INOUT t_wlogic);
END tristate;

ARCHITECTURE behave OF tristate IS
BEGIN
  tristate_proc: PROCESS(inval, enable, outval)
    VARIABLE predicted_state : t_logic;
  BEGIN
    CASE f_state(enable) IS
      WHEN '1' =>
        outval <= f_tech(f_state(inval))(tech);
      WHEN '0' =>
        outval <= f_convz(outval);
      WHEN 'X' =>
        predicted_state :=
            f_tech(f_state(inval))(tech);
        outval <= f_convu(predicted_state,
                          outval, tech);
    END CASE;
  END PROCESS tristate_proc;
END behave;
```

This model is for a tristate buffer component. The technology of the device is passed to the model through the generic *tech*. The architecture of the model contains a single CASE statement to implement the behavior of the tristate buffer. The CASE statement uses the logical value of the enable input to determine what action to take. If the enable input is a '1', then the tristate buffer is enabled, and the buffer will pass the input value to the output with the appropriate technology taken into account. If the enable input is a '0', then the tristate buffer is disabled, and the current output value of the tristate buffer is converted to a high-impedance strength, but maintaining the same logical value. Finally, if the enable input is a logical value 'X', then the tristate buffer will calculate the interval notation value from the *predicted_state* if enable is a '1' and from the current state if the enable is a '0', using function *f_convu*. The code that implements this function is in the package body for the STD_LOGIC package, described later.

```
FUNCTION f_convu ( newval  : IN t_logic;
                   lastval: IN t_logic;
                   tech    : IN t_technology )
                   RETURN t_logic;
```

The next set of constants are used to perform logical operations on values of type *t_state*. These tables are implemented as arrays of arrays, and the comments to the right of each value indicate the input values that will produce the appropriate output value, contained in the constant. These constants are called from the overloaded logical operator functions described earlier.

```
CONSTANT f_and : f_2_x_1 := (
   ( '0',      -- '0', '0'
     '0',      -- '0', '1',
     '0' ),    -- '0', 'X'
   ( '0',      -- '1', '0'
     '1',      -- '1', '1'
     'X' ),    -- '1', 'X'
   ( '0',      -- 'X', '0'
     'X',      -- 'X', '1'
     'X' )     -- 'X', 'X'     );

CONSTANT f_or : f_2_x_1 := (
   ( '0',      -- '0', '0'
     '1',      -- '0', '1',
     'X' ),    -- '0', 'X'
   ( '1',      -- '1', '0'
     '1',      -- '1', '1'
     '1' ),    -- '1', 'X'
   ( 'X',      -- 'X', '0'
     '1',      -- 'X', '1'
     'X' )     -- 'X', 'X'     );
```

```
CONSTANT f_nand : f_2_x_1 := (
   ( '1',     -- '0', '0'
     '1',     -- '0', '1',
     '1' ),  -- '0', 'X'
   ( '1',     -- '1', '0'
     '0',     -- '1', '1'
     'X' ),  -- '1', 'X'
   ( '1',     -- 'X', '0'
     'X',     -- 'X', '1'
     'X' )   -- 'X', 'X'      );

CONSTANT f_nor : f_2_x_1 := (
   ( '1',     -- '0', '0'
     '0',     -- '0', '1',
     'X' ),  -- '0', 'X'
   ( '0',     -- '1', '0'
     '0',     -- '1', '1'
     '0' ),  -- '1', 'X'
   ( 'X',     -- 'X', '0'
     '0',     -- 'X', '1'
     'X' )   -- 'X', 'X'     );

CONSTANT f_xor : f_2_x_1 := (
   ( '0',     -- '0', '0'
     '1',     -- '0', '1',
     'X' ),  -- '0', 'X'
   ( '1',     -- '1', '0'
     '0',     -- '1', '1'
     'X' ),  -- '1', 'X'
   ( 'X',     -- 'X', '0'
     'X',     -- 'X', '1'
     'X' )   -- 'X', 'X'     );

CONSTANT f_not : f_1_x_1 := (
     '1',     --   '0'
     '0',     --   '1'
     'X'      --   'X'        );
```

The STD_LOGIC package also contains some useful functions for modeling delay in the design. The package declaration contains function declarations for two functions that are useful in describing timing functionality. The first function *f_delay* is useful for describing the timing behavior of typical outputs that are always driven. Examples are the output of flip-flops, and gates. The second function *f_zdelay* is useful for describing the timing behavior of tristate, open collector, or open-emitter outputs. These functions are described in detail in the package body of the STD_LOGIC package.

```
FUNCTION f_delay( newlv   : IN t_logic;
                  delay01  : IN time;
                  delay10  : IN time)
                  RETURN time;

FUNCTION f_zdelay( oldlv : IN t_logic;
                   newlv : IN t_logic;
                   delay01 : IN time;
                   delay10 : IN time;
                   delayz0 : IN time;
                   delayz1 : IN time;
                   delay0z : IN time;
                   delay1z : IN time)
                   RETURN time;
```

The next two type declarations are used to describe the constant declaration *f_busres*. This constant is used to calculate the resolved value of two 46-state input values and is used to implement the resolution function (*f_logic_bus* is described later) of the 46-state value system. The two type declarations describe an array of array structure, in this example, 46 arrays of 46 entries each. This is the fastest possible method to implement the resolution function, by doing a table look-up two entries at a time.

Let's look at some examples to see how this will work. Below is shown three assignments using the *f_busres* constant, and the resulting values obtained. (This code is not in the package.)

```
a := f_busres(F1)(R0);
  -- a gets F1
a := f_busres(Z0)(WX);
  -- a gets WX
```

```
a := f_busres(R0)(R1);
  -- a gets RX
```

The first example shows how the value F1 is stronger than R0, therefore the resolution function will return F0. In the second example WX is stronger than Z0, and therefore WX is returned. In the final example both values are the same strength, but different logical values, therefore the result returned has a logical value of 'X'.

```
TYPE t_bus IS
   ARRAY(t_logic'LOW TO t_logic'HIGH) OF t_logic;

TYPE t_bus_tab IS
   ARRAY(t_logic'LOW TO t_logic'HIGH) OF t_bus;

CONSTANT f_busres : t_bus_tab := (


(U, U,
U, U, U, U, U,
U, U, U, U, U, U, U, U, U,
U, U, U, U, U, U, U, U, U, U, U, U, U,
U, U, U, U, U, U, U, U, U, U, U, U, U, U,
U, U, U ), -- U -  array for anything with U


( U,  D,
Z0, Z1, ZDX, DZX, ZX,
W0, W1, WZ0, WZ1, WDX, DWX, WZX, ZWX, WX,
R0, R1, RW0, RW1, RZ0, RZ1, RDX, DRX, RZX, ZRX,
RWX, WRX, RX,
F0, F1, FR0, FR1, FW0, FW1, FZ0, FZ1, FDX, DFX,
FZX, ZFX, FWX, WFX, FRX, RFX, FX ), -- D


(  U,  Z0,
Z0,  ZX,  Z0,  ZX,  ZX,
W0,  W1, WZ0, ZWX, WZ0, ZWX, WZX, ZWX, WX,
R0,  R1, RW0, RW1, RZ0, ZRX, RZ0, ZRX, RZX, ZRX,
RWX, WRX,  RX,
F0,  F1, FR0, FR1, FW0, FW1, FZ0, ZFX, FZ0, ZFX,
FZX, ZFX, FWX, WFX, FRX, RFX, FX ), -- Z0


(  U,  Z1,
```

```
ZX,  Z1,  ZX,  Z1,  ZX,
W0,  W1, WZX, WZ1, WZX, WZ1, WZX, ZWX,  WX,
R0,  R1, RW0, RW1, RZX, RZ1, RZX, RZ1, RZX, ZRX,
RWX, WRX,  RX,
F0,  F1, FR0, FR1, FW0, FW1, FZX, FZ1, FZX, FZ1,
FZX, ZFX, FWX, WFX, FRX, RFX, FX ), -- Z1

(  U, ZDX,
Z0,  ZX, ZDX,  ZX,  ZX,
W0,  W1, WZ0, ZWX, WDX, ZWX, WZX, ZWX,  WX,
R0,  R1, RW0, RW1, RZ0, ZRX, RDX, ZRX, RZX, ZRX,
RWX, WRX,  RX,
F0,  F1, FR0, FR1, FW0, FW1, FZ0, ZFX, FDX, ZFX,
FZX, ZFX, FWX, WFX, FRX, RFX, FX ), --ZDX

(  U, DZX,
ZX,  Z1,  ZX, DZX,  ZX,
W0,  W1, WZX, WZ1, WZX, DWX, WZX, ZWX,  WX,
R0,  R1, RW0, RW1, RZX, RZ1, RZX, DRX, RZX, ZRX,
RWX, WRX,  RX,
F0,  F1, FR0, FR1, FW0, FW1, FZX, FZ1, FZX, DFX,
FZX, ZFX, FWX, WFX, FRX, RFX, FX ), --DZX

(  U,  ZX,
ZX,  ZX,  ZX,  ZX,  ZX,
W0,  W1, WZX, ZWX, WZX, ZWX, WZX, ZWX,  WX,
R0,  R1, RW0, RW1, RZX, ZRX, RZX, ZRX, RZX, ZRX,
RWX, WRX,  RX,
F0,  F1, FR0, FR1, FW0, FW1, FZX, ZFX, FZX, ZFX,
FZX, ZFX, FWX, WFX, FRX, RFX, FX ), -- ZX

(  U,  W0,
W0,  W0,  W0,  W0,  W0,
W0,  WX,  W0,  WX,  W0,  WX,  W0,  WX,  WX,
R0,  R1, RW0, WRX, RW0, WRX, RW0, WRX, RW0, WRX,
RWX, WRX,  RX,
F0,  F1, FR0, FR1, FW0, WFX, FW0, WFX, FW0, WFX,
FW0, WFX, FWX, WFX, FRX, RFX, FX ), -- W0

(  U,  W1,
W1,  W1,  W1,  W1,  W1,
WX,  W1,  WX,  W1,  WX,  W1,  WX,  W1,  WX,
```

```
RO,  R1, RWX, RW1, RWX, RW1, RWX, RW1, RWX, RW1,
RWX, WRX,  RX,
FO,  F1, FRO, FR1, FWX, FW1, FWX, FW1, FWX, FW1,
FWX, FW1, FWX, WFX, FRX, RFX, FX ), -- W1

(   U, WZO,
WZO, WZX, WZO, WZX, WZX,
WO,  WX, WZO,  WX, WZO,  WX, WZX,  WX,  WX,
RO,  R1, RWO, WRX, RZO, WRX, RZO, WRX, RZX, WRX,
RWX, WRX,  RX,
FO,  F1, FRO, FR1, FWO, WFX, FZO, WFX, FZO, WFX,
FZX, WFX, FWX, WFX, FRX, RFX, FX ),--WZO

(   U, WZ1,
ZWX, WZ1, ZWX, WZ1, ZWX,
WX,  W1,  WX, WZ1,  WX, WZ1,  WX, ZWX,  WX,
RO,  R1, RWX, RW1, RWX, RZ1, RWX, RZ1, RWX, ZRX,
RWX, WRX,  RX,
FO,  F1, FRO, FR1, FWX, FW1, FWX, FZ1, FWX, FZ1,
FWX, ZFX, FWX, WFX, FRX, RFX, FX ),--WZ1

(   U, WDX,
WZO, WZX, WDX, WZX, WZX,
WO,  WX, WZO,  WX, WDX,  WX, WZX,  WX,  WX,
RO,  R1, RWO, WRX, RZO, WRX, RDX, WRX, RZX, WRX,
RWX, WRX,  RX,
FO,  F1, FRO, FR1, FWO, WFX, FZO, WFX, FDX, WFX,
FZX, WFX, FWX, WFX, FRX, RFX, FX ),--WDX

(   U, DWX,
ZWX, WZ1, ZWX, DWX, ZWX,
WX,  W1,  WX, WZ1,  WX, DWX,  WX, ZWX,  WX,
RO,  R1, RWX, RW1, RWX, RZ1, RWX, DRX, RWX, ZRX,
RWX, WRX,  RX,
FO,  F1, FRO, FR1, FWX, FW1, FWX, FZ1, FWX, DFX,
FWX, ZFX, FWX, WFX, FRX, RFX, FX ),--DWX

(   U, WZX,
WZX, WZX, WZX, WZX, WZX,
WO,  WX, WZX,  WX, WZX,  WX, WZX,  WX,  WX,
RO,  R1, RWO, WRX, RZX, WRX, RZX, WRX, RZX, WRX,
RWX, WRX,  RX,
```

```
FO,  F1, FRO, FR1, FWO, WFX, FZX, WFX, FZX, WFX,
FZX, WFX, FWX, WFX, FRX, RFX, FX ),--WZX

(   U, ZWX,
ZWX, ZWX, ZWX, ZWX, ZWX,
WX,  W1,  WX, ZWX,  WX, ZWX,  WX, ZWX,  WX,
RO,  R1, RWX, RW1, RWX, ZRX, RWX, ZRX, RWX, ZRX,
RWX, WRX,  RX,
FO,  F1, FRO, FR1, FWX, FW1, FWX, ZFX, FWX, ZFX,
FWX, ZFX, FWX, WFX, FRX, RFX, FX ),--ZWX

(   U,  WX,
WX,  WX,  WX,  WX,  WX,
WX,  WX,  WX,  WX,  WX,  WX,  WX,  WX,  WX,
RO,  R1, RWX, WRX, RWX, WRX, RWX, WRX, RWX, WRX,
RWX, WRX,  RX,
FO,  F1, FRO, FR1, FWX, WFX, FWX, WFX, FWX, WFX,
FWX, WFX, FWX, WFX, FRX, RFX, FX ),--WX

(   U,  RO,
RO,  RO,  RO,  RO,  RO,
RO,  RO,  RO,  RO,  RO,  RO,  RO,  RO,  RO,
RO,  RX,  RO,  RX,  RO,  RX,  RO,  RX,  RO,  RX,
RO,  RX,  RX,
FO,  F1, FRO, RFX, FRO, RFX, FRO, RFX, FRO, RFX,
FRO, RFX, FRO, RFX, FRX, RFX, FX ),--RO

(   U,  R1,
R1,  R1,  R1,  R1,  R1,
R1,  R1,  R1,  R1,  R1,  R1,  R1,  R1,  R1,
RX,  R1,  RX,  R1,  RX,  R1,  RX,  R1,  RX,  R1,
RX,  R1,  RX,
FO,  F1, FRX, FR1, FRX, FR1, FRX, FR1, FRX, FR1,
FRX, FR1, FRX, FR1, FRX, RFX, FX ),--R1

(   U, RWO,
RWO, RWO, RWO, RWO, RWO,
RWO, RWX, RWO, RWX, RWO, RWX, RWO, RWX, RWX,
RO,  RX, RWO,  RX, RWO,  RX, RWO,  RX, RWO,  RX,
RWX,  RX,  RX,
FO,  F1, FRO, RFX, FWO, RFX, FWO, RFX, FWO, RFX,
FWO, RFX, FWX, RFX, FRX, RFX, FX ),--RWO
```

```
(   U, RW1,
RW1, RW1, RW1, RW1, RW1,
WRX, RW1, WRX, RW1, WRX, RW1, WRX, RW1, WRX,
RX,  R1,  RX, RW1,  RX, RW1,  RX, RW1,  RX, RW1,
RX, WRX,  RX,
F0,  F1, FRX, FR1, FRX, FW1, FRX, FW1, FRX, FW1,
FRX, FW1, FRX, WFX, FRX, RFX, FX ),--RW1

(   U, RZ0,
RZ0, RZX, RZ0, RZX, RZX,
RW0, RWX, RZ0, RWX, RZ0, RWX, RZX, RWX, RWX,
R0,  RX, RW0,  RX, RZ0,  RX, RZ0,  RX, RZX,  RX,
RWX,  RX,  RX,
F0,  F1, FR0, RFX, FW0, RFX, FZ0, RFX, FZ0, RFX,
FZX, RFX, FWX, RFX, FRX, RFX, FX ),--RZ0

(   U, RZ1,
ZRX, RZ1, ZRX, RZ1, ZRX,
WRX, RW1, WRX, RZ1, WRX, RZ1, WRX, ZRX, WRX,
RX,  R1,  RX, RW1,  RX, RZ1,  RX, RZ1,  RX, ZRX,
RX, WRX,  RX,
F0,  F1, FRX, FR1, FRX, FW1, FRX, FZ1, FRX, FZ1,
FRX, ZFX, FRX, WFX, FRX, RFX, FX ),--RZ1

(   U, RDX,
RZ0, RZX, RDX, RZX, RZX,
RW0, RWX, RZ0, RWX, RDX, RWX, RZX, RWX, RWX,
R0,  RX, RW0,  RX, RZ0,  RX, RDX,  RX, RZX,  RX,
RWX,  RX,  RX,
F0,  F1, FR0, RFX, FW0, RFX, FZ0, RFX, FDX, RFX,
FZX, RFX, FWX, RFX, FRX, RFX, FX ),--RDX

(   U, DRX,
ZRX, RZ1, ZRX, DRX, ZRX,
WRX, RW1, WRX, RZ1, WRX, DRX, WRX, ZRX, WRX,
RX,  R1,  RX, RW1,  RX, RZ1,  RX, DRX,  RX, ZRX,
RX, WRX,  RX,
F0,  F1, FRX, FR1, FRX, FW1, FRX, FZ1, FRX, DFX,
FRX, ZFX, FRX, WFX, FRX, RFX, FX ),--DRX

(   U, RZX,
```

```
RZX, RZX, RZX, RZX, RZX,
RW0, RWX, RZX, RWX, RZX, RWX, RZX, RWX, RWX,
R0,  RX, RW0,  RX, RZX,  RX, RZX,  RX, RZX,  RX,
RWX,  RX,  RX,
F0,  F1, FR0, RFX, FW0, RFX, FZX, RFX, FZX, RFX,
FZX, RFX, FWX, RFX, FRX, RFX, FX ),--RZX

(   U, ZRX,
ZRX, ZRX, ZRX, ZRX, ZRX,
WRX, RW1, WRX, ZRX, WRX, ZRX, WRX, ZRX, WRX,
RX,  R1,  RX, RW1,  RX, ZRX,  RX, ZRX,  RX, ZRX,
RX, WRX,  RX,
F0,  F1, FRX, FR1, FRX, FW1, FRX, ZFX, FRX, ZFX,
FRX, ZFX, FRX, WFX, FRX, RFX, FX ),--ZRX

(   U, RWX,
RWX, RWX, RWX, RWX, RWX,
RWX, RWX, RWX, RWX, RWX, RWX, RWX, RWX, RWX,
R0,  RX, RWX,  RX, RWX,  RX, RWX,  RX, RWX,  RX,
RWX,  RX,  RX,
F0,  F1, FR0, RFX, FWX, RFX, FWX, RFX, FWX, RFX,
FWX, RFX, FWX, RFX, FRX, RFX, FX ),--RWX

(   U, WRX,
WRX, WRX, WRX, WRX, WRX,
WRX, WRX, WRX, WRX, WRX, WRX, WRX, WRX, WRX,
RX,  R1,  RX, WRX,  RX, WRX,  RX, WRX,  RX, WRX,
RX, WRX,  RX,
F0,  F1, FRX, FR1, FRX, WFX, FRX, WFX, FRX, WFX,
FRX, WFX, FRX, WFX, FRX, RFX, FX ),--WRX

(   U,  RX,
RX,  RX,   RX,  RX,  RX,
RX,  RX,   RX,  RX,  RX,  RX,  RX,  RX,  RX,
RX,  RX,   RX,  RX,  RX,  RX,  RX,  RX,  RX,  RX,
RX,  RX,  RX,
F0,  F1,  FRX, RFX, FRX, RFX, FRX, RFX, FRX, RFX,
FRX, RFX, FRX, RFX, FRX, RFX, FX ),--RX

(   U,  F0,
F0,  F0,   F0,  F0,  F0,
F0,  F0,   F0,  F0,  F0,  F0,  F0,  F0,  F0,
```

```
F0,  F0,   F0,  F0,  F0,  F0,  F0,  F0,  F0,  F0,
F0,  F0,  F0,
F0,  FX,   F0,  FX,  F0,  FX,  F0,  FX,  F0,  FX,
F0,  FX,  F0,  FX,  F0,  FX, FX ),--F0

(   U,  F1,
F1,  F1,   F1,  F1,  F1,
F1,  F1,   F1,  F1,  F1,  F1,  F1,  F1,  F1,
F1,  F1,   F1,  F1,  F1,  F1,  F1,  F1,  F1,  F1,
F1,  F1,  F1,
FX,  F1,   FX,  F1,  FX,  F1,  FX,  F1,  FX,  F1,
FX,  F1,  FX,  F1,  FX,  F1, FX ),--F1

(   U, FR0,
FR0, FR0, FR0, FR0, FR0,
FR0, FR0, FR0, FR0, FR0, FR0, FR0, FR0, FR0,
FR0, FRX, FR0, FRX, FR0, FRX, FR0, FRX, FR0, FRX,
FR0, FRX, FRX,
F0,  FX, FR0,  FX, FR0,  FX, FR0,  FX, FR0,  FX,
FR0,  FX, FR0,  FX, FRX,  FX, FX ),--FR0

(   U, FR1,
FR1, FR1, FR1, FR1, FR1,
FR1, FR1, FR1, FR1, FR1, FR1, FR1, FR1, FR1,
RFX, FR1, RFX, FR1, RFX, FR1, RFX, FR1, RFX, FR1,
RFX, FR1, RFX,
FX,  F1,  FX, FR1,  FX, FR1,  FX, FR1,  FX, FR1,
FX, FR1,  FX,  FR1, FX, RFX, FX ),--FR1

(   U, FW0,
FW0, FW0, FW0, FW0, FW0,
FW0, FWX, FW0, FWX, FW0, FWX, FW0, FWX, FWX,
FR0, FRX, FW0, FRX, FW0, FRX, FW0, FRX, FW0, FRX,
FWX, FRX, FRX,
F0,  FX, FR0,  FX, FW0,  FX, FW0,  FX, FW0,  FX,
FW0,  FX, FWX,  FX, FRX, FX,  FX ),--FW0

(   U, FW1,
FW1, FW1, FW1, FW1, FW1,
WFX, FW1, WFX, FW1, WFX, FW1, WFX, FW1, WFX,
RFX, FR1, RFX, FW1, RFX, FW1, RFX, FW1, RFX, FW1,
RFX, WFX, RFX,
```

```
FX,  F1,  FX, FR1,  FX, FW1,  FX, FW1,  FX, FW1,
FX, FW1,  FX,  WFX, FX, RFX, FX ),--FW1

(   U, FZ0,
FZ0, FZX, FZ0, FZX, FZX,
FW0, FWX, FZ0, FWX, FZ0, FWX, FZX, FWX, FWX,
FR0, FRX, FW0, FRX, FZ0, FRX, FZ0, FRX, FZX, FRX,
FWX, FRX, FRX,
F0,  FX, FR0,  FX, FW0,  FX, FZ0,  FX, FZ0,  FX,
FZX,  FX, FWX, FX,  FRX, FX,  FX ),--FZ0

(   U, FZ1,
ZFX, FZ1, ZFX, FZ1, ZFX,
WFX, FW1, WFX, FZ1, WFX, FZ1, WFX, ZFX, WFX,
RFX, FR1, RFX, FW1, RFX, FZ1, RFX, FZ1, RFX, ZFX,
RFX, WFX, RFX,
FX,  F1,  FX, FR1,  FX, FW1,  FX, FZ1,  FX, FZ1,
FX, ZFX,  FX,  WFX, FX, RFX, FX ),--FZ1

(   U, FDX,
FZ0, FZX, FDX, FZX, FZX,
FW0, FWX, FZ0, FWX, FDX, FWX, FZX, FWX, FWX,
FR0, FRX, FW0, FRX, FZ0, FRX, FDX, FRX, FZX, FRX,
FWX, FRX, FRX,
F0,  FX, FR0,  FX, FW0,  FX, FZ0,  FX, FDX,  FX,
FZX,  FX,  FWX, FX,  FRX, FX, FX ),--FDX

(   U, DFX,
ZFX, FZ1, ZFX, DFX, ZFX,
WFX, FW1, WFX, FZ1, WFX, DFX, WFX, ZFX, WFX,
RFX, FR1, RFX, FW1, RFX, FZ1, RFX, DFX, RFX, ZFX,
RFX, WFX, RFX,
FX,  F1,  FX, FR1,  FX, FW1,  FX, FZ1,  FX, DFX,
FX, ZFX,  FX, WFX, FX, RFX, FX ),--DFX

(   U, FZX,
FZX, FZX, FZX, FZX, FZX,
FW0, FWX, FZX, FWX, FZX, FWX, FZX, FWX, FWX,
FR0, FRX, FW0, FRX, FZX, FRX, FZX, FRX, FZX, FRX,
FWX, FRX, FRX,
F0,  FX, FR0,  FX, FW0, FX , FZX, FX , FZX, FX ,
FZX, FX , FWX, FX , FRX, FX , FX ),--FZX
```

```
(   U, ZFX,
ZFX, ZFX, ZFX, ZFX, ZFX,
WFX, FW1, WFX, ZFX, WFX, ZFX, WFX, ZFX, WFX,
RFX, FR1, RFX, FW1, RFX, ZFX, RFX, ZFX, RFX, ZFX,
RFX, WFX, RFX,
FX,  F1,  FX, FR1, FX , FW1, FX , ZFX, FX , ZFX,
FX , ZFX, FX , WFX, FX,  RFX, FX ),--ZFX

(   U, FWX,
FWX, FWX, FWX, FWX, FWX,
FWX, FWX, FWX, FWX, FWX, FWX, FWX, FWX, FWX,
FR0, FRX, FWX, FRX, FWX, FRX, FWX, FRX, FWX, FRX,
FWX, FRX, FRX,
F0,  FX, FR0,  FX, FWX, FX , FWX, FX , FWX, FX ,
FWX, FX , FWX, FX,  FRX, FX , FX ),--FWX

(   U, WFX,
WFX, WFX, WFX, WFX, WFX,
WFX, WFX, WFX, WFX, WFX, WFX, WFX, WFX, WFX,
RFX, FR1, RFX, WFX, RFX, WFX, RFX, WFX, RFX, WFX,
RFX, WFX, RFX,
FX,  F1,  FX, FR1,  FX, WFX, FX , WFX, FX , WFX,
FX , WFX, FX , WFX, FX,  RFX, FX ),--WFX

(   U, FRX,
FRX, FRX, FRX, FRX, FRX,
FRX, FRX, FRX, FRX, FRX, FRX, FRX, FRX, FRX,
FRX, FRX, FRX, FRX, FRX, FRX, FRX, FRX, FRX, FRX,
FRX, FRX, FRX,
F0,  FX, FRX,  FX, FRX, FX , FRX, FX , FRX, FX ,
FRX, FX , FRX, FX,  FRX, FX,  FX ),--FRX

(   U, RFX,
RFX, RFX, RFX, RFX, RFX,
RFX, RFX, RFX, RFX, RFX, RFX, RFX, RFX, RFX,
RFX, RFX, RFX, RFX, RFX, RFX, RFX, RFX, RFX, RFX,
RFX, RFX, RFX,
FX,  F1,  FX, RFX,  FX, RFX, FX , RFX, FX , RFX,
FX , RFX, FX , RFX, FX,  RFX, FX ),--RFX

(   U,  FX,
```

```
FX,   FX,   FX,   FX,   FX,
FX,   FX,   FX,   FX,   FX,   FX,   FX,   FX,   FX,
FX,   FX,   FX,   FX,   FX,   FX,   FX,   FX,   FX,   FX,
FX,   FX,   FX,
FX,   FX,   FX,   FX,   FX,   FX,   FX,   FX,   FX,   FX,
FX,   FX,   FX,   FX,   FX,   FX,   FX )--FX      );
```

```
END std_logic;
```

Next the package body for the STD_LOGIC package will be described. The package body contains the function bodies for all of the function declarations given, in the package declaration.

```
PACKAGE BODY std_logic IS
   --$ !VANTAGE_METACOMMENTS_ON
   --$ !VANTAGE_DNA_ON
```

The first function, *f_max_time*, is a local function used only internally in the package body to calculate the maximum of two time values.

```
FUNCTION f_max_time( t1, t2 : IN time )
      RETURN time IS
BEGIN
   IF (t1 > t2) THEN
      RETURN t1;
   ELSE
      RETURN t2;
   END IF;
END f_max_time;
```

The next set of functions are used to describe the overloaded-operator functions specified in the package declaration.

```
-- "=" operator.
FUNCTION "="    ( L : t_logic; R : t_state )
      RETURN boolean IS
BEGIN
   RETURN( f_state( L ) = R );
END;

FUNCTION "="    ( L : t_state; R : t_logic )
      RETURN boolean IS
BEGIN
   RETURN( L = f_state( R ) );
END;
```

```
-- "/=" operator.
FUNCTION "/="   ( L : t_logic; R : t_state )
     RETURN boolean IS
BEGIN
  RETURN( f_state( L ) /= R );
END;

FUNCTION "/="   ( L : t_state; R : t_logic )
     RETURN boolean IS
BEGIN
  RETURN( L /= f_state( R ) );
END;

-- "<" operator.
FUNCTION "<"   ( L : t_logic; R : t_state )
     RETURN boolean IS
BEGIN
  RETURN( f_state( L ) < R );
END;

FUNCTION "<"   ( L : t_state; R : t_logic )
     RETURN boolean IS
BEGIN
  RETURN( L < f_state( R ) );
END;

-- "<=" operator.
FUNCTION "<="   ( L : t_logic; R : t_state )
     RETURN boolean IS
BEGIN
  RETURN( f_state( L ) <= R );
END;

FUNCTION "<="   ( L : t_state; R : t_logic )
  RETURN boolean IS
BEGIN
  RETURN( L <= f_state( R ) );
END;

-- ">" operator.
FUNCTION ">"   ( L : t_logic; R : t_state )
```

```
        RETURN boolean IS
BEGIN
    RETURN( f_state( L ) > R );
END;

FUNCTION ">"    ( L : t_state; R : t_logic )
        RETURN boolean IS
BEGIN
    RETURN( L > f_state( R ) );
END;

-- ">=" operator.
FUNCTION ">="   ( L : t_logic; R : t_state )
        RETURN boolean IS
BEGIN
    RETURN( f_state( L ) >= R );
END;

FUNCTION ">="   ( L : t_state; R : t_logic )
        RETURN boolean IS
BEGIN
    RETURN( L >= f_state( R ) );
END;
```

The next set of function bodies describe the behavior of the overloaded logical operators, specified in the package declaration. Notice that these functions make use of the constants *f_and, f_or*, etc., to perform the actual logical operation. These functions mainly insure that the types of the operands are correct.

```
FUNCTION "and" ( l : t_logic;  r : t_logic )
        RETURN t_state IS
BEGIN
    RETURN( f_and( f_state(l) )( f_state(r) ) );
END;

FUNCTION "and" ( l : t_state;  r : t_logic )
        RETURN t_state IS
BEGIN
    RETURN( f_and( l )( f_state(r) ) );
END;

FUNCTION "and" ( l : t_logic;  r : t_state )
```

```
     RETURN t_state IS
BEGIN
  RETURN( f_and( f_state(l) )( r ) );
END;

FUNCTION "and" ( l : t_state;  r : t_state )
     RETURN t_state IS
BEGIN
  RETURN( f_and( l )( r ) );
END;

FUNCTION "or" ( l : t_logic;  r : t_logic )
     RETURN t_state IS
BEGIN
  RETURN( f_or( f_state(l) )( f_state(r) ) );
END;

FUNCTION "or" ( l : t_state;  r : t_logic )
     RETURN t_state IS
BEGIN
  RETURN( f_or( l )( f_state(r) ) );
END;

FUNCTION "or" ( l : t_logic;  r : t_state )
     RETURN t_state IS
BEGIN
  RETURN( f_or( f_state(l) )( r ) );
END;

FUNCTION "or" ( l : t_state;  r : t_state )
     RETURN t_state IS
BEGIN
  RETURN( f_or( l )( r ) );
END;

FUNCTION "nand" ( l : t_logic;  r : t_logic )
     RETURN t_state IS
BEGIN
  RETURN( f_nand( f_state(l) )( f_state(r) ) );
END;

FUNCTION "nand" ( l : t_state;  r : t_logic )
```

```
        RETURN t_state IS
BEGIN
    RETURN( f_nand( l )( f_state(r) ) );
END;

FUNCTION "nand" ( l : t_logic;  r : t_state )
        RETURN t_state IS
BEGIN
    RETURN( f_nand( f_state(l) )( r ) );
END;

FUNCTION "nand" ( l : t_state;  r : t_state )
        RETURN t_state IS
BEGIN
    RETURN( f_nand( l )( r ) );
END;

FUNCTION "nor" ( l : t_logic;  r : t_logic )
        RETURN t_state IS
BEGIN
    RETURN( f_nor( f_state(l) )( f_state(r) ) );
END;

FUNCTION "nor" ( l : t_state;  r : t_logic )
        RETURN t_state IS
BEGIN
    RETURN( f_nor( l )( f_state(r) ) );
END;

FUNCTION "nor" ( l : t_logic;  r : t_state )
        RETURN t_state IS
BEGIN
    RETURN( f_nor( f_state(l) )( r ) );
END;

FUNCTION "nor" ( l : t_state;  r : t_state )
        RETURN t_state IS
BEGIN
    RETURN( f_nor( l )( r ) );
END;

FUNCTION "xor" ( l : t_logic;  r : t_logic )
```

```
      RETURN t_state IS
BEGIN
   RETURN( f_xor( f_state(l) )( f_state(r) ) );
END;

FUNCTION "xor" ( l : t_state;  r : t_logic )
      RETURN t_state IS
BEGIN
   RETURN( f_xor( l )( f_state(r) ) );
END;

FUNCTION "xor" ( l : t_logic;  r : t_state )
      RETURN t_state IS
BEGIN
   RETURN( f_xor( f_state(l) )( r ) );
END;

FUNCTION "xor" ( l : t_state;  r : t_state )
      RETURN t_state IS
BEGIN
   RETURN( f_xor( l )( r ) );
END;
```

The next function in the package body is the resolution function for the type *t_wlogic*. This function has an input array which consists of the driver values for a signal. The resolution function will compute the resolved value of these driver values.

If the driver array passed to the function is 0 length, meaning no drivers are driving, then the result is the weakest state, D. If only one driver value is passed, so the length of the driver array is 1, then that driver is the resolved value. If more than one driver is passed, then the drivers are processed one at a time with the current result, to calculate the final result.

```
FUNCTION f_logic_bus( s : t_logic_vector )
      RETURN t_logic IS
   VARIABLE result : t_logic;  -- result so far
BEGIN
   -- If no inputs then default is D
   IF (s'LENGTH = 0) THEN
      RETURN D;
```

```
   ELSIF (s'LENGTH = 1) THEN
      RETURN s(s'LOW);

      -- Calculate value based on inputs
   ELSE
      result := D;
      -- Iterate through all inputs

      FOR i IN s'LOW TO s'HIGH LOOP
         IF ( s(i) = U ) THEN
            RETURN U;
         END IF;
         IF ( s(i) = D ) THEN
            NEXT;
         END IF;
         result := f_busres(result)(s(i));
      END LOOP;

      -- Return the resultant value
      RETURN result;
   END IF;
END f_logic_bus;
```

The next two functions in the package are delay functions. Function *f_delay* is used to calculate the delay for a signal that is always driven, and function *f_zdelay* is used to calculate the delay for a signal whose drive can be turned off. Function *f_delay* takes in two parameters, one for the rising delay (*delay01*) and the other for the falling delay (*delay10*). Based on the new state being scheduled (*newlv*), the appropriate delay is returned. If the new state is the value 'X', then the maximum delay value is returned.

```
FUNCTION f_delay( newlv : IN t_logic;
                  delay01 : IN time;
                   delay10 : IN time)
                   RETURN time IS
BEGIN
   CASE f_state(newlv) IS
      WHEN '0'  =>
         RETURN delay10;
      WHEN '1'  =>
         RETURN delay01;
```

```
      WHEN 'X'  =>
         IF (delay01 > delay10) THEN
            RETURN delay01;
         ELSE
            RETURN delay10;
         END IF;
   END CASE;
END f_delay;
```

Function *f_zdelay* works very similarly to function *f_delay*, except that there are six possible delay conditions to be handled. Along with the normal 0 to 1 and 1 to 0 delay conditions, there are also the Z to 1 and Z to 0 cases, and the 1 to Z and 0 to Z cases. The value Z in these cases means that the state has a high-impedance strength.

```
FUNCTION f_zdelay( oldlv   : IN t_logic;
                   newlv   : IN t_logic;
                   delay01 : IN time;
                   delay10 : IN time;
                   delayz0 : IN time;
                   delayz1 : IN time;
                   delay0z : IN time;
                   delay1z : IN time)
                   RETURN time IS
   VARIABLE old_strength : t_strength;
   VARIABLE new_strength : t_strength;
BEGIN
   -- Compute the strengths.
   old_strength := f_strength( oldlv );
   new_strength := f_strength( newlv );

   -- If both are 'Z', then take the highest
   -- of the four 'z' delays.
   IF ((old_strength <= 'Z') AND
        (new_strength <= 'Z')) THEN
      RETURN( f_max_time( delayz0,
                 f_max_time( delayz1,
                    f_max_time( delay0z, delay1z )
                            )
                        )
            );
   -- If the old strength is 'Z', then it
   -- must be delayz?.
```

```
  ELSIF (old_strength <= 'Z') THEN
    CASE f_state( newlv ) IS
      WHEN '0' =>
        RETURN delayz0;
      WHEN '1' =>
        RETURN delayz1;
      WHEN 'X' =>
        RETURN ( f_max_time( delayz0,
                             delayz1 ) );
    END CASE;
  -- If the new strength is 'Z', then it
  -- must be delay?z.
  ELSIF (new_strength <= 'Z') THEN
    CASE f_state( oldlv ) IS
      WHEN '0' =>
        RETURN delay0z;
      WHEN '1' =>
        RETURN delay1z;
      WHEN 'X' =>
        RETURN ( f_max_time( delay0z,
                             delay1z ) );
    END CASE;
  -- Otherwise, use f_delay TO compute
  -- the delay.
  ELSE
    RETURN( f_delay( newlv, delay01,
                     delay10 ) );
  END IF;
END f_zdelay;
```

The next function in the package body is the *f_convu* function. This function, as described in the package declaration, will calculate the proper 46-state value for a tristate output when the enabling signal is an indeterminate (X) value.

```
FUNCTION f_convu(  newval  : IN t_logic;
                    lastval : IN t_logic;
                    tech    : IN t_technology )
                   RETURN t_logic IS
  VARIABLE oldst : t_state;
  VARIABLE newst : t_state;
BEGIN
  -- Pickup states for values
```

```
oldst := f_state( lastval );
newst := f_state( newval );
CASE newst IS
   -- new value is false
   WHEN '0' =>
      CASE oldst IS
         -- from false to false
         WHEN '0' =>
            CASE tech IS
               WHEN ecl => RETURN RZ0;
               WHEN cmos =>RETURN FZ0;
               WHEN nmos =>RETURN FZ0;
               WHEN ttl => RETURN FZ0;
               WHEN ttloc => RETURN FZ0;
            END CASE;
         -- from true/unknown to false
         WHEN '1'|'X'  =>
            CASE tech IS
               WHEN ecl => RETURN RZX;
               WHEN cmos =>RETURN FZX;
               WHEN nmos =>RETURN FZX;
               WHEN ttl => RETURN FZX;
               WHEN ttloc => RETURN FZX;
            END CASE;
      END CASE;
   -- new value is true
   WHEN '1' =>
      CASE oldst IS
         -- from true to true
         WHEN '1' =>
            CASE tech IS
               WHEN ecl => RETURN FZ1;
               WHEN cmos =>RETURN FZ1;
               WHEN nmos =>RETURN RZ1;
               WHEN ttl => RETURN FZ1;
               WHEN ttloc => RETURN ZX;
            END CASE;
         -- from false/unknown to true
         WHEN '0'|'X' =>
            CASE tech IS
               WHEN ecl => RETURN ZFX;
               WHEN cmos =>RETURN ZFX;
```

```
                WHEN nmos =>RETURN ZRX;
                WHEN ttl => RETURN ZFX;
                WHEN ttloc => RETURN ZX;
             END CASE;
          END CASE;
       -- new value is unknown
       WHEN 'X'      =>
          -- from any value to unknown
          CASE tech IS
             WHEN ecl => RETURN RFX;
             WHEN cmos =>RETURN FX;
             WHEN nmos =>RETURN FRX;
             WHEN ttl => RETURN FX;
             WHEN ttloc => RETURN FZX;
          END CASE;
    END CASE;
  END f_convu;
END std_logic;
```

The STD_LOGIC package can be very useful as a starting point upon which to build a standard package for the designer's use. The standard types and functions provide a framework on which to build all the necessary functionality into the VHDL simulator to simulate large systems.

A copy of the STD_LOGIC package on floppy disk or cartridge tape can be obtained by contacting Vantage Analysis Systems directly.

Appendix

B

Technology Packages

In this appendix, five technology-specific packages will be presented. These packages allow the designer to write technology-independent models that can easily be mapped to any of the supported technologies by simply *using* the appropriate package.

The packages overload the logical operator functions, so that the operators return the appropriate 46-state values for the technology being targeted. For instance, when the CMOS package is included, CMOS values will be returned. When the ECL package is included ECL values will be returned.

An example of these packages in action is shown below. (This code is not included in the package.)

```
USE STD.std_logic.ALL;
USE STD.std_ttl.ALL; -- include the ttl package
ENTITY and2 IS
   GENERIC( rise, fall : TIME);
   PORT( a, b : IN t_wlogic;
         c : OUT t_wlogic);
```

```
END and2;

ARCHITECTURE behave OF and2 IS
BEGIN
   andproc : PROCESS(a, b)
      VARIABLE state : t_logic;
   BEGIN
      state := a AND b;
      c <= state after f_delay(state, rise, fall);
   END PROCESS andproc;
END behave;
```

The AND operator, with arguments *a, b*, is overloaded by virtue of the USE clause to calculate TTL technology values when assigning the new value to variable *state*. To make the *and2* model a different technology, all that is required is to USE a different package. Changing the USE clause from USE STD.STD_TTL.ALL, to USE STD.STD_ECL.ALL will change the output values from TTL states to ECL states.

The packages overload all of the logical operators for the *t_logic* and *t_wlogic* types.

```
--
--------------------------------------------------
--                copyright 1988
--          Vantage Analysis Systems,Inc.
--             ALL rights reserved
--
--    File name :  std_ttl.vhdl
--    Title     :  ttl overloaded operators.
--
--    Purpose   :
--
--        Provide standard logical operators
--        AND, OR, NAND, NOR, XOR,
--        and NOT which work on operands of
--        the std_logic type.
--
--    Author(s) :  KES
--
--
USE std.std_logic.ALL;
```

```
PACKAGE std_ttl IS
   --$ !VANTAGE_METACOMMENTS_ON
   --$ !VANTAGE_DNA_ON
   -- Logical operators.
   FUNCTION "AND" (l, r : t_logic )RETURN t_logic;
   FUNCTION "OR"  (l, r : t_logic )RETURN t_logic;
   FUNCTION "NAND"(l, r : t_logic )RETURN t_logic;
   FUNCTION "NOR" (l, r : t_logic )RETURN t_logic;
   FUNCTION "XOR" (l, r : t_logic )RETURN t_logic;
   FUNCTION "NOT" (l    : t_logic )RETURN t_logic;
END std_ttl;

--------------------------------------------------

PACKAGE BODY std_ttl IS
   --$ !VANTAGE_METACOMMENTS_ON
   --$ !VANTAGE_DNA_ON
   -- "AND" operator.
   FUNCTION "AND" ( l, r : t_logic )
     RETURN t_logic IS
   BEGIN
     RETURN( f_ttl( f_and( f_state( l ) )
                         ( f_state( r ) ) ) );
   END;

   -- "OR" operator.
   FUNCTION "OR" ( l, r : t_logic )
     RETURN t_logic IS
   BEGIN
     RETURN( f_ttl( f_or( f_state( l ) )
                        ( f_state( r ) ) ) );
   END;

   -- "NAND" operator.
   FUNCTION "NAND" ( l, r : t_logic )
     RETURN t_logic IS
   BEGIN
     RETURN( f_ttl( f_nand( f_state( l ) )
                          ( f_state( r ) ) ) );
   END;

   -- "NOR" operator.
   FUNCTION "NOR" ( l, r : t_logic )
```

```
      RETURN t_logic IS
   BEGIN
      RETURN( f_ttl( f_nor( f_state( l ) )
                          ( f_state( r ) ) ) );
   END;

   -- "XOR" operator.
   FUNCTION "XOR" ( l, r : t_logic )
      RETURN t_logic IS
   BEGIN
      RETURN( f_ttl( f_xor( f_state( l ) )
                          ( f_state( r ) ) ) );
   END;

   -- "NOT" operator.
   FUNCTION "NOT" ( l    : t_logic )
      RETURN t_logic IS
   BEGIN
      RETURN( f_ttl( f_not( f_state( l ) ) ) );
   END;
END std_ttl;


USE std.std_logic.ALL;
PACKAGE std_cmos IS
   --$ !VANTAGE_METACOMMENTS_ON
   --$ !VANTAGE_DNA_ON
   -- Logical operators.
   FUNCTION "AND" (l, r : t_logic )RETURN t_logic;
   FUNCTION "OR"  (l, r : t_logic )RETURN t_logic;
   FUNCTION "NAND"(l, r : t_logic )RETURN t_logic;
   FUNCTION "NOR" (l, r : t_logic )RETURN t_logic;
   FUNCTION "XOR" (l, r : t_logic )RETURN t_logic;
   FUNCTION "NOT" (l    : t_logic )RETURN t_logic;
END std_cmos;

--------------------------------------------------

PACKAGE BODY std_cmos IS
   --$ !VANTAGE_METACOMMENTS_ON
   --$ !VANTAGE_DNA_ON
   -- "AND" operator.
   FUNCTION "AND" ( l, r : t_logic )
      RETURN t_logic IS
```

```
BEGIN
  RETURN( f_cmos( f_and( f_state( l ) )
                       ( f_state( r ) ) ) );
END;

-- "OR" operator.
FUNCTION "OR" ( l, r : t_logic )
  RETURN t_logic IS
BEGIN
  RETURN( f_cmos( f_or( f_state( l ) )
                       ( f_state( r ) ) ) );
END;

-- "NAND" operator.
FUNCTION "NAND" ( l, r : t_logic )
  RETURN t_logic IS
BEGIN
  RETURN( f_cmos( f_nand( f_state( l ) )
                       ( f_state( r ) ) ) );
END;

-- "NOR" operator.
FUNCTION "NOR" ( l, r : t_logic )
  RETURN t_logic IS
BEGIN
  RETURN( f_cmos( f_nor( f_state( l ) )
                       ( f_state( r ) ) ) );
END;

-- "XOR" operator.
FUNCTION "XOR" ( l, r : t_logic )
  RETURN t_logic IS
BEGIN
  RETURN( f_cmos( f_xor( f_state( l ) )
                       ( f_state( r ) ) ) );
END;

-- "NOT" operator.
FUNCTION "NOT" ( l    : t_logic )
  RETURN t_logic IS
BEGIN
  RETURN( f_cmos( f_not( f_state( l ) ) ) );
```

```
   END;
END std_cmos;

--------------------------------------------------------

USE std.std_logic.ALL;
PACKAGE std_ecl IS
   --$ !VANTAGE_METACOMMENTS_ON
   --$ !VANTAGE_DNA_ON
   -- Logical operators.
   FUNCTION "AND" ( , r : t_logic )RETURN t_logic;
   FUNCTION "OR"  (l, r : t_logic )RETURN t_logic;
   FUNCTION "NAND"(l, r : t_logic )RETURN t_logic;
   FUNCTION "NOR" (l, r : t_logic )RETURN t_logic;
   FUNCTION "XOR" (l, r : t_logic )RETURN t_logic;
   FUNCTION "NOT" (l    : t_logic )RETURN t_logic;
END std_ecl;
PACKAGE BODY std_ecl IS
   --$ !VANTAGE_METACOMMENTS_ON
   --$ !VANTAGE_DNA_ON
   -- "AND" operator.
   FUNCTION "AND" ( l, r : t_logic )
      RETURN t_logic IS
   BEGIN
      RETURN( f_ecl( f_and( f_state( l ) )
                          ( f_state( r ) ) ) );
   END;

   -- "OR" operator.
   FUNCTION "OR" ( l, r : t_logic )
      RETURN t_logic IS
   BEGIN
      RETURN( f_ecl( f_or( f_state( l ) )
                         ( f_state( r ) ) ) );
   END;

   -- "NAND" operator.
   FUNCTION "NAND" ( l, r : t_logic )
      RETURN t_logic IS
   BEGIN
      RETURN( f_ecl( f_nand( f_state( l ) )
                           ( f_state( r ) ) ) );
   END;
```

```
   -- "NOR" operator.
   FUNCTION "NOR" ( l, r : t_logic )
     RETURN t_logic IS
   BEGIN
     RETURN( f_ecl( f_nor( f_state( l ) )
                          ( f_state( r ) ) ) );
   END;

   -- "XOR" operator.
   FUNCTION "XOR" ( l, r : t_logic )
     RETURN t_logic IS
   BEGIN
     RETURN( f_ecl( f_xor( f_state( l ) )
                          ( f_state( r ) ) ) );
   END;

   -- "NOT" operator.
   FUNCTION "NOT" ( l    : t_logic )
     RETURN t_logic IS
   BEGIN
     RETURN( f_ecl( f_not( f_state( l ) ) ) );
   END;
END std_ecl;
--------------------------------------------------
USE std.std_logic.ALL;
PACKAGE std_nmos IS
   --$ !VANTAGE_METACOMMENTS_ON
   --$ !VANTAGE_DNA_ON
   -- Logical operators.
   FUNCTION "AND" (l, r : t_logic )RETURN t_logic;
   FUNCTION "OR"  (l, r : t_logic )RETURN t_logic;
   FUNCTION "NAND"(l, r : t_logic )RETURN t_logic;
   FUNCTION "NOR" (l, r : t_logic )RETURN t_logic;
   FUNCTION "XOR" (l, r : t_logic )RETURN t_logic;
   FUNCTION "NOT" (l    : t_logic )RETURN t_logic;
END std_nmos;

PACKAGE BODY std_nmos IS
   --$ !VANTAGE_METACOMMENTS_ON
   --$ !VANTAGE_DNA_ON
   -- "AND" operator.
   FUNCTION "AND" ( l, r : t_logic )
```

```
    RETURN t_logic IS
BEGIN
    RETURN( f_nmos( f_and( f_state( l ) )
                          ( f_state( r ) ) ) );
END;

-- "OR" operator.
FUNCTION "OR" ( l, r : t_logic )
    RETURN t_logic IS
BEGIN
    RETURN( f_nmos( f_or( f_state( l ) )
                          ( f_state( r ) ) ) );
END;

-- "NAND" operator.
FUNCTION "NAND" ( l, r : t_logic )
    RETURN t_logic IS
BEGIN
    RETURN( f_nmos( f_nand( f_state( l ) )
                          ( f_state( r ) ) ) );
END;

-- "NOR" operator.
FUNCTION "NOR" ( l, r : t_logic )
    RETURN t_logic IS
BEGIN
    RETURN( f_nmos( f_nor( f_state( l ) )
                          ( f_state( r ) ) ) );
END;

-- "XOR" operator.
FUNCTION "XOR" ( l, r : t_logic )
    RETURN t_logic IS
BEGIN
    RETURN( f_nmos( f_xor( f_state( l ) )
                          ( f_state( r ) ) ) );
END;

-- "NOT" operator.
FUNCTION "NOT" ( l    : t_logic )
    RETURN t_logic IS
BEGIN
```

```
    RETURN( f_nmos( f_not( f_state( l ) ) ) );
  END;
END std_nmos;

--------------------------------------------------

USE std.std_logic.ALL;
PACKAGE std_ttloc IS
  --$ !VANTAGE_METACOMMENTS_ON
  --$ !VANTAGE_DNA_ON
  -- Logical operators.
  FUNCTION "AND" (l, r : t_logic )RETURN t_logic;
  FUNCTION "OR"  (l, r : t_logic )RETURN t_logic;
  FUNCTION "NAND"(l, r : t_logic )RETURN t_logic;
  FUNCTION "NOR" (l, r : t_logic )RETURN t_logic;
  FUNCTION "XOR" (l, r : t_logic )RETURN t_logic;
  FUNCTION "NOT" (l    : t_logic )RETURN t_logic;
END std_ttloc;

PACKAGE BODY std_ttloc IS
  --$ !VANTAGE_METACOMMENTS_ON
  --$ !VANTAGE_DNA_ON
  -- "AND" operator.
  FUNCTION "AND" ( l, r : t_logic )
    RETURN t_logic IS
  BEGIN
    RETURN( f_ttloc( f_and( f_state( l ) )
                          ( f_state( r ) ) ) );
  END;

  -- "OR" operator.
  FUNCTION "OR" ( l, r : t_logic )
    RETURN t_logic IS
  BEGIN
    RETURN( f_ttloc( f_or( f_state( l ) )
                          ( f_state( r ) ) ) );
  END;

  -- "NAND" operator.
  FUNCTION "NAND" ( l, r : t_logic )
    RETURN t_logic IS
  BEGIN
    RETURN( f_ttloc( f_nand( f_state( l ) )
                          ( f_state( r ) ) ) );
```

```
   END;

   -- "NOR" operator.
   FUNCTION "NOR" ( l, r : t_logic )
     RETURN t_logic IS
   BEGIN
     RETURN( f_ttloc( f_nor( f_state( l ) )
                            ( f_state( r ) ) ) );
   END;

   -- "XOR" operator.
   FUNCTION "XOR" ( l, r : t_logic )
     RETURN t_logic IS
   BEGIN
     RETURN( f_ttloc( f_xor( f_state( l ) )
                            ( f_state( r ) ) ) );
   END;

   -- "NOT" operator.
   FUNCTION "NOT" ( l    : t_logic )
     RETURN t_logic IS
   BEGIN
     RETURN( f_ttloc( f_not( f_state( l ) ) ) );
   END;
END std_ttloc;
```

This package provides the necessary tools to write technology-specific models using VHDL. The concepts in this package can be expanded to include higher-level functions such as shift, rotate, add, etc.

Appendix

C

Reading VHDL BNF

Once the basic concepts of VHDL are understood, the designer will want to try to write VHDL in a more elegant manner. To fully understand how to apply all of the syntactic constructs available in VHDL, it is helpful to know how to read the VHDL Bachus-Naur format (BNF) of the language. This format is in Appendix A of the IEEE Std 1076-1987 *VHDL Language Reference Manual* (LRM), pages A-1 to A-17. This format will specify which constructs are necessary versus optional or repeatable versus singular, and how constructs can be associated.

BNF is basically a hierarchical description method, where complex constructs are made of successive specifications of lower-level constructs. Our purpose for examining BNF is not to understand every nuance of the BNF but to put the basics to use to help build complex VHDL constructs. To this end, let us examine some BNF and discuss what it means.

The BNF for the IF statement is shown below:

```
if_statement ::=
  IF condition THEN
    sequence_of_statements
  {ELSIF condition THEN
    sequence_of_statements}
  [ELSE
    sequence_of_statements]
  END IF;
```

The first line of the BNF description specifies the name of the construct being described. This line is read as follows: "the IF statement consists of " or "the IF statement is constructed from". The rest of the description represents the rules for constructing an IF statement.

The second line of the description specifies that the IF statement starts with the keyword IF, is followed by a condition construct, and ends the clause with the keyword THEN. The next line contains the construct SEQUENCE_OF_STATEMENTS (discussed later). All of the constructs discussed so far are required for the IF statement because the constructs are not enclosed in any kind of punctuation.

Statements enclosed in brackets [ ], as in lines 6 and 7, are optional constructs. An optional construct can be specified or left out depending on the functionality required. The ELSE clause of the IF statement is an example of an optional construct. A legal IF statement may or may not have an ELSE clause.

Statements enclosed in curly braces { }, as in lines 4 and 5, are optional and repeatable constructs. An optional and repeatable construct can either be left out, or have one or more of the construct exist. The ELSIF clause is an example of an optional and repeatable construct. The IF statement can be constructed without an ELSIF clause, or have one or more ELSIF clauses, depending on the desired behavior.

The last line of the IF_STATEMENT description contains the END IF clause. This is a required clause because it is not optional [ ], and not optional and repeatable { }.

The IF statement contains two other constructs that need more description. These are the SEQUENCE_OF_STATEMENTS, and the CONDITION. The SEQUENCE_OF_STATEMENTS construct is described by the BNF shown below:

```
sequence_of_statements ::=
  {sequential_statement}
```

The SEQUENCE_OF_STATEMENTS construct is described by one or more sequential statements, where a sequential statement is described as shown below:

```
sequential_statement ::=
   wait_statement
   | assertion_statement
   | signal_assignment_statement
   | variable_assignment_statement
   | procedure_call_statement
   | if_statement
   | case_statement
   | loop_statement
   | next_statement
   | exit_statement
   | return_statement
   | null_statement
```

The | character means OR, such that a sequential statement can be a WAIT statement, or an ASSERT statement, or a SIGNAL ASSIGNMENT statement, etc. From this description, we can see that the statement part of the IF statement can contain one or more sequential statements, such as WAIT statements, ASSERT statements, etc.

The CONDITION construct is specified with the BNF description shown below:

`condition` ::= *boolean*_`expression`

Notice that the keyword *boolean* is italicized. The italics indicate the type of the expression required for the CONDITION. If a designer looks for a boolean expression construct to describe the syntax required, none will be found. The reason is that all expressions share the same syntax description. For our purposes, the boolean type of the expression is ignored, and the construct description can be found under the following description:

```
expression ::=
   relation {and relation}
   | relation {or relation}
```

```
| relation {xor relation}
| relation [nand relation]
| relation [nor relation]
```

To summarize, curly braces { } are optional and repeatable constructs, square brackets [ ] are optional constructs, and italicized pieces of a construct can be ignored for purposes of finding descriptions.

Index

ABOUT THE AUTHOR

Douglas L. Perry is currently a senior applications engineer with Synopsys, Inc. He is responsible for providing the technical direction and problem-solving capabilities necessary to make the accounts that he supports successful using logic synthesis tools.

He has been active in the computer-aided engineering (CAE) field for about 10 years, with positions at a number of CAE companies. Previous positions include: a software designer for Calma, Inc.; a software group leader at Daisy Systems, Inc. developing digital simulation and timing verification tools; and a software manager at Vantage Analysis Systems developing waveform display software. At Vantage he also created and taught VHDL training classes and developed a large portion of the STD_LOGIC package used throughout the book. He is currently a technical program co-chair of the VHDL User's Group.